D0820440

DRACONOMICON™
Metallic Dragons

ROLEPLAYING GAME SUPPLEMENT

Richard Baker • Ari Marmell

CREDITS

Design
**Richard Baker (lead),
Ari Marmell, Peter Lee,
David Noonan, Robert J. Schwalb**

Additional Design
**Logan Bonner, Kolja Raven Liquette,
Stephen Radney-MacFarland, Chris Youngs**

Development
**Stephen Radney-MacFarland (lead),
Logan Bonner, Peter Schaefer**

Editing
**Logan Bonner (lead),
Dawn J. Geluso, Joanna G. Hurley,
Jessica Kristine, Jean Nelson**

Managing Editing
Kim Mohan

Director of D&D R&D and Book Publishing
Bill Slavicsek

D&D Creative Manager
Christopher Perkins

D&D Design Manager
James Wyatt

D&D Development and Editing Manager
Andy Collins

D&D Senior Art Director
Jon Schindehette

Art Director
Mari Kolkowsky

Cover Illustration
Todd Lockwood (front), Chippy (back)

Graphic Designers
Keven Smith, Leon Cortez, Emi Tanji

Additional Graphic Design
Mari Kolkowsky

Interior Illustrations
**Dave Allsop, Kerem Beyit, Zoltan Boros & Gabor
Szikszai, Chippy, Wayne England, Jason A. Engle, Tomás
Giorello, Lars Grant-West, Ralph Horsley, Howard Lyon,
William O'Connor, Chris Seaman, Franz Vohwinkel**

Cartographers
Jason A. Engle, Stephen Radney-MacFarland

Publishing Production Specialist
Erin Dorries

Prepress Manager
Jefferson Dunlap

Imaging Technician
Carmen Cheung

Production Manager
Cynda Callaway

Game rules based on the original DUNGEONS & DRAGONS®
rules created by **E. Gary Gygax** and **Dave Arneson**, and the
later editions by **David "Zeb" Cook** (2nd Edition); **Jonathan
Tweet, Monte Cook, Skip Williams, Richard Baker,** and **Peter
Adkison** (3rd Edition); and **Rob Heinsoo, Andy Collins,** and
James Wyatt (4th Edition).

620-24210000-001 EN
987654321
First Printing:
November 2009
ISBN: 978 0-7869-5748-9

U.S., CANADA, ASIA, PACIFIC,
& LATIN AMERICA
Wizards of the Coast LLC
P.O. Box 707
Renton WA 98057-0707
+1-800-324-6496

EUROPEAN HEADQUARTERS
Hasbro UK Ltd
Caswell Way
Newport, Gwent NP9 0YH
GREAT BRITAIN
Please keep this address for your records

WIZARDS OF THE COAST, BELGIUM
Industrialaan 1
1702 Groot-Bijgaarden
Belgium
+32.070.233.277

DUNGEONS & DRAGONS, D&D, d20, d20 System, WIZARDS OF THE COAST, Player's Handbook, Dungeon Master's Guide, Monster Manual, Draconomicon, EBERRON, FORGOTTEN REALMS,
DRAGONLANCE, D&D Insider, Divine Power, Manual of the Planes, Martial Power, Scepter Tower of Spellgard, MAGIC: THE GATHERING, all other Wizards of the Coast product names, and
their respective logos are trademarks of Wizards of the Coast LLC in the U.S.A. and other countries. All Wizards characters and the distinctive likenesses thereof are property of
Wizards of the Coast LLC. This material is protected under the copyright laws of the United States of America. Any reproduction or unauthorized use of the material or artwork
contained herein is prohibited without the express written permission of Wizards of the Coast LLC. Any similarity to actual people, organizations, places, or events included
herein is purely coincidental. Other trademarks are property of their respective owners. Printed in the U.S.A. ©2009 Wizards of the Coast LLC.

VISIT OUR WEBSITE AT WWW.WIZARDS.COM/DND

CONTENTS

DRAGON LORE

If a man wishes to become a hero, then the serpent must first become a dragon: otherwise he lacks his proper enemy.
—Friedrich Nietzsche

FEW CREATURES can match the power and splendor of dragons. Armed with claws and fangs that can rend steel, armored in scales as tough as iron, faster than an eagle in flight, and strong enough to shatter castle gates, a full-grown dragon is an awesome foe. Dragons would be exceedingly dangerous creatures even if they were dumb, ordinary beasts, because of their size and power. But they are also gifted with cold, calculating reason and furnaces of elemental energy that provide them with terrible breath weapons.

In some places and times, dragons are scarcely more than legend, creatures so rare and mysterious that centuries pass without a sighting of one. In other times, dragons rule over the world, darkening the skies and destroying or subjugating lesser beings. The current age falls somewhere between these extremes. In the few centers of civilization, dragons are a rare sight. The typical farmer or merchant might see a dragon only once or twice in his life. But in the borderlands or the great wide wildernesses surrounding those domains, dragons are much more common.

This chapter explores the nature of metallic dragons and their place in the world. It includes the following topics.

✦ **Origins:** How metallic dragons arose in the world, and why they differ from their chromatic kin.

✦ **Physiology:** A summary of the physical traits that give dragons their unique strengths.

✦ **Life Cycle:** The stages of a dragon's life, from conception to death.

✦ **Outlook and Psychology:** A look at the workings of a typical dragon's mind, and how a dragon's power and self-absorption color its personality.

✦ **Society:** A discussion of the interactions of the highly social metallic dragons.

✦ **Religion:** How these prideful creatures view the deities, and which ones they consent to worship.

✦ **Metallic Dragons in Detail:** A brief look at each of the twelve kinds of metallic dragons.

RALPH HORSLEY

Dragons have soared through the skies of the world and roamed the far reaches of the cosmos since the earliest days of creation. They are the greatest of mortal creatures, although few in number compared to the myriad hosts of humankind or the numberless hordes of goblins or orcs. Although scores, perhaps hundreds, of dragons are remembered in the myths and the legendary histories of the mortal world, only a handful of sages know the tale of the world's first dragons.

FIRST DRAGONS

In the beginning of the world, the gods gave life to the naked substance of the world forged by the primordials. During the days of creation, the gods forged countless mortal vessels, giving rise to all the races, beasts, and plants that would populate the world. But the deity Io chose to bend his will toward creating mortal vessels that would not only live in the world of elements, but would give life and soul to the elements themselves. To contain the awesome power of elements given life, Io had to shape mortal vessels of tremendous strength and hardiness. And so he created the most powerful of all mortal creatures: the dragons.

Learned metallic dragons believe that each time Io created new dragons, he was in a different mood. The god's demeanor laid the seeds that determined what those dragons would eventually become. When Io was filled with compassion and the desire to help others, he created dragons that transformed into metallics after his death. When Io spawned dragons to sate his avaricious or destructive impulses, the god's dark emotions eventually warped those dragons into the first chromatic and catastrophic dragons. In the ages following Io's death, these seeds altered dragonkind into its various kindreds.

Naturally, catastrophic and chromatic dragons do not hold with this version of Io's story. Scourge dragons like it even less—according to this legend, scourge dragons are poor imitations of true dragons, created by jealous godlings that lacked Io's secret of fusing elemental energy with mortal form and soul. Scourge dragons detest this ages-old "slander," and deal harshly with any sage or scholar they find propagating the tale.

CHILDREN OF IO

Foremost among the gods in valor and physical power, Io fought and defeated many primordials in the Dawn War. Similarly, his mighty children stood at the forefront of all mortal beings in the fight to preserve creation from the unchecked elemental forces of the angry primordials. But Io finally met an enemy who was his match: the primordial Erek-Hus, the King of Terror. The King of Terror slew Io, and the primordials seemed on the verge of victory. Then, from Io's shattered body, two new gods arose: Bahamut, the Platinum Dragon, and Tiamat, the Chromatic Dragon.

Bahamut and Tiamat together defeated the King of Terror, but then Tiamat turned against the noble Bahamut and attempted to seize dominion over all dragons. Io was a deity who incorporated both honor and fury, ambition and resolve, a love of beauty and a desire to possess it. Tiamat inherited many of Io's darker traits, and she could not suffer the existence of an equal or allow any other creature to reign over dragonkind. Bahamut obtained more of Io's noble qualities and the greater part of Io's strength. The Platinum Dragon defeated Tiamat, and she retreated to the dark depths of Tytherion. She took little part in the rest of the war against the primordials. Bahamut went on to become a champion for the gods nearly as noble and powerful as Io had been.

THE WAR OF DRAGONS

The bitter strife between Io's heirs carried over to all of dragonkind. For a long age of the world, chromatic dragons battled furiously to throw down Bahamut and elevate Tiamat as the Queen of All Dragons. More than once, metallic dragons established wise

THE LEGEND OF PERFECTION

Though most dragons believe the different types of dragons arose after Io's death, many metallic dragons claim otherwise. According to the tales they favor, Io created each kindred in turn, growing in skill and understanding with each effort. The catastrophic dragons were Io's first effort to shape mortal vessels that could incorporate living elemental power. They were slaves to their own elemental natures; the elements within warped and twisted the draconic vessel. Io set them aside and shaped the chromatic dragons next, giving them bodies better suited to containing the elemental energy without being changed by it. But these dragons, while true to the physical form that Io intended, had souls that could not master the base passions of their own elemental nature. These too Io set aside. Finally Io forged the metallic dragons, now perfected in both body and soul to be masters of their nature, and not slaves to it. Naturally, the metallic dragons are Io's last and finest creation—or so the old and proud among metallic dragons claim.

and justly ruled kingdoms over the lesser mortals of the world only to watch their realms destroyed by furious hordes led by wrathful flights of chromatic dragons. But in time, the battles of dragon against dragon grew sporadic, and then ebbed to a rarely remembered collection of old challenges and vendettas. Dragons had grown fewer in number, and those that remained grew more strong-willed, more suspicious, and more self-absorbed as the ages passed. Io had made dragonkind too strong, too proud, to surrender its will to any cause for long, or to acknowledge the dominion of others—even their own kind.

Dragons have rarely united for any great cause. Old rivalries and suspicions dating back to the earliest days of Bahamut and Tiamat's war divide the races of dragonkind irreparably. Although the fiercest feuds are between chromatic and metallic dragons, plenty of suspicions exist between different varieties within each family. Silver dragons hate red dragons, but they also distrust the imperial ambitions of gold dragons and dislike the avarice of copper dragons. White dragons hate and fear the much stronger silver dragons, which often push them out of their chosen territory, but they are just as wary around red dragons, which are likely to demand tribute or kill them. In fact, for many dragons, their worst enemies are other dragons of their own color or kind.

Io's Charge

Tiamat's drive for dominion over dragonkind is not the only cause of strife between the various types of dragons. Metallic dragons see the world and their place in it differently from how their chromatic or catastrophic cousins do. They remember the words of Io and the stories of his deeds, and discern in them a great purpose for dragonkind. Metallic dragons believe that Io created dragons with their awesome strength, intelligence, and magical might in order to inspire and protect all the lesser mortals of the world. They believe that dragonkind is charged with defending the world against primordial forces that would destroy it, leading mortal civilization, and shaping the world's affairs to someday create the world that Io decreed long ago. Metallic dragons refer to this high purpose as Io's Charge—a great philosophy of existence shaped by ancient prophecies and revelations.

Not all metallic dragons know of Io's Charge, and some that do know of it don't care. Iron, adamantine, and cobalt dragons lead savage and reclusive existences and have little knowledge of the ancient history of their own kind. These dragons make their way in the world by their own wit, power, and judgment, seizing whatever territory or treasure they can and holding it for as long as possible. Other metallics regard Io's Charge as a dream of childlike naïveté, long ago poisoned by Tiamat's greed and ambition and lost forever in the sundering of dragonkind. The cynical among metallic dragons ignore Io's Charge outright, seeing no reason why they should exert themselves on any other creature's behalf. But though some dragons have forgotten it and others have abandoned it, Io's Charge still guides the actions of many of the world's most powerful metallic dragons. Gold, silver, mithral, and orium dragons are especially likely to honor Io's Charge and allow its ancient wisdom to inform their actions.

Those dragons that accept Io's Charge differ greatly (and sometimes violently) on what exactly it means and how it should be met. Gold dragons often interpret Io's Charge as a mandate to rule over lesser

KEREM BEYIT

creatures as a just monarch. Steel dragons tend to believe that Io's Charge is best served by safeguarding the freedom of lesser mortals to find their own path. Some dragons think that Io's Charge requires them to crusade mercilessly against races, societies, or institutions they find objectionable. Others believe that Io's Charge is best answered through providing guidance and inspiring examples to the other races of the world.

The other families of dragonkind have different views of Io's Charge. Catastrophic dragons regard the whole idea as pure fancy (if they've heard of it at all) and believe that Io left no great philosophy to guide dragonkind. Chromatic dragons and scourge dragons, on the other hand, believe that the great purpose of dragons is to do as they please with the world and its people. In their view, might makes right, and Io made them the most powerful creatures in the world so that they could subjugate, plunder, and destroy to their hearts' content. When chromatic dragons debate philosophy (a rare occasion, but it's been known to happen), they argue that metallic dragons have fatally misinterpreted and embellished the pure and simple purpose of Io's Charge, which is nothing more or less than the divine mandate to dominate the world and revel in its riches.

Good and Evil

Given their drive to dominion, the age-old war against chromatic dragons, and the complexities of Io's Charge, metallic dragons play many roles on the world stage. They are kings, counselors, and teachers that seek to bring out the best in others; prophets, visionaries, and oracles that steer the course of events to come; meddlers and manipulators, toying with the fates of kingdoms; protectors and guardians, sometimes benevolent and sometimes absolutely ruthless; gluttons and misers; tyrants and destroyers; great champions and wicked schemers. Just as humans and members of other mortal races do, dragons walk many paths in life.

More so than most other types of dragons, metallics discover and pursue great causes and high purposes. Some are just as brutish and shortsighted as the worst chromatics, of course, but most seek something more than comfortable lairs and plentiful food. Of course, the combination of powerful, long-lived, highly rational beings and great purposes is not necessarily beneficial for the rest of the world. It's unusual for metallic dragons to embrace wantonly evil causes, but many of the purposes they do conceive can be callous, ruthless, destructive, or tyrannical in the eyes of the lesser creatures caught up in draconic dreams.

Metallic dragons are much more likely than other dragons to incorporate humans and members of other sentient races in their machinations. An old,

powerful red wyrm might look at a rich dwarven kingdom and plan to despoil it, but a gold wyrm might plot something potentially worse: ways in which it can seize control of that realm for centuries to come and direct its growth and resources to the dragon's purposes. The red wyrm eventually leaves, but the gold wyrm might never finish its work.

With this example in mind, the three salient truths that one should keep in mind about the so-called "good" metallic dragons are these:

1. Not all metallic dragons are good.
Some metallic dragons are, in fact, of evil or chaotic evil alignment. Silver and gold dragons are not often evil, but it's not uncommon to find truly evil representatives of the baser metallic dragons, such as iron or cobalt dragons. Some evil metallic dragons regard weaker creatures as miserable rabble to be enslaved, plundered, or toyed with on a whim. Other evil metallic dragons harbor a twisted view of Io's Charge and shape human realms to fit their own dark desires, using whatever means are effective.

2. Unaligned metallic dragons often pursue dangerous objectives.
Dragons that aren't committed servants of evil might prove just as dangerous as those that are. Many of the more brutish dragons are highly territorial, quick to anger, or easily lured into hostile actions by the promise of rich rewards. Others regard the power and fortunes of their favored human tribes or realms to be a reflection of their own power. They build up the strongest, most loyal kingdoms to govern, whether these realms are savage, oppressive, warlike, corrupt, or decadent. Wiser, more patient dragons might easily become caught up in the game of toying with kingdoms and history, often to the great detriment of the people who attract their interest.

3. Even good dragons can be terrible enemies.
Powerful metallic dragons that serve good in the world can still pose threats to heroic characters. A good dragon might choose to destroy a band of heroes to defend some site or artifact, to fulfill an ancient oath, or to prevent a great evil. Given their long lives and their overwhelming pride and confidence, dragons think little of making the hard choices for lesser creatures and sacrificing the few for the good of the many. True compassion is rare indeed among dragonkind.

DRAGONS IN HERALDRY

As you might expect of the world's most majestic and powerful creatures, dragons are featured in all manner of heraldic devices and coats of arms. Though culture in the world isn't monolithic enough for widespread, unified systems of heraldry, everyone is familiar with the traits of dragons. Images of dragons can appear as charges (appearing in one of the divisions of a shield) or supporters (figures that stand to either side of the shield and appear to be holding it upright). Dragons are also used as crests, small figurines that top helmets.

Each variety of dragon symbolizes different qualities or virtues. Chromatic dragons in heraldry are viewed as martial, aggressive devices and usually belong to individuals or families who made themselves known through battle. Metallic dragons are regarded as devices signifying dominion and status, and they often reflect titles bestowed for loyalty and accomplishment. However, exceptions abound, and the dragons featured carry no real connotation of the owners' alignment or trustworthiness. A family whose coat of arms features a red dragon is as likely to be honorable and good as one whose coat of arms includes a gold dragon.

The dragons most commonly used in heraldry, and their heraldic qualities, are these:

Adamantine: Pride, immovability, or stoicism. Heroes who successfully defend some place against attack are often associated with this device.

Black: Death, tragedy, or terror. A black dragon device usually bears a negative connotation, but families that endure curses or heroes renowned for fearlessness in the face of the supernatural sometimes choose this device.

Blue: Ambition, superiority, knowledge. The blue dragon device often suggests arcane magic, but might also suggest arrogance. Families that include famous wizards often choose this device.

Copper: Wealth, prosperity, or mercantile interests, possibly also luck or good fortune. Families that have roots as merchants often choose copper dragons.

Gold: Divine right, nobility, or law. Gold dragon devices are considered royal in many lands and are usually reserved for the highest levels of the nobility.

Green: Cunning, revenge, beauty, or fey. Families sworn to overturn some ancient wrong might bear this device, as might those who claim eladrin or elven kinship.

Iron: Determination, courage, or zeal. The iron dragon connotes single-mindedness and ardor for battle, but it can also stand for mercilessness.

Red: Strength, power, or destruction. Families that took their lands by conquest often feature a red dragon in their heraldry.

Silver: Honor, duty, or sacrifice. The silver dragon is a favorite of families that include famous knights or paladins.

White: Rage, ferocity, or the hunt. The white dragon device often connotes a willingness to feud or a refusal to overlook slights.

WAYNE ENGLAND

Like their chromatic cousins, metallic dragons contain elemental magic bound inside their brawny reptilian frames. All varieties of dragons wield breath weapons directly related to the elemental energy that courses through their hearts and blood. Elemental energy also powers their magical abilities.

Metallic dragons advance through age categories as chromatic dragons do, growing stronger in every way as they progress through millennia of life.

THE DRAGON'S SCALES

While a chromatic dragon relies on tough, leathery scales to repel attacks, the scales of a metallic dragon are partly composed of metal. Large, overlapping, platelike scales armor the dragon's back and head, growing smaller and more flexible along its limbs. Softer, smoother scales lie side by side on the dragon's belly. Each scale is infused with whichever metal is natural to that dragon. For example, the scales of a gold dragon are infused with a more durable form of gold, and the scales of a bronze dragon are mineralized with an alloy of copper and tin. A metallic dragon's scales are innately magical, as intrinsic to its elemental nature as its heart or blood.

Although a metallic dragon's scales are largely inorganic, the dragon's body produces powerful enzymes that actively bond with and diffuse the metal content throughout their blood. Not only do these enzymes keep scales flexible, they also nourish the living parts of each scale and constantly thicken and replenish the nonliving parts throughout the dragon's life. When a scale is lost through injury or natural molting, it gradually becomes less organic and its metallic content solidifies as the enzymes dry out. This process leaves a dead, brittle scale interlaced with fine veins of pure inorganic metal. If properly smelted, a large detached scale can yield traces of pure metal. However, it is extremely tedious and time-consuming to separate the pure metal from the scales of a dead dragon, and in practice metallic dragon hides aren't worth any more than chromatic dragon hides.

Metallic dragon scales harvested for armor already benefit from being harder than steel, but lose their flexibility and become rigid. The residual metal content is weaker than the natural hardness of a dragon scale. Therefore, metallic dragon scales (with the exception of adamantine scales) do not greatly improve the protection value of armor made from dragon hide.

Many sages have noticed that in addition to its regular diet, a metallic dragon occasionally ingests metal objects appropriate to its kind. For example, a steel dragon can devour a mundane sword (with some care) and metabolize its substance. Although eating metal is by no means required for a metallic dragon, doing so increases the rate at which it regenerates lost scales.

INTERNAL ANATOMY

As with most aspects of their external anatomy, chromatic and metallic dragons share the same organs with virtually no exceptions. Much of what makes a dragon an elemental force to be reckoned with begins with its dense heart, the single most powerful muscle of a dragon's body. Both chromatic and metallic

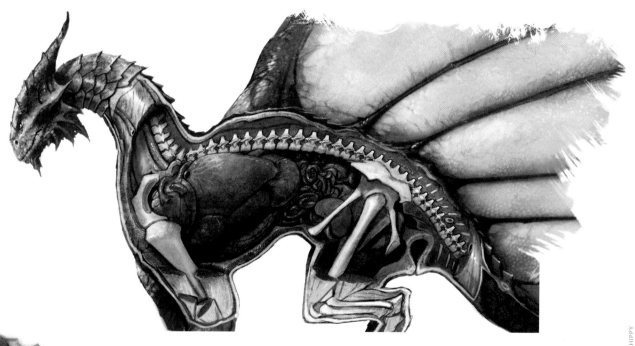

dragons have the same vocal range, enormous lung capacity, a fundamentum (a unique organ that concentrates elemental power in the blood), an upper stomach for gathering *breath weapon* blasts, and a gizzard for digestion. Moreover, both chromatic and metallic dragons boast a large brain mass with an extra lobe for controlling their *frightful presence* ability and their capacity for instinctive learning.

The parallels between chromatic and metallic dragons continue in the muscular and skeletal structures that shape their feline postures, from which only the decidedly reptilian neck and tail deviate. A dragon's heart pumps elemental energy throughout its body, making actions possible that would otherwise be impossible. The energy lets it instill fear, stave off exhaustion, and fly on membranous wings. Flushed with elemental blood pumped from the heart, a metallic dragon can stave off fatigue while remaining airborne for hours or days at a stretch. Dragon bones are hollow like those of birds, but immensely strong. The pectoral muscles of a dragon are among the strongest muscle groups in the body, and the tendons and ligaments are exceptionally tough and supple.

The elemental heart of a metallic dragon regulates body temperature regardless of external altitude, environment, or weather. Its heart can also slow down enough to permit hibernation, sometimes for hundreds of years. The elemental energy that flows through the body of a metallic dragon allows it to digest, process, and even subsume virtually anything it eats.

Looking for the origin of moral impulses, some sages have devoted considerable study to the variances in brain composition between chromatic and metallic dragons. Specifically, they have searched for any part of the brain that controls the inclination for good or evil tendencies. The truth, however disappointing, is that no such moral center exists. Dragons are good-natured or evil-minded based on the whims of personality, fate, and experience, much like humans and members of other mortal races, although some varieties of dragon are inclined to be more violent, domineering, and irascible than others.

DRACONIC ANATOMY

Draconomicon: Chromatic Dragons features a more extensive discussion of draconic musculature, skeletal structure, organs, and more. Metallic dragons are much like chromatic dragons in most of these particulars; refer to that supplement for more information.

SHAPECHANGING METALLIC DRAGONS

Most metallic dragons cannot assume the shapes of humanoids. Those that can have a considerable advantage over their peers, especially in matters of stealth and subterfuge. Shapechanged dragons normally assume the same appearance each time they change form. Other than that, no visual cues betray their true identities—they appear to be normal members of the creatures they imitate. However, some shapechanging dragons naturally include cosmetic characteristics that are borrowed from their metallic dragon bodies, such as eye or hair color that matches their scales. Age and gender of humanoid forms do not have to match those of dragons' natural forms. A male elder steel dragon, for example, could appear as a sprightly young female elf. Moreover, despite the radical difference in size between metallic dragons and humanoids, a disguised dragon's weight accurately reflects the dimensions of its current form. A dragon disguised as a bent and crooked old male human would weigh perhaps 150 pounds, not the thousands of pounds of its true draconic form.

Though a disguised dragon looks the same as a humanoid at a glance, telltale physical quirks can give them away. Although metallic dragons lose their bite, claw, tail, wings, and *breath weapon* in humanoid form, they retain their hit points, defense scores, resistances, and ability scores, leading savvy opponents to surmise that their target is a lot more resilient than appearances indicate.

When a dragon changes shape into humanoid form, the brain and heart make the polymorphic transition and function exactly the same way, pumping a font of magic-infused blood throughout the humanoid form. Sages have surmised that although a humanoid form lacks the mass of a metallic dragon, its elemental heart maintains the density of one. Finally, in addition to the brain, the extra lobe for controlling the *frightful presence* ability also crosses between forms, giving metallic dragons access to this one magical power in either body.

Though some varieties always develop the ability, every metallic lineage has a chance to produce shapeshifters. (See "Alternative Powers," page 219).

To truly understand dragons, one must imagine lifetimes that play out across thousands of years. Empires come into power, thrive, and fade into antiquity while ancient metallic dragons indulge the dream of blissfully long sleep. In many respects, dragons are creatures for which the passage of time holds little meaning. Although most are not immortal, the oldest of their kind living today have witnessed the rise and fall of ancient empires.

Dragons of any kind have the potential to live for several thousand years, but metallic dragons are the longest-lived of the dragon families, and often live half again as long as chromatic dragons do (barring death by violence, of course). Conjecture on the reason for this difference is rampant, but most sages believe that the metallic content infusing the scales, blood, organs, and flesh of metallic dragons concentrates the dragons' innate elemental power as they age, and helps them to resist the onset of decrepitude. The baser varieties of metallic dragons, such as brass and steel dragons, often reach ages of 2,500 to 3,000 years. Nobler, more powerful metallic dragons (silver, gold, and mithral) can live two to three times that span.

As with chromatics, metallic dragons experience six stages of life: wyrmling, young, adult, elder, ancient, and twilight. Although metallic dragons mature at the same rate as chromatics and reach adulthood at about the same time, they age more slowly after that and do not grow to elder or ancient status as quickly. (Of course, they remain ancient dragons long after chromatic dragons slip into twilight.)

MATING

Similar to chromatic dragons, metallic dragons become capable of mating halfway through their young stage of life, peak as adults, and diminish as elders and ancients. Not all dragons engage in the same mating rituals, but some patterns are common to most metallic dragons. Young dragons have little impulse to seek a long-term partner, but sometimes indulge in brief dalliances. These brief relationships rarely produce eggs, but if they do, the eggs are often fostered with older kin (or occasionally nondragons).

Adult dragons slowly awaken to a strong parental drive after establishing themselves in suitable lairs. Both parents closely watch the eggs, with either one becoming the caretaker while the other hunts for the couple, ensuring that one parent maintains a vigilant guard over the clutch. Because familial bonds are stronger among metallic dragons than among chromatics, these relationships rarely end until well after the wyrmlings hatch. Although either parent can raise wyrmlings alone, some metallic dragons—particularly orium, silver, and gold—stay together until their wyrmlings become young dragons.

Elder dragons, although still capable of reproduction, rarely mate. They are more inclined to foster or mentor the offspring of their own children. Ancient dragons do not normally seek out mates, but dragons that have not found a mate or produced descendants earlier in life sometimes choose to mate and lay eggs long after the time when most dragons do so. This

CHRIS SEAMAN

is especially true for ancient dragons that hold wide dominions or great power over the world and want to pass that power on to worthy heirs. Unlike with chromatic dragons, the desire for parenthood never truly goes away and finds many forms of expression throughout metallic dragons' lives.

Monogamy between metallic dragons is common, but each individual of a mated pair almost always maintains a separate lair, and the two spend most of their time apart. On rare occasions, mates form especially strong bonds and choose to reside together, sharing a lair for a few decades or even a century or two. Bronze, gold, orium, and silver dragons are the most likely to form these close bonds. However, once their wyrmlings have grown, most such pairs eventually separate—without young to hold them together, the dragons revert to their solitary ways.

EGGS

Female dragons control whether or not mating produces fertile eggs. If a female is not satisfied with the circumstances—for example, the size or location of the lairs, or the selection of possible mates—she rarely produces eggs.

Chromatic and metallic dragons are somewhat similar when it comes to laying eggs, with the exception that metallic dragons are more protective of their unhatched eggs. Female dragons lay eggs in small clutches of one to five; the precise count depends on the dragon's variety. Metallic dragons lay their eggs less frequently than chromatic dragons because their eggs' incubation time is considerably longer. Female metallic dragons keep their eggs within their bodies for 18 to 24 months. Eggs typically incubate for two to five years before hatching.

Egg shape and size are comparable to those of chromatic dragons, and egg color resembles that of the parents' scales. Eggs are highly resistant to damage from the *breath weapons* of the parents, but weaken as the wyrmlings grow ready to hatch.

HATCHING

Metallic dragon wyrmlings slowly leech nutrition from the mineral content of the inner shell wall while hibernating during most of their incubation period. Metallic dragons are known to carry on conversations with their eggs. The metal shells weaken during this time, until the wyrmlings rouse from their sleep ready to hatch. An awakened wyrmling quickly grows impatient, clawing, pushing against, and blasting what remains of the inner shell with an early version of its *breath weapon*. Hatching usually takes less than an hour.

Metallic dragon wyrmlings that hatch into the world as orphans are exceedingly rare. Such an event happens only when both parents have been killed but their eggs remained well hidden. Moreover, most metallic dragons are willing to foster orphaned

wyrmlings of their own line, so grandparents, aunts, or uncles can step in at need. Even evil metallic dragons are inclined to regard wyrmlings of their family line as potentially valuable minions or allies, and might go to the trouble of minding wyrmlings.

WYRMLING

Wyrmlings hatch from their eggs as predators that have instinctive knowledge imprinted on their minds. They are not automatically born with the knowledge of bygone generations, but they understood much of what their parents said to them while they were still in the egg. Consequently, after years of incubation, most dragons hatch with an understanding of their familial connections and basic lessons about hoards, hunting, lairs, and territory.

Wyrmlings are not merely born into the mantle of presumed superiority, but are hatched with a tailored understanding of how their supreme presence fits into the hierarchy of the world. They waste no time using their limbs, can usually fly halfway through their first day, and are eager to hunt by day's end. Indeed, after hatching, there is little that gives metallic wyrmlings pause; they are highly precocious creatures.

Wyrmlings live with a parent or parents for several years, but are already willfully independent, exploring outside the territory of their parents as they grow bolder and larger. They seek out and form relationships with other dragons of their familial line, although some especially territorial metallics such as adamantine and cobalt dragons have little tolerance for wandering wyrmlings. It isn't uncommon for wyrmlings to approach humanoids as well, drawn by curiosity, a desire for companionship, or some meddlesome impulse.

If a metallic dragon wyrmling does hatch on its own without the protection of a parent, it can easily survive into adulthood on its own, relying heavily on its inherited instincts and physical bearing. Even a small wyrmling is roughly equal to a large mountain lion in size and power. Its instincts, however, cause an orphaned metallic wyrmling to fixate on a parental figure should one be offered. Even if raised by dragons of a different kind or by lesser creatures, the wyrmling's powerful instincts keep it true to its kind, regardless of how contrary teachings might otherwise lead it astray.

YOUNG

Although young chromatic dragons leave home and must immediately fight for survival against a world hostile to their presence, a young metallic dragon can take measured steps away from its parent and be more discriminating about how it leaves home. When a metallic wyrmling grows into a young dragon, it becomes eager to find its own lair. Its mind has been intractably gripped by a primal desire to make

a home for itself and gather a hoard on which to sleep. It is now a powerful predator the size of a large horse, with deadly fangs and claws, and wings that can carry it for hours at a time. Once a young dragon departs from its parents' lair, it cannot return without an invitation, which is almost never offered.

Fortunately for the wyrmling, its years as an independent-minded creature were not idly spent. A young metallic dragon usually leaves its parental lair knowing exactly where it wants to establish its own territory, having already done the necessary reconnaissance as a wyrmling. Moreover, this lair will not be a temporary or transitional residence. The wyrmling studies the lands that interest it carefully to ensure that it can fulfill its needs for a draconic lifetime. Naturally, the young dragon strives to find territory that is rich, full of game, and unclaimed by other dragons—or at least larger and more powerful ones.

Adult

By the time a young metallic dragon comes into its own as an adult, it has established a lair that will serve it for the rest of its life. It is well on its way to gathering a significant hoard. If a metallic dragon plans to involve itself in humanoid affairs, either in its natural form or in a shapechanged guise, it sets the groundwork for those relationships during this time.

Although a metallic dragon becomes fertile approximately halfway through its "young" stage, a metallic dragon reaches its reproductive prime as an adult. After achieving the grandeur, independence, and predatory status of dragonhood it has so desperately craved since the earliest days of its life, an adult dragon begins to feel the drive to procreate. For one dragon this compulsion might be nothing more the urging of instinct, for another it could be a calm and calculated assessment of its biological needs, and for yet another it might manifest as a desire to achieve

even greater fame and renown by creating worthy heirs. As a metallic dragon enters the springtime of its life, a female studies potential suitors, and a male competes for and even fights over the right to mate with a desirable female.

In years when mates are not available, the dragon devotes its energy to relentlessly expanding its territory, adding to its hoard, and establishing itself as the master of all it surveys. Adulthood is the time when a metallic dragon conceives its grand purposes and plans and begins to put them into motion. A member of one of the less intelligent or determined varieties—for example, an iron dragon—might not contemplate any great purpose until much later in life, but a silver or gold dragon begins fulfilling its own interpretation of Io's Charge in the flower of adulthood.

Elder

Maturing into an elder dragon after several centuries of adulthood, a metallic dragon sits atop a veritable mountain of treasure, large enough to humble the wealth of a small barony. Regardless of this fact, the dragon's desire for more wealth remains insatiable. Any humanoid relationships established as an adult have long since come to fruition. An elder dragon holds a position of influence or leadership, as directly or indirectly involved in great affairs and endeavors as it cares to be.

As an elder, a metallic dragon can look back over multiple generations of progeny and feel pride and satisfaction in the families it has spawned. The drive to reproduce and the desperate need to establish territory have ebbed, which means an elder dragon is supremely self-confident. It is more patient and tolerant than a younger dragon. Even a violent and evil elder dragon is inclined to toy with weak enemies, or to solve problems by using subtle manipulation rather than sudden onslaughts.

CHAPTER 1 | *Dragon Lore*

CHRIS SEAMAN

Likewise, some elder wyrms find satisfaction in passing on their wisdom and life lessons to younger creatures—precocious wyrmlings and young dragons of their own familial lines, or sometimes humanoids of exceptional worth and charisma. Elder wyrms see the value in laying the foundations of legacies that will endure through the centuries, whether those legacies are in the form of destroyed enemies, mighty realms, or protégés that might go on to accomplish great deeds. They are sometimes willing to take under their wings younger descendants and orphaned dragons (provided they arrive with appropriate gifts) that are eager for their valuable and wizened insights about the world. A wyrmling raised by an elder dragon greatly benefits from the elder's experience and can become a formidable presence in the world.

ANCIENT

Metallic dragons that attain this robust age are at the height of their power. They can defeat entire armies or lay waste to whole kingdoms. They are not merely forces to be reckoned with, they are the standard by which cataclysms are measured. In the end, dealing with a metallic dragon of this stature becomes less about slaying the creature and more about appeasing its whims. Cities have been abandoned to accommodate their demands, religions have paid homage to their self-proclaimed divinity, and barbaric tribes have launched great raids to garner plunder fit to offer ancient draconic patrons.

It's not surprising that lesser creatures chafe under the influence of ancient dragons. Rare is the accord that strikes a comfortable balance with these oldest of wyrms. Even the best-intentioned ancient dragon monarch or guardian is inflexible and unapproachable by human standards. This is not to say that ancient metallics are incapable of friendship, but that they have reached a point in their lives when only the most heroic and worthy of lesser mortals are worth their attention.

An ancient dragon has mastered every endeavor that caught its interest over the centuries, from simple games to planar rituals. It no longer has patience for trivial details or petty machinations. Most ancient metallics want to build a legacy of gold, magic, and accomplishment that will last forever, sustained by their fearsome reputations. Others think nothing of indulging any appetite or whim that comes to them, utterly heedless of the effects on lesser creatures nearby. Humans and other folk are too frail and ephemeral to merit concern.

TWILIGHT

Metallic dragons entering their twilight years diminish in power for the first time in their lives. Although twilight dragons are a little less effective in battle, only the foolhardy would consider dragons in this chapter of the life cycle to be vulnerable. A metallic dragon in this stage knows it is slowly dying, and is prepared for this eventuality. It has created a legacy that spawned legends and listened as these stories proliferated, were forgotten, and reemerged as myth.

Not the least part of this legacy is the dragon's hoard. Every metallic dragon handles this matter differently, but regardless of a dragon's kind, the distribution of its hoard will never be left to chance. Some metallic dragons bequeath their hoards to descendants. Some leave entire inheritances to promising heirs or favored charges. Still others place their hoards into the hands of organizations they fostered, ensuring that their influence will persist in perpetuity. In any event, these preparations will have been set into motion long before a twilight dragon succumbs to the ravages of old age. In one instance, a mercury dragon created an elaborate web of clues, puzzles, and traps rumored to span continents, oceans, and planes of existence, parceling out its treasure one piece at a time. It took centuries to arrange, and only after its completion did the mercury dragon finally allow itself to die.

DEATH

Despite life spans that border on immortality, almost all dragons succumb to old age. (The exception is mithral dragons, which age but do not die; see page 166.) A metallic dragon, however, can choose the time and place of its demise. Whereas chromatic dragons often go out fighting, metallic dragons play out their final days exactly as planned: ceremonially, privately, publicly, religiously, or even by seeking out gods they worship. Few metallic dragons are interested in lying down to die without first arranging their personal matters. Some metallic wyrms are similar to chromatic dragons in their desire for glory, and those seek out a great rival for one last magnificent battle.

When a metallic dragon finally dies and its body is permitted to decompose naturally, its metal content breaks down and seeps into the ground, permeating the earth with veins of metal. Like chromatic dragons, metallic dragons are prone to environmental diffusion after death. The nature of the environmental change depends on the elemental energy of the dragon. For example, a gold dragon might diffuse into a fiery geyser or a scorching plain of stone.

DRAGONS IN TWILIGHT

Dragons in twilight fall to one to three levels lower than ancient dragons (see "Increasing or Decreasing Level," page 174 of the *Dungeon Master's Guide*). You can also decrease their ability to recharge powers, or give a penalty to initiative and Perception checks to represent the encroachment of age.

Only a foolish or inept sage would ascribe humanoid traits to dragons. Moral precepts that people apply are based on the incorrect assumption that these creatures have consciences. Most behave as they will, whether compassionately or pitilessly, not owing to alignment, but rather because their actions serve a larger purpose tied in with their goals. It would be fair to say that alignments have been imposed on dragons by humanoids to quantify the dragons' behavior and put themselves at ease.

DRACONIC DOMINION

Metallic dragons, unlike their chromatic or catastrophic kindred, rarely prey on humankind or rampage through human realms. They are not driven by the instinct to plunder or destroy. Instead, metallic dragons embody the draconic desire to dominate lesser creatures. A red wyrm might look on a human kingdom as a rich source of plunder and prey, but a gold wyrm sees that kingdom as something to be ordered to its own satisfaction. If it is especially benevolent, that gold dragon sees itself as a wise counselor, a loyal defender, and a stalwart ally of the realm. A different gold dragon might choose to reign openly over the realm, and another could be an inflexible tyrant and oppressor of the worst sort.

Even those metallic dragons that do not seek dominion over lesser races are often bound to them in other ways. Some are champions of good or evil, some are obsessed with old magic or ancient causes, and some are subtle manipulators engaged in a great game spanning the centuries. More than any other dragons, metallic dragons are interested and involved in the affairs of humanity.

DRIVES

Most metallic dragons, with the exception of those that can change shape, share little in common with humanoids when it comes to their base desires and needs. In the end, chromatic and metallic dragons share similar motivations, especially when they pertain to hunting. If prey runs, a dragon feels drawn to pursue and run the creature down—but not without caution if pursuing an intelligent creature. Having the mobility and stamina to travel great distances means a metallic dragon can chase a fleeing opponent indefinitely. It stops only when its food has been caught and eaten, because there is no excuse for returning home with an empty belly.

Metallic dragons, however rational when calm, have a primal imperative to attack and kill chromatic dragons on sight, sparing little thought for their own safety and pausing only when the likelihood of failure—not

death, but failure—is blatantly apparent. So powerful is this urge that if a metallic dragon reckons it can kill a nest of chromatic dragons at the expense of its own life, its instinctive mind deems that outcome acceptable. The compulsion to battle regularly causes metallic dragons to take on more than they can typically handle. Though dragons of all ages feel this urge, it's more powerful among young and adult metallics. Although chromatic dragons feel the same way toward metallic dragons, they already fight to survive in a world that vilifies their presence. For that reason alone, chromatic dragons pick their battles more carefully than metallic dragons do.

THE FAMILY LINE

Although the bonds of family are stronger among metallic dragons than among chromatic dragons, the bond between two metallic dragons that mate is limited to a finite time spent together for the wyrmlings' sake. After their offspring have departed from the lair, mated dragons are strongly drawn apart, back to solitude. If it wasn't for its powerful desire to extend its family line, a dragon would happily keep its own company. Even those dragons that have assumed humanoid forms for extended periods of time observe with bewilderment how humanoid couples and families can spend their entire lives with each other.

Although all dragons breed to ensure survival of their kind, the urge is particularly strong in metallic dragons. Sages attribute the reason to their longer gestation time and the innate awareness of how often their numbers are reduced by conflict against chromatic dragons. Metallic dragons also keep communication open among extended families. The more that a metallic dragon stays in contact with other metallics, though they are still separated by their respective territories, the easier it becomes to aid one's kin when the drive to fight chromatic dragons comes over them.

THE HOARD

Dragons of any kind deem their hoards—cascading piles of glittering coins, gems, and magic items—the marrow of existence. The hoard is why they hunt; it is the bed on which they sleep; it is the source of their self-worth. Dragons never grow bored with the acquisition of untold riches, even after thousands of years. This desire is, without a doubt, the single most important motivation in their lives. Even dragons that resist the natural inclination to possessively hoard wealth can still feel the instinct scratching in the backs of their minds, as if they are somehow missing out on treasure to which they are rightfully entitled.

Despite the constant lure of hoard-building, metallic dragons can still enjoy meaningful lives not consumed or overshadowed by the lust for wealth. Denying their nature, especially to themselves, would be futile. Better to remain introspectively aware of their weakness, to avoid letting it become an instrument of manipulation. As wyrmlings, dragons develop a psychological connection to treasure from which they never completely break free. More than leaving their parents, leaving the lair in which they were raised also means leaving the hoard around which they have played, not one coin of which travels with them abroad. When a wyrmling comes of age, it transitions from the considerable hoard of its parents to no hoard at all. This fact goes a long way toward explaining why young metallic dragons desperately start amassing wealth the moment they leave home.

THE STATUS IMPERATIVE

Any time a dragon interacts with a new creature socially, it immediately assesses how much of a struggle the new creature would put up in a fight. Dragons cannot suppress this instinct, even while conversing peacefully, because their predatory appetite creeps into the subtext of every spoken word. Try as they might to hide their hunting instinct, it translates through their unconscious body language. They size up creatures the way a humanoid might examine a piece of fruit in a marketplace.

For a dragon, establishing where it stands with a creature in combat allows it to adjust its posture accordingly. It lets the dragon know whether to behave arrogantly superior or—in the presence of more powerful opponents—to resort to bluster and subterfuge. Although one metallic dragon might keep this drive more in check than another, getting to know any potential prey is an automatic reaction that can't be controlled.

For this reason, disguising martial prowess is an effective way for some other creature to maintain the rapt attention of a dragon, which might otherwise categorize that creature as an insignificant threat or, worse yet, a possible meal. Not knowing where it stands against a new creature can infuriate or intrigue a metallic dragon. The dragon might invite an adventurer to a play a game of strategy, or make a sudden move to startle him or her into a revealing combat posture.

The benefits and downsides of someone concealing his or her true strength from a dragon are mostly situational. The dragon, driven by curiosity, will want to learn more about a mysterious adventurer, but then that person is the center of draconic attention, desired or not. A metallic dragon might initiate combat strictly for sparring purposes (but often without saying as much beforehand).

If adventurers intend to misrepresent themselves to a dragon, consider a skill challenge designed to fool the creature. Convincing a dragon to underestimate a potential foe might grant a bonus to attack rolls or initiative rolls. If a dragon is led to overestimate its foe, an adventurer might gain a bonus to Diplomacy or Intimidate checks. However, failing at such a ruse likely incenses the dragon, which brings an entirely different set of perils.

BEHAVIOR

Metallic dragons exhibit a broad range of dispositions, ranging from violent territoriality to predatory inquisitiveness to simple bemusement at humanoid antics. Most metallic dragons take great pride in their powers of observation and logical faculties. They see

LARS GRANT-WEST

themselves as dispassionate and rational—though some are just as short-tempered and easily provoked as the most antagonistic of red dragons.

HABITUAL CONDESCENSION

All dragons have an exceedingly high opinion of themselves. When they deign to engage in conversation with weaker creatures, dragons think they are demonstrating exceptional tolerance, and they expect that those they meet will be flattered by their attentions. Humanoids that find themselves in conversation with dragons would do well to show great appreciation for the honor; metallic dragons want their praises not only sung, but heralded loudly. Their need for affirmation does not stem from insecurity, but rather from a sense of entitlement. Metallic dragons that refrain from subjugating or preying upon humans do so because they're making a deliberate choice that goes against their true instincts. As such, they believe that in exchange for the gift of not being hunted and regularly eaten, humanoids should praise metallic dragons, and some dragons expect nothing less than outright worship.

Little separates the way chromatic and metallic dragons think. All dragons are supremely arrogant, incredibly self-centered, and strongly inclined to view lesser creatures strictly in the light of what possible uses they offer. It does not occur to dragons that humanoids exist for any other purpose than to serve the dragons' designs. The brief and trifling time that humanoids spend breathing requires direction, which they are gracious enough to provide. In the case of chromatic dragons, this attitude means they see humans and other humanoids as sources of food, treasure, or entertainment to be cruelly or callously exploited at will. Most metallic dragons, on the other hand, see humanoids as valuable resources, and carefully cultivate them over the centuries in order to achieve goals they deem appropriate. The rarest and kindest metallic dragons feel obligated to help humanoids build worthy realms and prosper.

Although it's not hard to imagine why dragons elevate themselves above virtually every other kind of creature (going by their physical stature and elemental power alone), pinning down the metallic dragons' inclination to nurture rather than neglect humanoids is more difficult. The divine answer points to Bahamut as the source, because the Platinum Dragon embodies all that was altruistic, charitable, logical, and patient in Io. The mundane answer, however, is that most metallic dragons are supremely rational creatures that see cruelty and callousness as wasteful. They therefore regard their humanoid neighbors with cold, dispassionate logic, which dictates that resources such as humanoids are best used with care. Some dragons come to believe that empowered humanoids are productive humanoids. Whether humanoids' power is real or imagined, they can achieve more when they are not devoured or robbed at random. Truly good dragons might still manipulate and sacrifice lesser creatures, but at least they do so based on the firm conviction that their guidance makes the world a better place.

The only time metallic dragons make any effort to suppress their natural arrogance toward lesser creatures is when they assume humanoid form to infiltrate their societies. To describe these occasions as trying for the dragon would be an understatement. A metallic dragon must constantly bite its tongue to blend in among the rabble. It takes practice, sometimes perfected over centuries, before a metallic dragon can make this transition seamlessly.

A DRAGON DOES AS A DRAGON WILL

Dragons are oblivious to societal impositions. The idea that a dragon would base a decision on anything other than its personal desires is entirely foreign. Even the most compassionate and fair-minded silver dragons choose to live by such virtues, not because other silver dragons or societies pressure them to do so, but because those qualities facilitate the achievement of their personal goals.

Where chromatic and metallic dragons differ is in how they interact with lesser creatures, and intelligent humanoids in particular. Although metallic dragons will not be swayed by humanoids' moral arguments, they at least recognize that people inhibit their own behavior with arbitrary laws and ethical rules (which goes a long way toward explaining why metallic dragons also regard them as lesser creatures).

When a metallic dragon listens to what a humanoid has to say, the dragon considers such an act as a privilege philanthropically bestowed, with the expectation that the dragon's time will not be wasted. A humanoid that uses this opportunity as an attempt to evoke a sense of duty in the dragon is doing nothing more than insulting the dragon, and might provoke a violent reaction. Unless a dragon favors a group of humanoids or an individual in some way, it will almost never be motivated to action by kindness.

This is not say that metallic dragons never grant aid or succor when requested, but that the supplicant must understand the dragon's egotistical disposition. The first step is for the requester to find a way to align his or her goals with the ambitions of the metallic dragon. Beyond that point, he or she must describe a way in which those goals can actively benefit the dragon. The benefit to the dragon need not be immediate. Even if it does not manifest until years or decades after an accord has been reached, the benefit is as valued by the dragon as if it had occurred right away.

It helps to think of metallic dragons not as good-natured, but rather exceedingly patient creatures that will not reflexively eat humanoids when they're hungry. If an adventurer manages to annoy a metallic dragon, there is little socially, and virtually nothing morally, that will stop the dragon from picking its teeth clean with the offender's bones.

ANYTHING WORTH DOING IS WORTH CONTEMPLATING

A metallic dragon is no more inclined than any other dragon to rush into a new endeavor. As a creature whose life spans centuries, it relishes the ability to thoroughly analyze a matter, dissecting the subject with its impressive intellect. It means to figure out all the ways in which it can either command the situation, profit from the undertaking, or both. Assuming that neither its life nor the lives of those it favors are hanging in the balance, a metallic dragon will not be hurried.

Maintaining intense focus, a metallic dragon can remain immersed in thought as it goes about its daily routine. In this state, it is aware of threats but unconcerned with how its presence and size might impact any environment through which it is passing. It doesn't acknowledge the immediate world around it, since it's too busy calculating all the possible advantages and drawbacks of some venture.

When a metallic dragon does finally arrive at a decision, it has not merely formulated a plan of attack, but also has several backup plans in case the main stratagem is somehow undermined. It has devoted considerable time to predicting any obstacles its plans might face and preemptively eliminating those hurdles before they can manifest. Mithral dragons are perhaps the most methodical when it comes to advance planning, but all dragons want absolute control over their schemes before taking a single step. They mean to win the battle before it begins, whether in business, negotiation, or warfare.

All that said, if a young or adult metallic dragon should encounter a chromatic dragon, it casts all its forethought aside and likely finds itself in a fight before assessing whether or not it can win the battle.

TEMPER

Metallic dragons choose to interact with humanoids peaceably only as an effective means to achieve their desires. Sting the pride of a metallic dragon, scorn its aid, or stretch its patience too thin, and it can unleash a force every bit as destructive as any chromatic dragon.

It doesn't take much to upset a metallic dragon. Perhaps too many intrusions have been made into its territory without proper acknowledgment, or the tribute for allowing humanoids to coexist in its domain has been consistently undercut. Whatever the case, the latest insult is merely the final straw in a series of perceived offenses, throwing the metallic dragon into a rage. Even if the offense is reasonable by humanoid standards, the dragon's reaction might seem completely out of proportion to the offense. For example, when a wandering wyrmling is killed by a poacher, its metallic dragon parent might raze the closest village for not policing its residents better.

WILLIAM O'CONNOR

Although individual metallic dragons might encounter each other accidentally, peaceably, or violently, dragon society is little more than a loose collection of familial relationships. Metallic dragons fulfill their own ambitions and serve their own purposes. They do not exist within societies so much as let societies take shape around them. Putting aside legendary occasions when metallic dragons of many kinds band together to oppose a common enemy, the closest they ever come to forming a rudimentary society is represented by their loyalties to children and kin. These lasting connections have tenuously united even the most territorial metallic dragons together.

The following four sections summarize how metallic dragons think and behave when they interact with other kinds of dragons or any kinds of humanoids.

OTHER METALLIC DRAGONS

When metallic dragons oppose one another, they remain tense and ready for battle. Whether the confrontation is over territory, treasure, or a mate, metallic dragons usually defer to (or flee from) more powerful wyrms, and demand submission from (or attempt to slay) weaker rivals. Evil or ill-tempered dragons are quick to attack when they have the advantage. Two dragons that recognize each other as equals often settle on cool, wary civility, watching carefully for mistakes or signs of treachery. However, the moment blood is spilled between metallic dragons, they no longer have any use for words. In any event, dragons won't compromise. A dragon that has the advantage over its rival claims the entire prize, whatever it might be. A dragon at a disadvantage retreats with nothing.

Negotiations between metallics follow this pattern: First, the two dragons instantly assess each other's age based on size, because seniority rules supreme. Second, a contest of knowledge ensues, in which the dragons compare what they know about a sought-after prize. Superior knowledge improves the standing of a dragon to its next older age category. The metallic dragon that has the oldest "effective age" is considered the rightful victor. Although many dragons respect this outcome and acquiesce to the superior wyrm, some dragons (usually brass, iron, mercury, or cobalt) raise the stakes one step further by challenging their rivals to trial by ritual combat, the result of which trumps all negotiations. Though these battles have been known to result in death, they usually end at first blood.

TERRITORIAL DISPUTES

When a metallic dragon accidentally enters the established territory of another, the average wyrm forgives the intrusion, but still boldly asserts its rightful claim. A more territorial metallic dragon, on the other hand, treats such an infraction as an opportunity to teach a younger wyrm a lesson—possibly a fatal one. Forgiveness, when offered, comes because a metallic dragon considers accidentally blundering into another dragon's territory to be a mortifying embarrassment. Metallic dragons consider territory, once staked by a metallic dragon of equal strength, to be sacrosanct. However, a covetous metallic dragon that desires the territory of a wyrm two or more age categories its junior considers such a domain ripe for the taking.

Metallic dragons of equal strength meet by invitation only (though older dragons often disregard this formality when associating with younger wyrms). If a message requests an audience, such as when a young dragon seeks tutelage from an older wyrm, a gift of treasure should accompany the request. The value of this treasure forever defines the relationship between the two dragons.

Metallic dragons that encounter each other in the wild outside their respective territories normally acknowledge one another openly, but travel their separate ways. Although some metallic dragons have been observed giving each other this respectful distance, many evil or bad-tempered metallic dragons use these opportunities to eliminate younger dragons that might eventually threaten their resources.

Generally speaking, the purpose of doing so must be extremely important for a metallic dragon to leave its territory and hoard. All metallic dragons accept that they suffer from a powerful attachment to their hoards. When they meet, unless they're actively attempting to thin the competition for resources or territory, they clear a path for one another. They silently acknowledge how vital a purpose must be to lure another dragon from its home. Although a metallic dragon would never characterize its attachment as a weakness, separating it from its hoard for too long can nonetheless be a tool of manipulation.

THE COUNCIL OF WYRMS

Obscure texts refer to an event known as "the Council of Wyrms." Much of the lore surrounding this event has been lost to history. What little can be assembled tells of the first metallic dragons coming together to form an accord shortly after Bahamut and Tiamat arose from Io's death. These dragons immediately recognized the chromatic spawn as their shared enemy and forged a lasting pact. They vowed to put aside their differences and monetary obsessions to wage war against chromatic dragons whenever the chromatics became a collective threat.

CHROMATIC DRAGONS

With few exceptions, a metallic dragon's rational persona disappears when it spots a chromatic dragon. It engages the dragon on sight, regardless of the consequences to itself or others. If the chromatic dragon is too daunting for one metallic dragon to handle, the metallic immediately seeks out allies and returns with greater numbers to assail the threat.

When battle is joined, metallic dragons fight savagely, eviscerating bellies, gouging eyes, and hamstringing legs. They slaughter chromatic dragon males, females, and wyrmlings without prejudice. After the slaughter ends, a metallic dragon resumes its normal personality as if nothing unusual had transpired, despite being covered in blood and gore. Once, when asked about its astonishing outburst of wrath, a silver dragon replied, "They cannot be allowed to reach critical numbers." Despite their drive to kill, most metallic dragons do not crusade against chromatic dragons. They merely deal with such wyrms as they appear.

Metallic dragons regard stories of cooperation and even forbidden love between the two groups of dragons as tales of fiction. Denials aside, reliable historical records document occasions when ancient and twilight metallic dragons cowed or manipulated chromatic dragons into their service, culminating with the chromatic dragons betraying their own kind, and resulting in the death of even more chromatic dragons.

CATASTROPHIC AND SCOURGE DRAGONS

Metallic dragons no more acknowledge catastrophic or scourge dragons than they would violent storms or enduring pestilences. In the eyes of metallic dragons, these other dragons fill necessary roles in the cyclical pattern of the world that metallic dragons witness countless times throughout their lives. Only when catastrophic and scourge dragons fail to respect this objectivity do metallic dragons take umbrage and offer resistance. A metallic doesn't care if a catastrophic or a scourge dragon runs roughshod over the world, as long as that dragon's interests aren't in its path.

HUMANOIDS

Metallic dragons see value in cultivating relationships with humanoids. This desire is so profound that after millennia of observing humanoid activities, some metallic dragons (including almost all mercury and steel dragons) have developed the innate magical ability to assume humanoid shapes. Their motivation

JASON A. ENGLE

is surprisingly simple: All metallic dragons crave power or wealth, and they frequently crave both. Indeed, whenever they seek influence or treasure, dragons are straightforward. As humanoids began propagating throughout the world, metallic dragons saw great potential in the scurrying little creatures, not for the sake of fostering their desperately short existences, but as creatures that could further the dragons' own agendas. Seeing this potential right away, metallic dragons realized that their goals could be more efficiently achieved through interaction rather than destruction.

Metallic dragons learned early on that to conduct any meaningful business with humanoids, they needed to relate (and be relatable) to them. Although that sometimes means assuming a friendly face, it can also mean impressing them with the majesty of draconic presence. After all, humanoids respond well to fear. In fact, many formidable metallic dragons greatly enjoy commanding armies of reliable humanoid minions to do their bidding.

Metallic dragons that can shapeshift have two faces: One for the social world (their humanoid guise) and one for the solitary life (their dragon form). As dragons, they want to be regarded with awe and feared by nations, but also left to their own devices. In their humanoid forms, they want to be easy to approach, to be respected by merchants, and to travel without fanfare. When they forge relationships with humanoids, shapeshifting dragons usually do so in humanoid form.

SOCIETAL ROLES

When they interact with humanoids, metallic dragons can take on many types of roles, from helpful to tyrannical.

ADVISOR

Metallic dragons that treat knowledge as the greatest treasure become sources of obscure information from which the rest of the world can benefit. These dragons act as oracles that foresee the future or librarians that share the lore stored in their minds. A dragon in the business of advising humanoids might stay highly accessible to encourage solicitation of their experiences or skills. Alternatively, a dragon might sequester itself from prying questions to meditate or research in peace. Gaining an audience with such a dragon is difficult, and usually requires braving treacherous terrain, but the knowledge it imparts is always valuable.

CUSTOMER

Metallic dragons that value quality over quantity rely on humanoids that specialize in acquiring rare goods. Humanoid crafters make a higher grade of product, and can make treasure to order. A business

that supplies a dragon connoisseur can earn a profit for countless generations. These transactions are usually conducted in settled or metropolitan regions. Alternatively, metallic dragons might hire adventuring humanoids to seek out coveted treasures. In such cases, metallic dragons that can change shape maintain their humanoid disguises while interacting with people.

GATEKEEPER

Metallic dragons sometimes stake claims to territory along dangerous or well-traveled humanoid routes. Once established, such a dragon demands tribute from humanoids that want to pass through the region. If they don't pay the toll, the dragon prevents movement through its domain. If the region is dangerous, the tribute guarantees that the dragon will protect travelers through the hostile area. Gatekeeper dragons can become integral parts of trading economies, regarded as yet another levy, tax, or toll.

GOD

If primitive humanoids want to worship a metallic wyrm as their deity, the dragon won't argue. Evil metallic dragons prefer having this type of relationship with humanoids, since it requires little effort in exchange for the praise and wealth that is heaped at their feet. In return for worship, metallic dragons grow fiercely protective of their worshipers. Dragonspawn, kobolds, lizardfolk, and troglodytes often become metallic dragon worshipers.

GUARDIAN

Metallic dragons that feel inclined to guide and protect lesser creatures adopt burgeoning centers of civilization, from small villages to teeming capitals. In exchange for the constant presence of the metallic dragon, the community directs major portions of its revenue to the dragon's hoard. The investment, however steep, is advantageous to both parties. With a dragon looking out for the populace, the community is shielded against outside threats, and its standing army (if it has one) becomes largely redundant. The civilization can focus on its own prosperity. This was the case in the dragonborn empire of Arkhosia, whose capital city became a meeting place for all metallic dragons. In addition to dragonborn, metallic dragons are likely to become guardians of dwarves, elves, halflings, humans, and tieflings.

MANIPULATOR

Whether puppeteering the politics of empires or bending the ears of prominent decision makers, metallic dragons operate behind the scenes, and as a result their influence is often not suspected. These dragons traffic in blackmail, favors, kickbacks, and (most important) knowledge. Such dragons nest near

the humanoid populations they control, and those that can change shape disguise themselves to blend in among the population. Metallic dragons either worm into the jeweled capitals of thriving nations or encourage humanoids to build in the dragons' domains, enticing the people by granting permission to harvest valuable minerals found there. As these settlements grow over time, the metallic dragon quietly remains in the background, pulling the strings of city leaders as needed.

TYRANT

Some metallic dragons find that nothing motivates lesser creatures more than fear. These dragons behave more like chromatics, with little regard for lives other than their own. Humanoids serve as mere tools, with a finite ability to manipulate, extract, and refine valuable minerals out of the ground. They are resources to be expended rather than individuals to be acknowledged. People in draconic regimes live under the constant threat of death or persecution, but metallics do recognize that some hope must be allowed. As such, they empower select humanoids with limited authority, if for no other reason than to police others of their own kind.

LANGUAGE

Although chromatic and metallic dragons are instinctive enemies, they aren't dissimilar enough to have developed independent languages. Chromatic and metallic dragons speak and write identical versions of Draconic. Some sages claim that the two types of dragons emphasize different parts of the same words, but these idiosyncrasies can also be attributed to personality and mood. See the "Language Details" and "Basic Vocabulary" sections on pages 24 and 25 of *Draconomicon: Chromatic Dragons*.

Metallic dragons follow the same naming conventions that chromatic dragons do. They can be named before birth, name themselves, adopt names they are given, or change their names to reflect major events in their lives. Metallic dragons that take humanoid forms, however, choose names for their shapes befitting the races and cultures they infiltrate. The only constant with these names is that they reflect the personas of the humanoids the metallic dragons become, as if the names help the dragons remember to stay in character.

WILLIAM O'CONNOR

Dragons of any variety worship deities only reluctantly, and they do so in a much different spirit from that of devout humanoids. Instead of humbling themselves before the deities, they strike bargains, seeing divine beings as strong allies and examples worth emulating. Dragons have little patience for pious rituals and behavioral restrictions. They tolerate such limitations only if it helps their pursuit of divine knowledge and righteous power.

BAHAMUT

The celestial platinum dragon who embodies the fairness, nobility, and strength of Io, Bahamut represents the foundation of metallic dragon worship and is universally respected by all metallic dragons, regardless of their faith. Strip away everything else, and Bahamut will always be the wyrm who drove Tiamat into a frightened retreat. Metallic dragons that battle against chromatics draw inspiration from his original struggle. When his worshipers conduct themselves in the world, they do so with the dignity of Bahamut. As they dispense justice onto lesser creatures, they ask what Bahamut would do in their place. When they charge into battle against those that oppress the weak, they believe that Bahamut invigorates their attacks.

Typical Followers: Bronze and silver dragons. Virtually all metallic dragons invoke Bahamut's name for strength as they launch into battle against chromatics.

BANE

The god of warmongering, subjugation, and tribute, Bane appeals to metallics that rule by fomenting fear. By honing their martial skill, his followers master fear and spread terror. Since dragons inspire fear merely by existing, Bane favors them. They can single-handedly wage war against an army or decide the outcome of a battle. Metallic dragons pay homage to Bane by fighting when they have not been asked to do so, and then demanding payment for their service. Metallic dragons also honor Bane by making sure neither side of a conflict definitively wins. They do so by switching sides to sustain the war or by leaking information to opposing sides.

Typical Followers: Brass, iron, and mercury dragons.

ERATHIS

Nothing is more important to dragon followers of Erathis than achieving stability through invention and lawfulness. Although dragons usually avoid living within societies, certain metallics protect

civilizations they have deemed worthy. Metallic dragons that protect rising empires as stalwart guardians, or that invisibly manipulate dynasties by guiding them toward prosperity, serve the goals of Erathis whether they mean to or not. As such, metallic dragons study her teachings to take advantage of any divine sanction their plans might already warrant.

Typical Followers: Gold and bronze dragons (which have expansionist tendencies), and silver dragons (which believe in the value of civilization).

IOUN

Virtually all metallic dragons embrace the god of knowledge and prophecy. As creatures of incredible patience and extended life, dragons seek Ioun's insights into both the nature of creation and the unforetold future. If metallic dragons hold any one deity in equal reverence to Bahamut, it would be Ioun for this reason. All dragons have an interest in the ability to accurately predict the future, especially those that work machinations that unfold across centuries. Dragons consider all the angles of a long-term venture before committing to a course of action. Despite how highly metallic dragons regard their own intellect, even they must acknowledge that complications can arise that they couldn't foresee. The ability to minimize those problems by looking into the future is more prized than platinum to many dragons.

Typical Followers: Mithral and orium dragons.

PELOR

A seasonal god who exemplifies summer, the sun, and time, Pelor opposes evil in all forms. Though many dragons are not moved by definitions of good and evil, metallic dragons that feel compassion for lesser creatures and save communities from suffering are quintessential forces for good. If the light of Pelor can help protect their charges, then so much the better.

Typical Followers: Gold, silver, and steel dragons.

TIAMAT

A metallic dragon would have to catastrophically lose its way before following the path of Tiamat, yet many have done exactly that. Tiamat represents all that is antithetical to metallic dragons, and especially to their predatory imperative to attack and kill chromatic dragons on sight. Still, with enough self-loathing, metallic dragons can become willing thralls of the draconic god. Although Tiamat is always a strict deity, she demands even more from her metallic converts than from the chromatics that revere her.

She constantly requires proof of their loyalty, usually by asking them to turn on their own kind. If a metallic dragon knows where to find wealth, regardless of familial bonds or lasting friendships, the dragon must plunder in Tiamat's name. In return, she promises the strength to prevail against those that would seek reprisal, and a swift death to weaker opponents.

Typical Followers: Iron dragons, and particularly greedy or envious adamantine and copper dragons.

EXARCHS

Deities operate in the mortal world primarily by proxy through their exarchs. In addition to heeding the prayers of worshipers, exarchs serve as divine intermediaries, determining what mortal events are worth mentioning to their patron gods.

The following are a few of the more prominent metallic dragon exarchs.

ATHEARSAURIV, EYE OF HEAVEN

Deity: Ioun
Dragon Variety: Mithral

Athearsauriv was an oracle who saw the future not as a fixed path but as an obstacle to be overcome. No venture was wasted, because she knew well in advance whether it would succeed or fail. No battle was lost, because she foresaw every feint or lunge before her opponents attacked. Eventually, Athearsauriv could foresee the future of an idea she idly contemplated: She no longer predicted the future, but could define what would happen. Ioun opened her realm to Athearsauriv out of necessity, and the dragon now guides the fates of mortals remotely.

Dragons that revere Athearsauriv request her visions, the bewildering accuracy of which is regarded as a mixed blessing.

EDARMIRRIK

Deity: Erathis
Dragon Variety: Gold

Edarmirrik, a glutton and master manipulator, infiltrated the family of a great dynasty while he was still a young wyrm. As an adult, he brokered commerce between every capital city on his territorial continent. Now an elder dragon, he manages the gold trade by proxy through a global merchant guild, shaving every gold coin in circulation to supplement his hoard. Erathis, pleased with the civilization the dragon had fostered, invited Edarmirrik to her domain. The dragon refused at first, but then the god assured him that he could still remain active in the world and sleep on his mountains of gold.

Dragons that revere Edarmirrik commend his single-mindedness and his expert management of humanoid societies.

THURKEARVAERI THE NIGHTDANCER

Deity: Bane
Dragon Variety: Mercury

Thurkearvaeri manipulated wars in the world, but never revealed her agenda to any mortal creature while doing so. She orchestrated battles in which opposing armies would clash, and ensured that the combatants would be enraged on a personal level by having their loved ones assassinated and framing a neighboring kingdom for the deeds. When a battle reached fever pitch, the mercury dragon would appear for the first time, admit her part in causing the hostilities, then join in the bloodshed. Bane fell in love with Thurkearvaeri and successfully enticed her to his realm.

Dragons that revere Thurkearvaeri are drawn by her mystery and her wickedly rational mind, as well as her bloodthirsty nature and her ability to manipulate humanoids into war on a grand scale.

VIVEXKEPESK

Deity: Bahamut
Dragon Variety: Brass

Vivexkepesk challenged every chromatic dragon he could find, young and ancient alike, and relentlessly hunted these creatures. As a side effect, his battles leveled towns, shook the earth, and shattered the landscape. The gods readied to smite Vivexkepesk to prevent this destruction, but Bahamut intervened, volunteering to personally fight the brass dragon and calm its dangerous rage. Miraculously, Vivexkepesk managed to keep the god constantly off balance. Seeing that the brass dragon merely wanted a challenging opponent, Bahamut offered him the opportunity to become an exarch, so he could fight Bahamut's greatest foes.

Dragons that revere Vivexkepesk respect his ferocious combat prowess and his refusal to back down, even when he's fighting a clearly superior opponent.

NO DEITY AT ALL?

Metallic dragons are prone to hubris when they compare themselves to gods, seeing the potential for their own deification. Although all dragons carry themselves with an arrogant sense of entitlement, metallic dragons' interactions with lesser creatures feed their ambitions. Metallics are often worshiped as gods in their own right. So although metallic dragons devoted to a deity do exist, they number far fewer than chromatic dragons, whose constant fight to survive causes them to seek a higher power's aid more frequently.

For the most part, the previous material in this chapter applies to all metallic dragons. What follows discusses each kind individually, offering further insight into their personalities, mannerisms, environment, and preferred means of hunting and fighting. These are not ironclad assertions; each kind of metallic dragon might prefer a certain type of treasure or environment, but metallics don't necessarily restrict themselves to the examples given.

In addition to the "main" metallic dragons, seven new varieties appear in this book. Some have appeared previously under other names, while others are recent discoveries, but all are as much a part of the metallic dragon family as the famous gold and silver dragons.

ADAMANTINE DRAGONS

Also known as cave dragons, or occasionally Underdark dragons, adamantine dragons are little known on the surface world. Although not the most intelligent of dragons, adamantine dragons are far smarter than their brutish, short-tempered behavior would suggest.

LAIRS AND TERRAIN

Adamantine dragons treat their territories as their personal fiefdoms, ruling over all creatures within. Although they demand obedience and respect at all times, they also take their duty as "ruler" seriously, protecting their subjects (or at least the obedient ones) from attack.

Most adamantine dragons dwell in the Underdark, in lairs filled with great caverns and twisting tunnels.

DRAGONS YOU CAN FIGHT

In previous editions of the DUNGEONS & DRAGONS® game, metallic dragons were portrayed as staunch defenders of good, and player characters rarely found reason to battle them. That's changed now. Although some metallics—especially among the silver and gold dragons—are fearsome champions against evil, you can't tell a metallic dragon's alignment just by looking at it anymore. Some metallic dragons are evil, and many are unaligned—which means they won't hesitate to battle heroes who intrude in their territory or interfere in their business.

Even otherwise benevolent dragons might find themselves at odds with good heroes. For example, a copper dragon might be momentarily overcome by its natural avarice, while a silver dragon might decide that honor demands that it slay intruders it catches in a shrine it is sworn to protect. Every dragon poses a potential threat to a party of player characters, regardless of the sheen on its scales.

The central lair has ledges or chambers at multiple heights, with at least two or three means of egress large enough for the dragon's bulk.

If Underdark (or at least underground) "kingdoms" aren't available, adamantine dragons lair in rocky mountain ranges, making their homes in caves surrounded with the comforting weight of rock. These adamantine dragons sometimes come into conflict with the equally territorial blue dragons that dwell in high, storm-shrouded mountains.

FAVORED TREASURE

Adamantine dragons prefer treasures that remind them of, or are native to, their home territory. For instance, an adamantine dragon whose Underdark "kingdom" includes rich veins of silver likely prefers silver treasures over other valuable metals or gems.

PHYSICAL CHARACTERISTICS

Adamantine dragons are a dark metallic hue. Some underground dwellers that have never seen a true black dragon call adamantines by that name. Their scales protrude in a bladelike fashion, ruffling like feathers when the dragon is irritated or hunting. An adamantine dragon has no horns per se, unless you count the row of spines that begins at the back of its head and runs the length of its body and tail. Its snout is sleeker than those of other dragons, vaguely resembling a snapping turtle's. Oddly, adamantine dragons smell not only like metal, but also vaguely oily, like a well-maintained blade or suit of armor.

DIET

Adamantine dragons prefer large amounts of smaller prey, a predilection developed over long years underground, where larger game is often unavailable. They particularly enjoy the taste of giant spiders and insects, but anything large enough for them to notice is large enough for them to eat. They don't make a habit of hunting sentient prey, but most won't turn it down if it's available. An adamantine dragon won't consume any of its "subjects" (see "Lairs and Terrain"), unless the only other option is starvation.

Unsurprisingly, given their physical abilities and favored terrain, adamantine dragons prefer to fight and hunt from the ground, flying to close on prey but then landing for the duration of the battle. That said, an adamantine dragon knows the terrain of its territory well and uses short flights to pass over obstacles intended to injure or impede its foes. Even in large caverns or mountain passes, an adamantine dragon prefers to patrol its territory on foot, the better to become familiar with the region.

PERSONALITY AND MOTIVATIONS

Highly territorial and exceptionally proud (even for a dragon), an adamantine dragon demands obedience and respect in its petty kingdom, and it might kill intruders without question. That said, if an explorer talks quickly and is respectful, an adamantine dragon won't necessarily be hostile. It might be willing to enter into treaties, agreements, or alliances with its neighbors.

On the other hand, offering a single insult is often enough to sour negotiations or trigger an instant attack. Adamantine dragons brook disrespect from nobody, and ignorance or carelessness is not an acceptable excuse.

RELATIONS WITH OTHER CREATURES

Adamantine dragons rarely encounter other metallic dragons, except when those that live in caves delve too deeply into the Underdark. However, they frequently clash with purple dragons, since the two kinds prefer the same type of territory. Although adamantine dragons are more powerful (assuming comparable age), purple dragons tend to be smarter, wilier, and more likely to use minions, making the contests more even.

Most frequently, adamantine dragons interact with other Underdark-dwelling sentient creatures, particularly humanoids. These include grimlock and troglodyte tribes, which adamantine dragons typically annex, and drow and duergar communities, with which they frequently war. Although adamantine dragons demand obedience from all creatures in their "kingdoms," they don't demand that their "subjects" do anything. (They're far less likely than purple dragons, for instance, to use humanoid spies or assassins.)

BRASS DRAGONS

Although weaker than many other varieties of dragonkind, brass dragons are still powerful creatures by any measure. They have a strong mercenary streak and often agree to serve as guardians or battle-champions for anyone willing to pay suitably well.

LAIRS AND TERRAIN

Brass dragons crave sunlight and dry heat, so naturally they prefer deserts, arid savannahs, and similar areas. They spend hours lying on sunning rocks high above the desert floor. Brass dragons also live in lands where hot, dry conditions are seasonal—for example, a temperate forest that sees little rainfall in the summertime. Brass dragons residing in such lands either migrate to warmer climes or retreat to subterranean lairs during the cool, rainy months.

Brass dragons make their lairs in rocky caves atop mesas, steep hills, or the walls of inaccessible canyons—preferably facing east, so they can enjoy

the morning sun. Typically, an intruder can access the lair only by scrambling or climbing up a long, exposed, barren slope that offers the dragon plenty of opportunity to spot the visitor's approach.

FAVORED TREASURE

Although they value all precious items, brass dragons are especially fond of handcrafted work in materials such as bone, wood, stone, or fabric (particularly weaving).

PHYSICAL CHARACTERISTICS

A prominent head crest shaped like a plowshare distinguishes brass dragons from other varieties. Young brass dragons are a dull, mottled brown. As they age, their color becomes more brassy, taking on a warm luster. They have a faintly acrid odor reminiscent of hot, oiled metal.

DIET

Brass dragons typically hunt on the wing and prefer to eat mountain goats, sheep, antelope, and other

TOMAS GIORELLO

such creatures. Only the most evil of brass dragons would choose to devour an intelligent creature, but a brass isn't above helping itself to a traveler's mount and leaving him or her stranded on foot. Well adapted for desert life, brass dragons can survive on almost no water.

PERSONALITY AND MOTIVATIONS

Placid and curious, brass dragons are among the most talkative of dragons and are slow to anger. Even in battle, brass dragons are rarely cruel or vengeful, and they frequently allow beaten enemies to retreat. However, they are still dragons—conceited, proud, touchy creatures. Like other dragons, brass dragons take offense at rude or disrespectful behavior. However, when other dragons might lash out in anger, brass dragons are more likely to break off a conversation and leave. Anyone foolish enough to persist in the face of such a clear warning sign deserves whatever he or she gets.

Shameless mercenaries, brass dragons readily strike deals to fight in exchange for rich rewards. The better ones rigorously fulfill their bargains, but less honorable members of the race are lazy and dishonest and have a nasty habit of breaking inconvenient deals if something better comes along. Pure self-interest governs most brass dragons, and they never take sides without first asking, "What's in this for me?"

RELATIONS WITH OTHER CREATURES

Brass dragons associate with desert-dwelling humanoids—usually dragonborn, humans, or gnolls. Older, more powerful dragons strike alliances with azers, fire giants, or efreets. Brass dragons make many acquaintances, ranging from other intelligent monsters such as sphinxes or nagas to notable humanoid princes, wizards, or bards. Evil brass dragons create networks of minions and informants instead. Either way, a brass dragon is exceptionally well informed about events in nearby territory.

Brass dragons strongly dislike brown dragons, since they prefer the same environments and compete for territory and influence.

BRONZE DRAGON

Duty-bound and honorable to a fault, bronze dragons commit themselves to order and are among the greatest and most devout champions of that ideal. To a bronze dragon, there is no greater calling than to ensure a universe governed by law, where chaos and corruption can gain no foothold. For most bronze dragons, enforcing justice in their lands is enough. But for a few, only absolute order can sate their ethical hunger—even if it means they must act as despots and tyrants, for the ends justify the means. As a

ZOLTAN BOROS & GABOR SZIKSZAI

result, bronze dragons come into conflict with other peoples, even when their values and beliefs are not worlds apart.

Lairs and Terrain

Bronze dragons choose lairs on rocky islands, granite cliffs overlooking the sea, or other coastal locales. Some bronze dragons eschew land altogether and stake out underwater territory in kelp beds, submerged caverns, or sunken ships. In rare cases, a bronze dragon might protect or rule a community of underwater creatures.

Freshwater bodies can sustain bronze dragons too, though adapting to these environments is slow and painful. Though rare in these environs, a bronze dragon might dwell in a large lake, inland sea, or even a deep river if the available prey can sustain it. Bronze dragons have little love for cold, and are unlikely to live in arctic climes, ceding those areas to cobalt and white dragons.

A bronze dragon's lair is usually accessible by water, its entrances concealed by the waves. Water-filled passages connect to dank and dripping mazes. The dragon uses natural caves to house servants, store treasure, and trap intruders. It might incorporate traps in the form of deadfalls, slides, and shifting tunnels. Often a secondary entrance, usually a chimney, allows the dragon an escape route. Such a passage, often disused and overgrown with creepers or buried under debris, can be even harder to find than the main entrance.

Favored Treasure

A bronze dragon's hoard consists of whatever the dragon can scavenge from the sea, sunken cities, lost ships, or vessels it attacks. Since saltwater can corrode most metals and other valuables, the dragon's hoard often consists largely of ceramics, statuary, and gemstones—durable goods that are immune to the effects of the dragon's environment.

Physical Characteristics

A ribbed and fluted crest sweeps back from a bronze dragon's cheeks and eyes, and the ribs end in curving horns, the largest growing from the top of its head. Webbing along its limbs and between its claws helps it swim. A bronze dragon's scales are a metallic dark brown, with a few highlights that look more like polished bronze.

Diet

Bronze dragons have voracious appetites, so they can't be too selective about what they eat. Most live on the sea's bounty, with kelp, fish, and crustaceans as their dietary staples. They prefer shark to other sea creatures, and often deplete local populations, leaving no sharks alive for leagues around. Like other metallic

dragons, bronze dragons don't consume intelligent creatures, though many make an exception for sahuagin, whose flesh is similar to shark meat.

Personality and Motivations

Bronze dragons have an elevated sense of purpose, believing their way is the proper way. Disagreement, they believe, arises from willful ignorance, and they have little patience for fools. A bronze dragon doesn't debate and doesn't argue, and if someone pushes the dragon, it might react with violence. In fact, most conflicts with bronze dragons arise from misunderstandings.

Bronze dragons see the world in black and white, right and wrong, and they choose not to appreciate the subtlety of gray. Disappointment and frustration with humanoid subterfuge might lead a bronze dragon to act rashly, destroying an entire population out of misapprehension. Even if it is later shown to have been wrong, the dragon would not feel regret and would see the tragedy as being brought on by the dishonesty of its victims.

Relations with Other Creatures

Bronze dragons are territorial creatures, and they do not tolerate trespassers or explorers in their lands—unless the interlopers offer some sort of tribute. A bronze dragon that settles near shipping lanes or in busy waters often demands payment to protect passing ships against sharks, sahuagin, pirates, and other dangers. Such dragons can be fierce guardians, but their prices are high, and many merchants go bankrupt meeting their demands.

On occasion, a bronze dragon might adopt a community and enforce its laws with an iron fist. It doesn't take long for the dragon to replace the ruler, and when it does, the community must abide by the dragon's rules or face extinction. Bronze dragons might rule over kobold, human, goblin, merfolk, or lizardfolk tribes. Older dragons extend their empires onto other planes, ruling devils, archons, and the like.

Bronze dragons detest evil aquatic creatures, and sahuagin are among their worst enemies. Blue dragons, though, are worse than even the sea devils, and their territories often overlap with those of bronze dragons. When a blue and a bronze meet, they clash violently, and if one retreats, it's never for long. Legends tell of bronze and blue dragons waging war for decades or centuries, with neither getting the upper hand. They spar and raid, striking and retreating until one gives up and flees for safer waters or, more likely, falls in battle.

COBALT DRAGON

Grim and sullen in demeanor, the fierce cobalt dragons measure success by the territories they rule and the lesser creatures they subjugate. They suffer no traveler to pass through their lands without bending knee and acknowledging their power, and anyone who refuses quickly comes to regret that error. Most cobalts rule over barbaric tribes or small, remote settlements, exacting instant obedience through claw, fang, and icy breath.

LAIRS AND TERRAIN

Cobalt dragons hate hot weather, preferring cold, gloomy lands—snowy forests, tundra, icebound mountains, or windswept downs and hills in northerly lands. Many cobalt dragons live in the Shadowfell, especially in the borderlands of Letherna or other portions that correspond to cold lands in the mortal world. They have little interest in spirits of the dead or necromantic power, instead dominating tribes or settlements of shadowborn humanoids such as shadar-kai.

Cobalt dragons make their lairs in glacial rifts, in low-lying caves hidden in wet gorges, or deep under the north-facing slopes of steep hills. Foes approaching a cobalt's lair on foot might face a difficult climb down an ice- or moss-covered cliff or might have to cross a swift, icy torrent to reach their destination. Cobalts think nothing of splashing through freezing water to enter or leave their lairs, but they rarely choose lairs that are accessible only by extended swimming.

FAVORED TREASURE

Cobalts prize lavishly decorated arms and armor, admiring the combination of workmanship and practicality. Bejeweled weapons litter their hoards, especially if the weapons feature blue or white gemstones. Cobalt dragons delight in arms and armor taken from long-dead challengers.

PHYSICAL CHARACTERISTICS

In addition to its dark, rich blue scales, a cobalt dragon's forward-curving, ramlike horns and its stocky build distinguish the creature. Its wing membranes are a pale blue, flecked with spots of darker blue. A cobalt has wide feet and diamond-shaped scales.

DIET

Cobalt dragons favor large game, especially moose, elk, and reindeer. They also have a taste for bear meat, and many a cobalt carries the scars of its early encounters with full-grown brown bears or dire bears. They prefer to hunt by night, when their keen senses give them a distinct edge over warm-blooded, diurnal prey. Since they're not strong fliers, they rarely try to take prey on the wing. Good-aligned cobalt dragons don't eat intelligent creatures, but unaligned and evil ones do—especially those they regard as pests or adversaries.

PERSONALITY AND MOTIVATIONS

The best way to describe the demeanor of cobalt dragons is possessive. They have a fierce, unyielding desire to hold and control anything they deem important—principally their wealth and their station. Wealth is easy to measure, of course. Like other dragons, cobalts are infatuated with their hoards, and they dream constantly of enlarging them. Cobalts measure their station by the extent of the lands they hold sway over, the strength of the people and creatures they dominate, and the tenacity with which they cling to power. Driven to demand the fear and respect of all others, cobalt dragons fiercely resist any development that might weaken their control.

Cobalt dragons are extremely forceful and demanding creatures. On meeting other intelligent creatures, they engage in physical intimidation and tests of will, determined to dominate any possible rival. Good-aligned cobalt dragons do so to determine the courage and worth of those they face; those who stand up to them win respect. Other cobalt dragons enjoy bullying the weak and are quick to maim or kill those foolish enough to show defiance without having the strength to back up their words.

Although many cobalt dragons are brutal, callous tyrants, the race isn't inherently evil. The best of them are indefatigable, defending the people they have come to rule, and they would rather die than permit an enemy to harm their subjects. However, most cobalt dragons defend their territories and subjects mainly to satisfy their own sense of station and their craving for respect, while feeling little moral obligation toward those they rule. To a cobalt, strength is the ultimate measure of worth. Minions and foes that prove strong win its grudging respect, and the dragon despises those that turn out to be weak.

RELATIONS WITH OTHER CREATURES

Cobalt dragons assert themselves as the masters of all they survey. From a young age, they begin to subjugate neighbors that are too weak to win their respect. They count most cold-dwelling races among their subjects, including barbaric dwarves or humans, lycanthropes, orcs, ogres, minotaurs, and trolls—the fiercer the better. More powerful cobalt dragons might rule over oni or frost giants, or force monsters such as manticores or wyverns into their service.

Among dragons, cobalts compete with white dragons, silver dragons, and shadow dragons. They sneer at white dragons, seeing them as stupid weaklings (although a young cobalt is smart enough to stay away from adult or older whites), and they resent the

WAYNE ENGLAND

superior strength of silver dragons. Shadow dragons make for deadly enemies, since they are strong enough to dominate all but the oldest and most powerful cobalt dragons. To a cobalt dragon, nothing matches the ignominy of serving as another dragon's thrall.

COPPER DRAGONS

Charismatic, sly, and witty, copper dragons are by far the cleverest and most interesting of dragons—or so they say. Schemers and thieves, coppers tend to be charming scoundrels. Even the evil members of the race flaunt their glibness and ironic sense of humor.

LAIRS AND TERRAIN

Copper dragons dwell in temperate hills and mountains. As exceptionally quick and nimble fliers, they prefer terrain that allows them to take advantage of their natural ability. They establish their territories near human settlements or frontiers. In fact, many copper dragons choose to live in the midst of human cities. Most have no natural ability to take on human shape, so city-dwelling copper dragons either hide in deep dungeons or vaults beneath the streets, or they come to an understanding with the local rulers that allows them to take up residence in outlying estates or royal palaces as "nobles," protectors, or advisors.

Copper dragons that have no such arrangements make their lairs in abandoned structures or ruins. An old castle, dungeon, or monastery is perfect, since such a place has thick walls and is highly defensible.

Lairs with commanding views of the nearby countryside are especially prized.

FAVORED TREASURE

Copper dragons value fine art of any kind, especially beautiful metalwork. Well-made jewelry captivates most copper dragons, inflaming the avarice in their hearts.

PHYSICAL CHARACTERISTICS

A copper dragon is lean and sinuous. It has a prominent pair of swept-back, scale-covered horns, cheek ridges, and jaw frills. Its scales are large, glossy bands or plates, smooth to the touch. Its eyes are bright turquoise. As a copper dragon ages, its scales take on a green tinge, like verdigris on an old statue.

DIET

In the wild, copper dragons eat small game and fowl. However, they often live close enough to civilized settlements to acquire a taste for human foods, especially wine. Not even the cruelest and most vile of copper dragons would deign to eat an intelligent humanoid. After all, a devoured victim can't appreciate the dragon's wit and beauty.

PERSONALITY AND MOTIVATIONS

Quick-witted, clever creatures, copper dragons cultivate their lively senses of humor. They delight in outfoxing and deceiving enemies, and they love a good jest—as long as it isn't directed at them. Most are insincere and facile in their dealings with other creatures, and a few are cruel and deceitful, deliberately spreading mayhem with malicious lies and subtle manipulation. The race suffers from covetousness—its chief weakness. All dragons are avaricious to one degree or another, but copper dragons are by far the greediest of the metallic dragons. So taken are they with their own charm, they can't help but believe that they deserve to have whatever they want.

RELATIONS WITH OTHER CREATURES

Humankind and the other civilized races fascinate copper dragons. The more covetous copper dragons associate with bandits, thieves, or brigands. More than one thieves' guild is secretly ruled by a copper dragon. Coppers also have good relations with fey creatures such as eladrins, elves, satyrs, and centaurs. Copper dragons don't like to associate with stupid or bloodthirsty monsters. They want to surround themselves with followers that can appreciate their cleverness and humor.

Red dragons are natural enemies of copper dragons. Reds sometimes compete with coppers for territory, and they have no appreciation at all for the wit and charm of their smaller rivals.

GOLD DRAGONS

Also called royal dragons or imperial dragons, gold dragons are the apex of an already unimaginably powerful race. Of all metallic and chromatic dragons, only mithral dragons might be more powerful—but they don't often overtly involve themselves in mortal events as golds do.

LAIRS AND TERRAIN

Gold dragons tend to favor gently rolling hills and open plains as sites for their lairs, but exceptions to this tendency abound. Gold dragon lairs can also be found in craggy mountains, in deep caves, and even in the midst of humanoid communities (though this last sort of lair is less common for gold dragons than for steel or silver). A gold dragon often settles near a society it has involved itself with or near a great source of magic it has chosen to protect. The actual terrain or climate is often a secondary concern, but golds do dislike living in frigid regions.

Though they have a few preferences, gold dragons can live almost anywhere. And, frankly, if a gold dragon wants to live somewhere, who's going to tell it otherwise? Territorial disputes are the most common cause of conflict between golds and other dragons, and unless there's a major age discrepancy in favor of the opposing dragon, the gold usually proves victorious.

FAVORED TREASURE

Gold dragons prefer magic items to other valuables, but a gold's hoard isn't likely to consist entirely of magic items. Gold dragons also enjoy well-crafted works of art they can admire, as well as collections of gems and raw ore that are not merely valuable but can serve as a backup larder.

PHYSICAL CHARACTERISTICS

Gold dragons are born with dull coloration that shifts to gleaming gold—and then to illuminated radiance—as they age. A gold is one of the most sinuous of dragons, graceful and flexible, and its wings are almost fanlike, running the length of its body. It has impressive horns, but they are ineffective as weapons. Facial tendrils, thin strands of muscle that appear almost mustachelike, descend from around its mouth and nostrils. These tendrils are neither strong nor dexterous, but are just prehensile enough to aid the dragon in cleaning food from around its mouth or between its teeth.

A gold dragon gives off a faint scent, which some adventurers liken to the smell of molten metal. They say this aroma is one of the few hints that a humanoid might be a shapechanged gold dragon in disguise.

DIET

Gold dragons prefer larger prey and deliberately hunt down dangerous monsters. In so doing, they combine their biological needs with their ethical leanings. When appropriate prey isn't available, a gold dragon is more willing than other dragons to subsist on inanimate matter—preferring gems and valuable metals, which befit its high status.

PERSONALITY AND MOTIVATIONS

Gold dragons are strong believers in the rule of order and the greater good, but they are also arrogant and dismissive, more concerned with unfathomable goals than with the needs of "lesser creatures." For every gold dragon champion that aids a community of humanoids, or rules it with a just and benevolent hand, there is another that has become a tyrant, demanding the obedience it deserves "by right," or crushing individual freedoms and creativity in the name of law. Even these dragons tend to view themselves as morally in the right, making the hard choices nobody else can.

Even when cooperating with or benevolently ruling other creatures, gold dragons seem dismissive of the concerns of lesser beings. This attitude isn't necessarily a sign that they don't care for the good of their subjects or allies (though some might not); rather, it's because gold dragons believe in their superiority over other races but don't necessarily understand what that means. A gold dragon watching over a community might not acknowledge the complaints, needs, or troubles of citizens because it truly doesn't realize how bad things are. Even after dwelling for years among humans, gold dragons are frequently shocked at just how weak and fragile such creatures are.

RELATIONS WITH OTHER CREATURES

A gold dragon sees itself as the pinnacle of living creatures and almost never acknowledges any other creature as its superior. It might do so for an older dragon, but that's only temporary. If a gold dragon serves as a mere advisor to a ruler or chooses to stay uninvolved in a region's events, it's because that dragon doesn't feel like taking on the burden of leadership, never because the dragon doesn't think it could do a better job.

Gold dragons and red dragons have a particularly strong rivalry—in part because reds resent the more powerful golds and scheme or gang up against them. Gold dragons rarely consume humanoids, unless the people in question are blatantly evil (or pose some threat to the dragon or its domain). Even a starving gold dragon won't consume a sentient being that it doesn't think deserves to die—though, of course, the definition of who deserves to die varies from dragon to dragon.

IRON DRAGONS

Violent and ill-tempered, iron dragons are undoubtedly the most brutish and vicious of the metallic races. Many iron dragons are evil, and most of the rest are, at best, a particularly hungry and dangerous variety of unaligned.

LAIRS AND TERRAIN

Iron dragons naturally favor settings that offer plenty of game and good cover. They build lairs in dense forest or broken hills—terrain that offers many hiding places for a large predator.

Iron dragons hide their lairs well. In the absence of truly inaccessible terrain, an iron dragon settles for the most difficult and tangled ground cover it can find. Caves in brush-filled forest ravines or briar-choked gulches are common iron dragon lairs. Given their tough, thick scales, iron dragons have no qualms about plunging through the thickest patches of thorny foliage. The lair usually consists of several large, unimproved antechambers—natural caves with uneven floors, jagged rocks, or hindering vegetation hanging down from the outside, often festooned with the rotting remains of previous meals—and a deeper, more comfortable den.

JASON A. ENGLE

Favored Treasure

Treasure of any sort fascinates dragons, but iron dragons particularly love the luster and feel of gold and silver coins—the more the better.

Physical Characteristics

Iron dragons have coarse, heavy, dark gray metallic scales. Although they might be confused with silver or mithral dragons, the other metallics tend to be much brighter in color, and their scales are smaller and finer. As it ages, an iron dragon develops rusty-brown streaks, especially on scales near major joints and on its wings.

Diet

Iron dragons prey on midsized game, such as boar, deer, or antelope. Most regard humanoids as prey too, and they prefer small, comparatively weak creatures, such as goblins, kobolds, gnomes, and halflings. Natural ambush predators, they lie hidden in deep thickets or old ruins alongside roads until a tempting target wanders within reach of a sudden charge. Good-aligned iron dragons refrain from devouring intelligent creatures (except for the occasional goblin), but evil ones prize intelligent prey and often roam far from their native forests in search of humanoid settlements, well-traveled roads, and other suitable hunting grounds.

Personality and Motivation

Iron dragons are governed by their base passions—hunger, greed, creature comforts (of the sort that appeal to dragons, anyway), and the desire to be feared and respected. The best of the race are sullen and reclusive, preferring their own company to that of others. Most iron dragons seek to sate their brutish impulses by devouring or robbing any creature foolish enough to intrude on their demesnes. They are not especially clever and can sometimes be outwitted through bribery, flattery, and other such tactics—their greed can easily override their natural sullenness.

Relations with Other Creatures

Young iron dragons are easily enticed into serving other monsters as guardians or champions. Goblins and their kin especially prize iron dragons for their fierceness and their susceptibility to bribes, gifts, and flattery. Larger and more powerful monsters, such as giants, can easily bully iron dragons. No matter how their allegiance is won, iron dragons make dangerous and unreliable servants. The larger they grow, the more demanding they become. Few goblin realms successfully keep an iron dragon under control for long after the dragon reaches adulthood, and only the most powerful of masters can retain the loyalty of an elder or an ancient iron dragon.

Iron dragons dislike all other dragons, but they especially resent green dragons. Both prefer the same types of forest environs, and the sly, malicious greens frequently frustrate and outwit iron dragons with their exceptional intelligence.

Mercury Dragon

Mercury dragons are a little bit crazy—but there's definitely a method to their madness. A mercury dragon craves variety above all else. If another creature offers a wide array of food to hunt and the opportunity to gather a hoard, a mercury dragon will serve that creature in an arrangement of convenience. Thus, mercury dragons can be found as champions, bodyguards, and assassins in the employ of greater powers.

Lairs and Terrain

Mercury dragons hail from volcanic mountain ranges in tropical climates, and though many of them remain in such locales throughout their lives, the variety has spread far and wide. Many a mercury dragon spends its youth scheming for a way to reach the Elemental Chaos and establish a lair there. For a creature that craves variety, the ever-changing landscape of the Elemental Chaos is the perfect place to construct a lair.

But the most common lair for a mercury dragon is one provided and maintained by someone else. As long as they receive the variety they crave, mercury dragons serve as bodyguards, messengers, or assassins for powerful mages, priests, or rulers—and sometimes more sinister forces. When a mercury dragon works for another creature, the dragon takes part of a larger fortress and makes a section its own, filling it with traps to frighten off any curious lackeys and to keep its personal hoard safe.

Like any dragon, a mercury dragon hates when interlopers or thieves enter its lair. But that hatred is tempered with curiosity about why "lesser creatures" would dare to invade its domain. The traps and guardians on the periphery of a mercury dragon's lair are often nonlethal, intended to capture, wound, or frighten intruders rather than kill them outright. These protections enable the mercury dragon to toy with intruders and extract some sort of unusual experience from the event, instead of just cleaning more corpses out of the bottom of a pit trap.

Favored Treasure

It should surprise no one that mercury dragons aren't good at assembling matched sets or cohesive collections. A mercury dragon's hoard is a hodgepodge of coins, jewelry, and items from scores of lands and dozens of eras. Older mercury dragons might seek out some items they've heard about but never seen, and they're avid treasure traders. If adventurers can acquire some rare item from a far-off land, a mercury dragon is often willing to part with treasures from its hoard in exchange, especially if the dragon is trading away a duplicate.

PHYSICAL CHARACTERISTICS

A mercury dragon has scales of whitish-silver and a sleek and serpentine body. Its frame lacks some of the muscular bulk that other dragons have, and its scales are smaller and more closely set. Mercury dragons are peerless shapechangers, capable of taking both a humanoid form (to blend in among civilized people) and an amorphous, liquid form (for defense and to slither where others cannot go).

DIET

A carnivore through and through, a mercury dragon always craves something different from whatever it just ate. This compulsion is more than just instinct; a mercury dragon forced to eat the same food meal after meal quickly becomes listless and difficult to awaken from sleep. Mercury dragons are enthusiastic hunters, cunning enough to plan elaborate traps for their prey. They toy with weaker prey before killing and eating it. From the viewpoint of the prey, this behavior amounts to cruelty. To the mercury dragon, it's another expression of its need to experience something different.

PERSONALITY AND MOTIVATIONS

A mercury dragon acts differently from time to time, depending on how much variety it has experienced lately.

If the dragon feels as though it's in a rut, it might attack an adversary right away, then snarl, "Tell me why I shouldn't finish you off." Because the magic of its breath weapon renders a mercury dragon invisible to its prey, it can boast while hidden. What sounds like garden-variety draconic arrogance is, from the dragon's perspective, legitimate questioning. If its adversaries can engage the dragon's interest, it might regard them as more than just a meal and a momentary diversion.

If a mercury dragon thinks its life has been varied enough lately, it talks first and fights later, using its *breath weapon*, natural maneuverability, and *quicksilver form* to elude those who challenge it. Even if the challengers are trying to kill it, the dragon talks to them to understand the stakes. After all, it would be a shame to kill someone who's more interesting when alive. And a mercury dragon shows some cunning when placed in the position of prey. It happily engages in a cat-and-mouse game with hostile pursuers, confounding them and getting them to exhaust themselves before turning the tables and attacking with its full might.

An adult or older mercury dragon can magically alter its shape to appear as an ordinary humanoid,

and these dragons tend to be more circumspect when not in their draconic forms. A mercury dragon might take humanoid form when hunting, serving its master on a specific mission, or when it craves to experience "life among the lesser races" for a time. But a mercury dragon lacks the steel dragon's affinity for civilized life, and the nuances of specific cultures are often beyond its understanding. Sometimes, even the basics of humanoid life are foreign to a mercury dragon. For instance, a shapechanged mercury dragon might walk into a butcher shop craving something new to eat, purchase a leg of lamb, and consume it raw on the spot while the butcher looks on in horror.

RELATIONS WITH OTHER CREATURES

A mercury dragon will enter into a working arrangement with almost any creature stronger or smarter than itself. Such arrangements tend to be feudal in nature: The mercury agrees to serve as a guardian, messenger, or hired killer in exchange for some combination of lair space, treasure, food, and the promise of varied experience. Such relationships last as long as the master can maintain the mercury dragon's interest—and not one moment longer. Draconic folklore is replete with tales of mercury dragons that eventually turned on their masters "just to see what happens."

Mercury dragons have a natural affinity with other creatures that split their time between the natural world and the Elemental Chaos, such as efreets. Mercury dragons often bargain with efreets for passage to the Elemental Chaos (and eventually for a place to start a lair). But efreets don't offer favors lightly, they and tend to be more shrewd negotiators than mercury dragons. Many a mercury dragon seeks vengeance on a particular efreet for a bargain that didn't turn out the way the dragon thought it would.

MITHRAL DRAGONS

No metallic dragon rivals the mithral for power and majesty. (Though golds are loath to acknowledge their inferiority to anyone.) Natives of the Astral Sea, mithral dragons have uncanny insight. Driven by visions and by Io's will, mithrals interact with other creatures only when doing so is necessary to advance their own enigmatic purposes. The few mithral dragons that appear in the mortal world do so to aid religious organizations or great causes—though such dragons can disappear as suddenly as they appear. Other mithrals traverse astral realms, inhabited or otherwise.

LAIRS AND TERRAIN

No two mithral dragons have the same type of lair, nor do mithrals regularly spend a great deal of time

on any given terrain. When a mithral does remain in one place, it dwells in a mine (where it can sense remnants of Io's divine will by reading gemstone deposits or veins of ore) or an abandoned temple (where it can attune itself to echoes of ancient faith).

On the Astral Sea, mithral dragons live in the domains of deities. Mithrals residing in such places maintain ties to their own deities, but also experience visions related to the dead god's existence.

FAVORED TREASURE

Mithral dragons do not discriminate about the types of treasure they collect: They take anything that furthers their goals. Unless their goals require wealth, mithrals don't hoard treasure.

PHYSICAL CHARACTERISTICS

A mithral dragon's scales flex with the muscles beneath them, and they glow faintly. As a mithral ages, the icy white scales of youth darken to silver with white streaks. At the height of a mithral's power, intricate white striations sharply contrast its darker base color. Patterns along the dragon's claws flare with energy during combat.

A ring of spikes crowns a mithral's head, and smaller spikes extend down its neck. The spikes stand on end when the dragon is excited—particularly when it's enraged. The dragon's wings consist of radiant energy instead of flesh.

DIET

Since living in the Astral Sea can make hunting difficult, mithral dragons developed as creatures that need little food to survive. As befits their omnivorous nature, many mithrals (both in the world and in the Astral Sea) create gardens or instruct followers to tend flocks. This delegation of tasks allows them to stay in their lairs and concentrate on their visions instead of hunting far and wide to find sustenance. Mithrals that have larger appetites make their lairs on verdant earthbergs within the Astral Sea, and they fiercely guard these precious properties.

PERSONALITY AND MOTIVATIONS

Mithral dragons retain strong connections to their home plane, the Astral Sea. They speak seldom, impressing upon listeners a sense of purpose too great for words—a purpose beyond mortal comprehension. Visions from Io guide mithrals of varied faiths and callings toward an end planned millennia ago.

Mithral dragons that live in the dominions of dead deities commune directly with Io's spirit. They take action when roused from ageless slumber by visions and dreams of vast import.

A mithral dragon might associate itself with any good or unaligned deity. Mithral dragons that follow evil deities usually venerate Zehir. Some mithrals

disfavor Bahamut, believing that Bahamut fails to further Io's plans and thus does not deserve devotion.

Mithrals destroy without hesitation any creatures that stand between them and their goals. Clever creatures can sway a determined mithral dragon only by convincing it that its goals—and, by extension, Io's will—are served by a temporary alliance.

RELATIONS WITH OTHER CREATURES

Mithral dragons that associate themselves with deities also associate with creatures that share their faith. Mithrals without deities keep to themselves, except when their long-term plans benefit from others' assistance. Mithrals that allow others to serve them are commonly evil.

Mithrals deride other dragons, particularly those that collect material goods solely to enlarge their hoards, such as copper dragons and red dragons.

ORIUM DRAGONS

Named after a crimson-hued metal used by ancient empires, orium dragons are likewise obsessed with the secrets of bygone ages. Orium dragons dwell among the crumbling ruins of forgotten fortresses and temples deep in the jungle. But those ruins are more than just a lair to these dragons. An orium dragon regards its home ruins as its most prized possession—a hoard composed of more than just coins and jewels. For an orium dragon, a life spent wresting the secrets from ancient ruins and restoring those ruins to their former glory is a life well spent. And woe to anyone that would trespass in an orium dragon's lair or try to thwart its efforts at reconstruction.

Why the obsession with the ruins of the past? More so than other kinds of dragon, orium dragons feel a strong drive to emulate the ancestral dragons in their bloodline. Many of those bloodlines were sworn to the service of ancient empires (and a few members of orium bloodlines even ruled kingdoms themselves). Thus, the present-day orium dragon sees the reconstruction of its ruined lair as act of homage, not an act of archaeology.

LAIRS AND TERRAIN

Orium dragons favor jungles because they like the climate and love the ruins hidden within those places. In particular, river deltas and sheltered valleys attract orium dragons, since those are locales where long-forgotten civilizations likely dwelled in ages past.

The lure of unexplored ruins sometimes draws orium dragons beyond their jungle homes. Colder climes make orium dragons less comfortable (and thus more irritable), but any orium dragon will put up with great discomfort if the lure of ancient secrets is strong enough. Although an orium dragon in a polar region would be rare indeed, it's not unusual to encounter one in a temperate climate. Orium dragons aren't accomplished swimmers or climbers, so ocean and mountain locales are unusual, though not unheard of.

After exploring a ruin and killing or subjugating any of its denizens, an orium dragon takes up residence in whatever structure was grandest in the ruin's heyday, often a temple, inner keep, or palace—even if that building is a shambles now. The dragon's servants start to reconstruct the building. If necessary, the workers take building materials from other parts of the ruins, and their reconstruction isn't necessarily accurate. As long as the building evokes the grandeur of a long-dead era, the reconstruction will please the orium dragon.

Still, the dragon might insist on changes to the structure for more practical reasons. For instance, older dragons need wider doorways to accommodate their bulk. And like any dragon, orium dragons want their treasure well protected, so many install traps or magic guardians to watch over their hoards. Orium dragons won't countenance changes that somehow diminish any remaining magic in the ruins or make it more difficult for the dragon to muse upon the ancient mysteries of the ruin.

Though the majority of orium dragons live in the natural world, more than a few call the Feywild home. Most of those are obsessed with the ancient societies of the Feywild and the strange magic of those civilizations. Some older orium dragons try to transport entire ancient ruins from the world to the Feywild, where they can then dream of bygone ages amid the vibrancy and splendor of that plane. Adventurers who encounter the architecture of Nerath or Bael Turath in the depths of the Feywild haven't discovered an extraplanar outpost of those ancient empires—they've stumbled upon the lair of an orium dragon.

FAVORED TREASURE

An orium dragon follows one simple rule when gathering treasure: the older the better. Antique jewelry, coins bearing unfamiliar portraits and mottos, and magic items with archaic decorations fill its hoard. The dragon gathers much of its hoard from the vicinity of its lair, but sometimes acquires items from distant places, especially if it sends its servants far afield in search of ancient mysteries.

PHYSICAL CHARACTERISTICS

An orium dragon is somewhat feline in appearance, with a lithe body and feet that look more like paws than reptilian appendages. Elder and ancient oriums use their long, prehensile tails as an extra weapon in battle. An orium dragon takes inordinate pride in its red metallic scales and spends much of its time grooming itself so that its scales gleam amid the mud of the jungle and the dust of the ruins. Older orium dragons sometimes inlay jade designs on their larger scales—part jewelry, part tattoo.

DIET

Orium dragons, though they are able hunters and true omnivores, would rather study the secrets of the ancients than gather food for themselves. As soon as it's old enough to make its way in the world, an orium dragon intimidates and browbeats other creatures—often a tribe indigenous to the area—into bringing food as tribute. This relationship quickly becomes symbiotic, with the orium dragon providing protection for the tribe in exchange for frequent "sacrifices" of wild game—and, in some cases, captives from rival tribes or trespassing adventurers.

PERSONALITY AND MOTIVATIONS

When characters first meet an orium dragon, they might be surprised at how taciturn it seems. Unlike other dragons, an orium dragon won't bluster or threaten when it first encounters strangers. Instead, it asks simple questions such as "Who are you?" and "Why have you come here?"

The orium dragon's questions are designed to categorize the strangers for its purposes. The vast majority of creatures that an orium dragon encounters fall into one of three categories: thieves, future servants, and food. The orium dragon's mild (for a dragon) demeanor lasts until it has figured out which category the strangers belong in. Then, food and thieves typically are attacked without warning, while future servants are treated to a display of power and intimidation that the orium dragon hopes will cow them into servitude. A typical orium dragon treats only other dragons as equals—and even then, it does so only after it's sure that the other dragon isn't out to steal from the orium's lair.

In the first few rounds of a battle, an orium dragon is quiet, uttering only the occasional grunt of pain (when hit) or derisive chuckle (when hitting). But as the battle goes on, the orium dragon will taunt and countertaunt adversaries who address it in Draconic. Most of an orium dragon's insults play on how young and inexperienced the opponents are—how they have no idea of the ancient power that surrounds them, couldn't possibly comprehend the magic of centuries ago, and so on.

Fundamentally, an orium dragon could be a useful ally for player characters. After all, adventurers and orium dragons tend to do the same things: go into ancient places and abscond with ancient treasure, lore, and powerful magic. But it takes superlative negotiation to persuade an orium dragon to see it that way, because its instinct to classify others into inflexible categories is so strong.

Relations with Other Creatures

Once a creature demonstrates a basic degree of loyalty and tractability, an orium dragon adopts it as a servant and protects it from others in exchange for tribute and labor in the dragon's lair. Humans (often hunter-gatherer tribes) and lizardfolk are the most common servants, but any creature capable of understanding commands and performing manual labor is a potential servant to an orium dragon.

Once it has moved into a lair, an orium dragon faces two main problems. First, in its zeal to establish a lair, it gives less interesting parts of the ruin only a cursory search. Thus, the remnants of the ancient civilization, any guardians it might have left behind, and other creatures that moved into the ruins before the orium dragon can threaten it—or at the least harass its servants.

Second, members of the orium dragon's servant tribe might reveal the existence of their master's lair, attracting the attention of adventurers and other dragons. An orium dragon has no compunctions about taking another orium dragon's lair, and other kinds of dragons might attempt to steal a jungle lair as well.

Silver Dragons

Silver dragons embody all that is honorable about dragonkind. Good silver dragons protect weaker creatures. The few silvers that turn to evil maintain their honor and reputation; they do not slaughter unworthy foes or engage in acts of petty malice.

Lairs and Terrain

Silver dragons love open spaces and lofty heights. They make their homes in mountain ranges, in castles constructed among the clouds, and in the Elemental Chaos. During periods of warm weather, they retreat to the coolest, loftiest heights.

Silver dragons spend less time in their lairs than other dragons do. Wanderlust and curiosity spur them to engage in far-ranging patrols. From time to time, silvers embark on months-long journeys to the corners of the world. Because they spend so much time away from their lairs, silver dragons choose lairs among the highest, least accessible mountain peaks. Those lairs bristle with defenses and traps to protect hoards from other dragons.

Favored Treasure

Silver dragons especially appreciate exceptionally crafted works of art. They collect carefully cut gems and intricate carvings, textiles, and jewelry.

Physical Characteristics

The luster of a mature silver dragon accentuates its prominent neck frills, a beaklike snout, plated facial armor, and long, backswept horns. From a distance, the exceptionally fine scales appear to blend together, lending the dragon the appearance of a sculpture.

Silver dragons have a scent reminiscent of rain and evergreen needles. Their powerful build places them among the strongest members of dragonkind.

Diet

Silver dragons, gifted with keen eyesight, hunt wild game such as mountain goats and deer. They fly gracelessly but dive with great accuracy and power. A silver commonly makes its kill by swooping from a mountainside perch. Silver dragons eat lightly for their size, taking prey only three or four times a month. They do not devour intelligent creatures, because they consider such behavior savage.

Personality and Motivations

Silver dragons are the knights-errant of dragonkind—fierce champions of great causes. Good silvers defend innocents, assure the prosperity of civilized kingdoms, and protect and nurture noble families and young heroes. Evil silvers are rare in the extreme; those that do exist serve tyrants, guard temples of evil deities, or attempt to use evil artifacts to reshape the world.

To a silver dragon, honor means more than life. Silvers choose silence over lies and keep their word, even when doing so places them in opposition against creatures of their alignment. For example, a good-aligned silver dragon sworn to guard an oracle from all intruders discourages any adventurers from consulting the oracle, regardless of their reason, and attempts to destroy those who disregard the warning—after offering them the option to retreat.

Relations with Other Creatures

Silver dragons admire civilized races, particularly individuals that have noble or heroic backgrounds. Silvers commonly associate with dwarves and dragonborn. In the Elemental Chaos, silvers ally with azers and djinns.

When a silver dragon wants to observe a lesser creature, it keeps its distance. A few silvers perform rituals to disguise themselves so they can walk among creatures of interest.

Silver dragons are natural enemies of red dragons, and they consider the formidable reds to be the worthiest of adversaries. In return, red dragons, which hate anything that has the potential to match or better them, kill silvers indiscriminately.

Silver dragons favor similar terrain to white dragons. When a white dragon catches wind of a silver, it stays out of the way.

KEREM BEYIT

STEEL DRAGONS

The sociable steel dragons prefer the company of humanoids to that of other dragons. Their reasons range from admiration to greed. Steels take humanoid form more often they remain in than their natural shape.

LAIRS AND TERRAIN

Because steel dragons live in towns and cities, they live as humanoids do—in houses—and establish humanoid histories and families. In case an enemy discovers its identity, a steel maintains a secondary lair in a ruin, such as a crumbling temple, castle, or tower. The harder it is for other creatures to reach such a site, the better. Wards, traps, and guardians protect these refuges.

FAVORED TREASURE

Steel dragons invest in property and business. A steel that maintains multiple identities might hold controlling shares in two or more enterprises. Steels outfit their homes with art, antiquities, tomes, magic items, finery, and servants.

PHYSICAL CHARACTERISTICS

Compared to other metallic dragons, a steel dragon has a slight build and a small head. Swordlike frills grow from its head, elbows, and digits. Its wings consist of overlapping blades that look like feathers, and the scales on the dragon's chest resemble shields. When a steel dragon adopts humanoid form, it retains something of its draconic nature: gray eyes, pale skin, hair the color of steel, or affectations such as steel jewelry.

DIET

A steel dragon adapts its omnivorous diet to suit its surroundings. A young steel, unaccustomed to assuming humanoid form, might take a while to realize that it needs less to eat in that form than when it's in dragon form. To the disgust and amazement of those around it, such a dragon might consume two to three times more food than a normal humanoid.

PERSONALITY AND MOTIVATIONS

Steel dragons favor humans over other humanoids because of the race's adaptability and cleverness. For this reason, they live in human cities when possible.

For all their fascination with humanoid races, steel dragons cannot tolerate authority. To them, the law serves its purpose only when it maintains order flexibly, so that the dragons can protect their interests and advance their aims. A steel might spark a rebellion to overthrow an oppressive regime, even if doing so could lead to the destruction of its adopted community.

RELATIONS WITH OTHER CREATURES

Steel dragons primarily keep the company of humans but also coexist with elves, half-elves, and dwarves. Steels particularly favor adventuring groups that operate on the fringes of established order and fight the despots that the dragons also oppose.

Opposition to tyranny pits steel dragons against gold dragons, bronze dragons, and chromatics. Disagreements with other dragons rarely blossom into violence, however; steel dragons cause trouble for their kin in subtler ways.

CHAPTER 2

DM's Guide to Dragons

The woman winked, and the flesh of her face started to flow like water. Her head lengthened as her auburn hair faded into thin air. Then her skin rippled, transforming into gray scales, and she loomed taller as her body stretched to accommodate its new, serpentine dimensions.

The voice, though an octave lower, was unmistakably the same: "Were you expecting me to be curled up on a pile of gold coins or something?"

EVERY DRAGON in a D&D game is there because a DM put it there. Some await intruders at the center of trap-infested lairs. Others cast long shadows across the countryside, pillaging at will. But metallic dragons in particular are too versatile to be defined by stereotypes. They can be wise counselors, deadly assassins, intermittent allies, or frustrating rivals.

In this chapter, you'll see ways to nudge metallic dragons off their piles of treasure and into the narrative of your game. In particular, you'll learn about:

✦ **Dragons in the World:** The many campaign roles a dragon can fulfill give you an arsenal of plot elements for any sort of campaign.

✦ **Draconic Encounters:** Because dragons are solo monsters, crafting encounters with them requires some care. In addition to the standard combat encounter, you'll see examples of social challenges, subdual battles in which the object is to convince the dragon of your worthiness, and traps used by dragons to guard their lairs.

✦ **Adventures:** In these adventure outlines, you'll see how dragons can be enemies, allies, neutral parties, or objects around which the entire narrative revolves.

✦ **Draconic Campaigns:** The players will admire and loathe the dragons they meet in these campaign arcs. As each campaign reaches its climax, the players will realize that some dragons are worthy of both admiration and condemnation.

✦ **Draconic Organizations:** Metallic dragons surround themselves with worthy allies, whether the dragons are trying to be a force for good in the world, to overthrow tyrants, or to safeguard an old prophecy. The characters might be just the allies they need.

RALPH HORSLEY

Metallic dragons are everywhere in the world of D&D, both geographically and thematically. A metallic dragon can be the most steadfast ally the characters have, or their most confounding enemy. Dragons have what adventurers want, whether that's ancient lore, access to power, or just a big pile of treasure. And metallic dragons specifically have a more nuanced, versatile history than their chromatic counterparts. They're not just "the good dragons." Some are noble, wise, and true, but others are as scheming, arrogant, and venal as any chromatic dragon.

METALLIC DRAGON PATRONS

A copper dragon working with the characters might be an advisor, suggesting future adventures and providing key clues. The dragon that sees itself as a customer, hiring the characters and insisting that they adhere to its contracts, will behave in a much different way. If the dragon wants to be treated as a god and issues edicts that it expects the heroes to follow without question, it adds a different flavor to your campaign. Yet in all three cases, the dragon's campaign role is the same: patron.

A patron is a powerful creature that sends the characters on missions, provides key campaign information, and sometimes delivers rewards. Played well, a metallic dragon patron can be one of the DM's best friends. It can deliver exposition and explain to the characters (and by extension the players) how the world works. Its lair can serve as the characters'

headquarters. The dragon can provide rewards out of its hoard, and it can send characters on all sorts of quests.

Dragons have a lot of attributes that make them good patrons. They have wide-ranging interests, so it's easy to justify almost any quest you want to send the characters on. They live in lairs, so they tend to stay in one place. And they're haughty and arrogant enough that you should have no problem hamming it up when you portray a dragon patron.

But dragon patrons also have some drawbacks. Because dragons are themselves powerful, consider ahead of time why the dragon sends the characters on quests. You want an answer ready when a character asks, "How come you don't just fly over there and do it yourself?" And because a dragon's power is tied to its age, a dragon patron doesn't increase in power at the same rate that the characters do. When the relationship between the patron and the characters changes with growing character power, you can decide whether you want that relationship to evolve into an alliance among equals or into a rivalry that the characters must contend with.

Draconomicon: Chromatic Dragons introduced the notion of draconic patrons. This campaign role is a relatively rare occurrence among chromatic dragons, but metallic dragons serve as adventuring patrons with far greater frequency. Some do so as a means of exercising their own power and authority through proxies, rather than risking their own lives or expending their own effort. Some do so purely for the social interaction. Some, such as chromatic

ZOLTAN BOROS & GABOR SZIKSZAI

dragons that serve as patrons, have their own agendas or evil schemes. And others, as in the tragic tale of the dragon known to mortals as Silvara (page 214), do so because they genuinely want to help other races overcome the evils that beset them on a daily basis.

Regardless of motivation, a metallic dragon patron normally provides the characters with funding, shelter, knowledge, and advice. (The latter often takes the form of cryptic hints rather than overt information, especially if the dragon wants to obscure its true motives, nature, or reasons for helping.) Only rarely does a draconic patron assist its adventurers in any physical capacity.

MISSIONS AND ENDEAVORS

Since metallic dragons tend to be both more subtle and more social than chromatic dragons, their reasons for using adventurers as proxies are rather broader and can be adapted to fit the needs of your campaign. Some of the most common reasons that dragons use proxies include the following:

✦ The dragon thinks the objective isn't terribly important or is too time-consuming to warrant the dragon's full attention.

✦ The dragon can't accomplish the objective on its own.

✦ The dragon thinks the objective is too dangerous to attempt itself.

There are times when a dragon might want to keep its involvement in an overall endeavor secret. The dragon might then engage proxies to pursue missions related to larger endeavors such as these:

✦ Guiding the fate of a mortal family, community, or organization from behind the scenes.

✦ Acquiring a magic item that the dragon doesn't want its rivals to know it has.

✦ Completing a goal or task that borders on violating (but doesn't quite break) an oath or religious precept.

✦ Thwarting an enemy without that foe knowing who was responsible.

Sometimes, the objective is a secondary reason for a dragon to use proxies. The dragon's actual reason might be something such as the following:

✦ To know if the characters can be trusted with a more important endeavor in the future.

✦ To learn if the mortals of the region might be able to develop sufficient skill and power to pose a threat, either to the dragon itself or to its allies or enemies.

✦ To determine if the characters are part of a particular prophecy or religious revelation and, if

they are, how best to manipulate them to the dragon's ends.

Another possibility is for the endeavor to be something the dragon wants the characters to find for their own good. Possibilities include:

✦ A magic item the characters can use to thwart some great evil (or some enemy of their patron's).

✦ A piece of knowledge or lore the characters will stumble across on their way to completing their assigned mission.

✦ An opportunity for the characters to grow more skilled (that is, gain levels), perhaps to make them ready for a particular enemy or so the dragon can make more effective use of them later.

INDIVIDUAL PATRONS

Unlike chromatic dragons, which tend to connect with humanoid adventurers only as adults or elder dragons, even very young metallic dragons might employ humanoids. This might be because they don't feel powerful enough to accomplish their objectives, or it might be a means of learning how to interact with the more powerful individuals in humanoid society. Similarly, although ancient chromatic dragons tend either to be loners or to have already established a network of slaves and servants as they age, metallic dragons retain their social nature even into their twilight years and, thus, might continue to take up the role of patron to adventurers.

Bronze, gold, mithral, orium, silver, and steel dragons are more likely to become patrons of adventurers than other kinds of metallic dragons. Bronze and gold dragons often prefer to have a few trusted operatives rather than a wider variety of proxies. Cobalt dragons contact humanoids only when the strength and power of a particular party impresses them, and copper dragons do so only when it seems more profitable than other alternatives. Brass, iron, and mercury dragons, which often find themselves working for others, almost never take up with adventurers, and adamantine dragons do so only when a party involves itself in events in or near the dragon's domain.

Draconomicon: Chromatic Dragons offered a number of sample chromatic patrons intended to serve as models for specific types of patrons. That book goes into detail, but here is a quick summary:

✦ The open patron is up front and honest with the characters about its purposes and draconic nature.

✦ The hidden patron keeps its draconic nature hidden and might work through proxies, but is otherwise truthful with the adventurers.

✦ The deceptive patron hides its true nature and also deceives the adventurers as to the true objectives of the quests it offers. It means to use the characters to further a goal they might not approve of.

✦ The intimidating patron demands obedience and expects, by virtue of its strength and power, to be obeyed.

These types of patrons are quite common among metallic as well as chromatic dragons. The roles of guiding patron and controlling patron (detailed below) can appear among chromatic dragons, but they are more common among metallic dragons.

As with the samples in *Draconomicon: Chromatic Dragons*, you can use these characters as they are or as models for designing your own patrons.

Jolvadiris, Guiding Patron: An adult steel dragon who has held multiple humanoid identities in several major cities, Jolvadiris serves as a patron for adventurers who have widespread reputations. In part, he enjoys interacting with impressive humanoids, but he also—like other guiding patrons—seeks to aid individuals and communities in bettering themselves. He does so partly to alleviate suffering and partly to maintain peace and stability in the region.

Many guiding patrons are up front about their draconic nature. Others, such as Jolvadiris, prefer to maintain a human guise, believing that those with whom they interact are more honest and cooperative that way. Unlike truly open patrons, guiding patrons have no compunctions about lying to or misleading their adventurers, often withholding the true purpose of their missions or the true nature of their endeavors. But unlike a deceptive patron, Jolvadiris believes that he does so for the good of the adventurers, allowing them to gain power and uncover secrets at their own rate.

Omalikos, Controlling Patron: A controlling patron, such as the elder orium dragon Omalikos, tends to be straightforward and to expect obedience from its associates. Unlike intimidating patrons that use personal strength and threats to enforce their dictates, Omalikos and his ilk rely on a sense of external authority. Some dragons, for instance, claim rulership of a region that includes the areas where the characters are operating, while others—such as Omalikos—take advantage of their greater knowledge of regional events, using that information to bribe, threaten, or browbeat others into obedience. Omalikos uses adventurers primarily to collect lost lore but also to expand his influence and knowledge of distant regions.

Most relationships with controlling patrons last a short time, unless the dragon holds some legal, moral, or religious authority over the characters. (Those dragons that do not, but that continue to attempt to enforce obedience, tend to shift into intimidating patrons.)

OTHER CAMPAIGN ROLES FOR A METALLIC DRAGON

If you don't develop a dragon as a patron for the characters, there are still plenty of ways to use a dragon—or more than one—in interactions or relationships with the adventurers.

Dragons have a wide array of tools. They are smart, conversational, and social enough to gather other monsters around them in order to engage in plots and schemes that eventually include adventurers. And they're physically dangerous. A dragon has the defenses and hit points to stand toe-to-toe with the toughest characters, but it's maneuverable enough that it doesn't have to. Many dragons are magically potent as well, and higher-level dragons have centuries of experience behind them.

Dragons also come with lairs, adventure sites you can populate in whatever way you want. And a lair provides adventurers with at least one inherent motivator: the pile of shiny coins and magic items the dragon sits on. Delving into a dragon's lair delivers a memorable session of D&D. If you want to use a metallic dragon as more than a monster the characters fight for one encounter, try some of the campaign roles described in the following sections.

Chapter 1 discusses the different ways in which metallic dragons interact with humanoids (such as the characters). But you also want to think about how the dragon interacts with your overall narrative—the role it plays in your campaign. A metallic dragon's campaign role doesn't limit it to interacting with the characters only in certain ways.

MYSTERIOUS STRANGER

One way a metallic dragon can keep your ongoing narrative in flux is by not appearing at all—or at least, not appearing as a dragon. Some metallic dragons, notably the steel and mercury dragons, can change shape into humanoid forms. A metallic dragon can be the hooded stranger in the corner of the bar, the old crone yelling words of prophecy in the bazaar, or the cloaked thief who absconds with the idol just as the characters reach the temple chamber.

If you introduce a dragon as a mysterious stranger, consider carefully the pacing of the "reveals" you do. You want the dragon to be mysterious, but you don't want it to stay mysterious indefinitely. This is a mystery the characters should solve over time. Let each interaction with a shapechanged dragon provide the characters with another clue about what the mysterious stranger is and why it's skulking about.

Also consider the payoff: the moment when the characters realize that they've been in the company of a dragon all along. Does that knowledge lead to a fight? A social challenge? A rescue from an otherwise catastrophic situation? No matter how it plays out, this is a moment rich with drama. Try to clear some space in your plot for the characters to enjoy the moment when the dragon ceases to be a mysterious stranger.

More so than other roles, the mysterious stranger role evolves into another role; the dragon, once it's revealed, becomes a rival, a patron, an occasional ally, or some other campaign role. In terms of the plot, it was performing that role all along. But for the players, confounded by the "Who is that guy?" puzzle, the dragon is a mysterious stranger until the moment they solve the mystery.

A metallic dragon without the ability to shapechange can be a mysterious stranger, too. In this case, it stays mysterious by keeping just out of reach. At first, the characters don't encounter the dragon at all. They come across the fresh corpses of enemies the dragon just defeated. Fast-forward a few sessions, and the heroes find smashed treasure chests and some reptilian footprints leading to a stained-glass window with a gaping hole in the middle. They stay one step behind the mysterious stranger for a long time, but each time they come a little closer and gain another clue to solving the mystery. Eventually, they might meet a survivor of the dragon's attacks. Perhaps after that they spy a glimpse of the dragon at a distance. The characters are now primed for the climactic scene: an actual confrontation with the no longer mysterious dragon.

Occasional Ally

Sooner or later, the characters are going to get in over their heads. When that happens, a metallic dragon can serve as the metaphorical cavalry, flying over the hill and forcing the characters' enemies to flee.

With their intelligence, physical potency, and maneuverability, dragons bring a lot to the table as allies for the characters. A dragon can fight, relay information, give transportation, and provide a safe place to stay when black-clad assassins are burning down every village the characters visit.

What metallic dragons don't do well is fight alongside the characters for extended periods of time. You have enough work to do without dealing with a solo monster as the characters' constant ally. Putting a dragon on the heroes' side in a battle is a fun change of pace once in a while, but when repeated, it loses its luster for the players and becomes a burden for you.

The key part of this campaign role is the word "occasional." Know ahead of time what factors prevent the metallic dragon from working with the characters full-time. Perhaps the dragon won't venture far from its lair, nor stay away too long. Maybe it has other allies that need its help more. Or maybe

CHRIS SEAMAN

it exacts a price (literal or figurative) for its assistance that the characters aren't always willing to pay. Finally, the dragon's personality might render it inherently unreliable.

Vexing Ally

Characters naturally want a dragon on their side, and this campaign role plays on that inclination. A vexing ally seems like an asset at first, but eventually grows to be more trouble for the characters than it's worth.

A vexing ally might be overzealous, seeking the same overall goal as the characters but seeking it in a way the characters regard as beyond the pale. The dragon might be more militantly religious than the characters, trying to convert everyone it meets. Or the dragon might be so arrogant, short-tempered, or indiscriminate in its diet that the characters can't deal with it even to reach a common goal.

The dragon might also be working toward a goal that seems to be in concert with the characters' goal at first, but gradually diverges over time. A copper dragon can find common cause with characters who are trying to drive ogres out of the nearby foothills, but when the dragon starts constructing a fortress-lair on the hill that overlooks the characters' home town, the characters might wish the ogres were still around.

Like the mysterious stranger campaign role, consider how you'll gradually reveal the vexing aspect of the dragon ally. Eventually, you want the heroes to face the fundamental choice: What do they do about this dragon? Should they rein it in somehow, keep it at arm's length, or confront it once and for all? That choice takes on added richness when the characters have had several interactions with the vexing ally, and each interaction has widened the gap between the characters and the dragon a little more.

Prepare the dragon's response to each of the possible solutions the characters could use to deal with their vexing ally. At this point, the metallic dragon takes on a new campaign role. Whether the dragon becomes an occasional ally, a rival, a villain, or something else entirely is up to you and your players.

Uncaring Obstacle

Sometimes you want a powerful figure in your campaign that fundamentally doesn't care about your campaign. It starts to look a little suspicious if every creature in the world is consumed with the drow incursions into the surface world (or whatever the overall conflict is in your campaign). It can be useful to have a powerful figure that isn't going to be drawn into the ongoing conflict—neither as an enemy nor as an ally. A metallic dragon's long outlook and tendency to hole up in its lair make it a good uncaring obstacle that the characters must contend with outside of your core narrative, which already has plenty of scheming factions and adversaries.

When you use a metallic dragon in this role, answer three key questions: What does the dragon have? How do the characters find out what the dragon has? What hoops will the dragon make them jump through to get it?

Metallic dragons own all sorts of stuff that adventurers want: rare magic items, powerful rituals, ancient lore, and so on. And you can seed a clue in an early part of your campaign that lets the characters know where to go to obtain these things. They might have to piece together several clues to figure out where the uncaring obstacle dragon is, or it might be as simple as another character telling them, "Only the iron dragon Arthanaclaur knows the secrets of the Twelve Portals."

Figure out what it takes for the characters to get what they want. The simplest solution is for them to battle the dragon in its lair, slay it, and reap the reward they came for. But a dragon might also give up what the characters want after negotiation (a skill challenge), after they answer three riddles (or solve any sort of puzzle), or after they undertake a quest for the dragon (a specific adventure).

How does this role differ from that of the occasional ally? It requires less work in terms of plotting, because the dragon is indifferent to the various machinations of the heroes and villains. It's also less likely to be a recurring campaign role. This dragon is in your campaign to make the characters solve a puzzle or undertake a quest, and it remains offstage thereafter. It's merely a delivery mechanism for a plot element, not a plot element in and of itself.

Rival

Metallic dragons often have nuanced personalities, and it's easy to have them ride the fence between ally and enemy. A metallic dragon rival might be working toward the same goal as the characters, or it might have schemes of its own that merely run parallel to their plans. The dragon might have the same patron as the characters, and might try to curry favor with the patron and make the characters look incompetent or untrustworthy in the process.

The key element to an ongoing rivalry is providing variety in each interaction with the characters. If the heroes simply fight the rival dragon each time they meet, the dragon just feels like a recurring enemy, not a full-fledged rival. Sometimes the rival dragon merely makes mischief when the characters are engaged in another challenge and then escapes before the characters can confront it directly. Sometimes the rival dragon is the opponent in a skill challenge or in another situation in which it will trade insults but not blows with the heroes. And don't forget one of the oldest plot twists in fiction: two rivals who are forced into a reluctant, temporary alliance to defeat a foe that neither could withstand alone.

That isn't to say you shouldn't let the characters fight their rival. They're going to ache for the chance after a while, and you should satisfy that urge. You have several tools to make sure that the battle doesn't end in death. You can make it a duel of honor (see page 50), have a more powerful creature intervene near the end of the battle, or merely play the rival dragon cautiously enough that it can escape a losing fight of its own volition.

As you introduce a rival dragon, have some idea of when you want to resolve the rivalry—one way or another. The characters become more powerful over time, but dragons tend to stay the same for decades. Make sure your rivalry comes to a dramatic conclusion before the characters' level is high enough to render the dragon rival inconsequential.

This campaign role differs from the vexing ally mostly in that it's not a gradual reveal. The characters feel the rivalry right away and must deal with it throughout the campaign. But a vexing ally can become a rival once the characters realize just how wrong they were to make it their ally.

VILLAIN

Metallic dragons are less likely to be evil than are chromatic dragons, but even so, there are more than a few bad apples among them. Good and unaligned creatures can make effective villains, too.

Just because a dragon is good doesn't make it wise or honorable. It can be as haughty, quick to anger, and driven by ignoble emotions as humanoids—or other dragons. A good dragon might see the characters as evildoers (whether that's accurate or not), as obstacles to its ongoing schemes, or as necessary sacrifices in order for good to triumph over evil.

An unaligned dragon can likewise be a center-piece villain in your ongoing campaign. It's easy to justify a dragon that's a callous mercenary, because draconic greed is legendary. And a metallic dragon could be egomaniacal enough to see itself as the arbiter of some sort of cosmic balance, battling the characters lest the forces of good become too powerful.

Truly evil metallic dragons are out there, too. Some are outwardly evil, but others play on the metallic dragons' heritage as children of Bahamut. They hide their evil behind metallic scales, sending their minions out on quests that appear beneficial but have a darker purpose. You can start a dragon in the patron or vexing ally campaign role, and then switch the dragon to a villain role when the characters realize that the dragon they've been fighting with or working for was evil all along.

DRAGONS IN THE BACKGROUND

Metallic dragons can be important when they aren't directly interacting with the player characters. Even when they're in the background, dragons are bound to catch the interest of the characters.

Strategic Weapon: When you need to threaten a town or a city with destruction, nothing does the job better than dragons circling in the sky overhead. Faced with this threat, the characters can try to negotiate with the dragons to keep them on the sidelines, find a magic countermeasure for an impending dragon attack, preempt the villain as he's about to launch the dragon attack, or evacuate the city. None of those responses involves a direct battle with dragons, and only one of them interacts with the dragons at all. The dragons are a plot element that remains in the background but drives the story forward.

Mass Transit: Dragons have fast overland flight speeds, making them an effective way to move characters from place to place—when used sparingly. There's something inherently cool about traveling on the back of a dragon, but that sense of the fantastic loses its luster if it becomes commonplace.

Border: The *terra incognita* at the edge of the map marked "Here be dragons" is a cartographic cliché. But viewed through the lens of the game world, that cliché becomes far more real: a far-off ridge that people dare not explore because they see brass dragons soaring overhead, for example. You can use the presence of powerful dragons to channel characters' explorations elsewhere until the heroes are powerful enough to face the dragons. At that point, they will have earned the right to cross the border you've set up.

Scenery: Dragons have a symbolic value that the players instinctively understand. A dragon signifies power, and it signifies the fantastic. You can put a dragon in the literal background of a scene to add power and a sense of the fantastic to what you're describing. Players are likely to respect a general who has a sleeping dragon curled up behind his tent, even if the dragon never wakes up and neither the general nor the characters mention the dragon in conversation.

When you put a dragon in front of the characters, you'll definitely get the players' attention. More so than any other monster, a dragon makes any encounter something the players will be talking about in the weeks and months to come. Players know that they'll be dealing with a solo monster that has potent attacks, high defenses, and at least some maneuverability. And they probably suspect that where there's a dragon, there's probably a dragon hoard.

But a dragon—especially a metallic dragon—is more than just a statistics block. You have a lot of tools at your disposal, including mixes of dragons and other monsters, subdual encounters, and social challenges.

COMBAT ENCOUNTERS

The obvious way to build a combat encounter with a dragon is to pick a dragon of an appropriate level and use only that dragon. Dragons are solo monsters, after all. Just because that approach is simple doesn't mean it isn't effective. A dragon has enough powers in its arsenal to keep the characters on their toes, and if they can defeat a solo dragon, they've earned their experience points and their treasure. More to the point, a dragon is designed to place roughly the same demands on the characters as five normal monsters would. Play that solo dragon, play it well, and that's all the encounter-building you need to do.

But sometimes the ongoing adventure (or your own sense of creativity) demands that you mix it up a little. Making a solo monster part of a larger encounter is tricky because you face two limiting factors: the experience-point budget for the encounter and the limits of what you can bring to life at the game table.

MANAGING THE XP BUDGET

The following tips can help you manage a dragon encounter without ruining the XP budget.

Raise the Encounter Level: A solo monster of a level equal to the party's level takes up the entire budget for an encounter of that level. So if you want to add monsters, you can make the encounter tougher (and they're fighting a dragon, so doing so makes some dramatic sense). Adding one standard monster of the dragon's level puts the encounter on the cusp of being one level tougher. If you add two standard monsters or one elite, you're at least one level tougher and sometimes almost two levels tougher.

Lower the Level, Then Add Monsters: If you want to add monsters without breaking the budget, you can use a lower-level dragon to begin with. If you use a dragon one level lower than the party's level, you can definitely add one monster and sometimes two monsters and keep the overall encounter at the same level as that of the characters. If you use

a dragon two levels lower, then you can add at least two—and often three—standard monsters.

And you can both downshift the dragon and raise the encounter level if you want an encounter in which the dragon is only a small part of the monster mix. (But be aware of the complexity issues described in "Managing the Encounter's Complexity.")

Use an Elite Dragon: Turn a normal solo dragon into an elite using the advice given on page 218.

Give the Characters an Advantage: If you want to add monsters to a solo dragon encounter without raising the encounter level, you can provide advantageous terrain or other equalizing factors to make for a fair fight. How you pull off this trick depends on the specifics of your adventure, but it's easy to justify the presence of almost anything in a dragon's lair. The characters might benefit from any of these advantages:

✦ Fantastic terrain such as blood rock, a font of power, or a pillar of life (all described on pages 67-68 of the *Dungeon Master's Guide*). Such terrain is an advantage for the characters only if they seize it before the monsters do. A small piece of terrain such as a single pillar of life might work against the characters if they cluster around it, letting the dragon use its *breath weapon* on everyone at once.

✦ A distraction that the dragon or some of the monsters must deal with. If the monsters must keep one of their number tending an ongoing ritual every round, for example, they can't focus their full attention on the characters. Although you don't need to immediately explain to the players how the distraction works, what's going on should be apparent after a few rounds of observation. If, for example, the dragon always flies back to the blue orb in the round after the orb flashes, then the characters can put that knowledge to work for them—and they'll have an interesting puzzle (what does the blue orb do?) when the fight ends.

✦ Reinforcements that enter the fight gradually. If the door opens at the start of round four and kobold cultists start pouring into the dragon's chamber, then you've added monsters but given the characters a key advantage: three rounds of focused attacks against the dragon.

✦ An unusual victory condition. The characters might be able to overcome the challenge of the encounter without beating every single monster down to 0 hit points. If the dragon yields as soon as it's bloodied, for example, it's not a solo monster. It's more like a supercharged elite, and your encounter planning should reflect that. Likewise, if the other monsters flee or surrender as soon as the dragon goes down, then the characters have a significant advantage.

ZOLTAN BOROS & GABOR SZIKSZAI

If you include an unusual victory condition, realize that it's more meaningful if the players know about it ahead of time. If the characters are tenaciously fighting the dragon, hoping to take it down and thus cow the kobolds into submission, that's tactically useful and a recipe for a dramatic encounter. But if they don't suspect that the kobolds will surrender, they might kill the kobolds first, denying themselves the advantage you intended and making the encounter more difficult than you planned.

Managing the Encounter's Complexity

Although it's tempting to build a dragon encounter with other monsters, interesting terrain, reinforcements, and an unusual victory condition, it's your ability to manage all those elements that determines whether anyone has fun in your game–including you. By itself, a solo dragon isn't too complicated, but don't mistake that solo dragon for an ordinary monster. When you start adding more monsters, complex terrain, and other factors to your encounter, it's easy for the overall complexity to creep past the point where you (or anyone) can comfortably manage it.

Just as you can give your encounter a bigger XP budget by increasing its level, you can allow yourself more complexity in your encounter by spending time preparing for it beforehand. One overlooked aspect of preparation is practice: running through the fight ahead of time. If you've practiced with the dragon a few times, you can run through its attacks without a lot of thought, position it favorably for *breath weapon* attacks without a lot of contemplation, and remember the details such as auras and recharges that a harried DM can easily forget. Another way you can improve your ability to handle complexity is by having good notes behind your screen. If you've pulled out all the relevant rules text and terrain information, you'll spend less time flipping through books and more time making the fight a challenge for the players.

One final consideration: As you build your dragon encounter, take a critical look at complexity that's invisible to the players, because it's rarely worth the effort. If reinforcements arrive through the north door, there's little point in having them arrive in a random round (the players aren't going to go through the encounter more than once, so it won't be a random round to them). Nor would it be worthwhile to have the type of reinforcements depend on a die roll or the specific situation in the dragon's lair. To the players, it's just monsters coming through a door.

Subdual Encounters

D&D has a long tradition of dragons that can somehow be subdued–defeated instead of killed. Subduing a dragon makes particular sense in the case of metallic dragons, which are usually less antagonistic than their chromatic counterparts. A subdual encounter provides the players with a fight that's out of the ordinary. And by preserving the dragon for future encounters, a subdual encounter can assist the ongoing narrative.

At its simplest, a subdual encounter is one in which the dragon stops fighting–and the characters win–when the dragon is bloodied. But the degree of the victory matters, so you will need to keep track of how many characters were bloodied during the course of the battle.

Why would a dragon fight this way? For two main reasons: honor and survival. Some dragons abhor needless bloodshed as inherently dishonorable, and those dragons are more likely to be metallic than chromatic. Other dragons will fight a subdual encounter for more pragmatic reasons. It's likely that the second half of the battle would go the same way as the first half, and if the dragon is bloodied, it's better to pay off or otherwise placate the intruders than to risk its life.

BUILDING A SUBDUAL ENCOUNTER

A dragon four levels higher than the characters is appropriate for a typical subdual encounter. If the battle ends when the dragon is bloodied, it effectively has fewer hit points than a typical solo of the party's level, but its defenses will be higher and its attacks more potent. But it's fundamentally a fair challenge, and the characters deserve the XP and treasure rewards for their victory. Award experience points for an encounter of the party's level, and account for an appropriate treasure parcel either directly (by having the dragon give the characters a gift from its hoard) or indirectly (by increasing the treasure elsewhere in the adventure). You can make part of the treasure reward depend on how many characters avoided becoming bloodied.

A subdual encounter is also a good way for the characters to earn assistance from a dragon. If they beat the dragon in a subdual encounter, the dragon is often inclined to be helpful. After all, those characters might start a fight to the death the next time. A subdued dragon will grant passage through its territory, part with important lore or clues, or end alliances with foes of the characters. Again, you can provide a graduated award. The dragon might part with only cryptic clues if the characters were all bloodied, offer more detailed lore if just one or two were bloodied, and give them an accurate map of their next destination if none of the characters became bloodied.

Many good and some unaligned dragons perform subdual battles as a matter of course; it's how they prefer to deal with hostile humanoids. They'll fight the characters normally until they're bloodied, at which point they'll stop attacking for a round, praise the characters for an honorable defeat, and then make arrangements for a reward. You don't have to tell the players ahead of time that it's a subdual battle, and if the characters want to continue the fight and deal with the consequences, they certainly can. Subdual battles usually work better, though, when characters know the ground rules: They're trying to remain unbloodied, and the battle will end when either the dragon is bloodied or all the characters are.

DUELS OF HONOR

A duel of honor functions as a subdual encounter—everyone knows ahead of time what the ground rules are. There's an additional complication for the characters: The dragon won't attack bloodied characters, but it expects that bloodied characters will retreat and observe the rest of the battle as spectators. A given dragon might or might not engage in duels of honor. There's no mandate that it has to, and an untrustworthy dragon might claim a duel of honor until defeat seems likely, at which point it breaks the rules and fights a standard battle.

Assuming that everyone follows the rules, a duel of honor makes the battle easier for the dragon than a normal subdual encounter would be, because it's easier for the dragon to knock characters out of the fight. A dragon three levels higher than the party's level is an appropriate challenge for a duel of honor.

When you run a duel of honor, consider its effect on the players—not just their characters. If you focus the dragon's attacks and spend action points early, the dragon might bloody one of the heroes in the first round or two. That player, assuming the characters adhere to the duel's rules, doesn't have anything to do except sit and listen until the fight is over. Spreading the dragon's damage around isn't optimal play, but it makes for better drama. Ideally, you want everyone to be just one attack away from being bloodied and to be sweating each roll of the dice.

Just as with a subdual encounter, if the characters break the rules in a duel of honor, there's a natural consequence: They have to deal with an angry dragon that's three or more levels higher than they are.

SOCIAL ENCOUNTERS

Countless exceptions exist, but characters are more likely to negotiate with a metallic dragon than a chromatic one. When the characters are talking to a dragon, you've already marked the interaction as important. Dragons have a gravitas unlike other monsters. Dragons demand respect. Including a social encounter with a dragon means you need to deliver on the implicit promise that talking to a dragon is something special.

Let your dragons truly be dragons. Make them casually arrogant, occasionally inscrutable, and perpetually scheming. Have each dragon demonstrate for the characters that it's the whole package: physically powerful, magically potent, and (in the case of older dragons) backed up with the experience of centuries. Dragons can still inadvertently display their weaknesses, though. A dragon should always underestimate smaller creatures (such as the characters), obsess about the treasures in its hoard, and harbor sinister ambitions against its rivals.

UNMASKING THE DRAGON

"What do you mean, 'Am I really just a minstrel?' " she asks, revealing a glimpse of a wry grin as she tosses her hair back. "Are you really just a soldier? And is your companion really just a priest?"

In this challenge, the characters are talking to a dragon that has used its *change shape* power or other magic to appear humanoid.

You can run this challenge in one of two ways. If the characters know that the individual they're conversing with isn't what he or she appears to be, then this challenge is an overt effort to figure out just what they're dealing with.

But it's also possible that the characters' suspicions are more vague: They know that something is amiss, but they don't know for sure that they're dealing with a shapechanged creature, much less that a dragon is in the mix. In this case, you should mix the skill checks called for below with other actions and checks. As the characters simultaneously work on the surface conversation (whatever the dragon is talking about), they're also probing to figure out what's unusual about the stranger they're conversing with. You can combine this social challenge with a negotiation and run two social challenges simultaneously.

Start the skill challenge as soon as a player expresses some suspicion or doubt that the social interaction taking place is as ordinary as it appears.

Level: 9 (800 XP).

Complexity: 2 (requires 6 successes before 3 failures).

Primary Skills: Diplomacy, Insight, Nature, Perception.

Diplomacy (DC 19, standard action): The character's quick talking or smooth manner has coerced some information out of the dragon that hints at its true nature. It could be that the dragon is beginning to trust the characters, or perhaps the hint was unintentional.

Insight (DC 14, minor action): The character picks up a clue from body language or a vocal mannerism that's decidedly not humanoid. With each success, reveal a further clue about what lies under the disguise. For example, "She's older than she appears," then "She's not human," then "Whatever she is, she's accustomed to being on all fours," and so on.

Nature (DC 19, minor action): The character notices something specifically draconic, such as a slow blink or a sinuous, reptilian stretch of the neck and shoulders. Only 1 success can be gained in this way.

Perception (DC 19, minor action): The character spots a strictly physical flaw in the dragon's disguise: a bit of telltale magical blur, or the faint outline of a scale on exposed skin. As with Insight checks, try to show the characters the truth gradually. First reveal evidence that suggests that they're indeed dealing with a disguised creature, and then provide better and better clues about what's under that disguise.

Secondary Skills: Bluff, Arcana, Dungeoneering, Religion.

Bluff (DC 8, standard action): The character isn't bluffing directly so much as he or she is using adroit conversation to draw the dragon into a lively, fast-paced exchange during which it might inadvertently reveal something. A successful Bluff check doesn't provide a success, but it grants a +2 bonus to the next Insight or Perception check.

Arcana, Dungeoneering, or Religion (DC 19, minor action): Success with any of these skills on a monster knowledge check doesn't provide a success in the challenge, but it eliminates the possibility that the creature has one of the origins associated with the skill in question. If the skill check is successful, tell the player, "You don't see any clues that would suggest a creature like the ones you've studied." Each of these skill checks can be attempted only once.

Success: The dragon admits what the characters are about to figure out: It's a dragon. If conditions are right, it changes back into its real form and deals with the characters as a dragon.

Failure: The characters get no indication they're dealing with a disguised dragon, but they might retain the suspicions they already have. The dragon cuts the interaction short if it can, and is uncommunicative if it can't get away from the characters.

BEGGING FOR MERCY

As you scatter to avoid the dragon's breath, it circles around, casually tossing your unconscious comrade to the ground at your feet. "You've proved your tenacity," the dragon growls. "But you're about to prove your foolishness. Do you want further demonstrations of how overmatched you are?"

There's no ironclad guarantee that an encounter with a dragon will be fundamentally fair. In this social encounter, the characters must negotiate a ceasefire with the dragon they're fighting—while surviving long enough to reach the end of the skill challenge.

Don't underestimate the players' willingness to press onward in the face of their near-certain demise. Before you bring this skill challenge into play, make sure you have a way of suggesting to the players that a social encounter might save their characters' lives. This might be as blatant as a "You might be able to talk your way out of this" clue.

This skill challenge begins when a character makes a Bluff, Diplomacy, History, Insight, or Religion check in hopes of ending hostilities. The dragon continues to fight the characters during this skill challenge, but it does so cautiously. If the characters do well (as described in the "Success" paragraph below), the dragon refrains from attacking for a round.

Level: 14 (XP 2,000).

Complexity: 2 (requires 6 successes before 3 failures).

Primary Skills: Bluff, Diplomacy, History, Insight.

Bluff (DC 18, standard action): The character engages in deception, trying to make the dragon believe the heroes are either weaker or more capable than they are. A failed check grants the dragon a +2 bonus to attack rolls against that character on the dragon's next turn.

Diplomacy (DC 18, standard action): The character tries to persuade the dragon to end the conflict peacefully.

History (DC 18, standard action): Reciting a past case in which a dragon spared mortals' lives and benefited from doing so, the character tactfully reminds the dragon of that event.

Religion (DC 23, standard action): The character quotes some analects of Bahamut about the nature of honorable mercy. This skill can be used to gain only 1 success.

Secondary Skills: Insight, special.

Insight (DC 11, minor action): By assessing the dragon's mood, the character gets an idea of how best to convince it to let the party live. Success on an Insight check does not provide a success in the challenge, but it grants a +2 bonus to either Bluff or Diplomacy checks until the end of the character's next turn; the DM determines which skill gains the advantage against the dragon. The character can share this information with allies.

Special: If no character has attacked the dragon for a full round, each character gains a +2 bonus to Diplomacy, History, and Insight checks. The first time the characters bloody the dragon, they earn 1 failure in the challenge. If the dragon attacks in a given round but doesn't hit anyone, the party earns 1 success.

Success: If the characters achieve 3 or more successes in a single round, the dragon waits for them to continue their argument and doesn't attack on its next turn. It still maneuvers, rolls recharges for its *breath weapon*, and otherwise prepares for the battle to resume. When the characters reach 6 successes, the dragon announces that the battle is at an end. It then converses with the characters—not as equals, but

as creatures wise enough to know their proper place in the world.

Failure: The dragon won't grant the characters even a temporary respite from its attacks. If the characters want to survive, they must retreat.

REQUESTING TRANSPORT

The dragon raises up on its hind legs and unfolds its leathery wings. "It is indeed true that none can travel through the Sorrowflame mountain passes," the dragon intones. "But we dragons spurn such petty inconveniences. The mountains cannot hinder dragons on the wing."

In this skill challenge, the characters negotiate with a dragon (or possibly several dragons) to persuade it to take them someplace using overland flight.

This encounter assumes a few facts: Travelers can't easily reach the destination (so the dragon knows that its service is valuable), getting there is neither easy nor impossibly difficult, and the destination isn't someplace the dragon often visits, so any wayfinding guidance the characters can provide will be useful. The skill challenge is most effective if the characters are under time constraints.

For the dragon to agree to take the characters where they want to go, they must convince it both that the journey is worth it and that they deserve of the honor of riding a dragon.

Level: 15 (2,400 XP).

Complexity: 2 (requires 6 successes before 3 failures).

Primary Skills: Diplomacy, Intimidate, Nature.

Diplomacy (DC 18, standard action): The character makes a direct appeal to the self-interest of the dragon, pointing out advantages of journeying with the characters and employing the obligatory flattery.

FRANZ VOHWINKEL

Intimidate (DC 18, standard action): As soon as one character uses Intimidate to argue that he or she is worthy of riding a dragon, have all the characters make Intimidate checks as the dragon assesses them collectively. If the dragon has seen the characters defeat an enemy, give them a +1 bonus to this check; give them a +2 bonus to this check if the characters have previously defeated the dragon. The heroes earn 1 success in the challenge if more characters succeed than fail. Intimidate can be used only once in this way, but it has an alternate use.

Intimidate (DC 23, standard action): The character delivers a threat or an ultimatum to the dragon, with a +2 bonus to this check if the characters have previously defeated the dragon. If this check succeeds, perform the Intimidate group check (described above), if you haven't already done so. If this group check fails to earn a success in the challenge, the dragon makes an attack roll against the character who delivered the threat or ultimatum. If that attack hits, the character is knocked prone or slammed into a wall, but takes no damage. This is only a warning: The dragon is punishing the character's temerity.

Nature (DC 18, standard action): The character demonstrates his or her knowledge of the journey ahead and its rigors and hazards. This skill can be used to gain only 1 success in the challenge.

Success: The dragon agrees to take the characters where they want to go, using overland flight. If battles happen during the journey, the dragon fights alongside the characters.

Failure: The dragon is unconvinced that the characters' journey is worthwhile, or that the characters are worthy of flying with it. The dragon will take the characters where they want to go only if they undertake a quest on the dragon's behalf first (see page 62 for some quest ideas). During the journey, it fights only when its own survival is at stake; the characters are otherwise on their own.

Debating the Scholar

"Your point about the eldritch connection is well taken, if artlessly expressed," the dragon says, slithering toward a bookstand in the corner.

"A dragon named Lorroch-Turhelion spoke of that connection more than twenty of your lifetimes ago—as part of a theory about interactions with the Feywild. She pointed out that the strength of the connection isn't nearly as important as its exact nature. She identified twelve categories, each divided by the relevant influence, origin point, and . . ."

With their native intellect and centuries long life spans, dragons are natural sages and lore-keepers. Convincing a dragon to part with that wisdom is no easy task. Nor is it easy to teach an elder or an ancient dragon something new, but that's exactly the goal of characters who find themselves drawn into an academic debate with a dragon.

This skill challenge deliberately doesn't specify the nature of the academic debate. That's a matter for you and your campaign to determine. Ultimately, the specific proposition under debate doesn't matter; it might be relevant to the characters' goals or it might just be a topic chosen by the dragon to test the lesser creatures that have the brashness to question draconic wisdom. Dragons are arrogant enough to savor an argument for its own sake, after all.

Setup: For the characters to convince the dragon that they're right, they must win the debate by using arguments that the dragon understands and respects.

Level: 24 (12,100 XP).

Complexity: 2 (requires 6 successes before 3 failures).

Primary Skills: Arcana, History, and whichever knowledge skill is relevant to the debate.

Specific Knowledge Skill (DC 24, standard action): The characters argue the merits of the proposition. This will involve an Arcana, Dungeoneering, History, Nature, or Religion check most of the time. History and Nature can be used in other ways to advance the characters' argument, as described below. Characters who speak Draconic gain a +1 bonus to the skill check.

History (DC 24, standard action): In his or her argument, the character references ancient authorities and obscure texts—but authorities and texts that a long-lived dragon would know and respect. A character who speaks Draconic gain a +1 bonus to the skill check.

Nature (DC 29, standard action): The character applies a uniquely draconic spin on the argument, mimicking dragon speech patterns and picking up on subtle behavior cues that only those who have studied dragons would spot. The characters can earn only 1 success with this approach.

Secondary Skills: Insight, special.

Insight (DC 24, minor action): The character reads the demeanor of the dragon, learning which lines of argument it finds particularly compelling. Use of this skill doesn't provide a success or failure in the challenge, but a successful check grants a +2 bonus to the next knowledge check a character attempts in the challenge.

Special: If the Consult Oracle ritual is performed before engaging the dragon in debate, it can give the characters a head start on constructing a compelling argument. It grants 1 automatic success on the skill challenge for every two questions answered by the oracular spirit.

Success: The dragon is convinced by the characters' arguments and impressed by their knowledge. The reward for success is usually something specific to your campaign, but it's reasonable for the dragon to offer a service or boon at this point. Furthermore, the characters earn a +1 bonus to skill checks in future skill challenges with this dragon.

Failure: The dragon contemptuously dismisses the characters' arguments, and if possible ends the interaction altogether. The characters take a -1 penalty to future Diplomacy checks or Intimidate checks made to influence this dragon.

ENEMY OF MY ENEMY

Water drips from the ceiling. Burning naphtha pools cast queer shadows on the cavern walls, throwing red light across the dragon's scales. One moment, a pale membrane covers its great golden eyes; the next, it stares at you, unimpressed by your swords and spells. "Speak quickly, little fools. It has been hours since my last meal."

Enemies threaten a nearby city, and although the citizens are willing to give their lives toward their community's defense, they are too few to stand against the approaching doom. Allies promise aid, but it will take a week at least for the reinforcements to arrive. The characters need to buy them time, and what better way to gain a few extra days than by stirring a dragon to fight on their behalf? Naturally, the dragon has little interest in the affairs of such feeble creatures, especially when they haven't paid it tribute in generations, and it would take a good argument to persuade the monster to stir from its lair.

The heroes must convince the dragon that the threat to the city is also a threat to itself.

Level: 8 (700 XP).

Complexity: 2 (6 successes before 3 failures).

Primary Skills: Bluff, Diplomacy, History, Insight, Nature.

Bluff (DC 19, standard action): The character fabricates a reason why aiding the heroes is in the dragon's best interest.

Diplomacy (DC 14, standard action): The character describes how the troubles affecting the city will ultimately trouble the dragon or flatters the dragon and makes it think the city has no chance to stand against the impending doom without its help. The characters might also offer treasure, service, or something of value in exchange for the dragon's assistance. A particularly generous offering can reduce the DC to 8 for a single check.

History (DC 14, standard action): The character reminds the dragon of a time when it has come to the aid of good people in the past, or when other dragons have done so, and how the legends of such events are flattering to the dragon and good for its reputation. This skill can be used to gain 1 success in this challenge.

Insight (DC 14, minor action): Careful attention helps the character know what the dragon wants to hear, whether it seeks an excuse to help or needs to see the benefit to itself. This skill can be used to gain 1 success in this challenge. A success also grants the party a +2 bonus to either Bluff or Diplomacy checks (characters' choice) for the duration of the challenge.

Nature (DC 14, standard action): The character recalls a useful fact about the dragon's diet, lair, or physiology for use as an advantage during the negotiation. This skill can be used to gain 1 success in this challenge.

Success: The dragon agrees to aid the community and promises to strike the enemies to slow their progress. If the characters completed the challenge with no failures, the dragon also helps defend the city when the menace finally arrives.

Failure: The dragon decides the characters and the city aren't worth the trouble and demands that the characters leave its lair at once, resorting to violence if they don't leave. If the characters achieved no successes in the challenge, the dragon automatically attacks.

RESTORING THE PEACE

Through the smoke and the burning buildings, you spy a gleaming beast, its scales shining in the light cast by the flames. The dragon turns its head toward you, revealing a bestial grimace that contorts its astonishing features into a visage of wrath.

A dragon known to be nonviolent is attacking a town that it had never bothered before. The townsfolk seek a peaceful solution, because the dragon's presence has kept vicious creatures away for many years. The adventurers must discover why the dragon is attacking and restore the peace. The dragon is still rampaging during this challenge, and the characters might be rescuing people or trying to delay the dragon as they play out the challenge. Each character can attempt only one skill check in the challenge per turn.

CHANGING LEVELS FOR SOCIAL ENCOUNTERS

You can adapt any of these social encounters to fit the level of the characters in your current adventure. Doing so is a simple matter of substitution. Replace the DCs noted in the skill challenges with the appropriate ones in the table below. First, use the table to determine whether the check for each skill used in a challenge is easy, moderate, or hard. Then replace that DC with the easy, moderate, or hard DC at the level appropriate for your game.

Party Level	Easy	Moderate	Hard
1st-3rd	5	10	15
4th-6th	7	12	17
7th-9th	8	14	19
10th-12th	10	16	21
13th-15th	11	18	23
16th-18th	13	20	25
19th-21st	14	22	27
22nd-24th	16	24	29
25th-27th	17	26	31
28th-30th	19	28	33

Level: 20 (8,400 XP).

Complexity: 3 (requires 8 successes before 3 failures).

Primary Skills: Diplomacy, Heal, History, Insight, Bluff, Perception.

Diplomacy (DC 27, standard action): Using careful questions so as not to anger the dragon further, the character tries to learn the reason for the dragon's wrath. This skill can be used to gain a maximum of 4 successes in this challenge, but each character can attempt a Diplomacy check only once.

Heal (DC 14, standard action): The character offers to treat the injuries the dragon has sustained in battle. A successful check grants the characters 1 success and removes 1 failure. The characters can gain only 1 success (and remove 1 failure) with this skill.

WAYNE ENGLAND

History (DC 22, standard action): The character reminds the dragon of the long alliance between it and the people of the land. This skill can be used to gain a maximum of 3 successes in this challenge.

Insight (DC 27, minor action): Examining the dragon's words and body language, a character can gain in inkling about the dragon's frustration. A character who succeeds on an Insight check can make a Bluff check during the following round (see below). A failed Insight check, in addition to counting as a failure in the challenge, also imposes a –2 penalty to Diplomacy checks until a successful Insight check is made. This skill can be used to gain a maximum of 3 successes in this challenge.

Bluff (DC 27, minor action): After a character gets a sense of the reasons behind the attack with an Insight check, he or she might downplay the severity of the dragon's problem or make false promises to aid the creature. A failed Bluff check, in addition to counting as a failure in the challenge, also imposes a –2 penalty to the next two skill checks in the challenge. This skill can be used to gain a maximum of 3 successes in this challenge.

Perception (DC 22, standard action): The character assesses the dragon's victims, the buildings or objects it has destroyed, and any other pertinent details to learn why the dragon is attacking. This skill can be used to gain a maximum of 2 successes in this challenge.

Secondary Skills: Intimidate, Nature.

Intimidate (DC 27, minor action): The character threatens the dragon with promises of retribution. A successful check grants the characters 1 success, but imposes a –2 penalty to Diplomacy checks and prevents further use of the Heal skill to gain success in this challenge. A failed check blocks further use of the Heal and Intimidate skills to gain success in this challenge. This skill can be used to gain 1 success in this challenge.

Nature (DC 25, minor action): The character searches his or her memory for useful lore about the dragon. A successful check grants a +2 bonus to all Diplomacy checks or Insight checks made until the end of the challenge.

Success: The dragon's wrath abates, and it confides in the characters the reason for its attack. If the characters offer to help the dragon with its predicament, it stops razing the countryside, but if the characters fail or don't resolve the problem fast enough, the dragon will right the wrongs committed against it, no matter the cost. If the characters completed the challenge with no failures, the dragon gives them a longer time in which to resolve the problem.

Failure: The dragon grows frustrated with the characters and turns its full wrath against them. The dragon fights until it becomes bloodied, at which point it flies away. If the characters achieved no successes, the dragon fights to the death.

Draconic Traps

All dragons value their progeny and their possessions–whether treasure, minions, or territory. They go to great lengths to safeguard those things from rivals and adventurers alike. Though not all dragons use traps, many metallic dragons employ a clever mix of traps and followers to protect their treasure. Copper dragons, in particular, delight in using traps in unexpected ways, finding dark humor in the plight of those that would dare rob them.

Niter Patch	Level 5 Lurker
Hazard	XP 200

When exposed to fire, the white encrustations covering the cavern's walls explode in fiery death.

Hazard: Ten squares scattered across the room's walls bear niter encrustations. When exposed to a fire or lightning attack, they explode into flame and create a zone of caustic salts to burn any creature that enters their area.

Perception
✦ DC 7: The character notices a glittering crust covering patches on the walls in its line of sight.

Additional Skill: Dungeoneering
✦ DC 12: The character identifies the encrustation as being niter.

Trigger
When a niter patch is caught in the area of a fire or a lightning attack, the patch makes an opportunity attack. Each trapped square explodes only once. A triggered niter patch can trigger other niter patches in the blast's area.

Attack ✦ Acid, Fire, Zone
Opportunity Action   Close blast 3
Targets: Each creature in the blast
Attack: +7 vs. Reflex
Hit: 1d6 + 4 fire damage.
Effect: The blast creates a zone of caustic salt that lasts until the end of the encounter. Any creature that enters the zone or starts its turn there takes 5 acid damage and grants combat advantage to all enemies (save ends). Creatures that are flying are immune to the zone's effect.

Countermeasures
✦ A character can neutralize one square of niter with a radiant melee or ranged attack, and he or she can neutralize multiple zones by using a close or area radiant power that encompasses more than one of them.
✦ A character can leap over the zone of caustic salt by making a DC 30 Athletics check (or DC 15 with a running start).

Upgrade to Elite (400 XP)
✦ Increase the attack bonus by 2.
✦ The hazard attacks when caught in the area of any close or area attack.

Tactics

A brass or a bronze dragon prefers to place niter patches at strategic locations in its lair, usually near the entrance or entrances. The dragon then uses its breath weapon to set off an entire patch. Orium and black dragons will sometimes nest on piles of niter, letting their enemies set them off.

Support Pillar	Level 6 Blaster
Hazard	XP 250

A pillar supporting the ceiling shatters, causing rocks to fall from above.

Hazard: Soon after the support pillar is damaged, it falls, causing the rocks above to fall in the immediate area.

Perception
No check is required to see the support pillar.

Additional Skill: Dungeoneering
✦ DC 12: The character notices structural imperfections in the pillar, indicating that it could easily shatter and cause the ceiling to collapse.

Initiative +6

Trigger
When the support pillar is damaged by any attack (AC 8, other defenses 6; hp 1), the support pillar rolls initiative. The trap makes a single attack on its initiative count, and then the trap is destroyed.

Attack ✦ Zone
Standard Action   Close burst 3
Target: Each creature in burst
Attack: +11 vs. Reflex
Hit: 3d8 + 6 damage.
Miss: Half damage.
Effect: The burst creates a zone of difficult terrain that lasts until removed.

Countermeasures
✦ At your discretion, certain powers or items could delay the support pillar's collapse–for example, *web*, *Bigby's icy grasp*, or a wall power.

Tactics

Support pillars are the type of hazard of which a dragon isn't always aware. When it is, it either shores up the ceiling to protect the lair or prepares to take advantage of it with intruders. The dragon's *breath weapon* is the safest way for it to activate the pillar. While waiting for the right time to activate the pillar, the dragon stays out of its area of effect in case a character gets any bright ideas.

When many support pillars are near each other, it creates a domino effect: One pillar collapsing triggers the next, and so on, which can make for a neat scene or bring down an entire cavern.

Dragontooth Passageway	Level 7 Lurker
Trap	XP 300

Fang-shaped blades arc out of a slit in the floor to slice into those that pass through this hallway.

Trap: A section of hallway–up to 4 squares by 1 square– contains a slit in the floor that giant blades slice through. A beam of light spans the corridor as a trigger.

Perception
✦ DC 14: The character notices the slit in the floor where the blades are hidden.
✦ DC 19: The character notices illuminated dust in the air where the triggering light shines through.

Additional Skill: Insight
✦ DC 14: A character notices an enemy moving oddly to avoid crossing the beam of light.

Trigger
When a character moves into a trapped square and breaks a beam of light, a rotating blade comes out of the floor and slices through all the trapped squares.

Attack
Opportunity Action   **Melee**
Targets: Each creature in the trapped squares
Attack: +12 vs. AC
Hit: 1d12 + 5 damage.

Countermeasures
✦ A creature that flies or jumps 5 feet above the trapped squares does not trigger the trap. Jumping it requires a DC 25 Athletics check (with a running start). A failed check triggers the trap.
✦ A creature can make a DC 19 Acrobatics check to avoid the blades or a DC 14 check if it is aware of the beam of light and avoids that instead. A failed check triggers the trap.
✦ A character can climb around the trapped squares with a DC 15 Athletics check. This climb takes 6 squares of movement.
✦ Invisible creatures do not break the light beam, so they do not trigger the trap.

Tactics

The blades of a dragontooth passageway are in the shape of a dragon's teeth, and such a trap is frequently edged with the teeth of dragons the lair's owner killed. This trap is often handy when the characters are in a hurry and are bound to be less cautious. It can be combined with another trap that requires quick action, such as a crushing walls room (see page 68 of *Dungeon Master's Guide 2*). Monsters that push characters into the beams of light can make this trap more deadly, but that action also can be seen as unfair.

Scatter Trap	Level 8 Obstacle
Trap	XP 350

Infused with ancient magic, the room sports hidden wards to scatter and frustrate intruders.

Trap: Six randomly positioned squares contain nearly invisible glyphs that damage and teleport creatures that enter their spaces. Once a square of the trap attacks, that glyph moves to a different square in the room.

Perception
✦ DC 19: The character notices a faint glow emanating from the closest square containing a glyph.

Additional Skill: Arcana (trained only)
✦ DC 24: The character perceives the glyph from which the faint light shines and identifies the space as containing some sort of teleportation trap.

Trigger
When a creature enters or begins its turn in a square containing a glyph, the scatter trap attacks that creature.

Attack ✦ Teleportation
Opportunity Action   **Melee 1**
Target: The triggering creature
Attack: +11 vs. Reflex
Hit: 1d8 + 5 damage, and the target teleports 1d4 squares to a random unoccupied space (roll 1d8: 1, north; 2, northeast; 3, northwest; 4, east; 5, west; 6, south; 7, southeast; 8, southwest) and is stunned and invisible until the end of its next turn.

Effect: The glyph moves to a random adjacent square (roll 1d8: 1, north; 2, northeast; 3, northwest; 4, east; 5, west; 6, south; 7, southeast; 8, southwest).

Countermeasures
✦ A character who makes a successful Athletics check (DC 10 or DC 5 with a running start) can jump over a single trapped square.
✦ An adjacent character can disable one trapped square with a DC 19 Arcana or Thievery check.
✦ With a DC 14 Arcana or Thievery check, an adjacent character can discharge one trapped square without being caught in the effect.

Upgrade to Elite (700 XP)
✦ Increase the DCs for Arcana, Perception, and Thievery checks by 2.
✦ The trap's attacks deal 2d8 + 6 damage, and the target is stunned (save ends).

Tactics

Dragons place scatter traps in chambers where they anticipate future battles and know they have enough room to stay off the floor, either by flying or using another form of movement (such as climbing). Other dragons inscribe glyphs that only they can see, allowing them to navigate the trapped area and lure enemies into the glyphs. If a dragon can see invisible objects and creatures, it specifically targets the invisible, stunned enemies.

Fire Egg Fabrication	Level 9 Warder
Trap	XP 400

The nest contains what looks like barrel-sized dragon eggs. But once an individual moves close, the eggs explode in a fiery burst.

Trap: One square is filled with a nest containing three to six artificial dragon eggs, primed to explode if disturbed.

Perception
✦ DC 19: The character notices that the dragon eggs are not real.

Trigger
When a creature moves adjacent to the square containing the fire egg fabrication or when the eggs in the nest are moved, the trap attacks.

Attack
Opportunity Action   **Close blast 3**
Targets: Each creature in the blast
Attack: +12 vs. Reflex
Hit: 3d8 + 5 fire damage and ongoing 5 fire damage (save ends).

Countermeasures
✦ A character can attack the fire egg fabrication (AC 18, other defenses 13; hp 1). If it is damaged, the trap attacks. A character who hits the trap from a sufficient distance, using a ranged, area, or close attack, can set off the trap without causing damage to himself or herself.
✦ A character can leap over the nest (and surrounding squares) by making a DC 30 Athletics check (or DC 15 with a running start).

Tactics

Many dragons use fire egg fabrications to safeguard their eggs. Often, they will leave them in fake hatcheries or among their treasure.

Dragontooth passageway

Curse of the Dragon's Death	Level 10 Lurker
Hazard	XP 500

The spirit of a dragon lives on long after its death, twisted by hate and anger.

Hazard: When a nondragon enters the room, a Medium invisible curse moves its speed toward the closest living creature and attacks to possess that creature.

Perception
✦ DC 16: The character notices a shimmering presence in the curse's square.

Additional Skill: Religion
✦ DC 15: The character identifies the shimmering presence as a curse of the dragon's death.

Initiative +7   **Speed** 5

Trigger
When characters enter the area, the hazard rolls initiative, moves, and attacks on its turn.

Attack ✦ Charm, Psychic
Standard Action   **Melee** 1
Target: One living creature
Attack: +13 vs. Will
Hit: 1d8 + 5 psychic damage, and the curse enters the target's space without provoking an opportunity attack. If the target starts its turn with the curse in its space, it is dominated until the end of its turn. The curse usually compels the target to attack one of its adjacent allies or make a charge attack against the closest ally.

Countermeasures
✦ A character can attack the curse (AC 24, other defenses 22; hp 20; vulnerable 5 radiant; the curse is invisible). Destroying the curse ends the hazard.
✦ If the curse is hit by an attack against Will, it can't dominate a creature until the end of the attacker's next turn.
✦ If the curse is hit by a radiant attack, it moves up to its speed away from its attacker. If the radiant attack scores a critical hit, the curse is destroyed.

✦ A creature can attempt an Arcana, Intimidate, or Religion check (DC 16) as a standard action to force the curse to shift 1 square to leave a creature's space.

Upgrade to Elite (1,000 XP)
✦ Increase the initiative modifier and speed by 2.
✦ Increase the attack bonus by 2.
✦ When the curse is in a creature's space and the creature charges, the curse moves with the target.

TACTICS

Pairing a curse of the dragon's death with creatures or traps that immobilize targets makes it easier for the curse to keep a creature dominated or to keep targets in range of the dominated creature's attacks.

FRANZ VOHWINKEL

Fake Lair Entrance — Level 12 Solo Warder
Trap — XP 3,500

A passageway into the dragon's lair suddenly reaches a large wooden door. When the door is opened to reveal nothing but a dead end, a heavy bronze door falls closed behind the intruders, trapping them as poisonous gas flows into the room.

Trap: A hallway approximately 2 squares wide and 6 squares long has a trapped wooden door at the end that, when triggered, causes a smooth bronze plate to be dropped, entombing the targets in a small area slowly filling with poisonous gas.

Perception
- DC 16: The character notices the sliding bronze door before it is dropped.
- DC 21: The character notices that the wooden door is trapped.

Additional Skill: Dungeoneering
- DC 21: The character notices that the passageway is not heavily trafficked.

Initiative +15

Trigger
The trap rolls initiative when the wooden door is opened. Immediately, the sliding bronze door falls and traps those inside the area. Poisonous green gas starts erupting from six hidden nozzles in the walls of the corridor.

Attack ✦ Poison

Standard Action   Melee

Target: Each creature in the sealed corridor

Attack: +17 vs. Fortitude

Hit: 1d6 poison damage for each round the trap has been active, up to a maximum of 6d6.

Miss: Half damage.

Effect: After 10 rounds, the bronze door lifts and the wooden door automatically closes itself, resetting the trap.

Countermeasures
- A character can disarm the wooden door's triggering trap with a DC 21 Thievery check. The character can now open the wooden door to reveal the blank wall.
- A character can try to slow the gas from exiting a vent with a DC 16 Athletics check. If successful, the damage rolled for the next attack is not increased by 1d6 this round.
- A character can try to permanently disable a gas vent with a DC 21 Thievery check. If successful, the damage rolled for the next attack is not increased by 1d6, and the maximum damage is 1d6 less per disabled vent.
- A character can try to lift the bronze door with a DC 21 Athletics check; one other person can assist from the inside, and two people can assist from the other side of the door.
- A character can attack the bronze door (AC 20, other defenses 16; hp 100; resist 10 all). Destroying the door allows characters to leave the trapped area.

Tactics

A fake lair entrance is designed to kill unwanted visitors without forcing the dragon to rouse from its rest. Even so, a dragon needs to know when the trap has been triggered in order to at least clear it of bodies. Some fake lair entrances ring alarms in the lair or magically alert the dragon. A dragon that investigates the alert might find heroes escaping from its trap.

A dragon that has a poisonour breath weapon might use a fake lair entrance as the real entrance to its lair. Once the trap has run its course, the blank stone wall behind the door clicks open. The dragon then refills the trap's gas supply from its own breath weapon.

Webs of Elemental Ice — Level 13 Obstacle
Hazard — XP 800

Strands of silvery ice spread across the cavern, stretching from floor to ceiling and wall to wall, forming a vast crystalline web.

Hazard: This trap covers a 7-by-7-by-7-square area, filling it with a web of elemental ice. Creatures entering spaces containing the ice trigger an attack from the trap.

Perception
No check is necessary to notice the webs of elemental ice.

Additional Skill: Arcana
- DC 25: The character recognizes the elemental ice for what it is, and that character and all allies gain a +2 bonus to Acrobatics checks made to navigate its spaces.

Trigger
When a creature enters a space containing the elemental ice web, the hazard attacks.

Attack

Opportunity Attack   Melee 1

Targets: Each creature in a square containing the hazard

Attack: +18 vs. AC

Hit: 1d10 + 6 damage, and the target is slowed and takes a -2 penalty to Will defense (save ends both). If the creature is already slowed, it becomes dazed (save ends) instead.

Countermeasures
- A character entering one of the hazard's spaces can make a DC 18 Acrobatics check to gain a +4 bonus to AC against the hazard's attacks until the start of the character's next turn.
- A character can attack a space containing the elemental ice web (AC 23, other defenses 18; hp 50; vulnerable 10 necrotic). Reducing the hazard's hit points to 0 clears the webbing from the space attacked.

Upgrade to Elite (1,600 XP)
- Increase the attack bonus by 2.
- Increase the hazard's hit points to 100.

Tactics

Carefully procured and harvested by cobalt, silver, and, occasionally white dragons, webs of elemental ice are considered both pleasing and useful in the defense of a dragon's lair. Often, one of these dragons will place these webs close to its favorite perch—to control those trying to attack it—or in areas close to its hoard—to slow down potential thieves.

Dragon Simulacrum — Level 15 Blaster
Trap — XP 1,200

Exquisitely carved from black basalt, the stone dragon's eyes glitter with malevolence.

Trap: The dragon simulacrum occupies a 2-by-2-square space. It triggers when caught in the area of a dragon's breath weapon and periodically spews a ball of explosive energy to scatter and punish the dragon's enemies.

Perception
No check is necessary to see the simulacrum.
Additional Skill: Arcana (trained only)
✦ DC 23: The character recognizes the dragon simulacrum's nature.

Initiative +9
Trigger
When a dragon catches the dragon simulacrum in the area of its breath weapon, the trap rolls initiative and attacks on its turn. The trap continues to attack until no nondragons remain in the room.

Attack ✦ Special (see text)
Standard Action   **Area** burst 1 within 10
Targets: Each creature in the burst
Attack: +16 vs. Reflex
Hit: 2d6 + 6 damage, and the simulacrum slides the target 2 squares.
Special: The trap's attack gains the same damage type as the breath weapon used to trigger it.

Countermeasures
✦ Characters standing in a space adjacent to the simulacrum gain a +2 bonus to defenses against the trap's attack.
✦ A character can attack the simulacrum (AC 23, other defenses 18; hp 125; resist 10 all).
✦ A character that catches the simulacrum in a close or area attack can choose to change the trap's damage type so that it matches the power's damage type. The power must have a damage type to alter the simulacrum's damage type.

Upgrade to Elite (2,400 XP)
✦ Increase the initiative bonus by 2.
✦ Increase the attack bonus by 2.
✦ Increase the area of the burst by 1.

TACTICS
A dragon places a simulacrum in a hall that leads to its lair and uses it to harry intruders. The dragon uses its *breath weapon* on the simulacrum to activate it, then retreats—possibly to recharge its *breath weapon* and return—while the heroes are busy with the statue.

Echo Gems — Level 17 Lurker
Trap — XP 1,600

Glittering crystals stab out from the room's walls and attune to energy created in their presence. Dragons keep these gems to further beef up their breath weapons.

Trap: This trap consists of eight 2-by-2 clusters of echo gems placed throughout the room. Creatures adjacent to the gems gain vulnerability to certain damage types.

Perception
No check is necessary to notice the echo gems.
Additional Skill: Dungeoneering
✦ DC 25: The character identifies the echo gems' function.

Initiative +0

Trigger
Whenever a space containing an echo gems cluster is in the area of a close or area attack, that cluster becomes attuned to the attack's damage type, if the attack has one. Each creature adjacent to that cluster gains vulnerable 10 to that damage type while adjacent to the cluster. Each time a cluster is in the area of a close or area attack that has a damage type, it becomes reattuned to the damage type of that attack.

The first time any of the trap's clusters is triggered, the trap rolls initiative. Each time the trap's initiative comes up, a random cluster that has been attuned makes an attack.

Attack ✦ Zone
Standard Action   **Close** burst 2
Targets: Each creature in the burst
Attack: +20 vs. Reflex
Hit: 2d8 + 7 damage of the type to which the cluster is attuned.

Countermeasures
✦ A character can attack the echo gems cluster (AC 31, other defenses 29; hp 80; vulnerable 10 thunder). If this attack hits the cluster and deals damage that has a type, the cluster becomes attuned to that damage type. Reducing the cluster to 0 hit points causes it to make the attack described above before it is destroyed, if the cluster was attuned.
✦ A character can make an Arcana check (DC 20) as a standard action to cause a cluster within 5 squares of the character to lose its attunement.

Upgrade to Elite (3,200 XP)
✦ Activate two different attuned clusters on the echo gems' initiative.
✦ Increase the vulnerability by 5.

TACTICS
Dragons place echo gems in their lairs to use the gems to amplify the effects of their breath weapons. A dragon keeps its clusters of gems constantly attuned to the damage type of its *breath weapon*, so the echo gem clusters in a dragon's lair have already been triggered.

Use a dragon with a breath weapon that has forced movement or that prevents the target from moving (such as adamantine, brass, bronze, cobalt, and iron dragons) to keep characters in range of the clusters' attacks. If the dragon has allies, include those that use the same damage type.

Lightning Siphon — Level 19 Blaster
Trap — XP 2,400

Crackling bolts of lightning lash out from the object and pull individuals closer.

Trap: When a character steps within 5 squares of a statue of a Large iron dragon, the statue starts blasting nearby creatures with ensnaring bolts of lightning.

Perception
✦ DC 22: The character notices an occasional spark coming from the mouth of the dragon statue.
Additional Skill: Arcana
✦ DC 27: The character identifies the trap as a lightning siphon.

Initiative +11
Trigger
When a creature comes within 5 squares of the dragon statue, the trap activates and rolls initiative.

Attack ✦ Lightning
Standard Action   Close blast 5
Target: Each creature in the blast
Attack: +22 vs. Reflex
Hit: 2d10 + 7 lightning damage, the trap pulls the target 3 squares, and the target is slowed until the end of its next turn.
Countermeasures
✦ An adjacent character can disable the trap with a DC 22 Thievery check.
✦ A character can attack the statue (AC 33, other defenses 31; hp 80; resist 5 all). Destroying the statue disables the trap.
Upgrade to Elite (4,800 XP)
✦ Increase the initiative bonus by 2.
✦ Increase the attack bonus by 2.
✦ Use two statues (activating only one each round), or make the statue Huge or Gargantuan.

Tactics

A lightning siphon is usually created by an iron dragon's allies or underlings. Encounters with lightning siphons rarely include actual dragons. Consider using monsters that have forced movement effects and customizing them with lightning resistance so they can survive fighting near lightning siphons. These traps are frequently placed near doorways to important areas or in long hallways, where it's difficult for creatures to walk around them without coming within 5 squares.

Grasping Stalagmites	Level 21 Obstacle
Trap	XP 3,200

Magically animated rocky tendrils come out of the floor and grab unsuspecting individuals.

Trap: Four stalagmites have been animated by a magic ritual to attack and restrain intruders.
Perception
No check is required to see the stalagmites.
Additional Skill: Arcana
✦ DC 31: The character notices that the stalagmites are animated.
Initiative +10
Trigger
When a creature moves within 2 squares of one of the grasping stalagmites, the trap activates and rolls initiative.
Attack
Standard Action   Melee 2
Target: One creature within melee reach
Attack: +24 vs. Reflex
Hit: 3d6 + 8 damage, and the target is grabbed. Only one target can be grabbed by a single stalagmite at a time, and the stalagmite cannot attack another target while it has a target grabbed.
Countermeasures
✦ A character can attack a stalagmite (AC 32, other defenses 29; hp 25; resist 15 all). Destroying a stalagmite does not affect other stalagmites.
Upgrade to Elite (6,400 XP)
✦ Increase the initiative bonus by 2.
✦ Increase the attack bonus by 2.
✦ Add four additional stalagmites to the room.

Tactics

Grasping stalagmites are a favorite ward of adamantine dragons and other dragons that lair in the deep. Often, dragons will watch areas with these traps from high above, and pounce on those that become ensnared.

Haunting Conscience	Level 24 Warder
Trap	XP 6,050

The dragon's hoard glimmers in the half light. But when it's approached, serpentine tendrils of golden mist curl from the coins and antiquities to doom those that would plunder the dragon's treasure.

Trap: The trap protects a dragon's hoard, occupying each square adjacent to the hoard and all squares containing the hoard. When the trap is triggered, it attacks and compels the triggering creature to protect the treasure at all costs.
Perception
✦ DC 24: The character notices a faint chemical smell emanating from the hoard.
Additional Skill: Nature
✦ DC 29: The character recognizes the odor as belonging to haunting conscience—an arcane mixture that can charm a dragon's enemies.
Trigger
When a creature other than the hoard's owner enters a trapped space, the trap attacks.
Attack ✦ Charm, Poison, Psychic
Opportunity Action   Melee 1
Target: Each creature in a trapped square
Attack: +27 vs. Will
Hit: 1d8 + 8 poison damage, and the target is dominated (save ends). A dominated creature screams at the top of its lungs to warn the dragon of the impending robbery (a free action), and attacks (or readies an attack against) the creature closest to the hoard that is not the dragon.
Aftereffect: The target is stunned until the end of its next turn.
Countermeasures
✦ A character forcibly moved away from the hoard can immediately make a saving throw to end the dominated effect.
✦ Slaying the dragon automatically disables the trap.
Upgrade to Elite (12,100 XP)
✦ A dominated creature deals 5 extra damage on its melee attacks.

Tactics

Haunting conscience, sometimes called dragoncall mist, is used by any dragon that can obtain it to guard the dragon's hoard. More territorial dragons, such as red dragons and adamantine dragons, will also use this strange substance at strategic spots around their territories, allowing the ruckus it causes to rouse them to violent action.

Metallic dragons are versatile enough creatures that you can drop them into an adventure without deeply connecting them to the framework of your ongoing campaign.

Many adventures that use metallic dragons play on the ambiguous nature of the creatures. Because a metallic dragon doesn't have the same reputation as a chromatic dragon, characters are likely to hesitate when they encounter one (rather than immediately charge into battle). As an adventure designer, you can play with that moment of discovery. Your adventure can reward characters who take the time to figure out what the metallic dragon is up to and whether the dragon's purpose is benign or sinister.

Adventure Hooks and Quests

You can use the following quests and hooks as written or as a guide. The number before each title refers to the level of the most potent dragon in the hook. Use this level as a rough guide for setting encounter levels.

4: The Secret Audition

The young gold dragon Yathnikarius leads a knightly order called the Sable Lancers, and is seeking recruits.

One of the values that Yathnikarius treasures most in his lancers is integrity. If a Sable Lancer pledges to do something, Yathnikarius expects him or her to carry out the pledge no matter how tempting the alternatives might be.

Accordingly, Yathnikarius has established a test for those he believes might make good Sable Lancers. He has a confederate hire the prospective recruits to deliver a sealed box to another confederate in a city two weeks' travel away. Yathnikarius engineers several ethical dilemmas that the prospects must resolve along the way.

+ **Mother in Distress:** A woman tells the heroes that goblins ran off with her child. In a skill challenge, the characters must follow the tracks and find the child. There are no goblins, and the woman is one of the Sable Lancers, but the child is real. If the characters can't find the child, or if they spurn the woman, they fail.

+ **Peacemaking:** Two travelers (both secretly Sable Lancers) are arguing about a wagon collision at a one-lane bridge, and the argument is about to turn violent. The prospects must engage in a skill challenge to defuse the situation. If violence erupts or if the prospects ignore the argument, they fail.

+ **Found Money:** The characters find an unconscious male human (a Sable Lancer) in a ditch. A cursory examination reveals that he has several hundred gold coins on him. If the characters take the cash or if they don't revive him, they fail the test.

+ **The Box Itself:** If the prospects open the box, its magic summons Yathnikarius, who reclaims it and scolds the prospects for lacking integrity.

Not every encounter is staged; some of the dangers of the road are all too real. The prospects must also deal with bandits on the road, various monsters that attack their camp at night, and a copper dragon that regards the road as its personal hunting grounds.

Quest Hook: Yathnikarius identifies some or all of the characters as potential members of the Sable Lancers (or a different organization in your campaign), so he arranges for them to deliver the golden box and face the tests along the way. You can reveal the truth at the end of the adventure, or seed clues along the way that it's all a pretense (such as the absence of goblins, the rich traveler's dubious story, or some flaws in the bridge incident that suggest it was staged). At the end of the adventure, Yathnikarius can become an active patron if the Sable Lancers have a role in your campaign, or membership in the Lancers can be merely a ceremonial honor.

Quest XP: Delivering the box and resolving the ethical dilemmas to the satisfaction of Yathnikarius earns a major quest reward of 875 XP.

Quest Hook: If the characters are already Sable Lancers, Yathnikarius might want them to stage one of the above ethical dilemmas for potential recruits who are delivering the box.

Quest XP: If the characters are convincing in their roles, they earn a minor quest reward of 175 XP.

Quest Hook: The copper dragon, Ghalladara, is infuriated and regards Yathnikarius's "tests" as trespassing on her territory. She sends the characters to disrupt Yathnikarius's test and frighten off his prospects. She doesn't want them dead, just out of her territory and out of Yathnikarius's clutches.

Quest XP: If the characters can mess up the test and scare off the would-be Sable Lancers, they earn a major quest reward of 875 XP.

9: The Golden Facade

It's a feud that has raged for centuries, one that makes a human rivalry look like a child's game. On one side are the descendants of Ravolensurax, an ancient gold dragon; on the other are the members of the bloodline of Inselios, a powerful shadow dragon (*Draconomicon: Chromatic Dragons*, page 199) who has an unmatched mastery of necromantic ritual magic. Nobody outside the two families knows what started the conflict, and, indeed, it might have been nothing

more than a territorial or moral dispute. Whatever the case, the families have warred on and off for generations in a struggle that shows no signs of abating.

One of Ravolensurax's bloodline, a young gold named Rovoluserras, was exploring the port city of Ylsinar in human form when the brood of Inselios learned of her presence. Now she remains in hiding, seeking some way to leave the city without revealing her true form or encountering the agents—living and undead, humanoid and draconic—of the enemy.

Quest Hook: While the characters are in or near Ylsinar, a stranger approaches and introduces himself as "Rav." He explains to them that his younger sister is somewhere in Ylsinar, and that she is in great danger. Without yet revealing their true nature as dragons, Rav explains that his family's enemies have learned his sister is somewhere in the city, and they are hunting her down. He needs the characters to find her, secretly escort her from the city, and remain at her side until others from his family can arrive to guard her. He offers 2,100 gp (two level 9 treasure parcels) for the safe rescue of his sister.

If an opportunity arises, he takes the heroes outside the city, reveals his true form, and explains his sister's dilemma. The characters must escort her to freedom without counting on her aid, since she must remain in human form for her own safety.

Quest XP: If the characters manage to escort Rovoluserras to safety without getting into such trouble that she's forced to reveal her true nature,

they earn a major quest reward of 2,000 XP. If Rovoluserras is forced to reveal herself along the way, that reward is reduced to 1,500 XP.

Quest Hook: Many of the agents of Inselios are subtle, but others are not so secretive. In their search for Rovoluserras, they have caused a number of mysterious deaths in Ylsinar. The characters might be caught up in the search for the perpetrators, either by chance or at the request of the city watch.

Quest XP: If the characters unearth and defeat Inselios's chief operatives in Ylsinar, they earn a major quest reward of 2,000 XP. Although Inselios can call upon a great many powerful creatures and will do so if Rovoluserras is exposed, his current agents in the city are not nearly so potent. If the characters identify these operatives and warn the city government but do not deal with the operatives, they earn only a minor quest reward of 400 XP.

12: THE INSIDE-OUT LAIR

Obsessed with defending his lair, the adult adamantine dragon Bothurion is something of a hobbyist among metallic dragons. For years, he has advertised the wealth of his hoard in an effort to entice thieves to test his defenses.

At first, this tactic brought Bothurion the challenge he wanted. But after many upgrades, Bothurion's lair became practically impregnable. The lair's reputation is well known, so few thieves dare try to steal something now. The few who made such

WILLIAM O'CONNOR

attempts died in the outer ring of defenses, leaving some of Bothurion's more fiendish traps untested.

With no one to test his obsession, Bothurion resorted to drastic measures. He kidnapped several capable adventurers, threw them atop his treasure hoard, and dared them to reach safety.

Bothurion observes their efforts from a scrying chamber within the lair. He has taken measures to prevent them from short-circuiting his test. For example, the adventurers have no *residuum* or other reagents to manage a portal ritual or other magical escape. But they do have their weapons, armor, and other key items, because Bothurion wants to see how his guardians fare against determined thieves. Bothurion won't reveal himself until the adventurers reach the periphery of his lair—if they last that long.

Quest Hook: The characters are among the captives who awaken to find themselves atop an immense pile of coins and jewels. They have no idea where they are, and must find their way out of Bothurion's lair. Along the way, they must navigate elaborate traps, various servants and guardians of Bothurion, and eventually Bothurion himself. If you want to add a strong social element to the adventure, you can include a number of nonplayer character captives, some with sinister motives of their own.

Quest XP: Escaping Bothurion's lair earns the characters a major quest reward of 3,500 XP—and all the treasures they manage to carry out with them.

Quest Hook: If you have enough players in your campaign (or additional friends who are willing to take part in a one-shot adventure), you can split the characters into two groups. The first group plays the adventure as described above. The second group is the rescuers, who quickly figure out what happened to their friends and then delve into Bothurion's lair from the outside.

Alternate playing sessions (or use two DMs simultaneously) between the groups until they're about to reunite, and then run a combined session in which both groups simultaneously fight Bothurion.

Quest XP: Characters who take part in only the escape or the rescue receive minor quest rewards of 700 XP per player in the group, since they have to get only halfway in or halfway out of Bothurion's lair.

14: SHELL GAME

Olenvale is the central and largest town in a network of more than a dozen coastal villages and hamlets that make up one large community. People travel freely among them (during the day, at least), and the various community leaders meet in council before making decisions that might affect their neighbors or the open trade that all the villages enjoy.

Olenvale and its communities also have a sort of guardian angel, albeit a guardian angel for hire. The bronze dragon Vahalapras protects the villages from

attack in exchange for a regular tribute of coin and cattle. Those towns that choose not to pay don't gain the benefit of the dragon's protection, but Vahalapras doesn't torment them.

Two days ago, Vahalapras returned to her lair after dealing with a small cadre of bandits to find all her defenses penetrated and her new clutch of eggs missing.

The dragon held onto her temper only through willpower and an intense focus on the duty she owes to those who pay for her protection. Rather than tear apart Olenvale and the other villages looking for her missing clutch, she has made the community leaders an ultimatum: They have one week to locate and return the eggs and to identify the party responsible for taking them. The leaders balked at the short time, but who argues with an enraged dragon that has lost its clutch? If they are unsuccessful, she'll hunt down the eggs and the perpetrators, going through anyone and anything in her way to do it.

Quest Hook: With only five days left, the Reeve of Olenvale and the other community leaders turn to outside help—the characters. The townsfolk are too poor to offer much in the way of financial reward. They can pony up a mere 500 gp among them (one-quarter the value of the smallest level 14 treasure parcel). Still, they beg the characters for their help and offer to let them keep the perpetrators' possessions as part of their reward. They have found one clue: an eggshell shard just off the northern road.

Obviously, you must decide who the responsible party is. It could be a group of citizens angry about the extra taxes imposed to pay the dragon's fee—if so, how could they possibly have overcome the dragon's defenses? Were the eggs stolen by evil wizards or by cultists of Tiamat, perhaps with the intention of corrupting the hatchlings into draconians? If so, how long do the characters have before the villains smuggle their prize out of the region?

Quest XP: If the characters track down the perpetrators, defeat them or deliver them to the dragon, and return her eggs, they earn a major quest reward of 5,000 XP. If the characters identify the perpetrators and deliver that information to Vahalapras along with her eggs but do not succeed in defeating or delivering the perpetrators, they instead earn 3,000 XP.

Quest Hook: In the process of hunting down the eggs and the thieves, the characters might learn how the thieves circumvented Vahalapras's traps and defenses. Alternatively, the dragon might ask them to find this out after the eggs are safely back in her lair.

Quest XP: If the characters learn how the thieves broke into the dragon's lair and deliver that information to her, they earn a minor quest reward of 1,000 XP.

Quest Hook: If the characters are unable to find the perpetrators in time, they might need to convince Vahalapras to postpone her attack on the villages (by succeeding on a very complex skill challenge) or fight the dragon themselves in order to protect the people of Olenvale.

Quest XP: If the characters successfully protect the people from Vahalapras, they earn two minor quest rewards totaling 2,000 XP. They should not gain both this quest XP and the quest XP offered for tracking down the perpetrators. They undertake this last quest only if the first one fails.

18: Unmask the Conspirator

Lord Naumonshra Kell has grand ambitions. Since his father's untimely death two decades ago, Lord Kell has repeatedly added to his lands through subterfuge or outright conquest. Now he's on the verge of declaring himself monarch of the Kingdom of Kell.

In many ways, the duchy of Kell is already acting like a full-fledged kingdom. It has a standing army, a knightly order devoted to defense of the realm, and a court where diplomacy and intrigue rule.

Naumonshra's ambitions have been thwarted of late, seemingly by simple bad luck. Some ambassadors from neighboring duchies have died of untimely but apparently natural causes. War plans locked in Lord Kell's map room disappeared, causing a season's delay in a key border war. The accumulation of power has always come easily to Lord Kell, so when things become difficult, he is certain that it's more than bad fortune holding him back. There must be a spy in his court, Lord Kell reasons—probably a saboteur in the pay of a duchy that's about to be absorbed.

Kell's suspicions aren't far from the truth. A steel dragon named Ralahirah has been lurking on the edge of Kell's court for several months, using shapechanging and espionage techniques to thwart Kell's dreams. Ralahirah has succeeded thus far, but hers is a dangerous game. She's simultaneously pretending to be two courtiers, and if they're ever expected in the same place at the same time, she risks being unmasked.

Quest Hook: Naumonshra Kell hires the characters to spend time in his court and find the spy. He figures that because they're new to the court, the characters can't be part of the conspiracy. Eventually, clues will lead to Ralahirah in one of her guises.

Quest XP: If the characters expose Ralahirah, they earn a major quest reward of 10,000 XP—even if she escapes to cause future trouble for Lord Kell.

Quest Hook: Ralahirah has been trying to single-handedly prevent the creation of the Kingdom of Kell, but now she has decided that it's too big a task for her to do alone. She directs the characters (either through subterfuge, through persuasion, or by hiring them outright) to foment revolution outside the castle walls. The characters must stay one step ahead of Kell's agents while periodically sneaking back into the castle to receive further instructions from Ralahirah.

Quest XP: Each time the heroes strike a blow against Lord Kell and his royal ambitions, they earn a minor quest reward of 2,000 XP.

22: The Good of the Many

Locrecean, an elder silver dragon who has devoted his life to opposing the cults and dragons devoted to Tiamat, finds himself in a terrible quandary.

For years, he has pitted himself against the efforts of Ezrian Vakka, a dragonborn warlock and priest of one of Tiamat's cults. Vakka and his humanoid and dragon congregants hatched vile schemes, and time and again, Locrecean—sometimes alone, sometimes with allies—was able to stop them. Locrecean was, however, never able to slay or capture Vakka.

And now it might be too late.

Vakka and his associates have hidden themselves somewhere within the metropolis of Kaddastrei. Once a major city in the empire of Nerath, it is still an enormous community with more than 20,000 inhabitants. Ensconced within, protected against divination and scrying rituals, the cult of Tiamat could remain hidden for years.

But Locrecean doesn't have years to find them. Vakka is mere weeks away from completion of a dark ritual that threatens not only every person in Kaddastrei, but all the communities for thousands of miles, if not farther. (The precise nature of this threat is left for you to develop as best suits your campaign.) He desperately doesn't want to do it, but if he has to, Locrecean will level Kaddastrei itself—killing tens of thousands of innocents—to ensure Vakka's destruction and to prevent the rise of an even greater evil.

What he needs is someone to offer him a better alternative.

Quest Hook: The characters have several ways to become involved in the hunt for Vakka's sect. At their level, they doubtless have a widespread reputation, so Locrecean could approach them for aid directly. Alternatively, the authorities of Kaddastrei might have become aware that something's not right in their city—perhaps Vakka's plan requires sacrifices or test subjects, so people have disappeared. The leaders then ask the characters to intervene. Once they have begun to do so, the silver dragon approaches them and explains what's happening.

Quest XP: If the characters locate Vakka's hideout, Locrecean can take on the cultists without destroying the city, but there will still be substantial loss of life. If Locrecean is badly wounded in the ensuing battle, he allows much of the cult to escape. In this instance, the characters earn a quest reward of 10,000 XP. If they aid Locrecean in this battle, or find some way to drive Vakka and his people from the city so the dragon can avoid collateral damage, they earn a quest reward of 14,000 XP. If the characters defeat Vakka and his cult without endangering the citizens or forcing Locrecean to take action, they instead earn the full major quest reward of 20,750 XP.

There's almost no limit to how much you can employ metallic dragons in your campaign. They're varied in alignment, motivation, level, campaign role, and the challenges they offer to players. The following campaign outlines feature dragons in a spectrum of roles.

AWAKEN THE SLEEPERS

The city of Shurral Deraen has long relied on a brood of silver dragons inhabiting the city's central spire to protect citizens against the predations of hordes of giants in the mountains to the north.

Recently, however, the dragons have spent more and more time in deep slumber, and the mages who serve as emissaries between the dragons and the city are worried that soon they'll be unable to awaken the dragons. Meanwhile, a frost giant jarl is attacking outlying communities, and growing ever more bold as his attacks don't provoke reprisals.

In this campaign, the connection to dragons isn't apparent at first. Only over time will the characters realize that what appears to be a giant invasion has its origin in an ancient rivalry between a cobalt wyrm and a silver wyrm.

HEROIC TIER:
SMOKE ON THE HORIZON

The giants in the Karralak Mountains, a mix of hill giants and frost giants, are restless. A few weeks after the mountain passes are clear of snow, everyone in the lowlands can see plumes of smoke floating south from the foothills—a sign that someone is occupying the old forts built by the giants centuries ago.

The farming communities of the lowlands aren't sure who's rebuilding the old forts, but the denizens of the mountains aren't waiting to find out. In a series of adventures, the characters must protect the farming villages against banditry from worg-riding goblins, hobgoblins, and bugbears. Through interrogation and evidence, the characters learn that giants from the northern wilds crossed the passes and pushed the goblins out of their mountain warrens.

In the final adventure in this tier, a band of ogres seizes the town of Harranton and declares it the "Throne City of Banakar the Ogre." The characters infiltrate the city and defeat the ogres, even as bandits, goblinoids, and other enemies of Shurral Deraen start gathering under Banakar's banner.

PARAGON TIER:
BEHIND THE CURTAIN

By defeating Banakar, the characters learn that he was acting under the direction of a frost giant jarl inhabiting Fort Ankherang in the Karralak Mountains. The characters travel to Shurral Deraen and inform the city leaders that the giants intend to march on the lowlands in a few months or sooner.

Because the heroes saved the town of Harranton, the city leaders invite them to enter the forbidden Tower of Dragons in the center of Shurral Deraen. They climb to the top in the company of the city's mages and find the silver dragons asleep. Even though the mages perform rituals of awakening over and over again, only one dragon regains consciousness: Launacathra. She reaffirms her commitment to defend Shurral Deraen and flies off to attack Fort Ankherang.

FRANZ VOHWINKEL

The city fathers, in a state of near panic, swear the characters to secrecy and send them into the Feywild to ask an orium dragon named Ossirian why the silver dragons won't awaken.

The journey to Ossirian's lair is an adventure itself through a Feywild domain ruled by fomorians and filled with hostile natives. After a tense negotiation, Ossirian provides a more powerful ritual that should enable the city's mages to counter whatever is making the silver dragons slumber.

The characters return to Shurral Deraen to find out that Launacathra hasn't returned and that one of the tower mages is missing. They must find the mage before he escapes the city or reveals that the dragons are sleeping, which would panic the citizenry.

While the mages start preparing the new awakening ritual, the characters must find a way to slow down the giants. They travel to Fort Ankherang, disrupt the giants' preparations there, and rescue a captured and groggy Launacathra. They also learn that the giants are offering tribute to a dragon—of an unknown variety—named Valkathator, whose lair lies far north of the mountain passes.

EPIC TIER: INVADERS BOTH OVERT AND SUBTLE

The characters and Launacathra return to Shurral Deraen with the invading giant horde only days behind them. The giants put the city under siege, and the adventurers must attack repeatedly to keep the invaders off balance long enough for the city's mages to complete the ritual. When the ritual is nearly finished, a huge cobalt dragon appears above the Tower of Dragons and flies inside. The characters run through the trap- and ward-filled tower interior and drive off the cobalt dragon before it kills all the mages and disrupts the ritual. The combined effort of the mages and the characters is sufficient to complete the ritual and awaken the silver dragons. They fly out of the tower and unleash their fury on the giants, who have just breached the city walls.

The giants die in battle with the silver dragons, but the dragons start to fall from the sky as the battle winds down. They're falling asleep again, and this time in full view of the citizens of Shurral Deraen—sparking a citywide riot. Amid the chaos, the characters follow the only clue they have: the cobalt dragon. The dragon is Valkathator, who was an ancient rival of the silver dragon that fathered Launacathra and the city's other dragons.

The characters and an increasingly sleepy Launacathra travel north through the remnants of the giant horde, over the mountain passes, and eventually up to Valkathator's lair, which lies within a blizzard cloud to the north. Launacathra succumbs to slumber just as the characters realize how Valkathator is making the other dragons sleep: by infusing the northern wind itself with magic. In a titanic battle, the characters defeat Valkathator, who is cast out of his lair into the brunt of the northern wind and suffers the fate he intended for all other dragons—a magically induced, unending slumber.

PROPHECY OF DOOM

For centuries, a loose conclave of mithral dragons has protected the eight *Wells of Futures Foretold*, powerful artifacts capable of not only revealing the future but altering it. Now something is killing those dragons one by one, and the remaining mithral dragons are in a panic because their prophecies aren't revealing who conspires against them. If all eight *Wells* fall into the wrong hands, the forces of evil will be able to remake the future into a dark, terrifying place.

HEROIC TIER: THE ORACLE IS CLOSED

Throughout most of this tier, the heroes undertake typical adventures: They fight bandits, delve into undead-infested tombs, and explore ancient ruins. Near the end of the tier, they find themselves caught up in a mystery involving a missing person, and they travel to the lair of a mithral dragon named Ahmidarius, because he is known as a peerless oracle.

After negotiating with Ahmidarius's dragonborn servants, they obtain permission to ascend into the clouds where his lair floats. They discover that despite the promises of Ahmidarius's trusted servants, the dragon has all the traps in his lair engaged, and he attacks the characters as soon as they reach his inner sanctum. After an abbreviated battle, the characters discover why Ahmidarius attacked them: He's expecting an attack from forces that he cannot identify even through his own divinations.

PARAGON TIER: SEEKING THE DRACOLICHES

With Ahmidarius's help, the characters resolve their missing-person mystery, but Ahmidarius receives an urgent mental message from his father, an ancient wyrm named Porothelion. The message says, "Come to my lair—you must save the *Wells of Future Foretold*."

Ahmidarius takes the characters into his confidence and makes whatever promises it takes to persuade them to venture into the Astral Sea with him to seek out his father's lair. They arrive to find Porothelion's lair occupied by hordes of undead led by a dreambreath dracolich (*Draconomicon: Chromatic Dragons*, page 202) known as Rhao the Skullcrusher. The characters and Ahmidarius take Porothelion's lair, but not before Rhao escapes, disappearing and taking one of Porothelion's towers with him. Porothelion is nowhere to be found—physically or psychically.

Ahmidarius receives another psychic message, this time informing him that "the conclave approaches."

Three ancient mithral dragons appear and explain that Porothelion was the guardian for one of the *Wells of Future Foretold*, stationary artifacts of unimaginable prophetic power. Dreambreath dracoliches are trying to seize all eight *Wells*, and have found a way to mask themselves from the scrying power of the artifacts.

The ancient mithral wyrms send Ahmidarius in search of Rhao the Skullcrusher. Then they tell the heroes to explore what lies beyond the planar portals in a heavily warded part of Porothelion's lair. The wyrms explain that before his disappearance (and presumed death), Porothelion was trying to track the dracoliches back to their lair. The newly constructed portals might indicate that he had succeeded.

The characters have various adventures beyond the portals. Eventually, they find the lair of a dreambreath dracolich in the Shadowfell.

EPIC TIER:
CATACLYSM ON THE SHADOWFELL

The characters report back to the ancient mithral dragons to find Ahmidarius absent. After receiving the characters' news, the conclave hastily assembles an invading force of dragons and allies the heroes were able to befriend in their adventures beyond the planar portals.

The campaign concludes with an assault on a black fortress in the Shadowfell where the dreambreath dracoliches dwell. The dracoliches can bend reality with the power of the five *Wells* they have seized, so the characters contend with the black fortress as much as they battle the dracoliches. The dracoliches have warped Ahmidarius to their cause, using the power of their corrupted *Wells* to turn him into an insane dracolich.

A LITTLE KNOWLEDGE . . .

Despite its grandiose, even ostentatious, name and customs, the Grand Assemblage of the League of Eternal Discovery—or the Assemblage for short—receives respect far and wide. The guild has knowledge of all manner of ancient wisdom and arcane secrets. From its universitylike hall in the ancient city of Pravarum, the Assemblage's members and reputation have spread almost unimaginably far in these days of dangerous roads and fearful travel.

And why not? The members of the Assemblage are among the most experienced adventurers, explorers, and arcane researchers the world has known since the fall of the great empires. Its members motivated by a shared desire to see all that can be seen, the Assemblage has grown from a tiny adventurers' guild into an organization that has scores of members.

Only those inducted into the Assemblage's highest orders know that several of the organization's patrons are members of an orium dragon family that uses adventurers as its eyes and ears in the world.

Yet even these few, and most of the dragons, remain unaware of a threat in their midst, a particularly driven orium wyrm who has goals for the organization far more sinister than the simple accumulation of knowledge.

A synopsis of the Assemblage, allowing you to use the organization in any campaign, can be found on page 75.

HEROIC TIER: APPRENTICE

After several early successes in their adventures, the characters are approached by a tiefling named Olfien. He says he is a member of the Assemblage and an emissary for Yuniosu, one of the Assemblage's greatest patrons. The characters have come to the patrons' attention, and they would like to work with the party on a freelance basis to better judge the characters' skills. To that end, Olfien hires the heroes for several adventures, nearly all of which revolve around the discovery or recovery of ancient magic or lore.

PARAGON TIER: JOURNEYMAN

After the characters undertake several adventures on his behalf, Olfien invites them to the city of Pravarum, where they will be officially inducted as members of the Assemblage. He introduces them to several valuable contacts, but the truly important meeting occurs after the ceremonies, when he takes them to meet Yuniosu—one of the orium dragons.

There, Yuniosu acknowledges that the characters would not normally have been told the secret of the group's patrons so soon, but the patrons needed to swiftly bring in people they could trust from outside. Several members of the Assemblage have vanished or died in recent months. Yuniosu and her relatives believe that someone within the guild might be responsible. The characters will continue to undertake adventures and explorations on behalf of the Assemblage, but their true objective is to get to know the members of the Assembly and attempt to learn who among them is the murderer—and why.

Over the course of their paragon adventures, the characters uncover several instances of corruption and conspiracy within the group, but all seem to be for prestige or power. None appears related to the murders, which increase in frequency. They also meet the other dragons of Yuniosu's family, including Konoktolta, the brood's mighty patriarch.

EPIC TIER: MASTER

Finally, as the murders and disappearances grow so frequent than the entire membership becomes aware of them, the characters learn that the perpetrator is Konoktolta. The secret-obsessed (and vaguely mad) orium wyrm has become convinced that knowledge of arcane magic is, in itself, too dangerous for the mortal races to have. He assisted his offspring in manipulating the Assemblage to use its members to hunt down arcane casters. Part of the plan is to assemble the most skilled arcanists in the region so they would be easy to exterminate.

With Yuniosu's help, the characters escape his initial attack. The early levels of the epic tier are spent attempting to save the lives of his other targets and to survive (or at least hide from) his wrath until the party has gained enough power that it can confront the dragon directly. Unwilling to fight to the death, Konoktolta escapes, leaving the characters to track him down before he can start his schemes over.

AN AGE OF ENDLESS STORMS

For centuries, Alkesandreth—a mighty silver dragon and a skilled ritual caster—has battled the evils of the mortal world. Demons, wicked cults, powerful necromancers, rival dragons—Alkesandreth fought them all, and won. Yet for all his efforts, the world is as wretched as ever, and the dragon has grown desperate.

In that desperation, Alkesandreth has turned to a sect called the Scions of the Unclouded Sun. A group consisting of powerful mortals, other dragons, and various sorts of angels, its members believe devoutly that evil flourishes in the world because dark forces—devils, demons, exarchs of vile gods—roam free while the gods of good maintain a "hands off" approach, leaving the fate of mortals to mortals.

Their goal is to force the gods to intercede in the day-to-day functioning of the world. In his study of the slow orbits of the planes, Alkesandreth believes he has discovered just how to do it. Soon, the gods will have no choice but to intervene in the world of mortals, stamping out evil once and for all. And the thousands—maybe millions—who must die to make it happen? They're simply a price that must be paid.

HEROIC TIER: FLOOD

The party's first adventures are of a standard variety. The only common theme is the weather: The region, wherever the characters travel, is beset with constant violent storms. Winds howl, rains flood low-lying regions, and lightning wreaks havoc as though deliberately targeting the structures of mortal races. As the season turns but the weather grows no better, the characters become aware that something is wrong. They begin encountering a variety of elemental creatures, such as slaad tadpoles running wild, or demons in the service of warlords or criminal guilds.

At the end of the heroic tier, perhaps seeking aid from sages or wizards, the characters learn that the world has come into conjunction with the Elemental Chaos—and that some mystical effect is holding the world there, turning what should have been only a brief period of turbulence into an ongoing danger.

PARAGON TIER: FIRE

Even as the heroes search for the cause of the prolonged conjunction, the Elemental Chaos's effect on the mortal realm grows stronger. The weather becomes unnatural, including rains of fire and snows of stone. Elementals, archons, and demons grow more common, demonic and primordial cults increase in power, and elemental dragons (*Draconomicon: Chromatic Dragons*, page 191) hunt the lakes and skies.

Staking out favorable areas, a number of dragons expand their territories, taking advantage of environments that do not harm them but prove hostile to invaders. It is during the characters' encounters with some of these dragons—perhaps while the characters defend besieged communities from their new would-be overlords—that they first hear of Alkesandreth. The silver dragon recently surrounded himself with

a cabal of powerful creatures and has spent the past several years gathering up enormous amounts of arcane reagents. The characters might assume he is a potential ally trying to end the conjunction, rather than the source who's maintaining it, but either way they have few options but to seek him out.

EPIC TIER: INFERNO

The conjunction trembles, and entire communities break loose from the earth and float into the skies, surrounded by clouds of gaseous flame. The characters must hunt down Alkesandreth, and only when they find him do they finally learn that the silver dragon is keeping the conjunction in effect. Although the characters are not quite powerful enough to take him on at his full strength, his devotion to maintaining the ritual allows the party to disrupt his plans, defeating many of his allies and demolishing the components necessary to continue the magic.

Even when the two worlds finally begin to drift apart, Alkesandreth refuses to give up on forcing the deities to intervene in the mortal world. Using the last of his great magics, he flees into the Astral Sea—and eventually to the Nine Hells. Whether to prevent him from finding some way to unleash an army of devils into the world or to keep one of the archdevils from gaining power over an already desperate and faltering silver dragon's soul, the characters pursue him into this realm of torment and suffering.

Here they must overcome him once and for all, even as they struggle to ensure that his death or defeat in Hell doesn't trap his soul there as a weapon for the devils to exploit.

THE BROKEN THRONE

At the height of the Empire of Nerath, one of its greatest kingdoms was the nation of Kindras, a heavily structured military power. Kindrasan soldiers made up a good portion of Nerath's armies, and its codex of laws heavily influenced the empire's code of justice. For all its might, however, when Nerath toppled, Kindras fell along with all the rest of the empire's subject regions. It left behind many independent towns and a few cities, all struggling to survive, all interconnected by a network of roads that has slowly deteriorated over the subsequent years. Where law once reigned, banditry is now the order of the day. Where caravans traversed roads in safety, now those few merchants brave or foolish enough to travel long distances do so with hired guards and one eye ever alert for the monsters that lurk in the overgrown wilds.

The bronze dragon Pelsemesios hopes to change all that. Working through a young local champion, a would-be queen by the name of Lady Casmerra, Pelsemesios hopes to see Kindras reborn into a kingdom of laws and civilization, a bastion of order and society in this wild, chaotic realm.

HEROIC TIER: CONSOLIDATION

A variety of patrons commission several groups, including the characters, to clear the region of dangers. After a few simple missions, their employer reveals herself as Lady Casmerra. She aims to consolidate the region into the kingdom of New Kindras. Using the characters to put the local criminals and robber barons on the defensive will allow Casmerra time to establish a permanent capital. She offers the characters long-term employment, perhaps positions in the new kingdom's military, if they assist her in establishing the rule of law.

"Queen" Casmerra frequently sends the characters to the outskirts of the slowing growing kingdom—little more than a few towns and cities so far—so they can deal with monstrous threats or local tyrants who refuse to yield to a larger authority. It is during these adventures that the characters first learn of Pelsemesios, the power behind Casmerra, and that he, too, seeks the return of order and civilization for the good of all who dwell in the region.

Pelsemesios's presence also inspires interference from his rivals. Throughout all the tiers, these enemies (some of them dragons and other monsters) ally with the leaders of rebellious communities to fight against the growing kingdom.

PARAGON TIER: REVOLUTION

The heroes discover during their infiltrations of the surrounding communities that Casmerra and Pelsemesios have been using their soldiers not only against military threats, but against any community that rejects the rule of New Kindras. The two have tried to avoid civilian casualties, and once they've gained control over a region, its citizens are granted the same rights and freedoms that residents anywhere else in the kingdom have. Nonetheless, Casmerra and Pelsemesios are using martial force to conquer those who reject their rule. Several villages have banded together and threaten the newly formed kingdom with armed revolt—a revolt that will fail, but that might destabilize the new government in the process.

If the characters confront them, the dragon and the queen point out that New Kindras can't enforce its rule over regions in which it lacks power. Under the watchful eyes of their soldiers, citizens of areas they conquer gain the benefits of codified laws and protection from the monsters and criminals that still lurk in the wild.

Do the characters stand with Pelsemesios and Queen Casmerra, acknowledging that the rule of law and safety of all take precedence over the rights of self-government for communities that want to maintain their independence? Or do they stand with the rebels against an expanding kingdom that seeks to make the world a safer place for all without regard for those who do not wish to be ruled?

Epic Tier: Retaliation

Regardless of the characters' decision, attacks by Pelsemesios's enemies intensify. The creators of New Kindras aren't the only would-be monarchs rising to power, and the growth of nations brings an outbreak of war. Many of the leaders hope to conquer other rising kingdoms before they reach their full potential.

These rival kingdoms span the planes, and magical warfare is the order of the day. Among the most dangerous rivals are:

✦ The efreet Sharamadras, whose dictatorship is based in the Elemental Chaos. Violent weather heralds her slave army's march into battle.

✦ Akkliar, a vicious devil who built his kingdom in the world so he could avoid the meddling of other devils. Rumors suggest that an archdevil—perhaps Asmodeus himself—is the power behind Akkliar's throne.

✦ Yorantadrios, the rival most strongly opposed to New Kindras. A much older sibling of Pelsemesios, Yorantadrios long ago became a dracolich. He has grown sinister and cruel since his transformation. Once this enemy is revealed, Pelsemesios claims he began building a kingdom to stop his brother's army of undead and draconic creatures.

The characters can fight alongside a kingdom, or they can try to end the conflict without taking sides.

The Pontifex Wyrm

Few full-fledged nations or kingdoms remain in a dark and lawless world, but surely Avaat Mahn comes close. A powerful, centuries-old city-state, Avaat Mahn claims dominion over every community within several days' travel of its great stone walls. Thousands of people in more than a dozen communities swear fealty to the Pontifex Council of Avaat Mahn. And, yes, perhaps their taxes are a bit higher, and perhaps their freedom to worship as they choose is curtailed. But at least the roads are far safer, the watch is more efficient, and the priests are ever ready with magic.

And those priests are common indeed, for Avaat Mahn is a strict theocracy, one in which the ruling clergy—the pontifices of the council—hold absolute power. Devoted exclusively to the god Ahn-Sur, the Pontifex Council rules in his name and teaches the people absolute obedience to the deity and to the theocratic authority of the state.

It's all a lie.

There is no deity named Ahn-Sur, even if most of the pontifices believe that there is. The gold dragon Suvankotha, who serves on the council in human form, concocted the entire religion. When he was much younger, Suvankotha decided to rule over the "lesser beings" of the region—for their own good, of course—and chose religious indoctrination rather than overt power as the means to achieve that rule.

Today, the temple of Ahn-Sur uses rituals to grant false divine power to its priests, and the Pontifex Council of Avaat Mahn rules over its people with an iron fist—keeping them safe, yes, but only in exchange for their worship and unquestioning obedience.

Heroic Tier: Followers

The characters begin the campaign as citizens of, or newcomers to, Avaat Mahn. So far in their lives, they've seen only the positive side of life in the city-state. The roads are safe, the peasants in the fields largely unmolested. Indeed, the heroes must travel a good distance to find adventure, and they are encouraged and supported by the Pontifex Council, which is eager to employ people capable of ensuring the region's safety.

Slowly, the characters learn more about some of the "threats" they're dealing with. Certain criminal gangs are, in fact, factions rebelling against the council's tyranny. Citizens of Avaat Mahn often disappear after questioning the council's rulings.

Paragon Tier: Apostates

Whether or not the characters act on what they have learned, the mere fact that they know it—that they've consorted with "heretics"—comes to the council's attention. Friends of the party begin to disappear, and the characters find themselves attacked by those they thought of as allies. Early in the tier, the characters must fight for their freedom and survival, even as they slowly begin to learn the truth of the Pontifex Council, the dragon in its midst, and the false god Ahn-Sur. They might have to escape Suvankotha's secret dungeon or rescue potential allies from deep within it.

In the latter levels of the tier, the characters are pitted directly against the forces of the Council. They cannot stand alone, but with the evidence they've found, perhaps they can convince enough citizens of the truth to raise a revolt against the theocracy. But even if they manage this, can they defeat Suvankotha?

Epic Tier: Believers

Now what? Perhaps the characters have thrown off the yoke of Suvankotha and the Pontifex Council, but they've left this theocracy with neither a government nor a spiritual center. They must find a way to maintain the rule of law and to introduce worship of the true gods (or at least some of them) to a populace bitter and betrayed by the one god they knew.

Furthermore, the characters must protect Avaat Mahn from other forces that have learned of its vulnerability. Warriors of dark gods see a chance to grab power, and portions of the populace that refuse to accept the truth see the heroes as heretics against Ahn-Sur. Lurking behind nearly all these threats are the offspring of Suvankotha. This entire family of dragons seeks blood vengeance on the characters and on the culture that betrayed their golden sire.

Some metallic dragons are social creatures. Some enjoy lording over "lesser beings," or at least believe they have the right and responsibility to do so. Some are determined to teach the humanoid races to fend for themselves. And some just need allies or servants that can reach places they cannot. Whatever the case, metallic dragons are far more likely than their chromatic counterparts to found, take over, or at least participate in humanoid organizations and factions. For the dragon, this offers a degree of influence and a pool of potential agents that it might not otherwise have. For the players, it offers the opportunity for their characters to interact, knowingly or unknowingly, with one of these great, potentially campaign-altering creatures.

The following examples can be used as is, or can serve as models for creating your own organizations.

THE BLOOD OF BARASTISS

Goal: The Blood of Barastiss, a community and religious sect that started out as an extended clan of lizardfolk, is motivated by religious zealotry in the name of a dragon that claims to be a primitive spirit-god. The Blood wants to swiftly expand its tribal borders, enslave and assimilate any communities in its way, and spread its particular religion.

Size: Small, located in a secluded region. The sect has not yet encroached on larger communities.

Alignment: Unaligned.

Philosophy: "Great Barastiss! Bring us meat and bone! Show us the weak so we can take what they do not protect! Great spirit, we bring more to worship at your idol!"

History: The Barastiss lizardfolk lived on a small island and worshiped ancestors and regional spirits. They warred with other primitive tribes, and the clan might have disintegrated had the iron dragon Ogtho-rilak not shown up to lead them. The dragon took the name Barastiss to emulate the clan's spirit-god and turned the group into the sect called the Blood of Barastiss. The Blood then assimilated other races into its ranks and spread to other islands and the nearby coast.

Leadership: The leader of the Blood is the iron dragon Barastiss. (He keeps his real name secret.) He poses as the avatar of the spirit the sect worships, communicating his wishes to the tribe's shaman, a greenscale lizardfolk named Varhisthist. The shaman relays those orders to Kromarrok, an orc who serves as the tribe's war leader and secular chieftain.

Headquarters: The heart of the Blood's territory lies on the island where the lizardfolk lived for hundreds of generations. Their greatest idol also stands atop the rocky hills of that island, making it the center of their worship.

Membership Requirements: The clan accepts members of all races. Petitioners must prove themselves with shows of might and participate in rituals with blood oaths to serve Barastiss.

Structure: The Blood's members come from various families and tribes that worship Barastiss. Other than the leaders mentioned above, the Blood doesn't have a hierarchy. The elder of a family holds authority over the younger members, and shamans have authority over the elders. When the sect conquers a region, it takes locals as slaves. Some of these slaves are married into tribal families, and their offspring are raised as members of the Blood.

Activities: The Blood's members can be brutal combatants, slave-takers, thieves, and (at times) cannibals. However, they aren't deliberately wicked, and they prefer to avoid the slaughter of noncombatants. Their slaves are well fed, worked hard but not abusively, and punished only when they show deliberate disobedience. The tribe occasionally trades with others beyond its borders, if it would be too difficult to take over those communities.

BLOOD OF BARASTISS LORE

History DC 8: The Blood of Barastiss, formerly Clan Barastiss, is an extended family of lizardfolk, kobolds, orcs, shifters, primitive humans, an occasional dragonborn, and a few other random humanoids. Members are united in religious worship of a being called Barastiss; they believe him to be the emissary—perhaps avatar—of a savage, primitive god. Although this fanaticism links them, the Blood's members also reinforce their family bonds through various blood-letting and blood-sharing ceremonies—such as the mingling of open wounds—and marriages between different creatures that would be considered taboo in most civilized cultures.

History DC 14: Clan Barastiss was a tribe of greenscale lizardfolk that worshiped a stone idol on a jungle island. An opportunistic iron dragon arrived to lead them, in the name of their god. Under his guidance, the clan became the Blood of Barastiss and spread to encompass all the tribes on the isle. It then grew, reaching the nearest shores of the mainland.

ADVENTURE HOOKS

The obvious purpose for the Blood of Barastiss is that of an adversary, pitting the characters against the soldiers of the tribe and perhaps, eventually, against the expansionist agenda of the iron dragon who rules them. Some possibilities include:

✦ The characters might be sent to rescue a noble shipwrecked on the tribe's island, only to discover that the noble has been captured by the Blood

ZOLTAN BOROS & GABOR SZIKSZAI

and is in imminent peril of being sacrificed to the "avatar" of the idol. The characters might discover that an artifact or treasure they seek is hidden in the buried vaults of a subterranean temple beneath the idol on a mysterious jungle isle; naturally, the Blood defends its sacred idol from any sort of intrusion. Or the Blood of Barastiss might launch a raid on a nearby coastal town at the dragon's direction, perhaps using a forgotten teleportation circle buried in the vaults beneath its idol.

✦ The tribe might not be simple adversaries in some adventures. Although many characters will want to see the spread of the Blood checked eventually, the sect is not the most evil power in the region. The heroes might find themselves forced to ally with members of the Blood against a more vile, more dangerous enemy–possibly the cult of a demon or an evil god, or maybe the servants of a dragon far worse than Barastiss himself. The characters would have to keep their allies in check, preventing them from unleashing their violence on those who don't deserve it, all the while walking on eggshells to avoid giving so much offense that the clan revokes its shaky alliance.

✦ The characters might be forced to prove themselves to the Blood, by a show of strength or prowess, or else negotiate with or bribe them, in order to pass through their territory on the way to an unrelated objective, to win back prisoners taken in a raid, or to earn the right to speak with, and gain certain information from, Barastiss or Varhisthist.

✦ Finally, the characters might take it upon themselves to end the threat of the Blood of Barastiss by proving to the members that the iron dragon is not, in fact, an avatar of their god. Precisely how the characters would accomplish this is up to them, but creative thinking on their part should be rewarded. Even if they succeed, though, will the tribe return to its old borders, or will someone or something else, perhaps with equally violent aims, take Ogthorilak's place?

THE GUARDIANS OF THE GATES

Goal: A diverse group called the Guardians of the Gates seeks out portals to other planes of existence. In truth, its leader Irthossalur wants to control the portals that access Sigil, the City of Doors (see Chapter 6 of *Dungeon Master's Guide 2* or page 25 of *Manual of the Planes*). This steel dragon believes she is the first line of defense for the city, and she wants to uphold the balance of power the Lady of Pain (see page 190 of *Dungeon Master's Guide 2*) has established.

Stated Goal: The Guardians are dedicated to watching over the portals that bridge the planes. In Sigil, the nature of the Guardians' work is more widely known. The Guardians allow natives of Sigil to pass through portals freely, since the society has no with to anger the Lady of Pain.

Size: Moderate, with most members clustered in small groups at portal sites rather than gathered in one central location. Even the main headquarters has no more than two dozen members.

Alignment: Unaligned.

Philosophy: "The world should look after the world, just as the Feywild should care for the Feywild and the Shadowfell should keep to the Shadowfell. When the grasp of evil extends between the planes, all planes are put in danger."

History: The Guardians of the Gates formed shortly after the god Vecna managed what no deity had ever done: He entered the City of Doors. Though Vecna was eventually thrown out of Sigil, the steel dragon Virtraxentyr started the Guardians of the Gates to protect the City of Doors. At first, he and his draconic children protected only gates into Sigil, but he quickly realized how economically powerful a mapped network of dimensional portals would be.

The society quietly constructed sites that would disguise the presence of portals, sites that also became lairs for Virtraxentyr's siblings and hatchlings. As the network grew, Virtraxentyr and his kin brought in more and more assistance by reaching out to humans, elves, and dragonborn.

Leadership: A protective steel dragon named Irthossalur is the current leader of the Guardians of the Gates. She spends most of her time disguised as a human known as Suzandra. The network of portals created over centuries of work has allowed Irthossalur to amass a great fortune in both material goods and interplanar knowledge. A council of twenty advisors, scattered across the planes, meets once a year to discuss business. Most of these advisors are Watchers, individuals who oversee specific portal sites.

Headquarters: Two buildings linked by a planar portal make up the Guardians' headquarters. A small building in Sigil connects to a similar structure in the world, nestled within the quiet village of Hornburg. In Sigil, the Guardians of the Gates use a front organization called the Planar Explorer Society, whose headquarters is within the Clerk's Ward. These two buildings also serve as Irthossalur's lair, since she loves the cosmopolitan nature of Sigil as well as the quiet and reserved inhabitants of Hornburg.

Membership Requirements: Characters must prove themselves to a Watcher. When one of the Guardians' permanent sites comes under attack by extraplanar foes, those who fend off the threat might be offered membership.

Structure: Around each portal the Guardians find, they set up a permanent enclave to guard and watch it. The Watchers who oversee these locations have a great deal of autonomy.

Activities: Most society members are explorers, spies, and scouts who secretly scour the world seeking functioning gates to other planes. Once a gate is discovered, the society establishes an appropriate cover operation to guard the location, such as an inn or a guard tower. Many of these sites also include teleportation circles, but the keys to operating these portals are kept secret. Teleportation circles that might have been compromised are destroyed. Portal seeking is a dangerous lifestyle, and those who undertake the challenge are richly rewarded by the Guardians.

Enemies: Any group or entity that plans an invasion between planes has reason to hate the Guardians. Fortunately for the Guardians, none of their enemies has devoted its full resources to dismantling the organization.

Rivals: Many powers within Sigil, and a smaller number in the world, oppose the restrictions the Guardians impose. Though natives of Sigil can pass freely, many travelers oppose the Guardians on principle, believing others should have the same right.

GUARDIANS OF THE GATES LORE

History DC 13: Guardians of the Gates members scour the world for portals to other planes and protect those portals against incursions. Since the presence of a portal could incite panic in a quiet village, the society works in secret.

History DC 20: The society is spread throughout the planes, maintaining a vigilant watch over planar traffic. When the Guardians find an active portal, they set up a permanent site to guard it. Each site has an established leader, known as a Watcher. Each Watcher is in charge of a small team that works to ensure that the local communities are not affected by the presence of the portal. Members of any race can belong to the society, but individuals are assigned to locations where they will blend in with the local communities. It is believed their main headquarters is located within Sigil, the City of Doors.

ADVENTURE HOOKS

Once the characters are ready for travel between the planes, they can partner with the Guardians.

✦ The characters come across a ruined tower invaded by a shadar-kai cult that has slipped into the world from the Shadowfell. If the heroes successfully fight off the invaders, the Guardians become patrons to the characters and provide further chances for adventures. The characters are tasked with tracking down additional portals to Sigil in unexplored lands. As the characters rise in power, they might be awarded an audience with Suzandra and be given more complex missions, such as destroying an archon stronghold that blocks traffic to the City of Brass or liberating a temple on a remote island in the Astral Sea that has been captured by devils.

✦ A Watcher decides that the characters shouldn't be allowed access to the gate hidden deep within an abandoned mine. This Watcher is a relative of Irthossalur and might fight the characters if they press the issue. If the characters cause the death of this relative, Irthossalur uses all her power to track down the murderers of her kin.

The Grand Assemblage of the League of Eternal Discovery

The Assemblage appears as part of the "A Little Knowledge . . ." campaign arc (page 68), but you can use it in any campaign.

Goal: The Grand Assemblage is a highly respected—if, as the name suggests, rather flamboyant—guild for adventurers and arcane scholars. The Assemblage doesn't have any secret motives.

Size: Small. Though it's large compared to other adventuring guilds, there aren't that many adventurers out there to fill its ranks.

Alignment: Unaligned.

Philosophy: "There's so much to learn from the lore of the ancients, and we need brave souls to delve into forgotten ruins and retrieve it. We all benefit from their heroic deeds."

History: The Assemblage formed as a circle of sages and wizards sharing occult and arcane lore. It grew slowly, until the founders began allowing more and more members after they realized doing so was the best way to obtain more lore. At this stage in the Assemblage's history, the orium dragon Yuniosu and her siblings approached the organization, becoming its greatest patrons. With their funding and guidance, the organization was able to spread and grow into the respected establishment of today.

Leadership: The official leader of the Assemblage is an elected guildmaster who holds the post for 10 years. The current guildmaster is Leore Esennarian.

The organization's true leaders, however, are members of an orium dragon family—the offspring and siblings of the ancient Konoktolta—who serve as the organization's primary patrons. The dragon Yuniosu is the primary contact with the organization. Like other orium dragons, members of Konoktolta's family gather knowledge and lore, and it is this purpose to which they put the members of the Assemblage.

Headquarters: The Assemblage's primary headquarters is its sprawling, multistructure campus in the city of Pravarum. It serves as a university to a few rich students. The Assemblage also maintains a few chapterhouses in villages and hamlets on the outskirts of civilization.

Membership Requirements: The Assemblage occasionally approaches adventurers who have solid reputations and invites them to join. Most members, however, petition to join (a process requiring them to supply a sufficient record of past accomplishments and discoveries).

Structure: The guildmaster decides policy, and each chapterhouse has an overseer. All other members are essentially equal. Yuniosu exerts her influence over whomever she sees fit, putting the right ideas in the right minds to get her way.

Activities: Members share information and rumors, offer advice and suggestions for the successful completion of adventures, and sometimes aid one another in their explorations (for a share of the profit, of course). The Assemblage makes membership as attractive to adventurers as possible. It provides access to libraries of lore, disseminates rumors and tales that might lead to rich dungeons, and introduces adventurers to allies who might prove useful on a given endeavor. At rare times, the Assemblage sells rituals and magic items to its members.

Grand Assemblage Lore

History or Streetwise DC 7: The Grand Assemblage of the League of Eternal Discovery is one of the most widespread adventurers' guilds. It's said that members have access to a library of lore, rumors of great treasures and challenges, and the advice of their peers. Accomplished adventurers can join for a minimal fee and the promise to turn over any ancient lore or lost knowledge they come across.

History or Streetwise DC 12: The Assemblage began as a small gathering of arcanists and sages who thought it more productive to share their knowledge. Slowly, as more and more individuals joined, the Assemblage expanded its membership to adventurers and explorers of all sorts, realizing that such individuals were most likely to make impressive discoveries.

History or Streetwise DC 17: Several wealthy patrons help bankroll the Assemblage in exchange for access to the information the group acquires. To the best of anyone's knowledge—and quite a few people have looked into it—there's nothing particularly sinister behind this, just genuine curiosity and fascination with lost lore.

Adventure Hooks

The Assemblage can introduce a wide variety of plot hooks to the characters—particularly if they become members. Want to feed them a rumor about a lost tomb, a rampaging dragon, an ancient artifact, or a forgotten shrine? Want to put them in touch with a particular employer? The halls of the Assemblage are the perfect place for doing so. The guildmaster might hire the characters to escort a scholar to a dangerous ruin so that the scholar can make a record of the mysterious hieroglyphics decorating the crumbling palace, entrust the characters with the task of recovering a treasure stolen from the organization's vaults decades ago by a rapacious lich, or even dispatch them on a planar journey to ask a question of a sphinx-guarded oracle. That said, the Assemblage doesn't have to be just a middleman; it can itself be the source of plots.

- Several members of the Assemblage vanished while pursing related goals. As the characters investigate, they discover that Handrakka, a moderately powerful dragonborn within the Assemblage, is behind the conspiracy. He was turned mad during an adventure into a deep mine. The solution to curing him—and thereby discovering where he has imprisoned the missing adventurers—requires delving back into the mine and facing the aberrant creatures dwelling there.

- Once within the ranks of the Assemblage, the characters find the political situation more complicated than they expected. They receive poor (or especially dangerous) assignments from the current guildmaster, Leore. Her term will be up soon, but her lackey Martoli is the frontrunner to replace her. Can the heroes find a suitable candidate who will give them more respect? If they find out about the orium dragons behind the Assemblage, they might be able to pull support from them.

- Other adventurers in the Assemblage might compete with the characters to acquire a specific treasure, or engage in political maneuvering to get one of their own elected as the next guildmaster.

- If the characters aren't members, the Assemblage can become an enemy—well, at least a rival—as its members constantly seek to beat the characters to their prizes and to outdo them in the public eye.

THE SOLEMN ORDER OF THE KNIGHTS OF SAINT VERCESIEN THE GOLD

Goal: Founded in memory of the gold dragon Vercesien, paladin and champion of Bahamut, the Solemn Order of the Knights of Saint Vercesien the Gold—or just the Knights of Vercesien—stands fast against the evils of the world. Its members struggle not merely to lighten the darkness between civilization's points of light but to expand those points, working for the day when the humanoid (and draconic) races can once again claim a wide empire where the people live safely, peacefully, and under the rule of law. The people of Four Winds and the other cities and roads the knights patrol swear that they've made a difference. In truth, the Knights of Vercesien are effective only on a local level. Their numbers are too small and their methods—patrolling roads and borders, hunting monsters and highwaymen—too narrow to have more than a localized effect.

Size: Small. The order is effective only in the areas around a few cities.

Alignment: Lawful good.

Philosophy: "We will remake the world as it was in the bright age of the past, when the light of just law illuminated all. The cities of peace will grow to become beacons that drive the darkness far away."

History: Vercesien lived several hundred years before the rise of the Empire of Nerath. Though not fond of humanoids on a personal level, the gold dragon took to heart the teachings of Bahamut and championed the cause of justice for all creatures. When he fell fighting in Bahamut's name, defending the city of Four Winds, followers of Bahamut revered his memory. It was only a few years later when several of Bahamut's knights, wanting to fight evil as freely as Vercesien had, formed the Solemn Order. The order spread from Four Winds to several major cities.

Leadership: The Aureate Shield—a council of three humanoids and a gold dragon—leads the order. By tradition, at least one of those humanoids must be a holy person devoted to Bahamut. Technically, the dragon leads the Aureate Shield, but a unanimous vote by the humanoids can overrule him. Currently, the members include Aureate Lord Emphanetrix, an adult gold dragon; Shield Lord Kelgas Evraine, a human warrior devoted to Bahamut; Shield Lady Renna Hyst, a half-elf arcanist and swordmaster; and Shield Lord Mahess, a dragonborn priest of Pelor.

Headquarters: An enormous, stone-walled fortress in the trade city of Four Winds houses the Knights' largest chapterhouse and the meeting hall of the Aureate Shield.

Membership Requirements: Knights frequently visit military and religious establishments, attempting to convince experienced "soldiers for good" to join. A sizable minority of enlisters simply approached a chapterhouse and petitioned to test for membership. Such tests measure both prowess and moral standing. Even gold dragons, with which the order maintains a reverent relationship, must be judged. By ancient tradition, only the Aureate Lord and other dragons (if any are members at the time) can judge them.

Structure: Beyond the Aureate Shield, rank is determined primarily by seniority, though the Aureate Shield or a chapterhouse's knight-prelate can grant advancement for exceptional service. Members are expected to obey higher-ranking knights without question, unless given an immoral order.

Activities: The Knights of Vercesien is an open organization. Though a few of its internal procedures and ceremonies remain secret, its existence and its goals are not. Vercesien chapterhouses accept visitors and hopeful applicants at all times.

KNIGHTS OF VERCESIEN LORE

History or Religion DC 15: Members of the Knights of Vercesien, an order made up primarily of fighters and paladins, fight against the monsters of the wilderness and expand the rule of civilization. Though its numbers aren't large enough to make a huge difference, the organization has rendered certain cities and highways relatively safe. The Knights

are associated peripherally with the worship of Bahamut, but there's no formal affiliation.

History or Religion DC 20: Saint Vercesien was a gold dragon devotee of Bahamut who fell in battle defending a human city from chromatic dragons. To this day, the gold dragon is the symbol of the order, and it's said that gold dragons participate in governing the organization.

The order is known for its use of drakkensteed mounts (see page 196) by its most skilled warriors.

History or Religion DC 25: Although most of the organization's members mean well, at times in the history of the group the self-interest of its leaders—or their unyielding interpretation of what "the rule of law" means—has resulted in the knighthood briefly becoming a tool of tyranny. Today, the knights look back on those days with shame and guard against the same thing happening again.

ADVENTURE HOOKS

The most effective use of the Knights of Vercesien in a campaign is to make the characters members, or at least allies, of the order. After all, what is it if not a group devoted to the same principles as many adventuring parties? The order can provide information and point the characters toward objectives they might not otherwise encounter. For example:

✦ The minions of Tiamat are natural enemies of the Knights; as members, the characters might be assigned to quash a cult of Tiamat causing trouble in a distant city, to recover a holy relic stolen by a cultist, or destroy an evil artifact that granted the cult the ability to command chromatic dragons to do their bidding.

✦ By interacting with the knights, the characters eventually meet with the Solemn Order's gold dragon leaders. A mission requires the heroes to travel to the frozen north. An ancient cobalt dragon lives there, and it holds a grudge against Aureate Lord Emphanetrix. The characters will need to speak to the dragon for its assistance, and navigate the twisting paths of draconic politics.

✦ The Knights of Vercesien can serve as foils or rivals for the characters instead of allies. They might both go after the same goal—a powerful artifact, perhaps—but for different reasons. A particularly stern leadership might have the knights seeking justice in the case of a "criminal" whose actions the characters thought were justified. Or a local knight-prelate's pride might be stung if the characters defeat an evil that his Knights could not, and he might then decide to move against them politically.

WILLIAM O'CONNOR

Dragons have created countless artifacts though the ages. Artifacts link directly to the dragons' essences or, in a few cases, to the power of dragon deities. Two of the more potent artifacts of dragonkind are described below.

BLOOD OF IO

The *Blood of Io* is appropriate for characters of the epic tier.

Blood of Io	Epic Level

This dragon-shaped crystal vessel contains droplets of blood spilled when a primordial's axe divided Io into the twin deities Bahamut and Tiamat. The user of this ichor taps into Io's ancient strength.

Wondrous Item

Property: Gain resist 5 acid, resist 5 cold, resist 5 fire, resist 5 lightning, and resist 5 poison.

Property: Your attacks deal 2d8 extra damage against targets of the elemental origin.

Property: You can speak and understand Draconic and can read Iokharic.

Power (Encounter ✦ Acid, Cold, Fire, Lightning, or Poison): Minor Action. You sip from the *Blood of Io*. Until the end of the encounter, you gain an at-will attack power that requires a standard action to use: close blast 5; +30 vs. Reflex; 4d6 + Constitution modifier damage of a type you choose from among acid, cold, fire, lightning, and poison.

Power (Encounter ✦ Healing): Minor Action. You sip from the *Blood of Io* and spend a healing surge. Instead of the hit points you would normally regain, you regain 50 hit points, and you gain resist 10 to all damage until the start of your next turn.

GOALS OF THE BLOOD OF IO

✦ Serve and protect chromatic and metallic dragons.

✦ Destroy draconic abominations such as draconians, dragonspawn, and dragons touched by the Far Realm.

✦ Oppose elemental creatures and their designs.

✦ Restore Io to proper form by merging his sundered halves—Bahamut and Tiamat—into one being.

ROLEPLAYING THE BLOOD OF IO

This small quantity of blood came from Io, the progenitor of dragons, and residual traces of the arrogant deity's will and intelligence still smolder within. Only the *Blood*'s owner can hear its whispers, at the rare times when it communicates verbally. The artifact prefers to convey its wishes through dreams. The *Blood* tries to fill its owner with the same burning hatred it feels against the primordials and elementals by showing flashes of past events: glimpses of the horrific first war between the deities

and the primordials, of Io's sundering, and of the birth of Bahamut and Tiamat from Io's divided body. It intersperses subliminal hints into these dreams, presenting visions of the course it wants its owner to take and the goals it wants to achieve. The *Blood* tests its possessor, urging the character to resume the war against primordials, to destroy elemental creatures, and to search for a way to knit together Io's halves.

CONCORDANCE

Starting score	5
Owner gains a level	+1d10
Owner is a dragonborn	+2
Owner performs a service for a chromatic or metallic dragon	+1
Owner kills an elemental (maximum 1/day)	+1
Owner attacks a dragon (maximum 1/encounter)	–1
Owner uses one of the artifact's powers	–1

PLEASED (16–20)

"Drinking the ichor reveals my true path and nourishes me. Nothing in the world can stand against me."

The *Blood* sees its owner as the catalyst of its rebirth and lends greater power to the character in hopes of restoring Io's ascendancy.

Property: Gain resist 10 acid, resist 10 cold, resist 10 fire, resist 10 lightning, and resist 10 poison.

Property: Gain a +5 bonus to Diplomacy checks and Insight checks against dragons.

Power (At-Will): Move Action. Fly a number of squares equal to your speed + 2. You must land at the end of the movement.

Power (Daily): Immediate Interrupt. Use this power when an enemy scores a critical hit against you or against an ally you can see. The hit is a normal hit instead.

Power (Daily ✦ Healing, Polymorph): No Action. Use this power when an attack reduces you to 0 hit points. You split into two identical creatures. Place a token for your duplicate in a space adjacent to you. You regain hit points equal to your bloodied value. The duplicate has hit points equal to your bloodied value.

Your duplicate acts immediately after you in the initiative order. It has the same senses, defenses, and other characteristics (such as speed and resistances) that you do.

You and your duplicate share your powers; for example, if one of you uses an encounter power, the other cannot use that power during that encounter.

Whenever one of you starts a turn in a space adjacent to the other, the one whose turn it is grants combat advantage to all attackers until the start of its next turn. If one of you is reduced to 0 hit points, that one fades away. Otherwise, the two of you merge at the end of a short or an extended rest.

SATISFIED (12–15)

"I have proven my worth to the Blood and so have proven my worth to all dragons."

The wielder erases the *Blood's* doubts, so the *Blood* sees the wielder as a possible agent of its rebirth and thus grants a measure of greater power.

Property: Gain a +2 bonus to Diplomacy checks and Insight checks against dragons.
Power (Daily ✦ Fear): Standard Action. You roar with terrifying wrath: Close burst 1; Charisma vs. Will; the target is dazed (save ends). *Aftereffect:* The target takes a -2 penalty to attack rolls until the end of the encounter.

NORMAL (5–11)

"I have yet to prove myself to the Blood. I must strive to live up to its expectations."

The artifact finds fault with its owner. It encourages the character to discard it so it can find a worthier champion.

UNSATISFIED (1–4)

"Little fluid remains in the vessel. I fear I have exhausted the Blood's patience."

Fighting dragons or excessively drinking the *Blood* erodes the artifact's goodwill. The owner must make amends soon, or the *Blood* will leave.

Property: Gain vulnerable 5 to all damage.
Property: Take a -5 penalty to Diplomacy checks and Insight checks against dragons.
Special: The *Blood* places you in harm's way. While marked by any creature, you grant combat advantage to all attackers.

ANGERED (0 OR LOWER)

"The phial is empty of even the Blood's scorn."

The *Blood* abandons all hope that its wielder will help it attain its goals. It withdraws its gifts and actively seeks to eliminate the character in favor of one better suited to its purpose.

Property: Gain vulnerable 10 to all damage.
Property: Take a -5 penalty to Bluff, Diplomacy, Insight, and Intimidate checks against dragons.
Property: Take a -5 penalty to death saving throws and to saving throws against effects from enemies that have the elemental origin.
Property: You can no longer use powers granted by the *Blood of Io*. (Its properties are still in effect.)

MOVING ON

"The Blood boils in the phial, signaling its imminent departure. I can take heart in having furthered its goals."

The *Blood of Io* has achieved all it can accomplish in mortal hands and is ready to complete its holy mission. It asks its bearer to deliver it to any ancient dragon that will carry the *Blood* to Bahamut or Tiamat when the dragon passes from the world.

If the owner finds an ancient dragon and the dragon accepts the *Blood of Io*, the owner gains a permanent +2 bonus to Bluff, Diplomacy, Insight, and Intimidate checks against dragons and permanently gains resist 10 acid, resist 10 cold, resist 10 fire, resist 10 lightning, and resist 10 poison.

If the owner gains a level before beginning a quest to find an ancient dragon or gains a second level without completing the quest, the artifact leaves the owner with a curse: In each encounter, the first time the character is hit by an attack that has a damage type, the character gains vulnerable 15 to that damage type until the end of the encounter. Remove Affliction can lift this curse if performed by an epic-tier ritual caster who worships Bahamut or Tiamat.

Until it moves on, the *Blood* retains all powers and properties appropriate for its concordance (or as if it is pleased, if its score is 21 or higher).

FRANZ VOHWINKEL

SEAL OF THE LAWBRINGER

The *Seal of the Lawbringer* is appropriate for characters of 16th level or higher.

Seal of the Lawbringer	Paragon Level

This round, platinum medallion features the holy symbol of Bahamut surrounded by seven stylized golden canaries. A fine platinum chain allows its owner to wear it as a pendant.

The *Seal of the Lawbringer* is a +5 *symbol of hope*. It has the following properties and powers.

Implement (Holy Symbol)
Enhancement: Attack rolls and damage rolls
Critical: +5d6 damage
Property: You can speak and understand Draconic and can read Iokharic.
Power (Encounter ✦ Cold): Minor Action. You attack with the *breath of Bahamut*: close blast 3; Constitution + 5 vs. Reflex; 2d6 + Constitution modifier cold damage, and the target is immobilized until the end of your next turn.
Power (Daily): Immediate Reaction. Use this power when an effect that a save can end targets you or an ally within 5 squares of you. The target gains a +5 bonus to saving throws against that effect.

GOALS OF THE SEAL OF THE LAWBRINGER

- ✦ Fight Tiamat and her servants.
- ✦ Protect the weak from evil.
- ✦ Defend civilization from chaos.

ROLEPLAYING THE SEAL OF THE LAWBRINGER

The *Seal of the Lawbringer* speaks in a calm, authoritative voice that only its bearer can hear. The owner's devotion to Bahamut's tenets increases the artifact's power. The *Seal* encourages its owner to pray to Bahamut often, especially after victory in battle. The *Seal's* ultimate gift is the ability for the character to transform temporarily into a platinum dragon; however, the transformation drains the *Seal's* power. The *Seal* seeks out not only owners who are already followers of Bahamut, but also heroes who have capably slain chromatic dragons and might be receptive to the power the *Seal* offers.

CONCORDANCE

Starting score	**5**
Owner gains a level	+1d10
Owner is a follower of Bahamut	+2
Owner kills a servant of Tiamat (maximum 1/encounter)	+1
Owner furthers a cause of Bahamut	+1
Owner, while above 0 hit points, allows an ally in combat to be reduced to 0 hit points	-1
Owner furthers a cause of Tiamat	-2
Owner uses the *Seal's* power to transform into a dragon	-5

PLEASED (16–20)

"I am one with the Lawbringer; his will is my will. I must protect the world from evil."

The bearer and the *Seal of the Lawbringer* are in tune with each other. Bahamut's power infuses the bearer.

Property: Gain resist 10 cold and resist 10 fire.
Property: On a missed attack from *breath of Bahamut*, the target takes half damage and is not immobilized.
Power (Daily ✦ Implement, Polymorph): Minor Action. Push each creature adjacent to you 1 square, and then transform into a Huge platinum dragon until the end of the encounter or until you end the transformation as a minor action. While you are in this form:
- ✦ Gain a fly speed equal to your speed + 2.
- ✦ Your hands are claws with a reach of 3 squares, granting you a +2 proficiency bonus to attack rolls while unarmed and making your unarmed attacks deal 1d10 damage.
- ✦ You cannot use an implement or a weapon other than the *Seal of the Lawbringer*.
- ✦ The *Seal's* enhancement bonus applies to all powers and unarmed attacks you use.
- ✦ Gain *dragon claw strike* and *platinum presence* (see below).

WAYNE ENGLAND

Dragon Claw Strike | Seal of the Lawbringer Attack

You lash out with platinum claws.

At-Will ✦ Implement
Standard Action   Melee 3
Effect: Make two melee basic attacks, each of which deals
   1d10 + Strength modifier damage.
   Level 21: 2d10 + Strength modifier damage.

Platinum Presence | Seal of the Lawbringer Attack

Your imposing stature fills foes with dread.

Daily ✦ Implement
Standard Action   Close burst 5
Target: Each enemy in burst
Attack: Charisma vs. Will
Hit: The target is stunned (save ends). *Aftereffect:* The tar-
   get takes a -2 penalty to attack rolls (save ends).

SATISFIED (12–15)

"The dawn of a new day nears."

The *Seal of the Lawbringer* recognizes its wielder's
strength and trusts the wielder with a portion of
Bahamut's might.

Property: *Breath of Bahamut* is a close burst 5 attack.
Power (Daily): Minor Action. Spend a healing surge to
   encase your skin in platinum scales. Gain resist 5 to all
   damage until the end of the encounter.

NORMAL (5–11)

*"I walk the path to freedom and strength, but the journey
is long."*

The *Seal* patiently and watchfully guides the
wielder on the best course of action.

UNSATISFIED (1–4)

*"I lack discipline and self-control. The Platinum One thinks
I am a coward."*

The *Seal* communicates with its bearer only
through dreams. In them, Bahamut takes the form
of an authority figure in the character's life, such as
a parent or tutor, and scolds the bearer. At the end of
such dreams, Bahamut takes his true form.

Property: Take a -2 penalty to all defenses.
Special: Once per day during combat, the *Seal* can make
   you attack a target within 5 squares of you. Roll a d20 +
   your level vs. Will; if the attack hits, you mark the target
   until the end of your next turn, slide 5 squares to a space
   adjacent to the target, and are dazed (save ends).

ANGERED (0 OR LOWER)

"The voice that once filled my soul is silent with contempt."

The *Seal of the Lawbringer* communicates with its
bearer only in dreams and only symbolically. The
bearer dreams of ignoring an innocent's plight and
then trying to reach Bahamut to no avail—drowning
in an ocean or being lost as a child. At the end of
such a dream, an image of Bahamut takes the place
of the dreamer but still does not become aware of the
dreamer's troubles; the bearer suffers the same aban-
donment the innocent suffered.

Property: At the start of each encounter, you lose a healing
   surge.
Property: Take a -5 penalty to all defenses.

MOVING ON

"I am ready for the Lawbringer's final trial."

When the *Seal of the Lawbringer* prepares to move
on, it assigns a final task to its bearer. It might ask the
bearer to restore a lost temple of Bahamut, to protect endangered innocents from a force of immense
power, or to stop machinations of Tiamat's followers.
Each morning after the *Seal* assigns the task, one of
the golden canaries on the *Seal* morphs into a ghostly
gold dragon, flies into the sky, and vanishes.

If the bearer finishes the task before the last
canary leaves, the bearer gains 1 point of concordance for each remaining canary. If the bearer
does not finish the task, the bearer loses 3 points of
concordance. If, during the final encounter of the
task, the bearer uses the *Seal*-granted power to turn
into a dragon, the level of concordance does not
change because the *Seal* moves on at the end of the
encounter.

When the *Seal* moves on, if it has a normal
or higher level of concordance, the final canary
becomes a gold dragon that thanks the bearer for
devotion to Bahamut before flying off. A +4 *symbol
of hope* marked with the holy symbol of Bahamut
remains in the bearer's possession. The bearer gains
a permanent +2 bonus to Charisma-based checks
and a permanent +3 bonus to his or her healing
surge value.

If the *Seal* is unsatisfied or angered when it moves
on, the final canary transforms into an elder gold
dragon (see *Monster Manual 2*, page 82), and the
Seal shatters and crumbles into worthless dust. The
dragon attacks the bearer, calling the bearer "the
Betrayer" and focusing its attacks on that character
even if other characters attack it. When the character
is reduced to 0 hit points, the dragon flies off, ending
the encounter. The character takes a permanent -2
penalty to Charisma-based checks and a permanent
-3 penalty to his or her healing surge value.

The *Seal of the Lawbringer* returns to the world only
when a need for it develops.

CHAPTER 3

DRAGON LAIRS

THE DRAGON'S lair is the most iconic adventure locale in the DUNGEONS & DRAGONS game. It challenges the characters with one of the toughest monsters in the game and provides one of the richest rewards—the dragon's hoard. Consequently, any dragon lair should be a spectacular and awe-inspiring encounter setting. This is especially true for metallic dragons, which have more refined tastes than their chromatic counterparts and seek out lairs that reflect their appreciation for aesthetics and the trappings of power. A younger and more brutish metallic dragon might settle for a dank cave, but any mature dragon that has even the most meager appreciation of beauty hungers for opulence and splendor in its lair.

Metallic and chromatic dragons often use the same settings for their lairs, with natural caverns and complexes proving the most common. Metallic dragons are more likely than chromatics to make their lairs near, or within, the communities of other creatures, or to dwell in specially constructed structures. (The latter are often built by humanoids employed, ruled, or enslaved by the dragon in question.) Because metallic dragons tend to be more social than chromatics—with other creatures, not just other dragons—they're more likely to choose lairs that other creatures can reach and enter on foot.

In this chapter, you'll find:

✦ **Designing a Dragon Lair:** A brief look at some of the characteristics of metallic dragon lairs.

✦ **Heroic Tier Lairs:** Encounters for characters of 1st–10th level.
  ✦ Goblin Folly (iron, 3rd level)
  ✦ The Terror of Prospect Hill (copper, 5th level)
  ✦ Tulkau Shayn (orium, 7th level)

✦ **Paragon Tier Lairs:** Encounters for characters of 11th–20th level.
  ✦ Mines of Bolmarzh (adamantine, 13th level)
  ✦ The Breaking Tide (bronze, 13th level)
  ✦ Methenaera the Mead-Keeper (silver, 18th level)

✦ **Epic Tier Lairs:** Encounters for characters of 21st level or higher.
  ✦ The Edge of Chaos (mithral, 23rd level)
  ✦ Citadel of the Golden Architect (gold, 24th level)
  ✦ The Earthen Dagger (mercury, 26th level)

CHIPPY

In many respects, a dragon's lair is as vital to a dragon-based encounter or adventure as the dragon itself. Whether it's a simple cave in a rocky mountain range, a great castle as ornate as any constructed by elves or dwarves, or a palace literally built of clouds and flames, a dragon's lair says everything about its master's persona, power, and goals.

At its simplest, a dragon's lair must serve as a repository for the beast's hoard and a relatively safe sanctum in which the dragon can relax without constantly worrying about intruders and thieves. Most such lairs, however, are far more. When you design a dragon's lair, try to consider the dragon's personality and goals as thoroughly as you would when building an adventure around the wyrm's activities. Is it almost impossible to access without the ability to fly? Is it riddled with traps or interwoven with twisting tunnels? Is it occupied by intelligent creatures that serve the dragon out of awe or fear or greed? Is it distant from communities of humanoids, or does it lie near them, so that the dragon can watch over these "lesser creatures"? Make each lair as unique and memorable as each dragon.

Metallic dragons often concern themselves with the comfort and convenience of their lairs more than with defensibility, but dragons as a rule are highly intelligent and suspicious creatures. Building formidable obstacles and carefully laid defenses for their lairs is one of the few menial tasks that dragons can apply themselves to without growing bored or impatient.

PURPOSE

Although chromatic dragons choose lairs that offer the best defensive advantages, metallics care about how convenient a location is in relation to the dragon's purpose. The first step in designing a lair is to ask why a dragon chooses to live in that spot. Some possible answers are discussed below.

Guarding a Site: The dragon is the appointed guardian of an important site: the vault of a wizards' guild, a sacred shrine, the sealed prison of a mighty demon, or a magic fountain. Whether the dragon was appointed to its duty or seized the locale for its own benefit, it must remain close to the place it intends to guard. Many such sites are inside the dragon's lair (or, to be more precise, the dragon establishes its lair around the site it guards). These lairs have fewer traits of draconic style because the dragon has to work around a site that was likely created by someone else.

Protecting Something: The dragon guards some item or secret instead of a site. The item it protects is portable, so the dragon can choose to live anywhere it likes, as long as it keeps the item safe. Sometimes the item is the dragon's hoard. Most lairs chosen for this purpose are exceedingly well hidden—for example, a natural cavern with a concealed entrance in a remote place or a lair disguised in the middle of some other site, such as a necropolis or ruined stronghold.

Ruling Others: The dragon has established itself as the lord or master of lesser creatures nearby—a human tribe or city, a goblin stronghold, a dragonborn village, or some settlement of humanoids. Some dragons are "talons-off" rulers that live in secluded, remote locations far from those they govern, relying on intermediaries to look after the day-to-day details of their realms. However, most dragons that rule over a domain enjoy basking in the fear, love, adulation, or tribute of their subjects; therefore, they choose to live somewhere highly conspicuous near their subjects.

With the resources of a community at its command, a dragon ruler can have a lair constructed or modified to its exacting standards. For example, a

EXTENDED ABSENCES

A metallic dragon might have a reason for leaving its lair for a extended time. A shapechanging gold dragon might spend years immersed in the court of a kingdom that interests it, while a silver dragon sworn to some great quest could scour the world for decades searching for someone or something. Other dragons might be lured away from their homes to ally with great heroes or spy out the secrets of hated rivals. A dragon contemplating an extended absence takes every precaution to make sure its home and hoard remains safe.

Concealment: Remote, natural lairs might be concealed by carefully contrived cave-ins, landslides, floods, or drifting snow or sand.

Guardians: Dragons that have access to the proper rituals or resources might use other monsters to safeguard their homes while they are away. Dragons that can't obtain suitable guardians might entrust the protection of their lairs to loyal minions or subjects, or ally with local powers willing to protect their lairs.

Warding Rituals: Likewise, dragons use ritual magic to bar entrance to their lairs or create alarms. The most powerful rituals let dragons teleport back to their lairs from wherever they might be wandering.

Removed Valuables: A dragon that expects to be gone for a long time might relocate its hoard to a new hiding place. This might be a place the dragon would want to live—for example, a cobalt dragon might burrow a tunnel into a glacier, stash its hoard inside, and then flood and freeze the passage to ensure that no other creature will approach its treasure while it's away.

ruling dragon might live in a spire at the city's center, a golden palace on a hill overlooking the town, a temple dedicated to its glory, or a magnificent cavern decorated by the work of generations of stonemasons.

Spying on Others: Many metallic dragons, especially copper and steel dragons, find humans and similar races fascinating. Some establish lairs in places where they can keep a close watch on people, especially if the dragons also have the ability to shapechange and mingle with crowds. A lair intended for spying might be built in a reconditioned sewer chamber, a deserted or ruined portion of a city, an abandoned fortification, or a noble estate (where a mysterious "lord" carefully guards the dragon's secret identity from all but a handful of loyal retainers). In the wilderness, a dragon might use a rarely visited area such as a sacred grove, a holy mountain, or a "taboo" valley as a lair, counting on tribal fears or laws to protect it from discovery.

Creating Comfort: Metallic dragons that have no other purpose to affect their choice of lair choose the most comfortable lairs they can find. A place offering a combination of natural beauty, a striking view, and restricted access is always serviceable. Dragons vary in their tastes, but any dragon is happy with a lair that is comfortable, defensible, and filled with items that it finds beautiful and interesting.

Attendants

Some metallic dragons value solitude, but many find room in their lairs for attending creatures that are anxious to please their draconic masters.

Sentries: Weak combatants aren't necessarily useless to a dragon. Even if they can't stand against enemies strong enough to challenge the dragon, they can sound alarms, seal gates, operate traps, and provide crucial time for organizing a lair's defenses.

Bodyguards: Creatures strong enough to stand beside their master in battle are obviously valuable. Dragons are careful not to use guards that are too powerful, since they don't want to become servants in their own homes. Bodyguards might include griffons or gargoyles, giants, elementals, or humanoids.

Counselors and Companions: Dragons are long-lived, highly intelligent, curious beings. The more sociable ones surround themselves with people whose company they enjoy, ranging from jesters or musicians hired for a few days' entertainment, to artists or scholars whose work is worth patronizing, to lifelong friends. Most attendants of this sort have no business in a battle, and they flee from attack.

Servants: A dragon might indulge itself with a staff of bodyservants—valets, cooks, maids, and other such trappings of wealth and luxury. Dragons that live near cities are more likely to maintain servants than those that live in remote wildernesses. Servants, though usually loyal and industrious, take no part in combat if they can avoid it.

Unusual Lairs

Dungeons, caves, or strongholds are all commonplace lairs for metallic dragons, but the most powerful and intelligent dragons are sometimes unwilling to settle for some dark, dank hole in the ground.

Draconic Palace: A draconic palace is a large, strong building constructed specifically to the directions of a powerful dragon monarch. Like the grand castle of a human king or queen, it combines practical defenses, awe-inspiring audience chambers, and decadent luxuries. A draconic palace normally stands atop a high hill, on a harbor or river island, or behind high walls in a wide field. Such a place uually has at least one side of the palace facing terrain the dragon can fly over, but that enemies on foot can't easily negotiate.

A draconic palace usually includes a spire or a high keep accessible only through flight, providing the dragon and its immediate family with an opulent retreat where they can sleep in safety. Portions of the draconic palace meant for both dragon and human access include wide hallways, spacious staircases, and huge, airy chambers that provide plenty of room to move for large, flying creatures. Some draconic palaces might also include humans-only portions (usually servants' quarters or barracks) with halls and doors scaled to human size. However, these are something of a defensive liability, and no dragon wants to leave places in its home where enemies might be able to lurk or move about outside its reach or knowledge.

Cloud Castles: Long, tedious, and extraordinarily expensive rituals can create a completely aerial home. A cloud castle is the gold standard of draconic homes. Some are free-floating, carried along wherever the wind takes them. Others are tethered so they roam only over a small area or remain motionless over a particular spot. Many dragons that dwell in such places still desire to have humanoid attendants, guards, and courtiers, so cloud castles routinely touch down at high hilltops or mountainsides where nonflyers can embark or disembark. A cloud castle might feature a well-guarded teleportation circle, stables for flying mounts, or a magic bridge that can bring visitors up from the ground at the master's will.

Demiplanes: Dragons of exceptional magical power might be able to create pocket dimensions to call their own. Few are much larger than several miles across, but their contents could include strange islets floating in mist; vast labyrinths or mazes; or cavern-worlds filled with lakes, forests, or anything else the creator desires. A demiplane lair is normally connected to the rest of the cosmos by some sort of magic gate. Intruders seeking access must first find where the door lies. Most of these are well hidden, accessed only through one specific, well-guarded locale in the world.

Iron dragon lair for five 3rd-level adventurers

Beneath the forest canopy of a secluded valley, a goblin band learns a fatal lesson when it foolishly "captures" an iron dragon. The game grows tiresome for the beast, which is confined in the goblins' lair. It's just a matter of time before its amusement turns into anger.

BACKGROUND

History DC 7: The goblins covet a forested vale, and they have long fought with the other inhabitants for mastery over these lands. Failure after failure diminished their numbers, driving them to desperate measures. A goblin hexer, a favored advisor within the tribe, proposed acquiring additional muscle to drive off the competition. In a rare moment of bravado, he suggested they capture a dragon and compel it into service. They set out to ensnare a young dragon, since the adults are too hard to handle.

History DC 12: The plan worked surprisingly well, and after a few days of searching, the goblins netted a young iron dragon named Thraesk. With their superior numbers, they marched the beast to their lair, but they didn't quite know what to do next. Now that the dragon is in their home, the goblins have begun to realize their mistake.

ENVIRONMENT

This "lair" includes both wilderness terrain and subterranean chambers.

The goblins live in a small cave complex beneath hills that extend north from a heavily forested valley. The hills feature more trees, moss-covered rocks jutting from the rocky soil, and occasional piles of bone and debris. Inside the cave complex, which is accessed through a tunnel at the base of the hills, the muddy floors are dotted with rank puddles. The goblins excavated the place, and their lack of crafting ability shows. Orange, hairlike roots thread through

---

THRAESK, THE IRON WIND

Young Thraesk is a curious iron dragon, inquisitive almost to a fault. Having escaped his mother's clutch only a century ago, Thraesk is intrigued by humanoids, and this fascination tends to get him into difficulty.

Thraesk was amused by the goblins' fumbling—yet daring—efforts, and he went along with them without any trouble. But being stuck in a dank and smelly cave was not how he intended to spend his time. Bored with the goblins' posturing, arguing, and occasional threats, the dragon is ready to leave. He might have left peacefully, but one of the goblins struck him—an unforgivable offense.

---

the walls and hang from the ceiling. Scattered about are stones, small shelves filled with human skulls, crude altars, and offerings to dark forces.

Illumination: Outside the cave complex, lighting depends on the time of day and the tree cover. Inside the warren, crude lanterns burn animal fat to fill the rooms with bright light.

As the characters draw near the lair, read:
Along the sides of the road, you see trees marked with crude warnings to trespassers. Animal carcasses litter the ground.

If the characters have been tracking the dragon and his goblin captors, you might consider running a complexity 1 or 2 skill challenge. Use Endurance, Nature, and Perception as primary skills, with moderate DCs. If the characters fail the challenge, they might run afoul of a wandering monster, be delayed by a natural hazard, or become temporarily turned around and arrive at the goblin warren later, only to find a rampaging dragon that has an axe to grind against all humanoids.

AREA 1: OLD WOOD
Underbrush grows between and around the trees blanketing the valley, making the going slow. The goblins have attempted to warn off intruders with skulls nailed to trees, rotting viscera hanging from low-hanging branches, and graffiti painted on rocks and trunks.

Tactical Encounter: "Escaping Goblins," page 88.

AREA 2: ENTRY GATE
The sentries at the entry gate are under strict orders to protect the chambers beyond and to make sure no one interferes. The goblins keep several wolves here for added security.

Tactical Encounter: "Uneasy Sentries," page 89.

AREA 3: CENTRAL CHAMBER
Chambers and tunnels make up the rest of the warren.

The main area, between the sleeping quarters to the east and the room to the west that has been cleared to hold the dragon, is a general storage room where the goblins keep food, water, and the junk they've stolen from caravans and other travelers. At the end of a short tunnel leading away to the southwest is a refuse pit that holds nothing of interest.

AREA 4: SLEEPING CHAMBER
A steep staircase descends 20 feet to the east and opens up into the goblins' cooking area and sleeping quarters, a room choked with lice-ridden blankets and bedrolls.

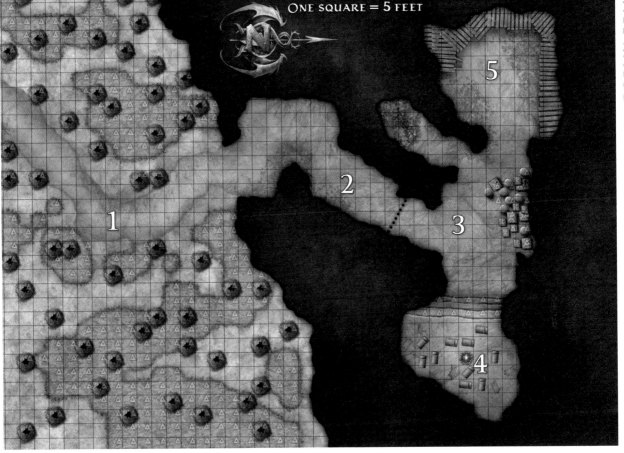

AREA 5: CHIEFTAIN'S CHAMBER

To the west, the central chamber widens as it forms the chieftain's hall. This room holds the dragon and many frightened goblins. Crude scaffolding rings the room, reachable by a ladder. Pieces of the chieftain and other goblins litter the floor, leavings from the angry dragon.

Tactical Encounter: "Standoff," page 90.

TREASURE

This set of encounters should provide the characters with three level 3 treasure parcels, one a magic item parcel and the other two monetary parcels.

DEALING WITH THE DRAGON

When the adventurers reach the third encounter, they find the dragon squaring off against the goblins. The dragon is uncertain about the characters' motives, and they need to prove their good intentions to have a chance of forming an alliance with Thraesk.

The characters need not refrain from combat in order to engage in this skill challenge. As long as they engage the goblins without affecting Thraesk, the dragon doesn't attack them unless it is provoked.

Level: 4 (XP 175).

Complexity: 1 (requires 4 successes before 3 failures).

Primary Skills: Bluff, Diplomacy, Insight.

Bluff (DC 10, standard action): The character offers aid under false pretenses, vowing to assist but plotting something else. On a failure, the dragon sees through the lies and uses one of its attacks against the character. Each character can attempt this skill check only once during the challenge.

Diplomacy (DC 15, standard action): The character earnestly vows to help the dragon defeat the goblins. Each character can attempt this skill check only once during the challenge.

Insight (DC 10, minor action): The first character who succeeds on an Insight check can tell that the dragon is angry about the situation the goblins have put it in and seems about evenly matched against them. This skill can be used to gain only 1 success in the challenge. A successful Insight check also grants a +2 bonus to the character and his or her allies when making Diplomacy checks for the remainder of the skill challenge. On a failed check, in addition to gaining 1 failure in the challenge, the character misreads the situation, seeing the dragon either as overmatched or in complete control of the situation.

Success: The dragon agrees not to attack the characters and works with them in fighting the goblins.

Failure: If the characters achieve 3 failures, the dragon sees them as threats and includes them in its attacks. Once all the goblins are defeated, the dragon turns on the adventurers.

Escaping Goblins

Encounter Level 2 (625 XP)

Setup

1 goblin underboss (U)
1 goblin cursespewer (C)
6 goblin cutters (G)

The goblin underboss and several of his underlings are fleeing the warren for their safety. The goblins want to escape the dragon, but they can't allow the adventurers to despoil their lair. The characters approach from the south along the road.

When the PCs notice the goblins, read:

Goblins are fleeing away from a hole in the base of the hillside ahead. Their fear turns into wrath when they see you.

Goblin Underboss (U)	Level 4 Elite Controller (Leader)
Small natural humanoid	XP 350

Initiative +4   **Senses** Perception +8; low-light vision
HP 110; **Bloodied** 55; see also *survival instinct*
AC 18; **Fortitude** 17, **Reflex** 15, **Will** 16
Saving Throws +2
Speed 5; see also *superior goblin tactics*
Action Points 1
ⓘ **Short Sword** (standard; at-will) ✦ **Weapon**
    +9 vs. AC; 1d6 + 4 damage. *Miss:* An adjacent ally makes a free basic attack.
Superior Goblin Tactics (immediate reaction, when missed by a melee attack; at-will)
    The goblin underboss and up to two allies within its line of sight shift 1 square.
Survival Instinct
    A goblin underboss gains a +3 bonus to defenses while bloodied.
Alignment Evil   **Languages** Common, Goblin
Skills Stealth +10, Thievery +10
| **Str** 18 (+6) | **Dex** 14 (+4) | **Wis** 13 (+3) |
| **Con** 15 (+4) | **Int** 11 (+2) | **Cha** 16 (+5) |
Equipment chainmail, short sword

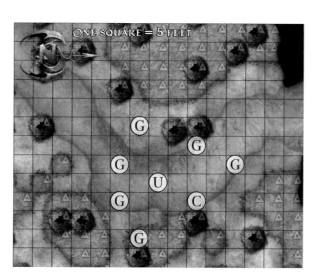

ONE SQUARE = 5 FEET

Goblin Cursespewer (C)	Level 2 Artillery (Leader)
Small natural humanoid	XP 125

Initiative +2   **Senses** Perception +2; low-light vision
HP 68; **Bloodied** 34
AC 14; **Fortitude** 14, **Reflex** 13, **Will** 15
Speed 6
ⓘ **Sacrificial Knife** (standard; at-will) ✦ **Weapon**
    +7 vs. AC; 1d4 + 3 damage.
ⓨ **Confounding Curse** (standard; at-will)
    Ranged 10; targets two creatures; +7 vs. Will; 1d6 + 3 damage, and the target grants combat advantage to allies until the end of the cursespewer's next turn.
✳ **Goblin Doom** (immediate interrupt, when a goblin within 5 squares is hit by a melee attack; at-will) ✦ **Poison**
    Area burst 2 within 10, centered on the goblin that was hit; the goblin explodes: +5 vs. Reflex; 1d10 + 3 poison damage, and ongoing 5 poison damage (save ends).
Goblin Tactics (immediate reaction, when the goblin cursespewer is missed by a melee attack; at-will)
    The goblin shifts 1 square.
Alignment Chaotic evil   **Languages** Common, Goblin
Skills Religion +5
| **Str** 11 (+1) | **Dex** 14 (+2) | **Wis** 12 (+2) |
| **Con** 16 (+4) | **Int** 9 (+0) | **Cha** 17 (+4) |
Equipment leather armor, sacrificial knife, wand

6 Goblin Cutters (G)	Level 1 Minion
Small natural humanoid	XP 25 each

Initiative +3   **Senses** Perception +1; low-light vision
HP 1; a missed attack never damages a minion.
AC 16; **Fortitude** 12, **Reflex** 14, **Will** 11
Speed 6; see also *goblin tactics*
ⓘ **Short Sword** (standard; at-will) ✦ **Weapon**
    +5 vs. AC; 4 damage (5 damage if the goblin cutter has combat advantage against the target).
Goblin Tactics (immediate reaction, when missed by a melee attack; at-will)
    The goblin shifts 1 square.
Alignment Evil   **Languages** Common, Goblin
Skills Stealth +5, Thievery +5
| **Str** 14 (+2) | **Dex** 17 (+3) | **Wis** 12 (+1) |
| **Con** 13 (+1) | **Int** 8 (-1) | **Cha** 8 (-1) |
Equipment leather armor, short sword

Tactics

At the start of combat, the underboss stands near the cursespewer and attacks any enemies who move adjacent to it. The cursespewer uses *confounding curse* and *goblin doom* each round on the cutters, which swarm the characters.

The underboss fights until either the cursespewer or all the cutters are defeated. The others flee if the underboss is slain.

Features of the Area

Underbrush: Squares of underbrush are difficult terrain.

Trees: Squares containing trees are difficult terrain and provide cover. Each tree requires a DC 7 Athletics check to climb.

UNEASY SENTRIES

Encounter Level 3 (750 XP)

SETUP

2 goblin sentries (S)
4 gray wolves (W)

Goblin sentries watch the warren's entrance, even as their fellows contend with the dragon inside the lair. The gray wolves are trained to attack any nongoblin that comes within 5 squares of the entrance. The goblins are more concerned about what's going on behind them than they are about watching for intruders, especially since the underboss fled just a few moments before. Thus, the goblin sentries (though not the gray wolves) are automatically surprised.

When the PCs enter this area, read:

Three wolves near the cave entrance turn toward you, bristling and growling. Beyond them, you see two goblins dressed in mail and hefting spears. Another wolf is with them. One of the goblins stands in front of a crude, red-painted wooden wall, and the other is visible behind the wall through a gate. Shrieks and growling noises sound from deeper inside the tunnel, and the sentries are totally distracted by the commotion.

2 Goblin Sentries (S)		Level 2 Soldier
Small natural humanoid		XP 125 each

Initiative +5   Senses Perception +6; low-light vision
HP 41; **Bloodied** 20
AC 18; **Fortitude** 15, **Reflex** 14, **Will** 12
Speed 5
⊕ **Spear** (standard; at-will) ✦ **Weapon**
    +9 vs. AC; 1d8 + 3 damage, and the goblin slides the target 1 square.
↗ **Hand Crossbow** (standard; at-will) ✦ **Weapon**
    Ranged 10/20; +9 vs. AC; 1d6 + 3 damage.
↯ **Trip Up** (standard; recharge ⚅)
    +7 vs. Reflex; 1d8 + 4 damage, and the target is knocked prone.
Goblin Tactics (immediate reaction, when missed by a melee attack; at-will)
    The goblin shifts 1 square.

Alignment Evil	**Languages** Common, Goblin	
Str 12 (+2)	Dex 16 (+3)	Wis 11 (+1)
Con 17 (+4)	Int 9 (+0)	Cha 8 (+0)

Equipment chainmail, light shield, spear, hand crossbow with 10 bolts

4 Gray Wolves (W)		Level 2 Skirmisher
Medium natural beast		XP 125 each

Initiative +5   Senses Perception +7; low-light vision
HP 38; **Bloodied** 19
AC 16; **Fortitude** 14, **Reflex** 14, **Will** 13
Speed 8
⊕ **Bite** (standard; at-will)
    +7 vs. AC; 1d6 + 2 damage, or 2d6 + 2 damage against a prone target.
Combat Advantage
    If a gray wolf has combat advantage against the target, the target is also knocked prone on a hit.

Alignment Unaligned	**Languages** —	
Str 13 (+2)	Dex 14 (+3)	Wis 13 (+2)
Con 14 (+3)	Int 2 (-3)	Cha 10 (+1)

TACTICS

The gray wolves attack the closest nongoblin, working in pairs to gain combat advantage so that they can knock their targeted enemies prone.

A goblin sentry lures the characters near the wall so its ally can help by stabbing with its spear. Failing this, the goblin behind the wall peppers controllers and leaders with crossbow bolts while the other goblin uses *trip up* to set up the gray wolves' attacks. The wolves fight to the death, but one or both of the goblins might decide to run off.

FEATURES OF THE AREA

Ceiling: The ceiling is 10 feet high.

Wall and Gate: Across the tunnel leading into the cave is a crude wooden wall with a gate in its center. The gate hangs on leather hinges. Pulling the gate open requires a DC 10 Strength check as a standard action. Openings in the gate and the wall allow creatures to attack through the barrier. Creatures on either side of the wall have superior cover against attacks originating from the other side of the wall. A 1-square wall section has AC 5, Fortitude 10, Reflex 5, and 20 hit points.

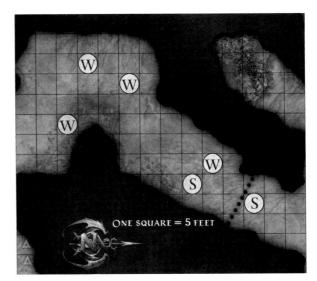

ONE SQUARE = 5 FEET

Standoff

Encounter Level 5 (1,100 XP)

or

Encounter Level 8 (1,975 XP)
with Thraesk

Setup

Thraesk, young iron dragon (T)
1 goblin hexer (H)
3 goblin skullcleavers (S)
5 goblin warriors (W)

This encounter is designed to unfold in area 5, where a group of relatively powerful goblins are trying to hold their own against an unhappy iron dragon. The characters should be drawn toward this area by the sounds of shrieks and growling they heard while they were involved with the sentries in the previous encounter. If the adventurers can win over Thraesk by succeeding on the skill challenge (see page 87), the dragon helps them fight the goblins. Otherwise, the characters become the third side in a three-way fight.

If the PCs head into area 4 right away, read:
Amid a clutter of bedding and dirty animal skins, you see several weak-looking goblins cowering before your approach.

Thraesk (T)	Level 4 Solo Lurker
Young iron dragon	
Large natural magical beast (dragon)	XP 875

Initiative +10   **Senses** Perception +8; darkvision
HP 212; **Bloodied** 106; see also *bloodied breath*
AC 18; **Fortitude** 16, **Reflex** 18, **Will** 15
Resist 15 lightning
Saving Throws +5
Speed 6, fly 6 (hover), overland flight 8
Action Points 2
⊕ **Bite** (standard; at-will) ✦ **Lightning**
   Reach 2; +9 vs. AC; 2d6 + 3 damage plus 1d8 lightning damage.
⊕ **Claw** (standard; at-will)
   Reach 2; +9 vs. AC; 1d10 + 3 damage.
⽬ **Double Attack** (standard; at-will)
   Thraesk makes two claw attacks.
↞ **Breath Weapon** (standard; recharge ⚄ ⚅) ✦ **Lightning**
   Close blast 5; +5 vs. Reflex; 2d8 + 3 lightning damage, and Thraesk pulls the target 3 squares. *Miss:* Half damage.
↞ **Bloodied Breath** (free, when first bloodied; encounter)
   Breath weapon recharges, and Thraesk uses it.
↞ **Frightful Presence** (standard; encounter) ✦ **Fear**
   Close burst 5; targets enemies; +5 vs. Will; the target is stunned until the end of Thraesk's next turn. *Aftereffect:* The target takes a -2 penalty to attack rolls (save ends).
↞ **Confounding Surge** (move; recharge ⚃ ⚄ ⚅) ✦ **Fear**
   Thraesk gains concealment and shifts 3 squares. All enemies adjacent to him at the end of this movement grant combat advantage until the end of Thraesk's next turn.
Alignment Unaligned   **Languages** Common, Draconic
Skills Acrobatics +11, Athletics +9, Stealth +11
Str 14 (+4)   **Dex** 18 (+6)   **Wis** 12 (+3)
Con 13 (+3)   **Int** 12 (+3)   **Cha** 12 (+3)

Goblin Hexer (H)	Level 3 Controller (Leader)
Small natural humanoid	XP 150

Initiative +3   **Senses** Perception +2; low-light vision
HP 46; **Bloodied** 23
AC 17; **Fortitude** 14, **Reflex** 15, **Will** 16; see also *lead from the rear*
Speed 6; see also *goblin tactics*
⊕ **Hexer Rod** (standard; at-will) ✦ **Weapon**
   +7 vs. AC; 1d6 + 1 damage.
↗ **Blinding Hex** (standard; at-will)
   Ranged 10; +7 vs. Fortitude; 2d6 + 1 damage, and the target is blinded (save ends).
↗ **Stinging Hex** (standard; recharge ⚄ ⚅)
   Ranged 10; +7 vs. Will; the target takes 3d6 + 1 damage if it moves during its turn (save ends).
❉ **Vexing Cloud** (standard; sustain minor; encounter) ✦ **Zone**
   Area burst 3 within 10; no attack roll; all enemies within the zone take a -2 penalty to attack rolls. The zone grants concealment to the goblin hexer and its allies. The goblin hexer can sustain the zone as a minor action, moving it up to 5 squares.
↗ **Incite Bravery** (immediate reaction, when an ally uses *goblin tactics*; at-will)
   Ranged 10; the targeted ally can shift 2 more squares and make an attack.
Goblin Tactics (immediate reaction, when missed by a melee attack; at-will)
   The goblin shifts 1 square.
Lead from the Rear (immediate interrupt, when targeted by a ranged attack; at-will)
   The goblin hexer can change the attack's target to an adjacent ally of its level or lower.
Alignment Evil   **Languages** Common, Goblin
Skills Stealth 10, Thievery +10
Str 10 (+1)   **Dex** 15 (+3)   **Wis** 13 (+2)
Con 14 (+3)   **Int** 9 (+0)   **Cha** 18 (+5)
Equipment leather robes, hexer rod

If the characters try to engage the warriors in combat, the goblins all flee toward area 5. (They would rather join up with their allies and risk the dragon's wrath than be dispatched on the spot.)

When the PCs approach area 5 and can see the dragon, read:
Goblins face off with an iron dragon that is backed into the far corner of this chamber. A robed goblin standing on scaffolding above the beast issues commands to other goblins.

When the characters arrive, roll initiative. Refer to "Tactics" for a summary of how the battle unfolds.

Tactics

When the characters appear on the scene, the goblins and the dragon stop arguing and start fighting. Thraesk uses his *frightful presence* on the goblins, spends an action point to use his *breath weapon*, and then moves to engage the nearest enemy in melee. The dragon singles out the characters for attacks only if they attack him first or otherwise provoke him.

While some of the characters involve themselves with the skill challenge, others might decide to attack the goblins or protect the characters who are

3 Goblin Skullcleavers (S)

3 Goblin Skullcleavers (S)	**Level 3 Brute**
Small natural humanoid	XP 150 each

Initiative +3   **Senses** Perception +2; low-light vision
HP 53; **Bloodied** 26; see also *bloodied rage*
AC 16; **Fortitude** 15, **Reflex** 14, **Will** 12
Speed 5; see also *goblin tactics*

⊕ **Battleaxe** (standard; at-will) ✦ **Weapon**
   +6 vs. AC; 1d10 + 5 damage, or 2d10 + 5 while bloodied.

Bloodied Rage (while bloodied)
   The goblin skullcleaver loses the ability to use *goblin tactics* and
   can do nothing but attack the nearest enemy, charging when
   possible.

Goblin Tactics (immediate reaction, when missed by a melee
   attack; at-will)
   The goblin shifts 1 square.

Alignment Evil   **Languages** Common, Goblin
Skills Stealth +9, Thievery +9
Str 18 (+5)   **Dex** 14 (+3)   **Wis** 13 (+2)
Con 13 (+2)   **Int** 8 (+0)   **Cha** 8 (+0)

Equipment chainmail, battleaxe

5 Goblin Warriors (W)

5 Goblin Warriors (W)	**Level 1 Skirmisher**
Small natural humanoid	XP 100 each

Initiative +5   **Senses** Perception +1; low-light vision
HP 29; **Bloodied** 14
AC 17; **Fortitude** 13, **Reflex** 15, **Will** 12
Speed 6; see also *mobile ranged attack* and *goblin tactics*

⊕ **Spear** (standard; at-will) ✦ **Weapon**
   +6 vs. AC; 1d8 + 2 damage.

⊙ **Javelin** (standard; at-will) ✦ **Weapon**
   Ranged 10/20; +6 vs. AC; 1d6 + 2 damage.

↗ **Mobile Ranged Attack** (standard; at-will) ✦ **Weapon**
   The goblin warrior can move up to half its speed; at any point
   during that movement, it makes one ranged attack without
   provoking opportunity attacks.

Great Position
   If, on its turn, a goblin warrior ends its move at least 4 squares
   away from its starting point, it deals 1d6 extra damage on its
   ranged attacks until the start of its next turn.

Goblin Tactics (immediate reaction, when missed by a melee
   attack; at-will)
   The goblin shifts 1 square.

Alignment Evil   **Languages** Common, Goblin
Skills Stealth +10, Thievery +10
Str 14 (+2)   **Dex** 17 (+3)   **Wis** 12 (+1)
Con 13 (+1)   **Int** 8 (−1)   **Cha** 8 (−1)

Equipment leather armor, spear, 5 javelins in sheaf

not fighting. Once the skill challenge is resolved,
Thraesk will be either an ally or an enemy of the
characters. Either way, the goblins have a stiff fight
on their hands.

   As the fight progresses, Thraesk moves toward and
then into area 3, intending to make his way out of the
goblin warren (but not before taking down as many
of his adversaries as possible).

   The goblin warriors focus their attacks on the
characters. Until the heroes attack them, the skullcleavers and the hexer devote all their effort to
attacking the dragon. Goblins, especially the warriors, might not hang around until the end of the
encounter.

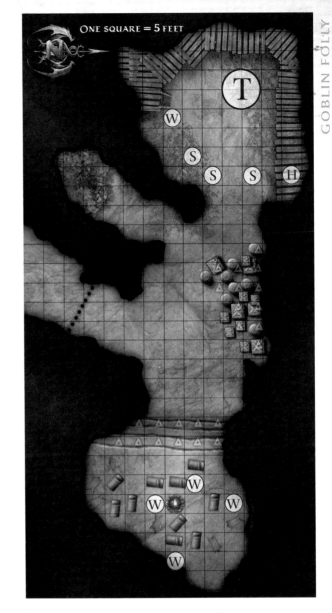

ONE SQUARE = 5 FEET

FEATURES OF THE AREA

   Ceiling: The ceiling is 10 feet high in area 3, 40
feet high in area 4, and 30 feet high in area 5.

   Plunder: The squares in area 3 containing a mix
of boxes, barrels, and crates count as difficult terrain.

   Scaffolding: The northern, southern, and western
walls of area 5 have scaffolding built to allow more
goblins to attend the now-dead chieftain. It stands
10 feet above the floor. A character can ascend the
ladder along the southern wall by spending 3 squares
of movement, or can climb up the side of the scaffold
with a DC 15 Athletics check. Scaffolding squares
have AC 5, Fortitude 10, Reflex 5, and 20 hit points.
If three or more squares are destroyed, the scaffolding collapses, dealing 3d6 + 4 damage to any creature
underneath it.

Copper dragon lair for five 5th-level adventurers

Deep in the northlands stands an imposing wooden stockade. Initially a source of horror and death for the surrounding communities, over the years it has been conquered, adapted to protect those that were once tormented, and finally left to the ravages of nature.

And now, like nature, the steading has come full circle. The fort on Prospect Hill has become the home of a band of highwaymen, led by a brutal tiefling warlock and accompanied by a copper dragon whose greed is much stronger than her small size and young age would suggest.

BACKGROUND

History DC 7: Some months ago, a gang of bandits moved into the principality of Kurich, an array of towns and hamlets a few miles from the permafrost of the north. Operating from an old fort atop a rise called Prospect Hill, and led by Chevkos, a sadistic tiefling, the bandits embarked on a campaign to rob and murder the locals.

While Kurich mobilized a militia to hunt down the bandits, Chevkos joined with a copper dragon named Korzinalikur. In exchange for a substantial share of the gang's profits, she became their primary enforcer and soldier, initially proving her worth by destroying the militia.

Today, the bandit gang all but rules the area from the fort on Prospect Hill, taking what they want from whom they want.

History DC 12: Chevkos worries that he might have made a devil's bargain. So far, Korzinalikur follows his orders and seems content to operate as an employee. However, she has begun suggesting the gang's next moves, and neither the tiefling nor his bandits have any doubt who would come out on top if–when–the dragon decides to run the show.

ENVIRONMENT

Anyone in the fortress's tower has a clear view of the surroundings, making it difficult for interlopers to approach undetected. The slope of Prospect Hill is not steep, but in combination with the thick grasses and soft soil, it counts as difficult terrain. The road leading up to the gate and the packed dirt inside the structure, however, are not difficult terrain.

When the PCs approach Prospect Hill, read:
The woods grow thin ahead, and the ground slopes up to form a large hillock. Atop it looms a fort. Enormous planks of wood form a stockade surrounding buildings constructed on an equally large scale. A great tower rises just east of the main gate, providing a clear view of the surroundings.

AREA 1: THE FRONT GATE

A wide gate in the wooden wall of the fort is the most obvious (and easiest) way to gain access to the inside. For details of how to open or break down the gate, see "Features of the Area" in the tactical encounter that begins on page 94. If the characters decide to try getting in by scaling the wall, that section of the encounter also has the necessary information.

Tactical Encounter: "Entering the Fort," page 94.

AREA 2: THE COURTYARD

The large area extending to the south and east from inside the front gate is devoid of any significant features except for a few trees. High walls, interrupted in a few places by doors, separate other parts of the fort from the courtyard.

Tactical Encounter: "Entering the Fort," page 94.

AREA 3: THE TOWER

The tower on the northern side of the fort stands 40 feet high and has a functioning ballista at its top. The

KORZINALIKUR

Korzinalikur isn't nearly as potent as she might seem at first glance. Since her birth she has been a somewhat sickly copper dragon, weaker than her clutchmates. Her family drove Korzinalikur out of their territory, forcing her to go find her own place to live. Seething at this treatment, and terrified that her weakened nature might prevent her from attaining the hoard and the respect that are hers "by right," Korzinalikur wandered the wilds for several years, feeding on roving animals and hunting desperately for an opportunity that lay within her capabilities.

She found it in Chevkos's offer. Korzinalikur sees her cooperation with the bandit gang not merely as the chance to build up her own wealth, but also a way to test the limits of her power. Slowly but steadily, she is becoming aware that, though she is weak for a dragon of her age, she is still the most potent force in the region. Like others of her kind, she is patient, willing to let the tiefling keep command of the bandits for now. In her heart, though, she has already begun to think of the fort, the treasure, and the bandits as hers—and she is developing designs on the entirety of Kurich. Korzinalikur works for the day when all the people of the region are devoted to enriching her hoard, and she can vent her simmering resentment upon those weaker than she is, in vengeance for the slights and abuses her family heaped on her.

interior of the tower is hollow, containing nothing but a set of stairs leading upward. (The map shows only the top of the tower.)

Tactical Encounter: "Entering the Fort," page 94.

AREA 4: DINING ROOM

Several of Chevkos's bandits currently occupy this dining room. The tableware, such as it is, is worthless, consisting of mismatched wooden and ceramic pieces.

Tactical Encounter: "Entering the Fort," page 94.

AREA 5: BARRACKS

This disheveled area—nothing more than an elongated room with sleeping pallets and tables scattered throughout—is the living quarters of the surviving members of Chevkos's bandit gang.

Treasure: The bandits have 50 gp among them.

Tactical Encounter: "Entering the Fort," page 94.

AREA 6: THE AUDIENCE CHAMBER

This room borders the lairs of both Korzinalikur and Chevkos. A wide pit in the center gives access to Korzinalikur's lair below (area 9), ringed by columns that extend to the floor below.

The secret door in the east wall, which provides an emergency exit, requires a DC 17 Perception check to locate.

Tactical Encounter: "The Central Lair," page 96.

AREA 7: CHEVKOS'S QUARTERS

This large bedroom serves as the living quarters for Chevkos and his four bugbear bodyguards.

The secret door (Perception DC 17 to locate) leads to spiral stairs that descend to a corridor that leads to area 9.

Tactical Encounter: "The Central Lair," page 96.

AREA 8: TREASURE ROOM

This room is kept locked. Chevkos and the bugbears each have a key. The bandit gang's treasures, other than the shares given to the various members, are kept here. The doors require a DC 18 Thievery check to unlock.

Treasure: This chamber contains wealth equivalent to one level 5 monetary treasure parcel.

AREA 9: KORZINALIKUR'S LAIR

The open chamber beneath area 6 serves as Korzinalikur's lair. It's smaller than the chamber above. A 5-foot-wide corridor (not shown on the map) leads underneath area 6 to the base of the spiral staircase that connects to the side of Chevkos's quarters.

When the fort was built, this area served as a gladiatorial arena, surrounded by an elevated concourse (area 6) from where spectators could watch the battles taking place below them. The corridor that connects this area with the spiral staircase outside area 7 provided a means for combatants to enter and exit the arena floor. Now, the pit makes a serviceable lair for Korzinalikur. The columns provide support for thick planks that form the walls of the pit, keeping the sides from collapsing.

Treasure: Korzinalikur's lair contains wealth or a magic item equivalent to one level 5 treasure parcel.

Tactical Encounter: "The Central Lair," page 96.

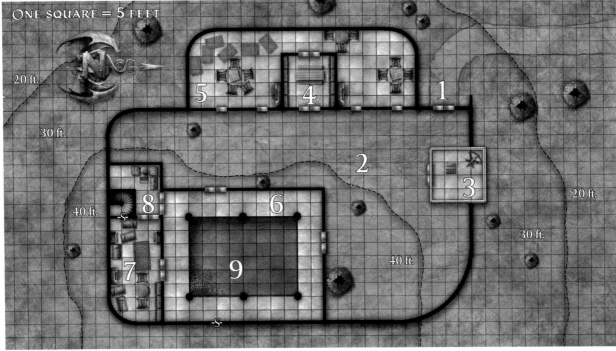

JASON A. ENGLE

Entering the Fort

Encounter Level 6 (1,315 XP)

Setup

2 Chevkos's crossbowmen (C)
3 Chevkos's guards (G)
10 Chevkos's lackeys (L)

To reach Chevkos, the characters need to find a way to enter the fort, probably through the gate. There's little cover, and the guards on the tower have a ballista they can fire at the characters. Two minions stand guard outside the gate. Once the characters enter, the bandits swarm out of their dining and sleeping rooms to intercept them before they reach area 6.

As written, this encounter assumes that the characters approach the fort from along the road and enter through the main gate. If they do not, the encounter can still occur largely as presented; adjust descriptions and tactics for the terrain, and possibly add ranged penalties for the crossbowmen.

When the PCs come within sight of the gate, read:

The tall wooden gates are barred. The entrance is guarded by a pair of bandits, and you can see two crossbow-wielding guards looking down from a tower a short distance to the east. You hear shouts of challenge and alarm from up ahead as the occupants take note of your approach.

When the crossbowmen first fire the ballista, read:

A heavy thump resounds from the tower, as a bolt the size of an ogre's spear flies toward you.

When the PCs enter the courtyard, read:

The earth inside this large area has been packed down, providing firm footing even on the hillside's slope. A pair of doors on the south side of the tower lead into the ground level of that structure. You also see a row of doors on the west wall and two other pairs of doors that give access to the southwestern portion of the complex.

When the bandits come out to fight, read:

Doors burst open across the western wall, and a tide of unwashed, unshaven bandits rushes at you.

If the PCs enter area 4, read:

You're standing in what looks like a slapdash dining room and beer hall. A long table and benches fill the center of the room, and shelves full of food are set into the walls.

If the PCs enter area 5, read:

A fireplace crackles away, warming a disorganized barracks. Scattered throughout are cots and sleeping pallets. A few rickety tables and old chairs are also visible.

---

2 Chevkos's Crossbowmen (C)	Level 4 Artillery
Medium natural humanoid, human	XP 175 each

Initiative +6   Senses Perception +4
HP 45; Bloodied 22
AC 16; Fortitude 16, Reflex 18, Will 16
Speed 6

⊕ **Short Sword** (standard; at-will) ✦ **Weapon**
   +9 vs. AC; 1d6 + 2 damage.

⊗ **Crossbow** (standard; at-will) ✦ **Weapon**
   Ranged 15/30; +11 vs. AC; 1d8 + 5 damage.

⌁ **Quick Shot** (standard; encounter)
   The crossbowman makes crossbow attacks against two different targets.

Alignment Unaligned		**Languages** Common
Skills Stealth +11		
Str 11 (+2)	Dex 18 (+6)	Wis 14 (+4)
Con 15 (+4)	Int 11 (+2)	Cha 11 (+2)

Equipment leather armor, short sword, crossbow with 20 bolts

---

3 Chevkos's Guards (G)	Level 4 Soldier
Medium natural humanoid, human	XP 175 each

Initiative +6   Senses Perception +3
HP 56; Bloodied 28
AC 20; Fortitude 18, Reflex 16, Will 15
Speed 5

⊕ **Longspear** (standard; at-will) ✦ **Weapon**
   Reach 2; +11 vs. AC; 1d10 + 4 damage, and the target is marked until the end of the guard's next turn.

⊗ **Crossbow** (standard; at-will) ✦ **Weapon**
   Ranged 15/30; +10 vs. AC; 1d8 + 3 damage.

✝ **Powerful Strike** (standard; requires a reach weapon; encounter) ✦ **Weapon**
   Reach 2; +11 vs. AC; 2d10 + 4 damage, and the target is knocked prone.

Alignment Unaligned		**Languages** Common
Str 18 (+6)	Dex 15 (+4)	Wis 12 (+3)
Con 16 (+5)	Int 11 (+2)	Cha 13 (+3)

Equipment chainmail, longspear, crossbow with 20 bolts

---

10 Chevkos's Lackeys (L)	Level 4 Minion Skirmisher
Medium natural humanoid, human	XP 44 each

Initiative +4   Senses Perception +3
HP 1; a missed attack never damages a minion.
AC 18; Fortitude 18, Reflex 15, Will 16
Speed 6

⊕ **Short Sword** (standard; at-will) ✦ **Weapon**
   +9 vs. AC; 5 damage.

⊗ **Hand Crossbow** (standard; at-will) ✦ **Weapon**
   Ranged 10/20; +9 vs. AC; 4 damage.

Combat Advantage
   A lackey deals 2 extra damage against any creature granting combat advantage to it.

Alignment Unaligned		**Languages** Common
Skills Stealth +7		
Str 16 (+5)	Dex 11 (+2)	Wis 12 (+3)
Con 14 (+4)	Int 10 (+2)	Cha 13 (+3)

Equipment leather armor, short sword, hand crossbow with 20 bolts

Ballista

The ballista on top of the tower can be fired by any creature adjacent to it. The creature can use the following attack.

⤤ **Ballista Shot** (standard; recharge special) ♦ **Weapon**
Ranged 20/40; +9 vs. Reflex; 3d8 + 4 damage, and the target is pushed 2 squares and knocked prone.

Make recharge rolls for the ballista at the start of the turn of the creature that last fired it. The power recharges on ⚅ ⚅ if two creatures are adjacent to the ballista (that is, loading it), or on ⚅ if only one creature is adjacent. The power doesn't recharge if no one is adjacent to the ballista.

Tactics

The crossbowmen use the ballista to attack once the characters have come within roughly 30 feet of the fortress (as soon as the players place their miniatures on the road at the edge of the tactical map). They continue firing after the characters move into the courtyard. The lackeys try to stand their ground near the gate, but they don't stay put if they notice ranged weapons or magic implements in the characters' hands.

When the characters are inside the walls, the guards and lackeys open the doors leading from the dining room and barracks and move a short distance into the courtyard.

When their numbers have been reduced to one guard or one crossbowman and two or three lackeys, the bandits surrender and beg for mercy.

The guards run out mainly to stop the characters from moving toward the southern end of the fort (where their leader is located). The guards protect the lackeys by marking foes and knocking enemies prone, giving the lackeys combat advantage.

A few lackeys might stop in doorways to fire their hand crossbows. If the characters come near, they retreat into the barracks.

Features of the Area

Illumination: Bright light outside and inside the fort at all times. (At night, lanterns illuminate the exterior and interior of the structure.)

Hillside Slope: The slope outside the fortress, with the exception of the road, is difficult terrain.

Trees: Squares containing trees inside and outside the fort are difficult terrain and provide cover. A tree can be climbed with a DC 12 Athletics check, and the trees range between 10 and 20 feet in height.

Doors: The entry gate to the fortress is barred (DC 12 Strength check to break or DC 17 Thievery check to jimmy the bar out of place). The doors to the tower are locked (DC 12 Strength check to break or DC 17 Thievery check to pick the lock). The doors leading to

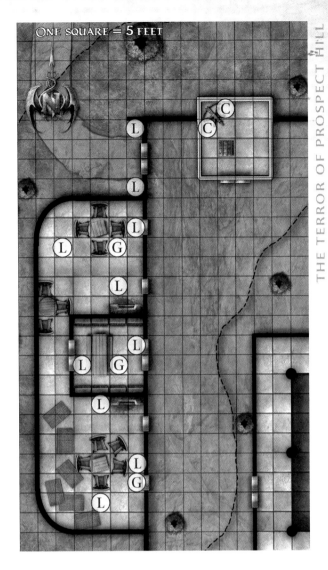

areas 4 and 5 are unlocked. The doors to area 6 are locked (see the next encounter).

Tower: The tower rises 20 feet above the top of the walls. Climbing the side of the tower requires a DC 18 Athletics check.

Outer Walls: The walls are 20 feet high and require a DC 17 Athletics check to climb. The tops of the wooden posts that form the walls are spiked; anyone who reaches the top of the wall is subject to an attack: +9 vs. AC; 1d4 + 2 damage, and the character must make a successful DC 17 Athletics check or fall.

Ceiling: Areas 4, 5, 7, and 8 have 20-foot-tall ceilings.

Benches, Tables, and Chairs: These features are difficult terrain. Jumping onto a bench or a table requires 2 squares of movement. In area 4, a character can tip over the long table to gain superior cover.

Fireplaces: At night, the two fireplaces in area 5 hold small fires; a character who enters a fire or begins his turn there takes 1d6 + 3 fire damage.

The Central Lair

Encounter Level 7 (1,550 XP)

Setup

Korzinalikur, elite young copper dragon (K)
Chevkos, tiefling heretic (C)
4 bugbear warriors (B)

During the previous encounter, none of the bandit gang's leaders emerged from their lair in the fort's central keep. Perhaps they assumed that their underlings could handle whatever the problem might be (and after all, it's not that hard to recruit new thieves and mercenaries). But once the characters gain control of the courtyard, neutralize the ballista, and move deeper into the complex, Chevkos and Korzinalikur fight back.

Each of the descriptions below assumes the characters first spot each foe at or near its starting point. Adjust the read-aloud text as needed if any of the monsters move before they are encountered, or if the characters manage to get into area 7 or 8 before going through area 6.

When the PCs enter area 6, read:
The center of the room drops away into a wide pit, from which wafts a vaguely reptilian scent. Several pillars rise from within the pit, clearly marking the edge.

Two bugbears instantly move toward you, morningstars raised high, and something begins to stir loudly in the shadowy depths of the pit.

When the PCs enter area 7, read:
This chamber serves as a lavish living area, far more extravagant than this place would seem to warrant. An old canopied bed sits in one corner, with several additional bedrolls scattered on the floor nearby. A heap of embers glows dully in the fireplace, radiating warmth throughout the room.

When the PCs see Chevkos, read:
Before you stands a short tiefling, clad in several layers of fancy clothes. Tiny bits of jewelry pierce his horns all over. He has a menacing glint in his eyes, and balefire crackles across his fingers. Two more bugbears loom nearby, clutching morningstars and grinning viciously.

When Korzinalikur first appears, read:
An enormous metallic form bursts upward from the pit, wings outspread and jaws agape. The light glints off its copper scales, and thin tendrils of sizzling spittle drip from the corners of its mouth.

Korzinalikur (K) — Level 6 Elite Skirmisher
Young copper dragon
Large natural magical beast (dragon) — XP 500

Initiative +10   **Senses** Perception +10; darkvision
HP 148; **Bloodied** 74; see also *bloodied breath*
AC 20; **Fortitude** 18, **Reflex** 19, **Will** 16
Resist 15 acid
Saving Throws +2
Speed 8, fly 10 (hover), overland flight 15; see also *flyby attack*
Action Points 1

⊕ Bite (standard; at-will) ✦ **Acid**
Korzinalikur shifts 2 squares before and after making the attack. Reach 2; +11 vs. AC; 1d10 + 4 damage plus 1d6 acid damage.

⊕ Claw (standard; at-will)
Reach 2; +11 vs. AC; 1d8 + 4 damage.

✦ Double Attack (standard; at-will)
Korzinalikur makes two claw attacks and then shifts 2 squares.

✦ Flyby Attack (standard; at-will)
Korzinalikur flies up to 10 squares and makes one melee basic attack at any point during that movement. She doesn't provoke opportunity attacks when moving away from the target.

↢ Breath Weapon (standard; encounter) ✦ **Acid**
Close blast 5; +7 vs. Reflex; 2d10 + 4 acid damage, and the target is slowed (save ends). *Miss:* Half damage.

↢ Bloodied Breath (free, when first bloodied; encounter)
Breath weapon recharges, and Korzinalikur uses it.

↢ Frightful Presence (standard; encounter) ✦ **Fear**
Close burst 5; targets enemies; +7 vs. Will; the target is stunned until the end of Korzinalikur's next turn. *Aftereffect:* The target takes a -2 penalty to attack rolls (save ends).

Alignment Unaligned   **Languages** Common, Draconic
Skills Acrobatics +13, Bluff +9, Insight +10
Str 16 (+6)   **Dex** 20 (+8)   **Wis** 14 (+5)
Con 18 (+7)   **Int** 12 (+4)   **Cha** 12 (+4)

Chevkos (C) — Level 6 Artillery
Medium natural humanoid, tiefling — XP 250

Initiative +8   **Senses** Perception +6; low-light vision
HP 60; **Bloodied** 30
AC 20; **Fortitude** 17, **Reflex** 18, **Will** 18
Resist 11 fire
Speed 6

⊕ Dagger (standard; at-will) ✦ **Weapon**
+10 vs. AC (+11 against a bloodied target); 1d4 + 2 damage.

⊙ Balefire (standard; at-will) ✦ **Fire**
Ranged 10; +9 vs. Reflex (+10 against a bloodied target); 1d8 + 5 fire damage, and ongoing 5 fire damage (save ends).

⊁ Serpent Curse (standard; encounter) ✦ **Illusion, Psychic**
Ranged 10; illusory snakes appear and attack the target; +9 vs. Will (+10 against a bloodied target); 1d6 + 5 psychic damage, and ongoing 5 psychic damage (save ends).

Cloak of Escape (immediate reaction, when Chevkos is hit by a melee attack; at-will) ✦ **Teleportation**
Chevkos teleports 5 squares.

Infernal Wrath (minor; encounter)
Chevkos gains a +1 power bonus to his next attack roll against an enemy that hit him since his last turn. If the attack hits and deals damage, Chevkos deals 5 extra damage.

Alignment Evil   **Languages** Common
Skills Bluff +15, Insight +11, Stealth +15
Str 15 (+5)   **Dex** 20 (+8)   **Wis** 16 (+6)
Con 18 (+7)   **Int** 13 (+4)   **Cha** 20 (+8)
Equipment dagger

4 Bugbear Warriors (B)		Level 5 Brute
Medium natural humanoid		XP 200 each

Initiative +5	**Senses** Perception +4; low-light vision	
HP 76; **Bloodied** 38		
AC 18; **Fortitude** 17, **Reflex** 15, **Will** 14		
Speed 6		

⊕ **Morningstar** (standard; at-will) ✦ **Weapon**
+7 vs. AC; 1d10 + 7 damage.

⸸ **Skullthumper** (standard; requires a morningstar and combat advange against the target; encounter) ✦ **Weapon**
+5 vs. Fortitude; 1d10 + 7 damage, and the target is knocked prone and dazed (save ends).

Predatory Eye (minor; encounter)
The bugbear warrior deals 1d6 extra damage on the next attack it makes against a target granting combat advantage to it. It must apply this bonus before the end of its next turn.

Alignment Evil	**Languages** Common, Goblin	
Skills Intimidate +9, Stealth +11		
Str 20 (+7)	**Dex** 16 (+5)	**Wis** 14 (+4)
Con 16 (+5)	**Int** 10 (+2)	**Cha** 10 (+2)
Equipment hide armor, morningstar		

TACTICS

Assuming the characters begin the encounter in area 6, the two bugbears in that area rush to attack. The bugbears that start in area 7 join the combat as soon as they can get there. All the bugbears try to stay in melee with the characters, to keep them away from Chevkos. The bugbears retreat if doing so is tactically sound, but they do not flee.

Korzinalikur erupts from the pit on her initiative count in the first round (requiring 4 squares of movement to do so). She initiates combat with her *breath weapon*, if she can use it without catching either of the bugbears in the blast. She then relies on *flyby attacks*, moving in and out of the chamber and through the entire fort, using the courtyard to circle around and attack from different angles.

If she becomes bloodied, Korzinalikur no longer cares about keeping the bugbears out of the area of her *breath weapon*. She attempts to escape if reduced to 40 or fewer hit points—she's not prepared to risk her life for the bandits—and surrenders if escape proves impossible.

Chevkos hangs back, using his ranged attacks to harry the characters. He uses *cloak of escape* whenever he is hit with a melee attack, teleporting to a place of relative safety in area 6 or even out into the courtyard if possible. He doesn't allow himself to be cornered in area 8. Even though Chevkos does his best to avoid being hit repeatedly, he does not abandon the fort and fights to the death.

FEATURES OF THE AREA

Illumination: Brightly lit, by sunlight or by lanterns.

Ceiling: The ceiling in areas 7 and 8 is 20 feet high.

Beds: A character can step up onto a bed with 1 extra square of movement. A DC 17 Strength check topples a bed over, allowing it to serve as cover for standing characters, and knocking prone any creatures standing on it.

Doors: Most of the interior doors are unlocked and designed to open from either direction. The doors to area 8 are locked and require a DC 18 Thievery check to open. Chevkos and the bugbears each carry keys.

Fireplace: At night, this spot holds a small fire; a character who enters the fire or begins his turn there takes 1d6 + 3 fire damage.

Pit: The pit is 20 feet deep. Climbing out requires a DC 20 Athletics check.

Secret Door: A DC 17 Perception check detects the secret door.

Spiral Stairs: The spiral stairs are difficult terrain. They lead to an underground passage that connects to Korzinalikur's lair.

Orium dragon lair for five 7th-level adventurers

From the steamy jungles of the south come rumors of the Alabaster City, a place lost to the mists of time, where every citizen was a sage and powerful magic fulfilled every whim of the city's denizens. No explorer can claim to know the location of the city, but lizardfolk wearing strange alabaster jewelry have been captured recently. Eager to save their own lives, the lizardfolk said they served an orium dragon named Zanathakla. She lives in the bottom of a vertical cave deep in the jungle known as Tulkau Shayn ("Gullet Cave" in the lizardfolk's dialect).

The captive lizardfolk claim that Zanathakla doesn't know where the Alabaster City is either, but she searches for it day and night and sends bands of loyal lizardfolk far and wide to look for it. So far, they have found the ruins of several smaller communities, and Zanathakla says the city will soon be theirs.

BACKGROUND

History DC 14: Zanathakla made Tulkau Shayn her lair about a year ago and quickly seized control of a large tribe of lizardfolk, which now treat her with reverence approaching outright worship. Most of the lizardfolk are in the jungle looking for clues to help find the vast ruins called the Alabaster City, because Zanathakla is obsessed with claiming the ruin's secrets for her own. Only a few of her followers are guarding Tulkau Shayn at any given time.

History DC 19: Gullet Cave has long been the source of superstition among the indigenous humans and lizardfolk. A stone outcropping resembling teeth runs along the north edge of the cave mouth, and the cave itself is 200 feet deep. For years, brave youths have crawled to the edge of Tulkau Shayn and peered into the inky blackness below. But until Zanathakla moved in with the lizardfolk tribe, no one knew how deep the cave was—or if it even had a bottom.

HOOK: DISCOVER THE ALABASTER CITY

Somewhere within the deep jungle lie the ruins Zanathakla seeks—the last remnants of the Alabaster City. People living near the jungle, or in the safer areas around its outskirts, know many rumors about the city but few facts. If the characters can find the location of the city, they might be able to recover what remains in its vaults, or the greater treasures of forgotten knowledge that lie in the vast libraries rumored to exist within the city.

Quest XP: 1,500 XP (major quest).

HOOK: RECOVER THE TRADE GOODS

A massive nearby river that winds through the jungle carries many merchant ships to towns and cities that dot the shoreline. The creatures under Zanathakla's command have begun attacking these merchants, usually taking preserved food and drink. They have also been known to steal tools. The river merchants ask the characters to retrieve their stolen goods and to end the threat of the lizardfolk raiders. See the descriptions of areas 2 and 7 in the following text for information about the items that belong to the traders.

Quest XP: 300 XP (minor quest).

ENVIRONMENT

Tulkau Shayn is a deep, vertical cave. The entrance opens in the center of the cave's ceiling, and the space within drops straight down 200 feet to a flat, rocky floor. The cave walls angle slightly outward; viewed from the side, the cave looks like an upright cone with the top chopped off.

Several side chambers branch off from the main chamber. Until the lizardfolk constructed the wooden pathway that spirals down the interior cave walls, those chambers were home only to flying creatures—mostly bats and stirges—that would ascend out of the cave each day to find food in the jungle.

Illumination: If there's daylight outside, the top 50 feet of the cave are in bright light and the next 50 feet in dim light. It's dark at the 120-foot mark, where the second encounter, "Stirge Chamber," takes place.

Walls: The cave walls are rough and have many handholds and footholds, but they slope outward, making a climb more difficult than it would otherwise be. Unless otherwise noted, climbing the cave walls in either direction requires a DC 20 Athletics check.

Side Chambers: Most of the side chambers don't contain encounters. Once the characters defeat the guards at the cave mouth, they have to pass a dangerous cave inhabited by stirges and gricks before reaching Zanathakla and accessing Tulkau Shayn's treasures.

Eventually lizardfolk search parties will return to the cave, but they might be too disheartened by Zanathakla's death to fight. (Or perhaps they're mad for vengeance; you make the call.)

AREA 1: CAVE ENTRANCE

When the characters make their way through the jungle and finally reach Tulkau Shayn (see the "Approaching the Cave" skill challenge on page 100), they find the cave's entrance guarded by lizardfolk that revere Zanathakla.

Tactical Encounter: "Cave Entrance," page 102.

AREA 2: LIVING CAVE

About 50 feet down inside the cave, connected to the entrance by way of the lashed wooden scaffolding the lizardfolk have built, is a large cave that serves as the lizardfolk's main living chamber.

When the PCs enter this cave, read:
The lizardfolk's bedding—mostly furs and fronds—lies in piles along the walls of this cave. In one corner, barrels contain fresh water and dried meat. In the center of the chamber lie several felled trees, rough wooden planks, and carpentry tools. The planks match those used in the walkway outside. A stone altar stands against the far wall, topped by a reddish statue of a dragon.

The barrels of food and water and the carpentry tools were stolen from river traders and can be returned as part of the "Recover the Trade Goods" minor quest.

Ceiling: The ceiling is 15 feet high along the perimeter of this area, rising to a peak of 25 feet near the chimney.

Treasure: A crude stone altar against the far wall holds a jade carving of a dragon worth 250 gp. The lizardfolk have smeared reddish mud on the idol to make it look more like Zanathakla, but a cursory examination reveals the jade underneath.

AREA 3: STIRGE DEN

This cave of pesky stirges has been easily bypassed by the lizardfolk, but now gricks also lurk inside, making it difficult for the characters to descend deeper into Tulkau Shayn.

Tactical Encounter: "Stirge Chamber," page 104.

AREA 4: ARTIFACT CAVE

Zanathakla and the lizardfolk keep the evidence of the Alabaster City in this side cave, which is 50 feet above the main cave floor and accessed by way of the wooden walkway. The artifacts include several chunks of alabaster masonry and stonework: cornices, column sections, and so on. Dozens of ceramic urns and pots litter the room, all painted in a distinctive zigzag pattern.

When the PCs enter the cave, read:
Ceramics and chunks of alabaster stonework litter this room, and a map hangs on one wall. Made of pieces of parchment stuck together with tree sap, the map shows the jungle nearby. It's divided into sections based on natural features and shows several ruins. Many of the areas have red "X" shapes marking them. Only a few areas are not struck through.

The large, patchwork jungle map created by Zanathakla shows civilized communities on the fringe of the jungle and Tulkau Shayn in the middle. Several sketches depict ruins, but almost all of these have "X" marks through them. More important for the characters, the jungle is divided into sections bounded by natural features such as rivers and mountain ridges. It should be obvious to the characters why most of the ruins sections are struck through—and what parts of the jungle Zanathakla and the lizardfolk haven't explored yet.

This map could be useful to the heroes if they're engaged in the "Discover the Alabaster City" quest. It doesn't tell them where to look for the Alabaster City, but it tells them something almost as useful: where not to look.

Ceiling: The ceiling is 10 feet high throughout this cave.

AREA 5: APPROACHING THE BOTTOM

As the characters come closer to the bottom of the cave, Zanathakla becomes aware of their presence. She is careful and cunning, and waits until they reach this point in the cave complex to attack.

Tactical Encounter: "Zanathakla's Wrath," page 106.

AREA 6: CAVE FLOOR

Zanathakla spends most of her time sleeping on the cave floor or examining particularly interesting objects discovered by the lizardfolk. Like all orium dragons, Zanathakla is keenly interested in uncovering the secrets of the past. In fact, her zeal has become an obsession, and she spends untold hours coiled up on the cave floor, dreaming of the day when she finds the Alabaster City, builds a new lair in the grandest building still standing, and has her servants bring her book after book full of ancient wisdom.

AREA 7: TREASURE CAVE

This chamber, level with the cave floor, is where Zanathakla has amassed a typical hoard for a young dragon. It's a good place for three level 7 treasure parcels: one magic item parcel and two parcels made up of art

EXPANDING THE LAIR

As written, "Tulkau Shayn" is the first step on an adventure that could take the characters to the Alabaster City. As a story element, the cave is a receptacle for a useful clue: the map in the artifact cave (area 4). You can easily turn this lair into a complete adventure site in its own right by enlarging and extending the side chambers. One or more of them could connect to an extensive cave network, full of all the monsters, traps, hazards, and treasure you can manage.

objects and coins. Lizardfolk captured the coins from river merchants who explored too deep in the jungle, and recovered the art objects and the magic item from the ancient ruins they've found. The lizardfolk don't enter this chamber; it is for Zanathakla alone.

If the characters return the coins to the traders (part of the "Recover the Trade Goods" minor quest), the traders compensate them with a magic item of equal value, which is more difficult to sell and therefore less valuable to the traders.

Ceiling: The ceiling is 15 feet high throughout this area.

Approaching the Cave

Getting to Tulkau Shayn is no easy task–the characters must journey across miles of trackless jungle to find the entrance to the deep cave. Each character can attempt up to two skill checks per day.

Level: 8 (XP 700).

Complexity: 2 (requires 6 successes before 3 failures).

Primary Skills: Endurance, Perception, Nature.

Endurance (DC 14, or DC 8 if the group is under the effect of an Endure Elements ritual): Select two characters in the group at random to make Endurance checks at the start of each day. They attempt to resist the effects of the oppressive heat and humidity, along with the general rigors of an overland hike through the wilderness. A failed check indicates that all members of the group grow weary and lose a healing surge, in addition to counting as 1 failure in the challenge. (If both characters fail their checks, all members of the group lose two healing surges and the characters gain 2 failures.)

Perception (DC 14, or DC 8 if the characters have a map): The character makes sure the group stays on course–or at least moves in a consistent direction. Success represents a relatively straight path through the jungle, and failure means the characters become lost or travel in circles. This skill can be used to gain a maximum of 2 successes per day.

Nature (DC 14): The jungle's many natural hazards–including quicksand pits, bogs, poisonous plants, and thorny undergrowth–can slow forward progress to a standstill. A successful Nature check maneuvers the characters around these hazards, while a failure represents delays as characters extricate themselves from the hazard and takes a longer path around it. This skill can be used to gain a maximum of 2 successes per day.

Secondary Skills: Streetwise.

Streetwise (DC 14): This check can be attempted only once, at the start of the skill challenge, while the characters are still in a civilized area. A character can try to secure a map to aid the party in locating Tulkau Shayn. Succeeding on this check does not count as a

success in the challenge, but it reduces the DCs for subsequent Perception checks, as shown above.

Success: The characters reach the entrance of Tulkau Shayn. After the final successful skill check, put the characters on the edge of the tactical map of area 1 and start the "Cave Entrance" encounter (page 102).

Failure: The characters walk into a monster lair. Choose one of the entries on the table below or roll a d6 to generate a random result. After handling the monster encounter, the characters still haven't reached Tulkau Shayn. They must repeat the skill challenge as a complexity 1 test (worth 350 XP and requiring 4 successes before 3 failures) to get there. With another 3 failed checks, they become hopelessly lost and are unable to find Tulkau Shayn without first returning to their starting point. However, they might discover some other strange ruin or adventure site deep in the jungle–maybe the Alabaster City itself.

JUNGLE ENCOUNTERS

d6	Encounter
1	3 grells (*MM* 144)
2	2 macetail behemoths (*MM* 31) and 3 ogre savages (*MM* 199)
3	2 bloodspike behemoths (*MM* 31) and 2 shambling mounds (*MM* 232)
4	2 spectral panthers (*MM* 213) and 3 displacer beasts (*MM* 70)
5	3 trolls (*MM* 254) and 2 bog hags (*MM* 150)
6	1 berbalang (*MM* 34)

THE ALABASTER CITY

The Alabaster City can have whatever traits work for your game, or it can be replaced with a different location you want the characters to go to next. Here are a few possible story hooks for the Alabaster City.

- ✦ Once ruled by rakshasa barons, the Alabaster City served as a library for dark lore and a site of ritual sacrifices. Ghosts of those slain still haunt the forgotten city, seeking those who can destroy their former captors.

- ✦ The Alabaster City fell into a giant sinkhole long ago and was covered over by the boughs of enormous trees. The great city is now inhabited only by ignorant troglodytes. They dwell amid the smashed alabaster ruins and have destroyed many of the tomes held within, burning them for warmth.

- ✦ The land where the Alabaster City lies is part of a worldfall (see *Manual of the Planes*, page 34) that links the world and the Feywild. When the Feywild's connection to the site is strong, the city becomes covered in vegetation and dangerous creatures spill over. The periods of Feywild influence last only a brief time, but make the city uninhabitable by civilized creatures.

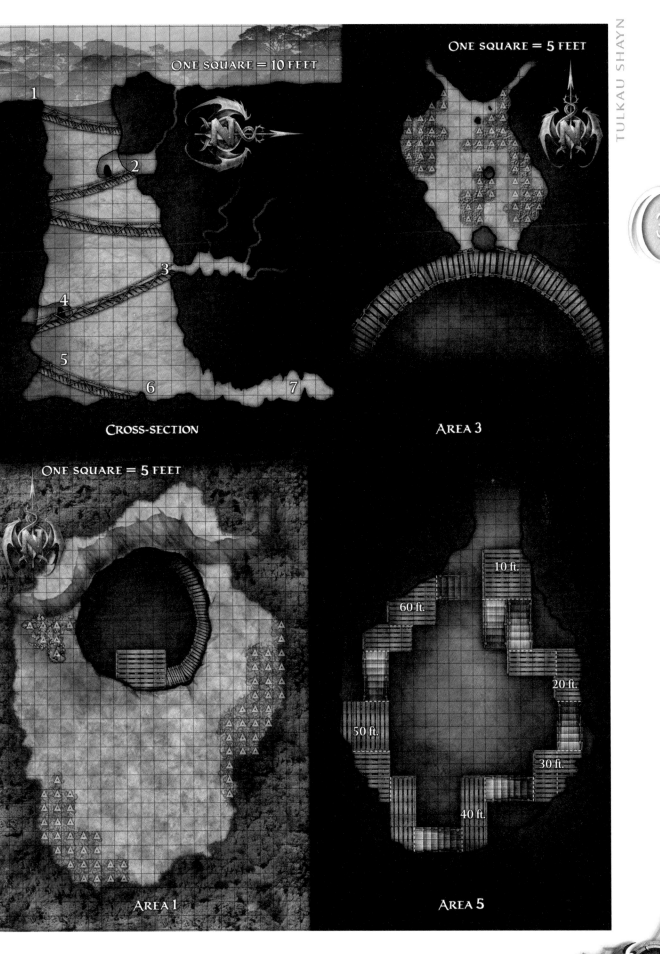

ONE SQUARE = 10 FEET

1

2

3

4

5

6   7

CROSS-SECTION

ONE SQUARE = 5 FEET

AREA 3

ONE SQUARE = 5 FEET

AREA 1

10 ft.

60 ft.

20 ft.

50 ft.

30 ft.

40 ft.

AREA 5

JASON A. ENGLE

CAVE ENTRANCE

Encounter Level 6 (1,450 XP)

SETUP

1 greenscale marsh mystic (M)
2 blackscale bruisers (B)
4 greenscale hunters (H)

The characters emerge from the jungle at the edge of a small clearing and find the entrance to Tulkau Shayn, but they must contend with lizardfolk guardians determined to drive them off.

When the PCs achieve the final success on the skill challenge to reach Tulkau Shayn, read:
The jungle canopy opens up as you enter a clearing. You see a massive pit dead ahead. An outcropping of rock on the pit's edge looks vaguely like a carnivore's teeth.

Perception Check
DC 14 *You spot a crest–like something you'd see on a reptile's head–over the edge of the pit for a brief moment, but then it's gone.*

When the PCs reach the edge of the pit, read:
Beyond the edge of the pit, you see a great cave that expands outward the deeper it goes. A wooden walkway attached to the cave walls spirals downward. You can see only a short way down before the cave becomes dark.

The lizardfolk are hidden just behind the edge of the pit, standing on the wooden platform when the encounter starts. It's possible the characters are hiding at the edge of the jungle. The lizardfolk guards are ready but not alert (*DMG* 36).

If both sides are trying to be sneaky, determine surprise:

✦ The character who has the lowest Stealth modifier makes a Stealth check against the bruisers' passive Perception check of 19.

✦ The lizardfolk make one Stealth check (using a +4 bonus) against the passive Perception checks of the party.

✦ If one group noticed the other one and wasn't noticed at the same time, that first group has surprise. Otherwise, no one has surprise.

Greenscale Marsh Mystic (M)	Level 6 Controller (Leader)
Medium natural humanoid (reptile)	XP 250

Initiative +4   **Senses** Perception +7
Marsh Blessing (Healing) aura 5; each ally that starts his or her turn in the aura regains 3 hit points.
HP 70; **Bloodied** 35
AC 19; **Fortitude** 15, **Reflex** 14, **Will** 19
Speed 6 (swamp walk)
⊕ **Spear** (standard; at-will) ✦ **Weapon**
  +7 vs. AC; 1d8 + 2 damage.
❀ **Swamp's Grasp** (standard; encounter) ✦ **Zone**
  Area burst 2 within 10; +9 vs. Reflex; the target is immobilized (save ends). The zone is difficult terrain until the end of the encounter.
❀ **Bog Cloud** (standard; recharge ⚅ ⚀⚀) ✦ **Poison**
  Area burst 2 within 10; +9 vs. Fortitude; 2d8 + 4 poison damage, and the target is dazed until the end of the marsh mystic's next turn.
Alignment Unaligned   **Languages** Draconic
Skills Athletics +10, Nature +12
Str 15 (+5)   **Dex** 13 (+4)   **Wis** 19 (+7)
Con 14 (+5)   **Int** 10 (+3)   **Cha** 12 (+4)
Equipment spear, bone breastplate

---

2 Blackscale Bruisers (B)	Level 6 Brute
Large natural humanoid (reptile)	XP 250 each

Initiative +6   **Senses** Perception +9
HP 86; **Bloodied** 43
AC 18; **Fortitude** 19, **Reflex** 16, **Will** 14
Speed 8 (swamp walk)
⊕ **Greatclub** (standard; at-will) ✦ **Weapon**
  Reach 2; +9 vs. AC; 1d10 + 6 damage, and the target is pushed 1 square.
† **Tail Slap** (standard; at-will)
  +7 vs. Reflex; 1d8 + 6 damage, and the target is knocked prone.
Alignment Unaligned   **Languages** Draconic
Skills Athletics +14
Str 22 (+9)   **Dex** 16 (+6)   **Wis** 12 (+4)
Con 16 (+6)   **Int** 5 (+0)   **Cha** 6 (+1)
Equipment greatclub

---

4 Greenscale Hunters (H)	Level 4 Skirmisher
Medium natural humanoid (reptile)	XP 175 each

Initiative +6   **Senses** Perception +8
HP 54; **Bloodied** 27
AC 17; **Fortitude** 15, **Reflex** 14, **Will** 13
Speed 6 (swamp walk)
⊕ **Spear** (standard; at-will) ✦ **Weapon**
  +9 vs. AC; 1d8 + 3 damage.
† **Sidestep Attack** (standard; at-will)
  The lizardfolk shifts 1 square and makes a melee basic attack.
Alignment Unaligned   **Languages** Draconic
Skills Athletics +10, Nature +8
Str 17 (+5)   **Dex** 15 (+4)   **Wis** 12 (+3)
Con 14 (+4)   **Int** 8 (+1)   **Cha** 8 (+1)
Equipment light shield, spear

TACTICS

The lizardfolk fight with tenacity; they're on their home turf, and they fear disappointing Zanathakla far more than they fear the adventurers.

The marsh mystic uses *swamp's grasp* as soon as it can, trying to lock down as many enemies as possible. Next it puts a *bog cloud* atop the area of *swamp's grasp* in the second round, then trails behind the hunters and bruisers so it can heal them.

The blackscale bruisers charge into battle, using their greatclub attacks to keep melee combatants far enough away to avoid counterattacks. Remember that they regain 3 hit points if they start their turns within 5 squares of the marsh mystic.

The greenscale hunters maneuver for flanking and combat advantage with *sidestep attack* as often as they can, and they're particularly alert for chances to attack characters who have been knocked prone by the bruisers. They have swamp walk, so they can move through the *swamp's grasp* area, but they aren't immune to poison, so they avoid the marsh mystic's *bog cloud*.

FEATURES OF THE AREA

Illumination: Bright light during the daytime, or dim light at night.

Platform: The area where most of the monsters are lurking is 5 feet below ground level. It takes 2 squares of movement to get from the platform to the clearing.

Walkway: The gently sloping walkway that trails downward from the platform is difficult terrain. The path is 5 feet wide (meaning that Large creatures must squeeze to move along it).

Cave: It's a 200-foot fall to the cave floor (20d10 falling damage), which is almost certainly fatal for anyone in this encounter. But in addition to the saving throw any creature receives if it's pushed, pulled, or slid off an edge, a creature that falls down the pit can make an Athletics check (DC 15) to grab onto the wooden walkway on the way down (as though it were falling while climbing). If the creature succeeds on the check, it takes 3d10 falling damage

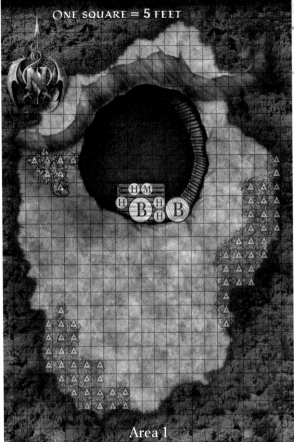

ONE SQUARE = 5 FEET

TULKAU SHAYN

Area 1

and lands on the wooden walkway 30 feet below the lip of the cave entrance. It takes 12 squares of movement upward along the walkway to reach the top of the cave.

Brambles: The large areas of brambles bordering the jungle to the southwest and the east are difficult terrain.

Rocks: The rock outcropping next to the slope on the northern end of the pit is an area of difficult terrain.

Cave Walls: The walls of the cave near the top of the opening are relatively easy to climb, requiring a DC 10 Athletics check.

CONCLUSION

If the characters engage in the time-honored tradition of throwing objects (especially torches and sunrods) down into the cave, they don't see Zanathakla, who is curled up below the wooden walkways. The characters do see the wooden walkway spiraling down into the cave and thus get a general idea of the cave's dimensions.

FALLING CREATURES

The precarious dropoff in this encounter is dangerous, and the blackscale bruisers have a power that pushes. Let the characters know this early by having a blackscale knock back a character who isn't near the edge. Treat that event as a warning to the characters; anyone who goes close to the edge after that is a fair target.

After a creature falls and catches itself, it takes more than one move action for that creature to return to the top of the pit. For the lizardfolk, you can remove the monster from the map (and not tell the players that it caught itself), then bring it back after skipping one of its turns.

Stirge Chamber

Encounter Level 7 (1,700 XP)

Setup

2 gricks (G)
2 dire stirges (D)
2 cave stirge swarms (S)

The jungles around Tulkau Shayn are infested with stirges and other flying beasts. Some of these creatures enter the chambers within the great cave by traveling through the smaller openings and chimneys that reach to the surface. When Zanathakla and the lizardfolk first moved into the cave, they tried to eradicate the dangerous pests in the stirge chamber to no avail. When they killed a group of them, another would take their place. Now the lizardfolk bypass the danger by smearing a pungent salve on themselves when they plan to pass by the chamber. The salve, which smells like dung mixed with rotten eggs (and that might be what it's made of), covers their scent and allows them to pass without attracting the stirges.

When the PCs approach the pots filled with the smelly salve, read:
A pair of pots sit on each side of the walkway just ahead of an opening on the north wall. A makeshift sconce with a single torch hangs over the pot closest to the cave wall. Even from a distance, you can smell that something rancid is in those pots.

Nature Check
DC 16 *After examining the contents of the pots, you figure out that it is some sort of scent-blocking salve used by lizardfolk hunters.*

If the characters stop and rub the salve on themselves, they can pass the cave without causing the stirges to immediately attack. However, a new threat has recently moved into the caves. A pair of gricks now prowl the chamber, attacking any creature attempting to pass. If the gricks bloody a character, the scent of blood draws the stirges, which then join the fight.

2 Gricks (G)		Level 7 Brute
Medium aberrant beast		XP 300 each

Initiative +4   **Senses** Perception +10; darkvision
HP 96; **Bloodied** 48
AC 19; **Fortitude** 19, **Reflex** 14, **Will** 15
Resist 5 against effects that target AC
Speed 6, climb 4
⊕ **Tentacle Rake** (standard; at-will)
   +10 vs. AC; 2d6 + 4 damage, and ongoing 5 damage (save ends).
Expert Flanker
   A grick gains a +2 bonus to attack rolls against an enemy it is flanking.
Alignment Unaligned   **Languages** —
Skills Endurance +11, Stealth +9

Str 18 (+7)	**Dex** 13 (+4)	**Wis** 14 (+5)
Con 16 (+6)	**Int** 2 (−1)	**Cha** 7 (+1)

2 Dire Stirges (D)		Level 7 Lurker
Small natural beast		XP 300 each

Initiative +10   **Senses** Perception +3; darkvision
HP 60; **Bloodied** 30
AC 21; **Fortitude** 17, **Reflex** 19, **Will** 16; see also *bite*
Speed 2, fly 6 (hover)
⊕ **Bite** (standard; at-will)
   +12 vs. AC; 1d6 damage, and the target is grabbed and takes ongoing 10 damage until the grab ends. A dire stirge doesn't make attack rolls while grabbing a target and gains a +5 bonus to its AC and Reflex.
Alignment Unaligned   **Languages** —
Skills Stealth +11

Str 10 (+3)	**Dex** 16 (+6)	**Wis** 10 (+3)
Con 12 (+4)	**Int** 1 (−2)	**Cha** 4 (+0)

2 Cave Stirge Swarms (S)		Level 6 Brute
Medium natural beast (swarm)		XP 250 each

Initiative +6   **Senses** Perception +7; darkvision
Swarm Attack aura 1; each enemy that starts its turn within the aura takes 5 damage.
HP 84; **Bloodied** 42
AC 18; **Fortitude** 15, **Reflex** 16, **Will** 17
Resist half damage from melee and ranged attacks; **Vulnerable** 10 against close and area attacks
Speed 2, fly 6 (hover)
⊕ **Bloodsucking Swarm** (standard; at-will)
   +9 vs. AC; 1d8 + 4 damage, and ongoing 5 damage (save ends).
Alignment Unaligned   **Languages** —
Skills Stealth +11

Str 8 (+2)	**Dex** 16 (+6)	**Wis** 19 (+7)
Con 14 (+5)	**Int** 1 (−2)	**Cha** 4 (+0)

Tactics

Simple hunters, the creatures that issue forth from this chamber use straightforward tactics as they try to claim their next meal.

When the characters enter the side chamber or travel along the walkway to the midpoint between the two entrances, the gricks attack. Skilled hunters, they attempt to find a soft target, flank that target, and fell it before moving on to the next. The gricks know the deep cave is dangerous, and they try not to come too close to the edge. They also attempt to bull rush (+10 vs. Fortitude) creatures that stand on the edge.

The stirges latch onto the closest creature until that creature is dead or has escaped.

The cave stirge swarms flutter in a position where they can deal damage to the most enemies. If enemies are not clustered together, a swarm usually stays near a dire stirge that has grabbed a creature, keeping the grabbed enemy in its *swarm attack* aura.

The stirges and the swarms are not intelligent, but have enough of a survival instinct to flee into the two narrow tunnels to the north if they are reduced to one-quarter or fewer of their hit points.

FEATURES OF THE AREA

Illumination: Darkness. The characters can light the torch above the pot of salve, providing bright light in a 5-square radius.

Walkway: The gently sloping walkway along the southern edge of this area is difficult terrain. From here to the bottom of the cave, the path is 10 feet wide.

Rubble and Guano: Large areas of rubble are mixed with bat and stirge guano in the cave. These squares are difficult terrain.

BATS!

Dozens, possibly hundreds, of bats live in this cave and try to avoid the dangerous stirges and gricks that have moved into their territory. The sounds of combat or the intrusion of bright light startles them. You can use these bats to add some variety to the encounter.

Create a 4-square-by-4-square area of bats along the north wall of the chamber at the end of the first round in which an attack is made or a bright light hits the back of the cave. At the end of each round, determine whether the bats move and what effect they have. Roll separately for movement and behavior, or choose the bats' behavior. The bats don't take sides, and often have both characters and monsters within the squares they occupy.

d6	Move	Behavior
1–2	0	Swarm creatures (creatures in squares of bats take a –2 penalty to defenses)
3–4	3	Cloud vision (creatures in squares of bats gain concealment)
5–6	6	Impede movement (squares of bats require 1 extra square to move into)

You'll also need to decide how the bats are affected by powers used in their area (especially burst or blast powers). For instance, if a character uses *fireball* on the area, you might shrink the area of bats to 2 squares on a side or eliminate it entirely.

Salve (Optional Rule): Creatures wearing the pungent salve from the pots outside the cave are unaffected by the bats.

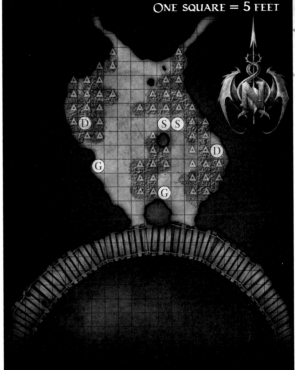

ONE SQUARE = 5 FEET

TULKAU SHAYN

Cave: As in the previous encounter, it's possible a monster might be pushed off the edge of the walkway. In addition to the saving throw any creature receives if it's pushed, pulled, or slid off an edge, a creature that falls down the pit can make an Athletics check (DC 15) to grab onto the wooden walkway on the way down (as though it were falling while climbing). If the creature succeeds on the check, it takes 3d10 falling damage and lands on the wooden walkway 30 feet below. It takes 12 squares of movement upward along the walkway to get back to the location of the stirge lair. A creature that fails the Athletics check falls 80 feet (and takes 8d10 falling damage).

Narrow Tunnels: The passages leading northwest and northeast away from the stirge chamber are only large enough for the stirges and the swarms to negotiate. The characters and the gricks cannot move through them, not even by squeezing.

CONCLUSION

Once they have made it past the stirge chamber, the characters are free to make their way toward the bottom, where Zanathakla lies in wait. They might stop off in area 4 (see page 99) before moving all the way to the cave floor.

ZANATHAKLA'S WRATH

Encounter Level 9 (2,150 XP)

SETUP

Zanathakla, young orium dragon (Z)
2 greenscale darters (D)

As the characters descend into Tulkau Shayn, they attract the ire of Zanathakla, the orium dragon who makes her lair here. They battle Zanathakla while perched on increasingly unstable platforms.

When the characters descend to the 60-foot-high platform, read:
A series of wooden platforms has been affixed to the inside walls of the cave with pegs and wooden beams. Shallow flights of stairs connect the platforms, making a spiraling pathway down into the darkness.

Perception Check
DC 21 *There are alcoves in the rock wall on the far side of the cave, and you can see a twitch of movement in them. There's definitely something alive in there.*

Under ordinary circumstances, there's no way the characters can sneak down to the alcoves or the cave floor. The wooden platforms creak loudly, and the characters are silhouetted against the open sky above.

The characters can't see Zanathakla. She remains on the periphery of the cave floor, where the

platforms block the heroes from getting a look at her even if they have a powerful light source.

The battle begins when one of two events occurs: A character heads down the stairs from the 60-foot-high platform, or a character spots the creatures in the alcoves to the south (the greenscale darters) and attacks them. Zanathakla flies up through the middle of the cave, lands on a platform, and breathes at the biggest cluster of enemies she can find.

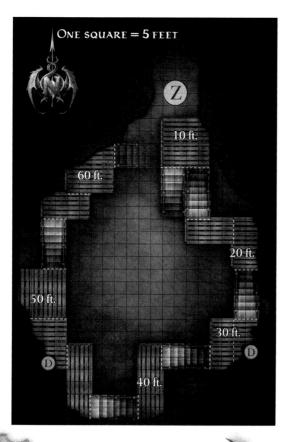

ONE SQUARE = 5 FEET

Zanathakla (Z)	Level 9 Solo Soldier
Young orium dragon	
Large natural magical beast (dragon)	XP 2,000

Initiative +9   **Senses** Perception +9; darkvision
HP 392; **Bloodied** 196; see also *bloodied breath*
AC 25; **Fortitude** 23, **Reflex** 21, **Will** 20
Resist 15 acid
Saving Throws +5
Speed 6, fly 8 (hover), overland flight 12
Action Points 2

⊕ **Bite** (standard; at-will) ✦ **Acid**
    Reach 2; +16 vs. AC; 1d10 + 6 damage plus 1d6 acid damage.

⊕ **Claw** (standard; at-will)
    Reach 2; +16 vs. AC; 1d8 + 6 damage, and the target is marked until the end of the dragon's next turn.

➵ **Stone Rend** (standard; usable only while a wall is within reach; at-will)
    Zanathakla tears stones from the walls and throws them: ranged 10; +14 vs. AC; 2d6 + 5 damage.

↯/➵ **Draconic Fury** (standard; at-will)
    Reach 2; Zanathakla makes two claw attacks and one bite attack, or makes one bite attack and one *stone rend* attack.

⟵ **Breath Weapon** (standard; recharges when one of Zanathakla's vaporous spirits is reduced to 0 hit points) ✦ **Acid**
    Close blast 5; +14 vs. Fortitude; 2d8 + 4 acid damage, and a Zanathakla vaporous serpent minion (see below) appears in any single unoccupied square in the blast. It acts just after the dragon in the initiative order.

⟵ **Bloodied Breath** (free, when first bloodied; encounter)
    Breath weapon recharges, and Zanathakla uses it.

⟵ **Frightful Presence** (standard; encounter) ✦ **Fear**
    Close burst 5; targets enemies; +14 vs. Will; the target is stunned until the end of Zanathakla's next turn. *Aftereffect:* The target takes a –2 penalty to attack rolls (save ends).

Alignment Unaligned	**Languages** Common, Draconic

Skills History +10, Insight +9, Intimidate +11

Str 21 (+9)	**Dex** 17 (+7)	**Wis** 11 (+4)
Con 18 (+8)	**Int** 12 (+5)	**Cha** 15 (+6)

Zanathakla Vaporous Serpent	Level 9 Minion Brute
Medium elemental beast	XP –

Initiative as dragon   **Senses** Perception +1
HP 1; a missed attack never damages a minion.
AC 21; **Fortitude** 20, **Reflex** 19, **Will** 18
Resist 15 acid
Speed 6, fly 4

⊕ **Bite** (standard; at-will) ✦ **Acid**
    +13 vs. AC; 10 acid damage.

Alignment Unaligned	**Languages** –

Str 17 (+7)	**Dex** 10 (+4)	**Wis** 4 (+1)
Con 12 (+5)	**Int** 4 (+1)	**Cha** 4 (+1)

2 Greenscale Darters (D)	Level 5 Lurker
Medium natural humanoid (reptile)	XP 200 each

Initiative +10   **Senses** Perception +9
HP 50; **Bloodied** 25
AC 18; **Fortitude** 14, **Reflex** 17, **Will** 14
Speed 6 (swamp walk)

ⓐ **Club** (standard; at-will) ✦ **Weapon**
+10 vs. AC; 1d6 + 1 damage.

➶ **Blowgun** (standard; at-will) ✦ **Poison, Weapon**
Loading the blowgun takes a minor action; ranged 6/12;
+10 vs. AC; 1 damage, and the greenscale darter makes a
secondary attack against the same target. *Secondary Attack:* +8
vs Fortitude; the target takes ongoing 5 poison damage and is
slowed (save ends both).

Sniper
A hidden lizardfolk darter that misses with a ranged attack
remains hidden.

Alignment Unaligned   **Languages** Draconic
Skills Athletics +8, Stealth +11

Str 13 (+3)	**Dex** 18 (+6)	**Wis** 15 (+4)
Con 14 (+4)	**Int** 8 (+1)	**Cha** 8 (+1)

Equipment club, blowgun with 20 poisoned darts

TACTICS

Part of the challenge for the characters is the acid-damaged platforms along the cave walls, so make the monsters move even when they don't need to. That will entice the characters to run—and eventually jump—from platform to platform.

Zanathakla prefers to perch on the platform either ahead of or behind the characters, then breathe her corrosive breath. She's surprised by the damage to the platforms, but she quickly realizes what an advantage it is, and she's proud enough to taunt characters who are standing on a damaged platform. When one of her vaporous serpents appears, she sends it along the platforms to engage the characters in melee. (Unlike ordinary vaporous serpents, a serpent created by Zanathakla's breath has a fly speed.)

Zanathakla fights to the death.

The greenscale darters stay in their alcoves as long as possible, then retreat (either to their alcoves or to the ground below) once they see a platform collapse. The darters try to ascend and escape into the jungle when Zanathakla dies, and they surrender if they can't escape.

FEATURES OF THE AREA

Illumination: Darkness.

Floor: The cave floor is difficult terrain—a jumble of rocks and bones from Zanathakla's meals or sacrificial victims thrown into the pit in ancient times.

Stairs: The stairs are difficult terrain for a creature ascending them, but normal terrain for a creature descending.

Platforms: Each section of platform is marked with its elevation above the cave floor. If a creature is pushed, pulled, or slid off a platform, it takes 1d10 falling damage per 10 feet as normal.

Zanathakla's corrosive breath weakens the pegs holding the platforms to the wall or to other sections of platform. Each section of platform or staircase (marked off with dashed lines on the map) can withstand Zanathakla's breath weapon twice before collapsing.

Each platform or staircase follows the same pattern as it is hit multiple times.

1. The wood visibly weakens.
2. The platform or staircase begins to sway and lurch. It's now challenging terrain, requiring a DC 14 Acrobatics check to cross. A creature that fails the check falls prone in the first space it tries to move into.
3. The third hit causes the platform or staircase to fall apart, and any creature standing on it plummets to the cave floor and takes falling damage. (The height of a fall from a staircase depends on which end of the staircase the creature is closer to when it collapses.)

Getting Back Up: A creature can get back to a platform by climbing. The sloping walls make the climb tough, requiring a DC 20 Athletics check.

CONCLUSION

When Zanathakla is defeated, the characters are free to explore Tulkau Shayn and have unfettered access to the other locales described in the overview (pages 98–99)—unless you decide to make this lair into a full-blown adventure site, in which case their adventure is just beginning.

DANGEROUS PLATFORMS

The unstable platforms in this encounter make it exciting. You want the characters to have an inkling of what's going to happen, so make sure you describe the effect of Zanathakla's *breath weapon* on the platforms, and track how many times Zanathakla's *breath weapon* touches each part of the structure. The *breath weapon* is a close blast 5, so Zanathakla will often hit multiple platforms and staircases with her breath each time she uses it.

Stunts: Also keep the rules for Acrobatic stunts in mind. Though the base DC is normally 15, adjust it as needed to make this encounter fun. The standard DCs for 7th level are 8 (easy), 14 (moderate), and 19 (hard). Describe various hanging ropes, fortuitous handholds, and other objects the characters can use to move quickly from one section of the scaffolding to another. The rubble at the bottom of the pit can contain handy objects—such as grappling hooks—that a character could use after being removed from the fight by a fall.

Adamantine dragon lair for five 13th-level adventurers

In the deeps of the Underdark lie the long-abandoned duergar mines of Bolmarzh. These are now the domain of the adamantine dragon Vanathia, who rules over the grimlocks and gargoyles infesting the chambers and passages of the old gray dwarf delving.

BACKGROUND

History DC 11: A few years ago, a young adamantine dragon named Vanathia discovered the old duergar mine while searching for a suitable lair. Vanathia settled into her new home and grew to adulthood in the hidden mines.

In recent months, she has plundered several caravans and demanded tribute from nearby villages in the surface lands, creating a serious problem for the local merchants and townsfolk. The call has gone out for someone to best the dragon before her depredations cause utter ruin.

History DC 18: Decades ago, a clan of duergar discovered a great chasm in the Underdark. Its walls glittered with veins of gold, and the gray dwarves quickly established a mining outpost they called Bolmarzh—in their tongue, "Secret Treasure." For years, the duergar worked the hidden mine, carving out living spaces for themselves in the surrounding caverns. Eventually, a large and fierce tribe of grimlocks discovered the duergar outpost. The grimlocks pillaged Bolmarzh and erected a crude shrine to the dark god Torog, in celebration of their victory over the gray dwarves. The outpost lay abandoned for a long time, visited occasionally by grimlocks that came to worship at their shrine.

ENVIRONMENT

The old duergar stronghold alternates between finished chambers and natural tunnels. Chambers that have "straight" walls are at least partially finished, with flagstone floors and walls of dressed stone blocks. Natural caverns have rough rock walls, but the floors have been smoothed and leveled. The exception is the floor of the Great Chasm (area 5), which is littered with heaps of broken rock from the duergar mining.

Although most of the monsters in the mines don't need light, Vanathia prefers a little illumination; several *everburning torches* are located in the lair at the locations indicated on the map. The sound of falling water echoes loudly throughout most of the complex, so Perception checks made to listen take a -5 penalty everywhere except areas 1, 2, and 3.

Vanathia uses grimlocks of the tribe she defeated as her guards and servants. She also commands the loyalties of a large clutch of gargoyles that inhabit the upper reaches of the chasm. At any given time, several small parties of grimlocks and gargoyles are out hunting in the caves and passages surrounding the old mines. (In fact, it might be an encounter with one of these raiding parties that reveals Bolmarzh's existence to a group of adventurers.) In addition, several monsters—a galeb duhr, a beholder, and others lurking in the far corners of the mines—are under the dragon's dominion and serve her loyally.

ENTERING THE MINE

The old duergar mines can be accessed from below or from above. Surface explorers are likely to discover the doors in area 1, which lie in a deep crevice or alcove of an otherwise unremarkable cavern. The cavern outside the doors of Bolmarzh might lie beneath another dungeon or connect through a series of natural caverns to a lonely mountainside

VANATHIA, THE BLACK STORM

The mines of Bolmarzh offered Vanathia a strong, secret, defensible home, while the upper reaches of the adjoining chasm provided her with easy access to passages leading up to the abundant hunting of the surface world. In time, the grimlocks discovered the dragon's presence and launched a furious attack to drive Vanathia out of her home. However, the dragon repelled their assault, followed the grimlocks back to their own lair, and slew their chieftain. Vanathia demanded the tribe's fealty, and the grimlocks yielded to her. The best warriors of the tribe must serve the dragon in her lair, doing her bidding. The grimlocks serve Vanathia grudgingly, but they dare not defy her—or disappoint her.

An adamantine dragon newly grown to adulthood, Vanathia is proud and ambitious. The draconic hunger to hoard items of value and to dominate lesser creatures burns brighter in her heart every day.

Vanathia is not cruel or malicious, but she is ruthless and quick to anger—any show of defiance provokes her into a furious attack. Intruders in her domain can expect no mercy, although supplicants who come bearing gifts might be given a chance to respectfully present their requests. Vanathia has a haughty, calculating demeanor, but she is a dragon of her word and sticks to any bargain she agrees to. Of course, that means she expects others to do the same. She hunts down and destroys anyone breaking their word to her.

cave. Vanathia's servants scour the nearby caverns and dungeons regularly, hunting game and gathering various edible fungi and lichens.

Travelers approaching from the deep Underdark are more likely to stumble across the southwest end of the Great Chasm and follow it up to the Lower Gate (area 8). Grimlocks and gargoyles in Vanathia's service roam the tunnels and caverns that connect the chasm to the deeper parts of the Underdark, patrolling against raids by other Underdark monsters.

This lair description assumes that the characters are approaching from the upper side (area 1).

The mines extend for several hundred yards to the southwest, following the chasm. Vanathia's lair occupies only part of the old excavations.

AREA 1: THE FRONT DOOR

The old duergar-forged doors to the mines still stand. The doors are not locked or barred; the grimlocks go in and out frequently, and they've fallen out of the habit of securing the doors.

When the PCs see the doors, read:
A deep alcove leading down from this cavern ends in a strong set of iron doors, covered in faded Dwarven runes. You can make out the distant sound of falling water from somewhere beyond.

If any PCs know Dwarven:
The doors read: "Herein lie the Halls of Bolmarzh. Death to those who enter uninvited."

Rusty Doors: A character who makes a DC 23 Perception check realizes that the doors are no longer seated evenly on their posts, and they will scrape loudly over the stone when pulled open. This noise alerts the monsters in area 2 unless the characters lift the doors slightly while opening them or take other measures to open the doors quietly.

Hidden Window: A small spy-hole at the back of an alcove near area 2 (Perception DC 27 to notice) looks down on the door from about 15 feet overhead. No one is keeping watch at the spy-hole the first time the characters venture into this area.

AREA 2: THE HIGH HALL

This room once served as the banquet room and audience chamber for the duergar lord that ruled Bolmarzh. For Vanathia, it is a guardroom where grimlocks and gargoyles stand watch to intercept intruders. In addition, Vanathia is entertaining a small delegation of duergar visitors that are interested in working Bolmarzh's rich veins again. The dragon has instructed her minions to allow the gray dwarves to camp here while she considers their offer.

The doorways that connect this area with areas 1 and 4 open into the hall underneath the balcony;

creatures moving into the room can't see anything on the balcony on their side of the room, although they could see across the room to the balcony on the far side.

A short passage from the balcony leads to a hidden window overlooking the doors in area 1. The window is about 1 foot square and 15 feet above the floor of area 1.

Tactical Encounter: "The High Hall," page 112.

Development: If the characters leave the mines and return later, Vanathia replaces slain guards with new ones (see the tactical encounter for more information).

AREA 3: STOREROOMS
When the PCs enter the area, read:
These chambers look like old storerooms. The floors are littered with rank furs, gnawed bones, stone flakes, and other such detritus.

Development: If Vanathia sends for more guards after the characters make their initial foray into the mines, twelve grimlock minions and three grimlock berserkers occupy these rooms.

AREA 4: THE SMELTER

Long ago, this chamber served as the center of the mining operation in the chasm. The remnants of the duergar excavations are still here.

When the PCs enter the area, read:
A ramshackle old sluice box bisects this room, fed by a dark, swift stream that spills out of a crevice high on the north wall. A waterwheel stands at the front of the sluice, connected by rotting pulleys to a bellows and furnace, both of which have rusted away to junk. Below the sluice box, a small footbridge crosses the stream, which flows southward out of the cavern to the sound of a waterfall. East of the stream, a double door leads out of the room to the south.

The stream is not deep; a character can wade it easily. The waterfall is in the portion of the stream south of area 4 and north of the pool in the end of the chasm. A character who makes a DC 18 Athletics check can ride out the waterfall (it's only a 20-foot drop) without incident. A character who fails this check takes 1d10 damage. In either case, the character ends up in the shallow pool on the other side of the waterfall.

Secret Door: A secret door (Perception DC 27 to notice) is set in the southeast corner of the room, leading into area 7.

AREA 5: THE GREAT CHASM
This long rift is 300 feet high. A shallow stream meanders through it. Two bridges cross the stream and the rubble-covered terrain adjacent to it. The ledges that border the chasm are 60 feet above the lower surface. Characters who travel down the waterfall from area 4 and find themselves in the pool must scale one of the sides of the ledge (Athletics DC 15)

to reach the higher terrain. Staircases that descend toward the south are cut into the ledges, following the slope of the chasm as it contonues south and west.

The chasm continues off the far edge of the map, leading into more excavations and eventually connecting with passages in the deeper Underdark. (You can map out and populate this area as you see fit, if you want this area to extend beyond the immediate vicinity of Vanathia's lair.) In the roof over the higher reaches of the chasm, vertical chimneys wind another hundred feet or so to exits hidden in the steep hills that lie on the surface. The dragon can't fly through these passages, but she can climb them easily enough. (These chimneys are not depicted on the map; they serve only to provide Vanathia with a way of leaving the mines if she manages to escape.)

Tactical Encounter: "Chasm Battle," page 114.

AREA 6: TOROG'S SHRINE

Off to the side of the chasm, 60 feet above the floor, is a cave that holds a small shrine dedicated to Torog. The grimlocks venerate the King that Crawls, although Vanathia could care less about the grimlock's religious observances. Before the dragon conquered them, the grimlocks occasionally raided the surface world for suitable sacrificial victims.

When the PCs enter this area, read:
This chamber has a high, stalactite-covered roof 30 feet overhead. In the far end of the area stands a pair of twisted rock pillars fitted with rusty manacles; the south wall of the cave has been crudely chiseled into the image of a monstrous, eyeless face with a fanged maw and writhing tentacles. Humanoid bones—mostly skulls and crushed ribcages—litter the floor.

Tactical Encounter: "Chasm Battle," page 114.

AREA 7: SECRET TUNNEL

The duergar built this tunnel to serve as an escape route in case some enemy seized the Lower Gate (area 8) and trapped them in the large southern chamber. The secret doors on either end are well hidden (Perception DC 27). The 5-foot-wide and 5-foot-high passageway between them is interrupted by staircases that descend from north to south. Vanathia knows about the secret tunnel, but she has never used it because it would be a difficult squeeze for her to get through it.

When the PCs enter the area, read:
This is a low and cramped passageway. The stairs are covered with thick dust.

AREA 8: THE LOWER GATE

The heart of the old duergar stronghold was the cavern that now serves as Vanathia's lair. Here, the

miners lived in barracks-buildings. To protect their dwellings, the gray dwarves walled off the mouth of the cavern and built another strong gate, which now suits Vanathia quite well. The doors are not locked or barred, but hidden sentries keep watch inside.

When the PCs enter this area, read:
The steps descending the chasm wall meet a much lower ledge here, only 10 feet above the chasm floor. To the south and west, the chasm continues off into darkness. To the east stands a double door of iron, at the top of a short flight of stairs.

Development: If the characters leave the complex and return, the doors are barred (break DC 28) and several grimlock guards are posted here to defend the entry.

AREA 9: VANATHIA'S LAIR

The duergar called this great cavern the Glimmervault, after the luminous crystals dotting its ceiling. It is so large that they were able to build free-standing buildings of thick stone blocks in this room to serve as the miners' barracks, their chieftain's home, and their chapel. Vanathia has knocked down most of the buildings to give her plenty of elbow room, but the stone footings remain.

The dragon keeps one of her loyal gargoyles close at hand at all times, to act as a messenger and major domo. Vanathia also has another ally in her lair—a galeb duhr that works slowly to shape and sculpt the lair to suit the adamantine dragon's whims. In exchange for its service as a guard, miner, and interior decorator, Vanathia allows the galeb duhr to feed on the rare crystals and rich veins found in the old duergar mines.

Tactical Encounter: "Vanathia's Lair," page 116.

AREA 10: DRAGON'S HOARD

This stone building once served as the personal quarters of the duergar chieftain of Bolmarzh. It is now Vanathia's private den, as well as the location of her hoard.

When the PCs inspect the building, read:
Unlike the other buildings in this cavern, this one is mostly still intact. Inside the wide doorway, a great pile of silver and gold coins lies in the center of the room, with several eye-catching gems and pieces of jewelry carefully arranged around it.

Treasure: Vanathia's hoard consists of a level 16 magic item, 6,000 gp, 22,000 sp, a sapphire-studded gold bracelet worth 800 gp, five diamonds worth 500 gp each, and a mithral goblet fashioned in the shape of dancing nymphs, worth 500 gp. This pile of valuables equals parcels 3 and 5 of a level 14 treasure.

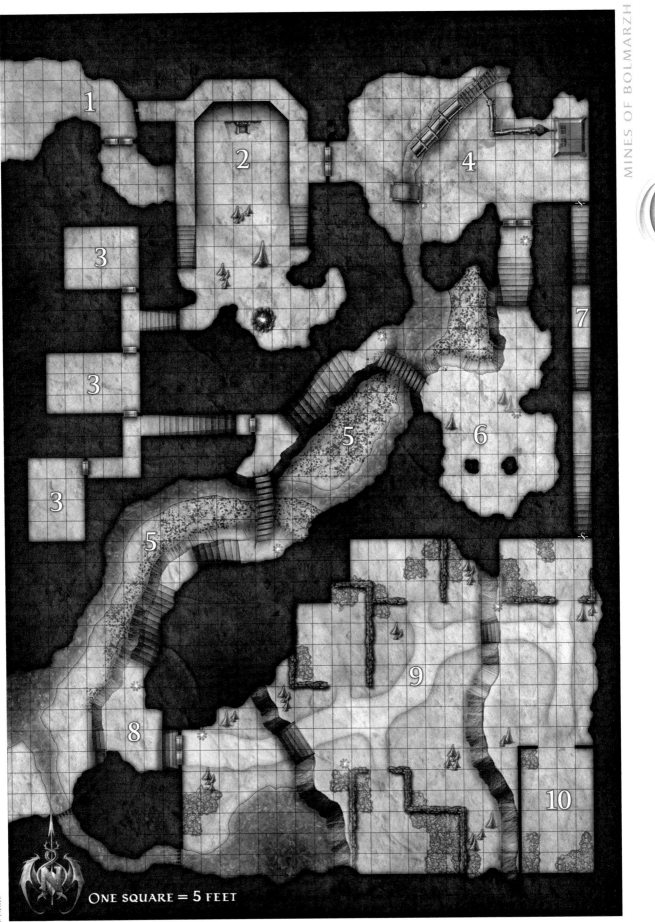

ONE SQUARE = 5 FEET

JASON A. ENGLE

THE HIGH HALL

Encounter Level 14 (5,000 XP)

SETUP

2 gargoyle harriers (G)
2 duergar hellcallers (D)
4 grimlock ambushers (A)

If the characters managed to open the door from area 1 silently, they surprise the monsters. The positions of the grimlocks and duergar on the map assume that the characters gain surprise. Otherwise, the noise of the old door squealing open alerts them. The grimlocks hide along the wall under the balcony to either side of the archway and surprise the characters with a sudden rush as soon as a character enters the room, while the duergar take cover behind the stalagmites. In either event, don't place the monsters on the map until the characters enter the room.

When the PCs enter the room, read:
This chamber is a natural cavern improved by careful stonework, its floor paved with flagstones, and three of its four walls finished in plain stone blocks. The ceiling still has its glistening stalactites, and the wall to the south is made of pale white stone. A balcony circles the room about fifteen feet above the floor, and a couple of stone statues gaze down on the floor below. An old stone dais stands in the northern part of the room.

If the PCs surprise the monsters, read:
Several gray-skinned savages with eyeless faces crouch in scattered locations near the west wall of this rom. On the other side of the room, a pair of dwarflike creatures sit near a small, dimly glowing fire, conversing in their guttural language.

Place the duergar and the grimlocks in the squares indicated, and resolve the surprise round.

If the monsters surprise the PCs, read:
Several gray-skinned savages with eyeless faces and greataxes rush the archway, shrieking in battle fury. Behind them, a pair of dwarflike creatures with red-black skin and beards of stiff, rust-colored hair jump out from behind stalagmites and begin hurling quills plucked from their beards.

Allow the characters Perception checks (DC 25) to detect the gargoyles for what they are. If the gargoyles go undetected, don't place them on the map. The gargoyles have combat advantage against the characters the first time the gargoyles act in the battle.

---

2 Gargoyle Harriers (G)	Level 11 Lurker
Medium elemental humanoid (earth)	XP 600 each

Initiative +13   **Senses** Perception +13; darkvision
HP 89; **Bloodied** 44
AC 27; **Fortitude** 23, **Reflex** 21, **Will** 21
Immune petrification
Speed 6, fly 8

⊕ **Claw** (standard; at-will)
  +16 vs. AC; 2d6 + 6 damage.

† **Flyby Attack** (standard; recharges after using *stone form*)
  The gargoyle flies up to 8 squares and makes a melee basic attack at any point during the move, without provoking an opportunity attack from the target. If the attack hits, the target is knocked prone.

Stone Form (standard; at-will)
  The gargoyle becomes a statue and gains resist 25 to all damage, regeneration 3, and tremorsense 10. It loses all other senses and can take no actions in stone form other than reverting to its normal form (as a minor action).

Alignment Evil   **Languages** Deep Speech, Primordial
Skills Stealth +13
Str 21 (+10)   **Dex** 17 (+8)   **Wis** 17 (+8)
Con 17 (+8)   **Int** 9 (+4)   **Cha** 17 (+8)

---

2 Duergar Hellcallers (D)	Level 12 Artillery
Medium natural humanoid, dwarf (devil)	XP 700 each

Initiative +10   **Senses** Perception +13; darkvision
HP 96; **Bloodied** 48
AC 24; **Fortitude** 23, **Reflex** 23, **Will** 25
Resist 10 fire, 10 poison
Speed 5

⊕ **Mace** (standard; at-will) ✦ **Weapon**
  +19 vs. AC; 1d8 + 5 damage.

➷ **Infernal Quills** (standard; at-will) ✦ **Fire, Poison**
  Ranged 10; +19 vs. AC; 1d8 + 3 fire and poison damage, and the target takes ongoing 5 fire and poison damage and a -2 penalty to attack rolls (save ends both).

➷ **Quick Quill Strike** (minor; encounter)
  The duergar hellcaller makes an *infernal quills* attack.

⇐ **Asmodeus's Ruby Curse** (standard; encounter) ✦ **Fear, Psychic**
  Close blast 5; targets enemies; +16 vs. Will; 3d8 + 5 psychic damage, and the duergar hellcaller slides the target to the nearest space outside the blast. This forced movement provokes opportunity attacks.

❊ **Quill Storm** (standard; encounter) ✦ **Fire, Poison**
  Area burst 2 within 10; +17 vs. Reflex; 1d8 fire and poison damage, and the target takes ongoing 10 fire and poison damage and a -2 penalty to attack rolls (save ends both).

Devilish Sacrifice (immediate interrupt, when an enemy makes a melee attack roll against the duergar hellcaller; encounter)
  The hellcaller shifts to the nearest space beyond the triggering enemy's reach. A legion devil hellguard (MM 64) appears in the hellcaller's former space and becomes the target of the enemy's attack. The devil acts immediately after the hellcaller's initiative count.

Alignment Evil   **Languages** Common, Deep Speech, Dwarven
Skills Arcana +11, Dungeoneering +13, Religion +11
Str 14 (+8)   **Dex** 19 (+10)   **Wis** 14 (+8)
Con 18 (+10)   **Int** 11 (+6)   **Cha** 22 (+12)
Equipment leather armor, mace

4 Grimlock Ambushers (A)	Level 11 Skirmisher
Medium natural humanoid (blind)	XP 600 each

Initiative +9   **Senses** Perception +7; blindsight 10
HP 110; **Bloodied** 55; see also *offensive shift*
AC 26; **Fortitude** 25, **Reflex** 23, **Will** 23
Immune gaze
Speed 6

⊕ **Greataxe** (standard; at-will) ✦ **Weapon**
+16 vs. AC; 1d12 + 5 damage (crit 2d12 + 17).

↯ **Offensive Shift** (immediate reaction, when an enemy moves within 2 squares of the grimlock ambusher and attacks an ally of the grimlock; recharges when first bloodied)
The grimlock ambusher shifts and makes a melee basic attack against the enemy.

Alignment Evil   **Languages** Common, Deep Speech
Skills Athletics +15, Endurance +12

Str 20 (+10)	**Dex** 14 (+7)	**Wis** 15 (+7)
Con 14 (+7)	**Int** 9 (+4)	**Cha** 9 (+4)

Equipment greataxe

TACTICS

The grimlock ambushers try to overwhelm the heroes with a quick rush. After that, they fight in a loose pack, so that two or three can use their *offensive shift* reaction at once when an enemy provokes it. The ambushers try to save a move action to shift away from enemies after attacking, so that enemies have to move up to attack them and provoke the *offensive shift* of their allies. The grimlocks happily mob any foes knocked prone by the gargoyles' attacks.

The gargoyles prefer *flyby attack*, beginning and ending each swoop on the balcony. They are patient and cunning foes, and they are willing to forego a turn of attacking to assume *stone form*. This act recharges *flyby attack*, so the gargoyles end up attacking every other round.

The duergar begin the battle by using *quill storm*, but only if they can catch at least two enemies in the burst. *Infernal quills* is their default attack. They try to hang back away from the melee, and they are quick to use *devilish sacrifice* or *Asmodeus's ruby curse* to keep enemies from closing on them. If necessary, they climb the stairs up to the balcony to stay out of easy melee reach. The duergar have no particular loyalty to Vanathia or their grimlock allies, and they don't hesitate to flee by any convenient exit once most of the dragon's servants have fallen.

FEATURES OF THE AREA

Illumination: Glowing coals from the duergar campfire provide 5 squares of dim light.

Ceiling: The ceiling in this chamber is 30 feet above the floor (15 feet above the balcony).

Balcony: The room is ringed by a stone balcony 15 feet above the floor. The squares directly underneath the balcony are open, so creatures can move under the overhang. The overhang blocks line of sght and line of effect between creatures on the balcony and beneath it on the same side of the room.

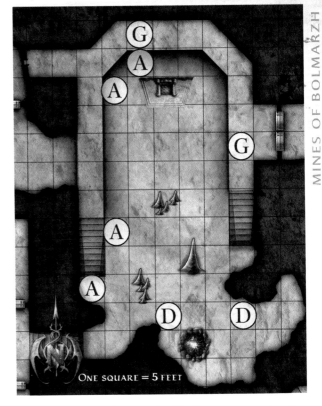

ONE SQUARE = 5 FEET

Iron Doors: The iron double doors connecting to areas 1 and 4 are not locked. They have AC 5, Fortitude 10, Reflex 5, and 60 hit points.

Stalagmites: Stalagmites are difficult terrain. They provide cover to Medium or smaller creatures. Each stalagmite has AC 5, Reflex 5, Fortitude 10, and 40 hit points.

Dais and Throne: This square is difficult terrain. The throne provides cover to Medium or smaller creatures. The throne has AC 5, Reflex 5, Fortitude 10, and 20 hit points.

Fire Pit: The square containing these embers is difficult terrain. A creature that enters the fire pit or starts its turn there takes 5 fire damage.

Spy-Hole Window: The spy-hole offers superior cover against attacks from area 1.

DEVELOPMENT

If the characters leave the mines and return later, Vanathia sends for more grimlocks to serve as guards. Four grimlock berserkers and two additional gargoyle harriers are alert against future intrusions. The door leading to area 1 is barred (DC 28 to break it down), and one of the gargoyles is posted at the spy-hole to keep watch for intruders. Any duergar slain in this room are not replaced.

TREASURE

The duergar carry substantial wealth in their belt pouches: 25 pp, 300 gp, and a total of three fine emeralds worth 400 gp each. These valuables equal parcel 9 of a level 14 treasure.

CHASM BATTLE

Encounter Level 13 (4,800 XP)

SETUP

1 beholder eye of flame (B)
1 eidolon (E)
3 grimlock berserkers (G)

The beholder and the grimlocks can see (or sense) the doors leading from areas 3 and 4 from their positions, and are also aware if anyone enters this area by coming down the waterfall, so it's unlikely that the characters can surprise them. If a character attempts to get into this area without attracting notice, allow the character a Stealth check (DC 27). On a success, the character has slipped through the door or into the pool unseen, but any subsequent movement puts the character in view of the monsters—without some means of staying unseen, the character is noticed.

If the PCs enter this area through the doors in area 4, read:

You stand on a landing overlooking an illuminated chamber to the south and a rubble-strewn chasm leading off to the southwest. A steep dropoff separates the chamber from the floor of the chasm. In the distance, you can make out a wooden bridge that spans the chasm and the stream that runs through it.

If the PCs enter this area through the door leading from area 3, read:

Ahead of you is a wide ledge with a set of ascending stairs that frames one side of a huge chasm. You can see light beyond the top of the stairs to the northeast, and another torch to the south casts light on a wooden bridge that crosses the chasm.

If any PCs enter this area through the waterfall, read:

You find yourselves in a shallow pool looking south into a giant crevasse that continues as far as you can see. Overhead, a bulbous monster covered in chitinous plates of fiery red glares down at you, prepared to attack.

If the PCs move into area 6, read the text on page 110 and continue:

Three more of the eyeless savages you encountered earlier are stationed in various spots throughout the shrine. Although they can't possibly see you, each one turns in your direction and snarls as you come closer.

Place the grimlocks and the beholder on the map. Allow the characters to attempt DC 23 Perception checks; if any character succeeds on this check, place the eidolon, too—the character realized that it was another creature. If all the characters fail these checks, mark the position of the eidolon, but don't acknowledge that it's another creature. Until the eidolon takes its first action, the characters mistake it for an idol of some kind.

Beholder Eye of Flame (B)	Level 13 Elite Artillery
Large aberrant magical beast	XP 1,600

Initiative +11   **Senses** Perception +15; all-around vision, darkvision

Eyes of the Beholder aura 5; at the start of each enemy's turn, if that creature is within the aura and in the eye of flame's line of sight, the eye of flame uses one random *eye ray* power against that creature.

HP 204; **Bloodied** 102; see also *fiery burst*

AC 26; **Fortitude** 26, **Reflex** 27, **Will** 28

Saving Throws +2

Speed fly 6 (hover)

Action Points 1

⊕ **Bite** (standard; at-will)
+18 vs. AC; 2d6 damage.

⌁ **Central Eye** (minor; at-will)
Ranged 8; the target gains vulnerable 10 fire, and any attack that deals fire damage to the target also deals ongoing 5 fire damage (save ends both).

⌁ **Eye Rays** (standard; at-will) ✦ see text
The eye of flame can use up to two *eye ray* powers (chosen from the list below), at least one of which must be a *fire ray*. Each power must target a different creature. Using *eye rays* does not provoke opportunity attacks.
1—Fire Ray (Fire): Ranged 8; +17 vs. Reflex; 2d8 + 6 fire damage.
2—Telekinesis Ray: Ranged 8; +17 vs. Fortitude; the target slides 4 squares.
3—Fear Ray (Fear): Ranged 8; +17 vs. Will; the target moves its speed away from the eye of flame by the safest route possible and takes a -2 penalty to attack rolls (save ends).

⬅ **Fiery Burst** (when first bloodied and again when the eye of flame drops to 0 hit points) ✦ Fire
Close burst 2; +17 vs. Reflex; 2d8 + 6 fire damage.

Alignment Evil	**Languages** Deep Speech	
Str 10 (+6)	**Dex** 20 (+11)	**Wis** 19 (+10)
Con 18 (+10)	**Int** 14 (+8)	**Cha** 23 (+12)

3 Grimlock Berserkers (G)	Level 13 Brute
Medium natural humanoid (blind)	XP 800 each

Initiative +7   **Senses** Perception +8; blindsight 10

HP 156; **Bloodied** 78

AC 25; **Fortitude** 27, **Reflex** 22, **Will** 23

Immune gaze

Speed 6

⊕ **Greataxe** (standard; at-will) ✦ Weapon
+16 vs. AC; 1d12 + 6 damage (crit 2d12 + 18).

⊺ **Power Attack** (standard; requires greataxe; at-will) ✦ Weapon
+14 vs. AC; 1d12 + 12 damage (crit 2d12 + 24).

⊺ **Frenzied Attack** (standard; at-will)
The grimlock berserker makes two greataxe attacks against a bloodied enemy.

Grimlock Rage
When a grimlock berserker bloodies an enemy, it gains 10 temporary hit points.

Alignment Evil	**Languages** Common, Deep Speech	
Skills Athletics +17, Endurance +14		
Str 22 (+12)	**Dex** 12 (+7)	**Wis** 15 (+8)
Con 16 (+9)	**Int** 7 (+4)	**Cha** 9 (+5)

Equipment greataxe

Eidolon (E)	Level 13 Controller (Leader)
Large natural animate (construct)	XP 800

Initiative +8 **Senses** Perception +9
Fearless Followers aura 5; each ally in the aura is immune to fear.
HP 132; **Bloodied** 66
AC 28; **Fortitude** 26, **Reflex** 22, **Will** 23
Immune disease, fear, sleep
Speed 5

⊕ **Slam** (standard; at-will)
　Reach 2; +19 vs. AC; 2d8 + 6 damage.

↗ **Divine Retribution** (immediate reaction, when an enemy attacks the eidolon while *hallowed stance* is active; at-will) ✦ **Radiant**
　Divine radiance strikes the creature that attacked the eidolon: ranged 20, +17 vs. Reflex; 2d8 + 5 radiant damage. *Miss:* Half damage. This attack does not provoke opportunity attacks.

↗ **Vengeful Flames** (immediate reaction, when an enemy kills one of the eidolon's allies in the eidolon's line of sight; at-will) ✦ **Fire**
　Divine fire engulfs the enemy: ranged 20; +17 vs. Reflex; 1d8 +5 fire damage, and ongoing 5 fire (save ends). This attack does not provoke opportunity attacks.

Hallowed Stance (standard; at-will) ✦ **Radiant**
　The eidolon assumes a meditative stance. Until the end of its next turn, the eidolon gains resist 20 to all damage, and all allies in its line of sight deal 1d8 extra radiant damage on their melee attacks. If the eidolon moves, the effect ends.

Alignment Unaligned	**Languages** —	
Str 22 (+12)	**Dex** 14 (+8)	**Wis** 16 (+9)
Con 20 (+11)	**Int** 7 (+4)	**Cha** 11 (+6)

TACTICS

The grimlock berserkers prefer to hack their enemies to death with axes, but they are well aware of the opportunity the ledge over the chasm offers–they begin the battle with a charge and a bull rush against any enemies next to the edge (+13 vs. Fortitude, counting the charge bonus). The grimlocks use *power attack* with abandon unless they have trouble scoring hits. The grimlocks fight to the death.

The eidolon remains in the shrine, assuming its *hallowed stance* (which grants its allies 1d8 extra

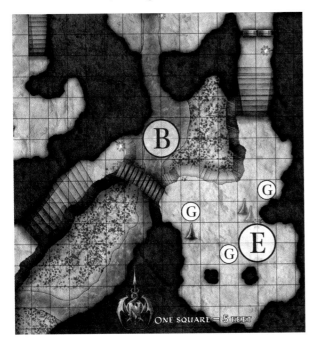

ONE SQUARE = 5 FEET

radiant damage on their melee attacks). It remains in *hallowed stance* until one of the grimlocks falls, using *divine retribution* if attacked or *vengeful flames* when its allies fall. After the first grimlock falls, the eidolon abandons its stance and wades into battle, pummeling enemies. The eidolon fights until it is destroyed.

The beholder hovers out over the chasm, staying out of melee reach of enemies on the ledge and 10 to 20 feet above the level of the ledge. It concentrates its *central eye* and *fire ray* on enemies who are capable of hitting it at range, and it uses its *telekinesis ray* to hurl other foes into the chasm. If the rest of the monsters have been defeated, the beholder retreats once it becomes bloodied, flying up into the higher reaches of the chasm until it is safely out of sight.

FEATURES OF THE AREA

Illumination: *Everburning torches* (shown on the map) provide bright light to a radius of 5 squares.

Waterfall Noise: The sound of the waterfall spilling out into the chasm is loud here. Perception checks made to listen for sounds take a –5 penalty.

Ceiling: The ceiling of the chasm (area 5) is about 200 feet above the ledge. The ceiling of the shrine (area 6) is 20 feet high.

The Chasm: The ledge outside area 6 is 60 feet above the chasm floor. Any creature that falls off the ledge takes 6d10 falling damage. A creature forced over the edge by a push, pull, or slide effect is allowed a saving throw before going over the edge; on a success, the creature falls prone at the edge. The chasm walls are rough (Athletics DC 15 to climb).

Bridges: The bridges are rickety wooden spans that creak under any amount of weight. Small creatures can move across a bridge without difficulty. Medium creatures treat a bridge as difficult terrain. Large creatures must attempt a DC 15 Acrobatics check to cross. A bridge has AC 4, Fortitude 12, Reflex 4, and 20 hit points.

Debris: The chasm floor is littered with broken rock and heavy rubble. It counts as difficult terrain.

Stream: The stream is only 2 feet deep, but the bottom is slippery; it counts as difficult terrain.

Stalagmites: Stalagmites are difficult terrain. They provide cover to Medium or smaller creatures. Each stalagmite has AC 5, Reflex 5, Fortitude 10, and 40 hit points.

Doors: The iron doors connecting with areas 3 and 4 are not locked. They have AC 5, Fortitude 10, Reflex 5, and 60 hit points.

DEVELOPMENT

If the beholder survives the fight, it hides near the top of the chasm until it recovers. If the characters leave the mines without slaying the dragon and return later, the beholder is back at its post, guarding the bridges.

VANATHIA'S LAIR

Encounter Level 15 (6,200 XP)

SETUP

1 galeb duhr rockcaller (R)
1 gargoyle harrier (G)
Vanathia, adult adamantine dragon (V)

The doors at area 8 are unlocked; Vanathia's servants come and go at all times, although they're in the habit of knocking respectfully and waiting to be invited inside. The dragon has a good view of the Lower Gate and won't be surprised by anyone entering the room from that direction.

Characters who descend through the secret tunnel (area 7) can surprise the monsters, since Vanathia doesn't expect anyone to enter from that direction, and the other monsters don't know about the tunnel. Allow characters who carefully open the secret door a Stealth check against the dragon's passive Perception (DC 25) to get the drop on her.

When the PCs enter area 9 through the double doors, read:

This grand cavern climbs toward the east in three stepped tiers, separated by steep 10-foot escarpments. The ceiling glitters with luminous crystals, and a small pool feeds a swift stream that flows out through a culvert. An old flagstone pathway leads up to the middle and upper tiers, where the ruins of several small stone buildings stand. Most of the buildings have been reduced to empty, rubble-filled shells.

A dragon with dark, glossy, metallic scales lies at the far end of the cavern, surveying the chamber from the highest ledge. A winged gargoyle crouches near the dragon, attending its master.

Place the dragon and the gargoyle as shown on the map. Don't place the galeb duhr until a character climbs to the second tier of the room or it takes an action, since it's not visible from the entrance of the room.

When the PCs see the galeb duhr, read:

Amid the ruins of the building to the north, a strange rock-creature lurks. It has a roughly humanoid shape but no discernible head—its face is in the center of its stony chest.

If the PCs address the dragon, read:

"Fools!" the dragon hisses. "You dare to invade the domain of Vanathia? Beg for your lives, and I may spare you. Otherwise . . . prepare to die."

Vanathia is willing to allow the characters to surrender, but only if they do so at once. If any character fails to throw down his or her weapon or implement, the dragon attacks.

Vanathia (V)	**Level 14 Solo Soldier**
Adult adamantine dragon	
Large natural magical beast (dragon)	XP 5,000

Initiative +14 **Senses** Perception +16; darkvision
HP 564; **Bloodied** 282; see also *bloodied breath*
AC 30; **Fortitude** 27, **Reflex** 26, **Will** 25
Resist 20 thunder
Saving Throws +5
Speed 8, fly 10 (hover), overland flight 15
Action Points 2

⊕ **Bite** (standard; at-will)
  Reach 2; +19 vs. Reflex; 2d6 + 6 damage, and ongoing 5 damage (save ends).

⊕ **Claw** (standard; at-will)
  Reach 2; +19 vs. Reflex; 1d10 + 6 damage.

↯ **Draconic Fury** (standard; at-will)
  Vanathia makes two claw attacks and then makes a bite attack against a different target.

↯ **Wing Buffet** (immediate reaction when an enemy enters or leaves an adjacent square)
  Reach 2; +19 vs. Fortitude; 1d8 + 6 damage, and the target is knocked prone.

↯ **Tail Snap** (minor action; at-will)
  Reach 2; targets a prone creature; +19 vs. Reflex; 1d10 + 6 damage, and the target is slowed and weakened (save ends both).

↞ **Breath Weapon** (standard; recharge ⚄ ⚅) ✦ **Thunder**
  Close blast 5; +17 vs. Fortitude; 3d8 + 6 thunder damage, and the target is knocked prone. *Miss:* Half damage.

↞ **Bloodied Breath** (free, when first bloodied; encounter)
  Breath weapon recharges, and Vanathia uses it.

↞ **Frightful Presence** (standard; encounter) ✦ **Fear**
  Close burst 5; targets enemies; +17 vs. Will; the target is stunned until the end of Vanathia's next turn. *Aftereffect:* The target takes a -2 penalty to attack rolls (save ends).

Alignment Unaligned	**Languages** Common, Draconic
Skills Insight +16, Intimidate +13	

Str 23 (+13)	**Dex** 21 (+12)	**Wis** 18 (+11)
Con 21 (+12)	**Int** 11 (+7)	**Cha** 12 (+8)

Gargoyle Harrier (G)	**Level 11 Lurker**
Medium elemental humanoid (earth)	XP 600

Initiative +13 **Senses** Perception +13; darkvision
HP 89; **Bloodied** 44
AC 27; **Fortitude** 23, **Reflex** 21, **Will** 21
Immune petrification
Speed 6, fly 8; see also *flyby attack*

⊕ **Claw** (standard; at-will)
  +16 vs. AC; 2d6 + 6 damage.

↯ **Flyby Attack** (standard; recharges after using *stone form*)
  The gargoyle flies up to 8 squares and makes a melee basic attack at any point during the move without provoking an opportunity attack from the target. If the attack hits, the target is knocked prone.

Stone Form (standard; at-will)
  The gargoyle becomes a statue and gains resist 25 to all damage, regeneration 3, and tremorsense 10. It loses all other senses and can take no actions in stone form other than to revert to its normal form (as a minor action).

Alignment Evil	**Languages** Deep Speech, Primordial
Skills Stealth +13	

Str 21 (+10)	**Dex** 17 (+8)	**Wis** 17 (+8)
Con 17 (+8)	**Int** 9 (+4)	**Cha** 17 (+8)

Galeb Duhr Rockcaller (R)	Level 11 Controller
Medium elemental humanoid (earth)	XP 600

Initiative +5   **Senses** Perception +12; tremorsense 10

HP 118; **Bloodied** 59

AC 25; **Fortitude** 26, **Reflex** 21, **Will** 22

Immune petrification, poison

Speed 4 (earth walk), burrow 6

ⓘ **Slam** (standard; at-will)
+16 vs. AC; 2d8 + 4 damage.

↓ **Rolling Attack** (standard; at-will)
The galeb duhr rockcaller moves up to 4 squares and then attacks an adjacent target; +14 vs. Fortitude; 2d8 + 6 damage, and the target is pushed 1 square and knocked prone.

⌁ **Earthen Grasp** (standard; at-will)
An earthen fist rises up to restrain the target. Ranged 10; +14 vs. Fortitude; the target is restrained (save ends). The target must be in direct contact with the ground, or the attack fails. The rockcaller can use *earthen grasp* against only one creature at a time.

⌁ **Rocky Terrain** (minor; at-will)
Ranged 10; up to 4 squares within range become difficult terrain. The squares need not be contiguous, but the affected terrain must consist of earth or stone.

Alignment Unaligned   **Languages** Dwarven, Giant

Skills Stealth +10

Str 19 (+9)	**Dex** 10 (+5)	**Wis** 15 (+7)
Con 22 (+11)	**Int** 13 (+6)	**Cha** 13 (+6)

TACTICS

Vanathia is an aggressive and overly confident combatant. She begins a battle by rushing into the middle of her foes and using her *breath weapon*, and then uses *tail snap* against an enemy on the ground. Then she spends an action point to use *frightful presence*. In the next round, she mauls foes with *draconic fury* and moves to attack the enemy who seems most dangerous to her. She saves her last action point for when her *breath weapon* recharges, so that she can use her *draconic fury* and *breath weapon* in the same round.

If Vanathia is reduced to 100 hit points or fewer, she attempts to flee by the nearest exit, or she surrenders if flight is not possible. If she has to, she'll squeeze to flee up the secret passage.

The gargoyle stays well away from the dragon, harrying any character who tries to hang back out of the fight. It uses *flyby attack* on its first attack, and it retreats to use *stone form* if it becomes bloodied or finds two or more characters attacking it at the same time.

The galeb duhr seeks to hinder characters attacking the dragon in melee. It uses *rocky terrain* to make it difficult for enemies to shift around Vanathia and *earthen grasp* to restrain any defender trying to mark the dragon. It avoids melee until the dragon becomes bloodied or it is attacked directly by enemies.

FEATURES OF THE AREA

Illumination: The luminous crystals of this cavern fill the room with dim light. In addition, *everburning torches* at the locations shown on the map provide bright light in a 5-square radius.

Ceiling: The ceiling of the cavern is 40 feet above the lower portion of the room, 30 feet above the middle portion, and 20 feet above the uppermost portion.

Ruined Walls: Crossing a wall counts as moving into a square of difficult terrain, even if the square on the opposite side is clear. The walls provide cover against attacks that cross the walls.

Stalagmites: Stalagmites are difficult terrain. They provide cover to Medium or smaller creatures. Each stalagmite has AC 5, Reflex 5, Fortitude 10, and 40 hit points.

Escarpment: The escarpments are 10 feet tall (Athletics DC 15 to climb). Any creature pushed off an escarpment takes 1d10 damage from the fall.

Pool: The pool is 5 feet deep. It counts as difficult terrain.

Doors: The iron double doors leading to area 8 are not locked. They have AC 5, Fortitude 10, Reflex 5, and 60 hit points.

TREASURE

Vanathia's hoard lies in the intact stone building in the southeast corner of this cavern (area 10). For details, see page 110.

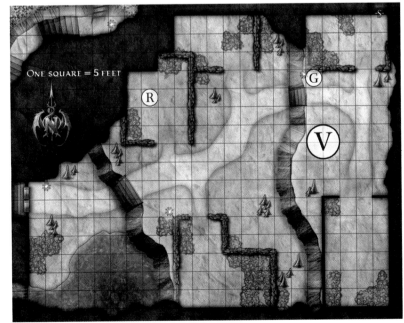

ONE SQUARE = 5 FEET

Bronze dragon lair for five 13th-level adventurers

Off the coast of the great Aelathric Ocean, near the Bay of Fins and the multitude of small port towns that line its shores, stands an array of small islands and protruding reefs. Tiny fishing villages, communities that trade their catch with the citizens of the larger towns on shore or the merchants who pass by in their galleons, inhabit some of them.

Others are inhabited by dwellers far less friendly.

Here, the dangers to passing ships go far beyond hidden sandbars and daggerlike reefs waiting to gouge the hulls of unsuspecting ships. For it is here, in a deep grotto on one of these isles, that a savage pack of sahuagin make their home—and here, too, dwells Xyphreneus, the bronze dragon who rules them.

Background

History DC 11: A few years ago, Xyphreneus, a bronze dragon, expanded his territory across portions of the coast and the Aelathric Ocean, including the Bay of Fins. When he learned of the constant sahuagin raids that had been going on for generations, he decided to take steps.

Not quite, as it turned out, the steps that the people of the surrounding communities might have hoped for.

With a few swift shows of strength (and of the consequences for those that disobeyed), Xyphreneus usurped command of the sahuagin tribe. The sahuagin baron, Uvokula, has managed to save face by claiming he has taken on Xyphreneus as a partner, a fellow predator who has seen the wisdom in the ways of Sekolah the shark god.

Today, the sahuagin tribe does not conduct random raids on villages and ships. Rather, it has become Xyphreneus's tax collector, levying tribute from every citizen, every town, every passing ship. After all, as the dragon sees it, he's performing a service, preventing the sahuagin from engaging in their bloody raids. The least the locals can do is show their appreciation and make it worth his while. And as for those who don't? Well, if they won't pay for the service, he's hardly going to keep the sahuagin from attacking them, is he?

The result is that, although the violence and bloodshed have decreased, the economic damage to the communities in the Bay of Fins is staggering. The villages are already poverty-stricken, and shortages might soon become an issue. What the people here need is someone who can deal with the dragon and the sahuagin both . . .

History DC 18: For as long as humans and halflings have dwelt on the Bay of Fins, they have had to suffer the depredations of the sahuagin, as well as the giant sharks they use as mounts and hunting animals. The earliest communities here were wiped out entirely, slain to the last individual. But as the Empire of Nerath grew, the Bay of Fins became ever more important to seaborne traffic, and ever larger towns sprung up around it. Before long, the land-dwellers greatly outnumbered the sea devils; the sahuagin attacks changed from wars of extermination to hit-and-run raids, intended to steal valuables and carry off handfuls of citizens as food, as blood sacrifices to their shark god, or both. And if the humans and halflings were too numerous for the sahuagin to pose a terminal threat, so were the sahuagin too stealthy and too brutal for the land-dwellers to defeat.

The result was a peculiar equilibrium. This isn't to say that the local magistrates and militias were happy about losing citizens to the sea devils. They took what steps they could to impede the sahuagin, but the occasional raids and fatalities were accepted as a risk of dwelling in the area; one might as well rail against the weather as expect the sahuagin to relent. On rare occasions, the sahuagin sent a few of their number to trade with the locals for goods they could not acquire in their raids, and the people—though often simmering with anger over those they lost—knew better than to attack those emissaries, lest the sahuagin retaliate with attacks far more fearsome than those that had come before. And so it went, for generations uncounted.

Environment

The waters around the chain of islands (outside the area depicted on the map) are rough, requiring a DC 15 Athletics check to swim. The tidal currents around and between the islands all have a strength of 3 squares, the direction depending on whether the tide is going out (flowing north) or coming in (flowing south). (See "Aquatic Combat," *DMG* 45.) Ledges and rocky outcrops on the isles are slippery, requiring a DC 25 Athletics check to climb.

Most of the sahuagin tribe is elsewhere, not within the grotto that contains the dragon's lair. As the characters search the island chains for the grotto, they might have additional encounters with sahuagin (*MM* 224), war sharks (see the statistics block on page 120), or a few citizens of the island-based fishing villages who worry that the characters will only antagonize the dragon and make matters worse.

As the PCs approach the grotto entrance, read:
Almost invisible behind a veil of chopping waves and the occasional jagged outcropping, a wide cave entrance gapes open, leading into the darkened interior of the stony isle.

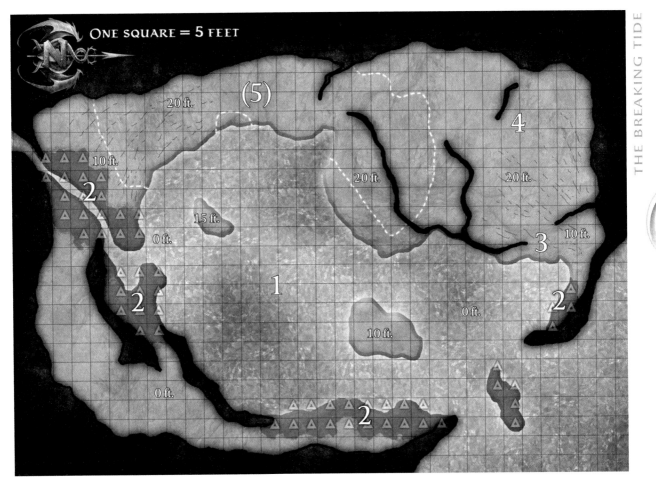

ONE SQUARE = 5 FEET

AREA 1: THE INLET

About half the area in and around the lair is aquatic, taking the form of an inlet that provides access to the caverns along the shore. The water here is deep and the tide strong (as potent as it is outside the grotto). The former leaders of the sahuagin tribe dwell here, eager to take out their frustrations on intruders.

Tactical Encounter: "Feeding Frenzy," page 120.

AREA 2: THE SHORES

The edges of the earth in these areas of the caverns are waterlogged, with layers of pebbles above soft and shifting sands. Although these areas offer a way to reach the higher ground deeper inside the grotto, the soggy terrain makes travel slow and difficult.

Tactical Encounter: "Feeding Frenzy," page 120, or "On the Rocks," page 122.

AREA 3: ROCKY SLOPES

Other than climbing the slippery, sheer sides of the cliffs that border most of the inlet, the only way to get up to the cavern's higher levels is by ascending these steep slopes. The rock in and around the areas marked 3 on the map is challenging terrain, requiring a character to make a DC 18 Athletics check in order t move across it in either direction.

Tactical Encounter: "Feeding Frenzy," page 120, or "On the Rocks," page 122.

AREA 4: XYPHRENEUS'S LAIR

This cavern, 20 feet above the water level and separated from the rest of the grotto by several thin but strong rock walls, is the home of the bronze dragon.

Treasure: Xyphreneus's lair contains wealth and magic items equivalent to one level 14 treasure parcel and half of another one.

Tactical Encounter: "On the Rocks," page 122.

AREA 5: THE CAVERN BELOW

This cavern, smaller than the one that houses Xyphreneus, is the home of the dragon's lieutenant–a dragonborn raider–as well as the sahuagin leaders, when they're not in the water. This cave runs beneath a portion of the dragon's lair and under the ledge leading from the southern slope up to the lair. The entrance is marked by the semicircle of dashed lines between the two other sets of dashed lines that describe the northern and southern edges of the area.

Treasure: The cave contains wealth equivalent to half of a level 14 treasure parcel, partly on the floor and partly on the person of the dragonborn.

Tactical Encounter: "On the Rocks," page 122.

JASON A. ENGLE

Feeding Frenzy

Encounter Level 14 (5,000 XP)

Note: The XP value for this encounter is slightly higher than normal, due to the aquatic environment, which greatly favors the monsters.

Setup

2 Aelathric sahuagin priests (P)
Uvokula, sahuagin baron (U)
1 war shark (W)

Moving into the grotto is hard enough, given the tides and the various rocky isles. It becomes harder once the leaders of the sahuagin tribe engage the characters with the full intent of slaughtering them and then consuming the flesh from their bones. In fact, they'll probably eat the bones, too.

The following descriptions assume that the characters are using boats or other aquatic vessels. If they're swimming, flying, or riding aquatic or aerial mounts, adjust the information accordingly.

When the PCs enter the cave, read:
The choppy waters swirl around you, waves rebounding off the stone wall and tides threatening to yank and spin your boat this way and that. Jagged reefs and small isles protrude from the dark sea, threatening to stave in the side of your vessel with the slightest contact. Great walls of stone rise up to either side, coated with ocean salt and bouncing echoes in all directions.

Perception Check
DC 26 (or 21 if the PCs are underwater) *Barely visible beneath the violent waters, you catch a glimpse of a dark-scaled creature, humanoid yet inhuman, moving swiftly toward your hull.*
DC 27 (or 22 if the PCs are underwater) *Beyond them, a third creature–larger, with four gaunt arms and grasping claws–rises from the darkened depths.*
DC 29 (or 24 if the PCs are underwater) *What at first seemed to be an undersea boulder suddenly moves, its body twisting sharply and cutting through the sea in your direction. A dorsal fin slicing the surface of the water like a blade is all the evidence you need that the beast must be a shark of prodigious size.*

Tactics

The sahuagin and the shark move to attack, leaving their starting points, once the characters have moved a reasonable distance into the grotto. (Assume they attack once the characters move to the east or west side of the large island. If, however, the characters attempt to moor their boat to the shore or climb up onto land before reaching either of those points, the monsters move in to attack anyway.)

2 Aelathric Sahuagin Priests (P)	Level 13 Artillery
Medium natural humanoid (aquatic)	XP 800 each

Initiative +11   **Senses** Perception +12; low-light vision
HP 102; **Bloodied** 51
AC 25; **Fortitude** 24, **Reflex** 25, **Will** 26
Speed 6, swim 8
⊕ **Trident** (standard; at-will) ✦ **Weapon**
    +18 vs. AC; 1d8 + 6 damage.
↗ **Trident** (standard; at-will) ✦ **Weapon**
    Ranged 3/6; +20 vs. AC; 2d8 + 6 damage. The sahuagin priest must retrieve its trident before it can throw it again.
↗ **Water Bolt** (standard; at-will)
    Ranged 10 (20 while in water); +20 vs. AC; 2d6 + 4 damage (3d6 + 6 while in water).
↗ **Spectral Jaws** (standard; recharges when a target saves against this effect)
    Ranged 20; spectral shark jaws appear and bite the target; +18 vs. Will; 3d8 + 4 damage, and the target takes ongoing 5 damage and a –2 penalty to all defenses (save ends both).
Blood Frenzy
    A sahuagin gains a +1 bonus to attack rolls and a +2 bonus to damage rolls against bloodied enemies.
Alignment Chaotic evil   **Languages** Abyssal, Common
Skills Intimidate +15
Str 18 (+10)   **Dex** 20 (+11)   **Wis** 22 (+12)
Con 18 (+10)   **Int** 13 (+7)   **Cha** 18 (+10)
Equipment trident, holy symbol, kelp robe

Uvokula (U)	Level 14 Elite Brute (Leader)
Large natural humanoid (aquatic)	XP 2,000

Initiative +12   **Senses** Perception +9; low-light vision
Blood Healing (Healing) aura 10; each ally within the aura that starts its turn adjacent to a bloodied enemy regains 5 hit points.
HP 340; **Bloodied** 170
AC 26; **Fortitude** 28, **Reflex** 26, **Will** 25
Saving Throws +2
Speed 6, swim 8
Action Points 1
⊕ **Trident** (standard; at-will) ✦ **Weapon**
    Reach 2; +17 vs. AC; 3d4 + 4 damage.
⊕ **Claw** (standard; at-will)
    Reach 2; +17 vs. AC; 1d6 + 3 damage, and ongoing 5 damage (save ends).
↗ **Trident** (standard; at-will) ✦ **Weapon**
    Ranged 3/6; +17 vs. AC; 3d4 + 4 damage. Uvokula must retrieve his trident before he can throw it again.
✦ **Baron's Fury** (standard; at-will)
    Uvokula makes a trident attack and two claw attacks.
Blood Hunger
    Uvokula gains a +2 bonus to attack rolls and a +5 bonus to damage rolls against bloodied enemies.
Alignment Chaotic evil   **Languages** Abyssal, Common
Skills Intimidate +16
Str 24 (+14)   **Dex** 20 (+12)   **Wis** 14 (+9)
Con 20 (+12)   **Int** 14 (+9)   **Cha** 18 (+11)
Equipment trident, headdress

The priests remain at a distance, lobbing ranged attacks at the characters. They prefer to focus on obvious ranged combatants, allowing Uvokula and the shark to deal with the party's front-liners.

Uvokula attempts to drag or knock foes into the water, where he has the advantage. If doing this proves impossible, he makes melee attacks against characters in a boat or on the shore.

War Shark (W)	Level 14 Skirmisher
Large natural beast (aquatic, mount)	XP 1,000

Initiative +16   **Senses** Perception +9
HP 139; **Bloodied** 69
AC 28; **Fortitude** 26, **Reflex** 28, **Will** 23
Speed swim 11

⊕ **Bite** (standard; at-will)
+17 vs. AC; 3d6 + 5 damage.

Deft Swimmer (while mounted by a friendly rider of 14th level or
   higher; at-will) ✦ **Mount**
   The war shark's rider gains a +2 bonus to AC against
   opportunity attacks. While in water, the rider also gains a +2
   bonus to attack rolls against creatures without a swim speed.

Waterborn
   While in water, a war shark gains a +2 bonus to attack rolls
   against creatures without a swim speed.

Alignment Unaligned		**Languages** –
Str 21 (+12)	**Dex** 24 (+14)	**Wis** 14 (+9)
Con 19 (+11)	**Int** 2 (+3)	**Cha** 9 (+6)

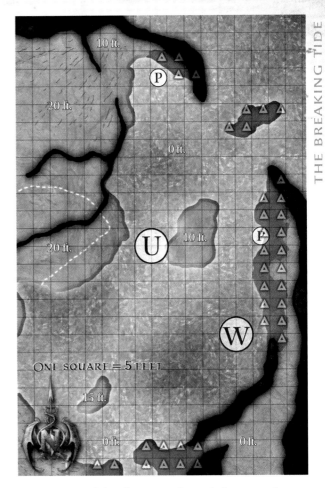

Uvokula prefers to keep close enough to his allies
for his *blood healing* aura to benefit them, but he does
not give up any tactical advantage, or retreat from
melee, to do so.

All three of the sahuagin fight to the death.

The shark goes after any character in the water,
preferring wounded targets over those who have not
been damaged by the sahugain.

The shark attempts to flee if the sahuagin are dead
and it is reduced to 34 or fewer hit points.

FEATURES OF THE AREA

Illumination: The grotto is dimly lit, by sunlight
coming in through the opening and by phosphorescent fungi along the rocks and the walls.

Ceiling: The ceiling of the grotto stands 70 feet
overhead.

Current: The current pushes each creature and
object in or on the water 3 squares at the start of its
turn, unless they spend movement to prevent it. (See
"Aquatic Combat," *DMG* 45.) The boat moves on its

pilot's turn. (If the characters haven't designated a
pilot, have them do so at the start of combat.) The
current moves either north or south, as you choose,
for the duration of the encounter. A creature or object
pushed up against the shoreline inside the grotto
stops moving in the square adjacent to the shore.

Echoes and Waves: Due to the ambient sounds
of water inside the cavern, all creatures take a –2 penalty to Perception checks to listen.

Island Reefs: If the characters' boat is pushed into
one of the islands, either by a bull rush or by the tidal
currents, roll a +14 attack against the boat's AC of 26.
On a hit, the hull is damaged, and the boat begins
to sink. The process takes 1d4 + 1 rounds, at which
point, if they have not already climbed onto land, the
characters find themselves in the water.

Cliffs: It requires a DC 23 Athletics check to
climb any of the cliffs at the water's edge.

Sandy Shores: Areas of wet sand on the shoreline (marked with triangles on the map) are difficult
terrain.

Stone Outcrops: Blackened areas on the map are
upthrust stone that blocks line of sight and serves as
impassable terrain.

Water: The water is rough (DC 15 to swim), due
to the waves and currents. The water is 10 to 15 feet
deep along the shores, but it swiftly drops off to as
deep as 90 feet near the cave entrance.

RAMMING THE BOAT

Uvokula or the war shark might attempt to ram any vessel
the characters occupy. Treat this as a bull rush attack
against the Fortitude defense of each character in the
boat, and against AC 26 for the boat (roll once for each
character and again for the boat, as though it were an
area attack). If the boat is hit, it moves 1 square, as with a
normal bull rush. This movement might cause the boat to
beach itself on one of the low-lying patches of wet sand.
It might also push the boat into one of the island reefs
(see "Features of the Area"). A character who is hit must
make a saving throw. Those who save are knocked prone
in the boat; those who fail the saving throw are knocked
overboard into the water. A character who is already
prone inside the boat does not risk falling overboard
during such an attack.

On the Rocks

Encounter Level 15 (6,675 XP)

Setup

1 dragonborn raider (D)
5 Aelathric sahuagin guards (S)
Xyphreneus, adult bronze dragon (X)

Once the characters emerge from the waters and begin exploring, it's only a matter of time before they encounter the draconic master of the sahuagin band—and unless they've come to offer great riches in tribute, he's not especially pleased to see them.

The read-aloud text below assumes that the characters first encounter each creature at its starting point as indicated on the map, but this won't always be the case. Modify your descriptions accordingly.

When the PCs first land on any area 2, read:
The soft sand squelches out from beneath your feet. Beyond, the earth appears firmer, the rocks—and the footing—more steady.

When the PCs approach any area 3, read:
A slope rises ahead; it looks slick, but not too hard to traverse. Beyond, stretches of rocky floor lead to several caves.

When the PCs enter area 4, read:
Atop the slopes stands a cavern, divided into several smaller chambers by winding walls of natural, water-carved stone. Beyond the scent of the ocean, you can make out a musky odor, faintly reptilian in nature.

As your eyes adjust, you spot something moving deep in the darkness of the cave, something with a long, sinuous neck and unfolding wings.

In a voice that sounds like the crashing of the waves against unyielding rock, the great beast speaks. "I am Xyphreneus. I trust you have come to offer me proper tribute."

When the PCs approach area 5, read:
An opening in the cliff wall leads beneath the ledges on the western side of the grotto.

When the PCs enter area 5, read:
The cavern under the grotto smells strongly of fish. In the shadows, several scaled humanoids similar to those who attacked you in the water glare in your direction.

Perception Check
DC 26 *Another figure, covered not in fishlike scales but reptilian ones of glossy black, creeps toward you, a dagger clutched in each clawed hand.*

Tactics

The dragonborn and the sahuagin attack as soon as they see the characters, unless the characters are

---

Xyphreneus (X)	Level 14 Solo Brute (Leader)
Adult bronze dragon	
Large natural magical beast (aquatic, dragon)	XP 5,000

Initiative +12   **Senses** Perception +13; darkvision
HP 507; **Bloodied** 253; see also *bloodied breath*
AC 26; **Fortitude** 28, **Reflex** 25, **Will** 25
Resist 20 lightning
Saving Throws +5
Speed 6, fly 8 (hover), overland flight 10, swim 6
Action Points 2

⊕ **Bite** (standard; at-will) ✦ **Lightning**
Reach 2; +17 vs. AC; 2d8 + 8 damage plus 3d6 lightning damage.

⊕ **Claw** (standard; at-will)
Reach 2; +17 vs. AC; 2d8 + 10 damage.

⊣ **Double Attack** (standard; at-will)
Xyphreneus makes two claw attacks.

⬅ **Breath Weapon** (standard; recharge ⚄ ⚅) ✦ **Lightning**
Close blast 3; +15 vs. Reflex; 3d8 + 5 lightning damage, and Xyphreneus pushes the target 2 squares. If the attack hit at least one target, Xyphreneus makes a secondary attack against a creature within 10 squares that was not a target of the primary attack. *Miss:* Half damage. *Secondary Attack:* +15 vs. Reflex; 2d10 + 5 lightning damage, and Xyphreneus pushes the target 1 square.

⬅ **Bloodied Breath** (free, when first bloodied; encounter)
Breath weapon recharges, and Xyphreneus uses it.

⬅ **Frightful Presence** (standard; encounter) ✦ **Fear**
Close burst 5; targets enemies; +13 vs. Will; the target is stunned until the end of Xyphreneus's next turn. *Aftereffect:* The target takes a -2 penalty to attack rolls (save ends).

Xyphreneus's Command (immediate reaction, when an enemy moves adjacent to an ally; at-will)
The ally can make a melee basic attack against the triggering creature and then shift 1 square.

Restorative Dive (minor; while bloodied and completely submerged in water; encounter) ✦ **Healing**
Xyphreneus regains 120 hit points, and each ally in water within 5 squares regains 20 hit points.

Alignment Unaligned	**Languages** Common, Draconic
Skills History +13, Intimidate +16	
Str 26 (+15)	**Dex** 21 (+12)	**Wis** 13 (+8)
Con 21 (+12)	**Int** 12 (+8)	**Cha** 20 (+12)

Two Fights or One

This encounter unfolds in one of two ways, depending on what happens first.

If the characters enter area 5 before meeting Xyphreneus, then they find the dragonborn and the sahuagin in their positions as indicated on the map, and combat takes place between the two groups. (When the characters resolve this battle, they should realize that there's still a dragon to be dealt with somewhere in the grotto.)

If the characters find the lair and confront Xyphreneus before entering area 5, the dragon lets out a roar that brings the dragonborn and the sahuagin running. At the start of the fourth round after the characters begin conversing or fighting with Xyphreneus, two of the other creatures enter the lair through the southern opening and join the fray. Two more appear in the fifth round and the final two a round later.

Regardless of the order of events, the encounter isn't over until all the monsters are dealt with.

Dragonborn Raider (D) — Level 13 Skirmisher

Medium natural humanoid — XP 800

Initiative +13   **Senses** Perception +13

HP 129; **Bloodied** 64; see also *dragonborn fury*

AC 27; **Fortitude** 23, **Reflex** 24, **Will** 21

Speed 7

⊕ **Katar** (standard; at-will) ✦ **Weapon**

+19 vs. AC (+20 while bloodied); 1d6 + 4 damage (crit 2d6 + 10).

↓ **Twin Katar Strike** (standard; at-will)

If the dragonborn raider doesn't take a move action on its turn, it shifts 1 square and makes two katar attacks, or vice versa.

⟵ **Dragon Breath** (minor; encounter) ✦ **Acid**

Close blast 3; +14 vs. Reflex (+15 while bloodied); 1d6 + 3 acid damage.

Combat Advantage

A dragonborn raider deals 1d6 extra damage against any creature granting combat advantage to it.

Dragonborn Fury (only while bloodied)

A dragonborn gains a +1 racial bonus to attack rolls.

Infiltrating Stride (move; recharges after the dragonborn raider attacks two different enemies with *twin katar strike*)

The dragonborn raider shifts 3 squares.

Alignment Unaligned   **Languages** Common, Draconic

Skills History +8, Intimidate +9, Stealth +16

Str 18 (+10)	**Dex** 21 (+11)	**Wis** 14 (+8)
Con 17 (+9)	**Int** 10 (+6)	**Cha** 12 (+7)

Equipment leather armor, 2 katars

5 Aelathric Sahuagin Guards (S) — Level 12 Minion

Medium natural humanoid (aquatic) — XP 175 each

Initiative +9   **Senses** Perception +8; low-light vision

HP 1; a missed attack never damages a minion.

AC 26; **Fortitude** 24, **Reflex** 23, **Will** 22

Speed 6, swim 6

⊕ **Trident** (standard; at-will) ✦ **Weapon**

+17 vs. AC; 6 damage.

↗ **Trident** (standard; at-will) ✦ **Weapon**

Ranged 3/6; +17 vs. AC; 6 damage. The sahuagin guard must retrieve its trident before it can throw it again.

Blood Frenzy

A sahuagin gains a +1 bonus to attack rolls and a +2 bonus to damage rolls against bloodied enemies.

Alignment Chaotic evil   **Languages** Abyssal, Common

Str 22 (+12)	**Dex** 17 (+9)	**Wis** 14 (+8)
Con 20 (+11)	**Int** 10 (+6)	**Cha** 12 (+7)

Equipment trident

conversing with the dragon. Once Xyphreneus attacks, the other creatures engage in combat. They fight to the death while Xyphreneus lives, but if the dragon is slain and they are bloodied, they attempt to escape.

Unless the characters try to offer Xyphreneus tribute (which might require a skill challenge), he grows irritated that they've bothered him (not to mention that they've slain some of his most potent servants, if they visited area 5 first) and attacks.

Xyphreneus prefers to engage in melee, opening with a breath attack and *frightful presence* (using an action point to do both in the same round), and then making claw, bite, and *wing smash* attacks until his *breath weapon* recharges. If more complex tactics are necessary, he circles through the cavern to attack from multiple angles, or else grabbing foes, moving over the water, and dropping them or diving in.

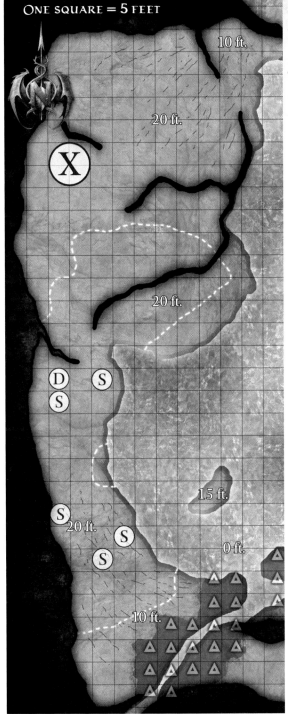

ONE SQUARE = 5 FEET

Xyphreneus is proud and refuses to accept defeat. Only if all his allies are slain and he is reduced to fewer than 40 hit points does he try to escape.

FEATURES OF THE AREA

Illumination: Dim light from phosphorescent fungi along the rocks and the walls.

Ceiling: The ceiling inside area 5 is 15 feet tall.

Stone Outcrops: The blackened areas in and around Xyphreneus's lair are upthrust stone that blocks line of sight and serves as impassable terrain.

Other Features: See the previous encounter.

METHENAERA THE MEAD-KEEPER

Silver dragon lair for five 18th-level adventurers

Twelve casks of mead—a gift from the dwarven deity Moradin—once filled the hoard of the ancestors of the elder silver dragon Methenaera. Anyone who drank it saw visions of the future. Methenaera's line kept the mead safe for centuries.

Two casks remain. Methenaera will grant them only to seekers she deems worthy of drinking this elixir of deities.

BACKGROUND

History DC 20: After the defeat of the primordials in their war against the gods, Moradin spent time in the northern mountains, constructing a fortress of polar ice. He befriended the local silver dragons, including Methenaera's ancestors, that loved his mead. In time, Moradin tired of the snow and, leaving casks of the mead as a gift to the dragons, returned to his dominion in the Astral Sea.

Centuries of blizzards transformed Moradin's ice fortress into a glacier indistinguishable from other glaciers in the mountain range. The dragons tapped the casks only when they needed prophetic power.

During the fall of Nerath, powerful heroes traveled north in search of Methenaera's mother and the casks, hoping to find a way to forestall the empire's collapse. Those who drank from the casks saw the future and returned to their ruined homes, sadder and wiser.

After the empire's fall, few sought the casks. Methenaera guards the last two, waiting for the day when she might honor Moradin and her ancestors by ensuring that the last of the mead goes toward a worthy cause.

HOOK: DRINK OF METHENAERA'S MEAD

When the characters search for clues about their ongoing quests, they can learn about Methenaera and the mead casks and then seek the mead for assistance. As they discover (if they find Methenaera and gain her trust or at least her cooperation), the mead serves as a component in prophetic rituals known by Moradin's high priests. Who better to fetch the casks from Methenaera than the adventurers? Other uses for the mead might develop as your storyline proceeds.

Quest XP: 2,000 XP (minor quest).

HOOK: THE ROLL OF CLAIMS

In addition to the remaining casks of mead, Methenaera maintains a chronicle of all who have claimed casks of mead in the past. Her ancestors passed down a scroll called the Roll of Claims, which identifies each person or group that claimed a cask of mead and gives the reason each sought the mead, a brief personal history, and the destination where the recipient was planning to go.

The character who takes on this minor quest might be seeking information about a hero from ages past. A more self-serving character might want to add his or her name to the list simply to gain more fame or greater pride.

Quest XP: 2,000 XP (minor quest).

METHENAERA, THE MEAD-KEEPER

Like the other dragons of her line, Methenaera worships Moradin above all other gods. She honors the wishes of her ancestors, who personally knew the god and drank his mead when it was still plentiful. Over the years, the casks have diminished in number as worthy crusaders have come seeking the mead's prophetic visions. Methenaera compels herself to live up to her family's legacy. The greatest shame she could suffer would be letting evil or meek creatures drink from the mead. The silver dragon's test of combat guarantees that any people who comes to collect will prove their dedication with blood.

After dwelling in her lonely cave for so long, Methenaera has little talent for conversation and no tolerance at all for idle chatter. When she does speak, her voice is stern, bordering on aggressive (at least when she's talking to those she hasn't yet fought). She peppers her speech with references to Moradin and invokes his name for success in battle.

Methenaera creates formations of ice crystals with her breath, and these creations jut up from the floor of her cave. Forming these abstract shapes is both a way to pass the time and a way to worship Moradin as the god of creation.

Environment

A journey to Methenaera's cave by land begins in the logging town of Nordkell, about a hundred miles south of the cave. Characters must contend with winding mountain roads, bad weather (snowstorms and blizzards, even in the summer), and a monster-infested landscape.

For those seeking to use magic to reach Methenaera's cave, the nearest teleportation circle is in Himmerdun, a dwarven fortress about fifty miles south of the cave. The dwarves have trained hippogriffs that can fly through the mountains in good weather.

Frost Giants: A clan of frost giants knows of the legend of Moradin's mead and would love to find the cave entrance. They have seen Methenaera flying at a distance, but she stays far enough away from them that they have not attacked her.

Moradin's Ice Fortress: One of the dozens of glaciers within a few leagues of Methenaera's cave is Moradin's fortress. Avalanches, blizzards, and the accumulation of ice have worn away the spires and battlements and covered the entrances. Interior chambers remain intact.

Who knows what ancient treasure—and guardians—the fortress might contain? Methenaera wants access; she might send the characters on a quest to find and map the fortress, which could help to convince her that the characters are worthy to drink the mead.

Cave Entrance: Methenaera's cave entrance, covered with a crust of snow, is barely wide enough for the silver dragon to squeeze through. It lies at the edge of a snow-covered alpine meadow.

Ice Stream: A cold stream from a spring higher up the mountain runs underneath the snow and into the cave. Within the cave, a thin sheet of ice covers the stream, which meanders through the upper chamber before dropping down a chute to emerge farther down the mountain.

Area 1: Upper Chamber

Four ice archons have served Methenaera's line of dragons since Moradin left for his dominion. The archons guard this chamber. They rest within the two black obelisks on the chamber floor.

Tactical Encounter: "Upper Chamber," page 126.

Area 2: Lower Chamber

When she is not soaring over the mountains and surveying glaciers in a search for intruders or food, Methenaera sleeps in the northern part of the lower chamber, curled around the two casks of mead.

Tactical Encounter: "Lower Chamber," page 128.

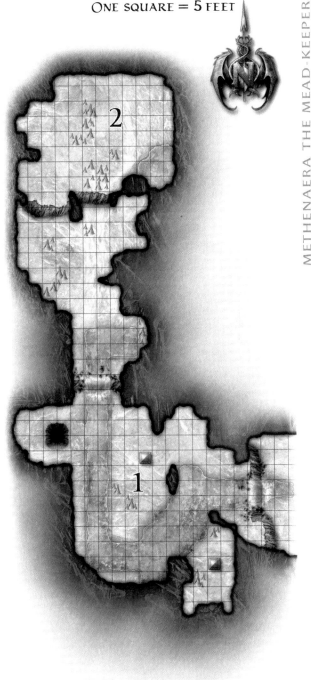

JASON A. ENGLE

Upper Chamber

Encounter Level 17 (9,000 XP)

Setup

1 ice archon frostshaper (F)
1 ice archon hailscourge (H)
2 ice archon rimehammers (R)

Before the characters reach Methenaera, they must contend with her ice archons.

When the PCs reach the cave entrance, read:
You enter the cave and stop at the edge of a 20-foot cliff. The stream pours down the cliff face and continues below, to the northwest. The irregularly shaped cave is about 70 feet long and nearly as wide. Rock protrusions block parts of the cave from view.

In the middle of the cave floor, a black stone obelisk glows briefly. Two dark-armored creatures made of living ice and wielding massive mauls appear and move slowly toward you.

Perception Check
DC 20 *In a reflection on an icicle, you see a dark shape around the corner to your left—perhaps another obelisk?*

The dark shape is a second obelisk—one that's producing a frostshaper and a hailscourge.

Arcana Check
DC 20 *Calling upon a sliver of knowledge from your memory, you discern that the obelisks are directly associated with the guardian creatures they spawn. It's possible that you can dismiss the creatures by ruining the obelisks.*

2 Ice Archon Rimehammers (R)	Level 19 Soldier
Medium elemental humanoid (cold)	XP 2,400 each

Initiative +15   **Senses** Perception +12
Icy Ground (Cold) aura 1; enemies treat squares within the aura as difficult terrain.
HP 185; **Bloodied** 92
AC 35; **Fortitude** 35, **Reflex** 32, **Will** 31
Immune disease, poison; **Resist** 30 cold
Speed 6 (ice walk)
⊕ **Maul** (standard; at-will) ✦ **Cold, Weapon**
   +25 vs. AC; 2d6 + 7 damage plus 1d6 cold damage, and the target is slowed (save ends). Against a slowed target, the ice archon rimehammer deals 2d6 extra cold damage.

Alignment Chaotic evil	**Languages** Primordial

Str 24 (+16)   **Dex** 18 (+13)   **Wis** 16 (+12)
Con 25 (+16)   **Int** 14 (+11)   **Cha** 15 (+11)
Equipment plate armor, maul

Ice Archon Frostshaper (F) Level 20 Controller (Leader)	
Medium elemental humanoid (cold)	XP 2,800

Initiative +14   **Senses** Perception +14
Icy Aura (Cold) aura 5 (while not bloodied); cold creatures within the aura gain regeneration 10. Enemies treat the squares within the aura as difficult terrain.
HP 190; **Bloodied** 95
AC 34; **Fortitude** 32, **Reflex** 28, **Will** 32
Immune disease, poison; **Resist** 30 cold
Speed 6 (ice walk)
⊕ **Ice Blade** (standard; at-will) ✦ **Cold, Weapon**
   +23 vs. AC; 2d6 + 8 cold damage.
↗ **Ice Javelin** (standard; at-will) ✦ **Cold, Weapon**
   Ranged 5; +23 vs. AC; 2d6 + 8 cold damage, and the target is slowed until the end of the ice archon frostshaper's next turn.
❄ **Icy Burst** (standard; recharges when the ice archon frostshaper hits with a melee attack) ✦ **Cold**
   Area burst 1 within 5; +23 vs. AC; 3d8 + 8 cold damage, and the target is slowed (save ends). *Miss:* Half damage, and the target is not slowed.

Alignment Chaotic evil	**Languages** Primordial
Skills Intimidate +23	

Str 26 (+18)   **Dex** 19 (+14)   **Wis** 18 (+14)
Con 22 (+16)   **Int** 14 (+12)   **Cha** 27 (+18)

Ice Archon Hailscourge (H)	Level 16 Artillery
Medium elemental humanoid (cold)	XP 1,400

Initiative +11   **Senses** Perception +10
HP 120; **Bloodied** 60
AC 30; **Fortitude** 28, **Reflex** 27, **Will** 26
Immune disease, poison; **Resist** 20 cold
Speed 6 (ice walk)
⊕ **Slam** (standard; at-will) ✦ **Cold**
   +19 vs. AC; 1d6 + 4 cold damage.
↗ **Ice Shuriken** (standard; at-will) ✦ **Cold**
   Ranged 6/12; +21 vs. AC; 1d6 + 4 damage plus 1d6 cold damage.
↗ **Double Attack** (standard; at-will)
   The ice archon hailscourge makes two *ice shuriken* attacks.
❄ **Hail Storm** (standard; recharge ⚃ ⚄) ✦ **Cold**
   Area burst 1, 2, 3, or 4 within 20; +21 vs. AC; 2d8 + 4 cold damage. *Miss:* Half damage. The ice archon hailscourge determines the burst radius.
Frost Shield (immediate interrupt, when attacked by a ranged, close, or area attack; encounter) ✦ **Cold**
   The ice archon hailscourge gains resist 20 to all damage against the triggering attack.

Alignment Chaotic evil	**Languages** Primordial

Str 18 (+12)   **Dex** 16 (+11)   **Wis** 14 (+10)
Con 18 (+12)   **Int** 14 (+10)   **Cha** 15 (+10)
Equipment plate armor

Tactics

Only a direct order from Methenaera can call off the ice archons. Because they have ice walk, the archons do not make Acrobatics checks to avoid slipping.

The rimehammers move slowly toward the characters; they would rather fight in the chamber than in the entrance, so they can lure characters onto the ice over the stream. Once engaged in melee, the rimehammers focus their attacks on slowed characters. Knowing the ice is thin, the rimehammers shift every round to avoid breaking through it. Their *icy ground* aura can keep the characters from shifting and puts them at greater risk for falling through the ice.

The frostshaper comes around the corner and drops an *icy burst* on as many characters as possible, even if that means catching other ice archons (which have cold resistance) in the burst. Next, the frost-shaper moves 5 squares behind the rimehammers to envelop them in its *icy aura*. It uses *ice javelins* against characters who are not slowed.

The hailscourge stays near the frostshaper and drops *hail storms* on the characters. (Again, the rimehammers' cold resistance should protect them.) When it cannot use *hail storm*, the hailscourge makes a *double attack*.

Although the archons are of chaotic evil alignment, they don't always behave accordingly (see the section about the obelisks in "Features of the Area").

FEATURES OF THE AREA

Illumination: During the day, the upper chamber has bright light at the top of the cliff and dim light below it, because the icy sheen on the walls is reflective. At night, the chamber is dark.

Obelisks: One of Methenaera's ancestors, after fending off a group of intruders that proved especially troublesome, used a ritual to construct these obelisks and bind a pair of ice archons into each one. The archons appear and attack when anyone not authorized by Methenaera enters the upper chamber. Each obelisk has AC 5, other defenses 10, and 40 hit points. Destroying an obelisk releases the archons

that were bound to it, whereupon those creatures flee out the entryway.

Walls: The cave walls are rough, but omnipresent ice makes climbing difficult. A character attempting to climb the walls must make a DC 25 Athletics check.

Cliffs: The cliffs at the entrance and dividing the upper chamber from the lower chamber are 20 feet high and require a DC 25 Athletics check to ascend or descend.

Thin Ice: The ice-covered stream that runs through the chamber is challenging terrain. When a character enters the first ice square in a turn, the character must succeed on a DC 17 Acrobatics check or fall prone in that square.

In addition, the ice is thin enough to be dangerous. A character who stays in a particular ice square from the start of his or her turn until the end of that turn hears the crack of ice and makes a saving throw. Success results in the character falling prone in an adjacent square as the ice gives way in the square he or she had occupied. On a failed saving throw, a character falls through the ice in his or her location and slides to a randomly determined adjacent square.

The water under the ice is 10 feet deep. A DC 10 Athletics check as a move action allows the character to swim to a square that contains open water. After that, a DC 20 Athletics check as a move action allows the character to climb into an adjacent, unoccupied square.

The stream runs west and then north, cascading from the upper chamber to the lower chamber.

Ice Crystals: To amuse herself in her spare time, Methenaera delicately breathes on the ground to coax jagged and complex ice crystal sculptures from it. Ice crystal stands are difficult terrain and provide cover. Each square of ice crystals has AC 8, other defenses 8, and 3 hit points.

Pit: The pit in the northwest corner is 50 feet deep. The walls are especially icy (Athletics DC 28 to climb). A narrow passage at the bottom of the pit slopes downward and emerges from the mountain a quarter-mile away.

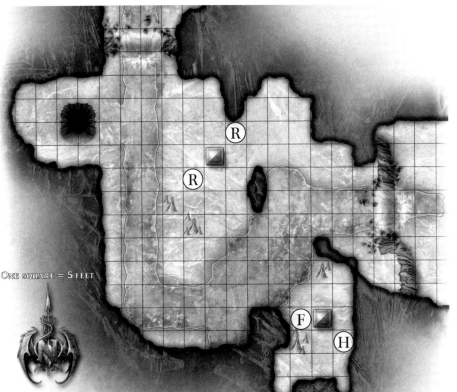

ONE SQUARE = 5 FEET

Lower Chamber

Encounter Level 18 (10,000 XP)

Setup

Methenaera, elder silver dragon (M)

Methenaera wants to fight; even if the characters try diplomacy, a battle ensues. Methenaera fights until bloodied, at which point she offers to surrender a cask of mead. Because this is a subdual encounter (described on page 49), Methenaera is the equivalent of an 18th-level adversary, and the encounter is worth a corresponding amount of XP.

When the PCs reach the point where the stream seeps into crevices in the wall, read:

The cavern seems to be at least 100 feet long. You can tell that the northern part has a lower floor, because you cannot see the floor of that part from where you stand. The near part of the cavern is empty except for stands of ice crystals.

An immense silver dragon rises into view in the northern end of the chamber.

"You have come for the casks of mead so potent it quenches the thirst of a deity," says the dragon. "I, Methenaera, do not surrender them meekly. Prove your worthiness in battle, or perish."

Tactics

Because this is a subdual encounter, Methenaera is effectively a creature with 525 hit points. Show off a variety of powers and tactics quickly to give the characters a full display of her draconic power in the short time they'll be fighting her.

Methenaera opens with a *breath weapon* attack against as many characters as possible. She uses this power in combination with *Methenaera's onslaught* and plays a game of cat and mouse while she's waiting for these powers to recharge.

Methenaera uses *Methenaera's onslaught* as often as she can, usually targeting characters who have vulnerable 10 to all damage thanks to her *breath weapon*.

If neither of her main two attacks has recharged, Methenaera strikes at one enemy, then flies to the north or south part of the chamber. She lets the characters contend with the cliff and the ice crystals, and counts on her *threatening reach* to keep melee combatants at bay. If she's fighting against a powerful ranged attacker, she flies to within 2 squares of that character and attacks it with *tail slam*.

Methenaera uses *frightful presence* early, as soon as characters flank her or otherwise hem her in. After she uses *frightful presence*, Methenaera flies away, landing behind ranged combatants and far from stunned defenders and melee strikers. She drops into a central location (rather than along a wall

or in a corner) and uses *wing slice* and opportunity attacks (with *threatening reach*) against characters who surround her. Because Methenaera is a solo monster with a four-level advantage on the heroes, her defenses are high: She can provoke opportunity attacks with little worry about the consequences.

Features of the Area

Illumination: Darkness.

Ice Crystals: To amuse herself in her spare time, Methenaera delicately breathes on the ground to coax jagged and complex ice crystal sculptures from it. Ice crystal stands are difficult terrain and provide cover. Each square of ice crystals has AC 8, other defenses 8, and 3 hit points. If faced with a choice of foes to attack and finding no tactical advantage to attacking one over another, Methenaera attacks characters who damage her ice crystals.

Methenaera (M) — **Level 22 Solo Brute**
Elder silver dragon
Huge natural magical beast (dragon) — XP 20,750

Initiative +14 **Senses** Perception +18; darkvision
HP 1,050; **Bloodied** 525; see also *bloodied breath*
AC 34; **Fortitude** 36, **Reflex** 34, **Will** 34
Resist 25 cold
Saving Throws +5
Speed 8, fly 8 (hover), overland flight 15
Action Points 2

⊕ **Bite** (standard; at-will)
　Reach 3; +25 vs. AC; 3d8 + 8 damage.

⊕ **Claw** (standard; at-will)
　Reach 2; +25 vs. AC; 2d8 + 8 damage.

↯ **Tail Slam** (standard; at-will)
　Reach 4; +23 vs. AC; 4d6 + 8 damage, and the target is dazed (save ends).

↯ **Methenaera's Onslaught** (standard; recharge ⚄ ⚅ ⚁)
　Methenaera makes a claw attack against each enemy within reach. She also makes one bite attack or *tail slam* attack.

↯ **Wing Slice** (immediate reaction, when an enemy flanking Methenaera attacks her; at-will)
　Reach 2; targets the triggering enemy and an enemy flanking with the triggering enemy; +25 vs. AC; 2d8 + 8 damage.

↩ **Breath Weapon** (standard; recharge ⚄ ⚅) ✦ **Cold**
　Close blast 5; +25 vs. Reflex; 3d8 + 8 cold damage, and the target gains vulnerable 10 to all damage (save ends). *Miss:* Half damage.

↩ **Bloodied Breath** (free, when first bloodied; encounter)
　Breath weapon recharges, and Methenaera uses it.

↩ **Frightful Presence** (standard; encounter) ✦ **Fear**
　Close burst 10; targets enemies; +21 vs. Will; the target is stunned until the end of Methenaera's next turn. *Aftereffect:* The target takes a –2 penalty to attack rolls (save ends).

Threatening Reach
　Methenaera can make opportunity attacks against each enemy within her reach (3 squares).

Unstoppable
　Methenaera makes saving throws against ongoing damage at the start of her turn as well as at the end of her turn.

Alignment Unaligned **Languages** Common, Draconic
Skills Athletics +26, Insight +18
Str 30 (+21) **Dex** 16 (+14) **Wis** 14 (+13)
Con 26 (+19) **Int** 14 (+13) **Cha** 15 (+13)

One square = 5 feet

Casks: Methenaera keeps the mead casks at the base of the eastern cliff, hidden amid stands of ice crystals. If a character picks up a cask (which weighs 20 pounds) without permission, Methenaera attacks that individual, even if another character has marked her.

Cliffs: The cliffs bisecting the lower chamber are 30 feet high and require a DC 25 Athletics check to ascend or descend.

Icy Floor: Unlike the ice-covered stream in the upper chamber, the stream in the lower chamber has thick ice that does not break under the characters' feet. The stream seeps into the eastern wall.

The ice over the stream and over the pool east of the cliffs is challenging terrain. When a character enters the first ice square in a turn, the character must succeed on a DC 17 Acrobatics check or fall prone in that square.

TREASURE

Methenaera's hoard is concealed at the bottom of the frozen pond in the southeast corner of the area where she begins the encounter. It consists of one level 19 magic item and 29,000 gp in monetary treasure.

Of course, her hoard also includes the two remaining casks of mead. A character who takes a drink of the mead gains the information he or she would receive from a Consult Oracle ritual (see page 302 of the *Player's Handbook*) and a Voice of Fate ritual (see page 314 of the *Player's Handbook*). The amount of information gained, as normal, depends on the result of the drinker's Religion check.

One cask contains enough mead for every member of the party to have one drink. If a character drinks from a particular cask more than once, the mead has no further effect for that character. The mead retains its potency if the casks are taken from the lair.

Also present with the casks, if you see fit, is the Roll of Claims (see the adventure hook on page 124).

CONCLUSION

When Methenaera becomes bloodied, she cries, "Enough! I yield. Let this bloodshed end, and I will release a cask to you." On her next turn, she flies away from the characters—to the casks if no characters are near them—and waits for the heroes to stand down. If they stop fighting, Methenaera performs the Raise Dead ritual on any slain character.

If the characters continue to fight, they draw the silver dragon's anger. She becomes more aggressive and focuses fire on individual enemies. She usually targets healers first, and becomes willing to make coup de grace attacks against anyone she drops. When Methenaera falls to fewer than 200 hit points, she repeats her offer of a cask. If the characters decline this offer, she flies to the casks, grabs them up, and attempts to escape. Now the characters will need to destroy her if they want to retrieve the mead.

Methenaera takes her duty seriously—and that duty is not merely to attack those who enter the chamber. Her aim is to ensure that Moradin's mead is used for a good cause. She respects anyone who is able to defeat her, and might even serve as a patron to the characters after her defeat. Since Methenaera's ancestors imbibed Moradin's mead, she has occasional, faint glimpses of the future and notions of Moradin's will. She can provide the characters with quests that advance the will of the god of creation and hints about how to best accomplish their goals.

Methenaera also needs heirs to guard the mead after her death. If she truly trusts the characters, she might charge them with protecting the mead while she travels far away to find a mate.

Mithral dragon lair for five 23rd-level adventurers

The strange bastion of Vyc Zaleeth sits upon an earth mote swaying between competing tides of a sea of fire and an ocean of water amid a particularly turbulent area at the edge of the Elemental Chaos. For centuries the Vyc Zaleeth monastery has been a place of ascetic contemplation, where githzerai ponder the nature of chaos at its very edge and develop its counterbalance through their mental discipline. Its strange disciplines were progressed peacefully by generations of monks and initiates that called this place home. Murmuring a constant concert of chants and mantras, the monks of Vyc Zaleeth found sanctuary from the universe and its petty conflicts. That is, until a mithral dragon and a small army of angelic mercenaries murdered them and took over their monastery to pursue a prophecy.

In less than a day, the dragon Astridaria and her angels destroyed all that the githzerai had built and defended for more than half a millennium. As despicable as these actions are, worse still are the dragon's ultimate plans for Vyc Zaleeth—to reignite the war between the creatures of the Elemental Chaos and the powers of the Astral Sea.

BACKGROUND

Given enough time, or if the story of how the characters come to Vyc Zaleeth gives them an opportunity, the characters can learn the following background information about Astridaria and her assault on the monastery. Even if the characters stumble upon Vyc Zaleeth, they might discover these plot threads through clues or by interrogating the mithral dragon's allies, or Astridaria might reveal them herself when the characters battle the dragon.

Arcana or History DC 22: Since she hatched, Astridaria has received visions of war between the Elemental Chaos and the Astral Sea. Urged by these auguries, she called together a force of angel

---

MEMORY CRYSTALS

When Astridaira attacked Vyc Zaleeth, she carefully preserved the githzerais' memory crystals. Repositories of the monastery's wisdom, these crystals come in many sizes, but none are larger than a short sword. Creatures trained in Arcana can make a DC 25 Arcana check to access a crystal as a standard action and then can "read" its memories in a manner similar to how a literate creature might read a book. The smallest crystals hold 1 to 10 pages worth of information, while the largest can hold the equivalent of 10,000 pages of information. These crystals can be used as both ritual books and scrolls.

---

mercenaries cast adrift when their deity died. Thus she took control of Vyc Zaleeth. A dark naga named Galzaik, for reasons unknown, has also aided Astridaria.

Arcana or History DC 26: At the heart of Vyc Zaleeth is a psychic resonance crystal. Astridaria's visions beckon for her to convert the crystal into a weapon of radiant energy powered by her fundamentum.

Arcana or History DC 28: The conversion is nearly complete. Astridaria awaits new visions to guide her next step.

HOOK: PREVENT ASTRIDARIA'S WAR

If you run an adventure in or around the Elemental Chaos, the heroes can come upon Vyc Zaleeth—a seeming beacon of order and radiance in the churning chaos—during their explorations. Because the monastery has a permanent teleportation circle, characters might hope to teleport safely from there to the Plane Below, only to find cosmic skulduggery unfolding there. Alternatively, a divine agent or a deity such as Ioun can catch wind of Astridaria's plans and encourage the characters to perform the Planar Portal ritual to travel to the monastery and stop Astridaria.

Quest XP: 28,000 XP (major quest).

ENVIRONMENT

Whether the characters arrive by the Planar Portal ritual or by other means, they first clearly see Vyc Zaleeth from the teleportation circle. The circle lies just outside the Chamber of Meditation entrance that faces the ocean of water. That entrance—and two others on either side of the crooked tower, each 20 feet wide—slants down into the tower, which winds from the top of the earth mote to a crown of crystal that once served as a psychic beacon. The crystal bristles with radiant energy so powerful that it sears the flesh of those who come near it and kills creatures that touch it.

The monastery's outer walls consist of pocked black stone flecked with iridescent blue crystals. Pools of primordial water or liquid fire—depending upon which sea a wall faces—collect in the pockets.

Teleportation Circle: When creatures use the teleportation circle to arrive at the monastery, the sound of a gong echoes down the nearest corridor to alert those within the Chamber of Meditation. Emblazoned at the edges of the circle is the sigil sequence needed to mke use of this circle for permanent teleportation. The characters can transcribe the pattern in 5 minutes.

Crowning Crystal: A creature that starts its turn within 10 feet of the crowning crystal takes 25

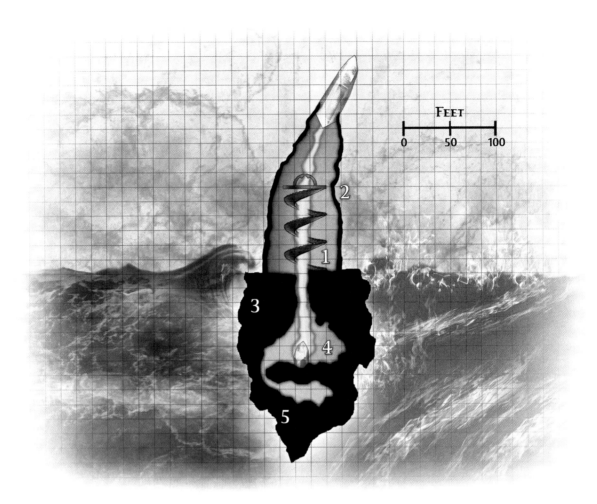

radiant damage. A creature that starts its turn touching the crystal takes 100 radiant damage.

Outer Walls: The outer walls' organic shape and puddles of dangerous liquid make them difficult to climb, requiring a DC 25 Athletics check.

Area 1: Chamber of Meditation

The Chamber of Meditation was once the focal point of monastic life at Vyc Zaleeth. Ringed with numerous alcoves that served as the githzerai's living quarters, it features an altar, a spiral staircase ascending to a platform, and a central chasm. Astridaria's angels wait in this chamber until Astridaria unleashes the next part of her plan.

Tactical Encounter: "Rage of Angels," page 132.

Area 2: Platform

From a platform high in the tower, made of blue translucent energy, a select group of angels and the dark naga Galzaik constantly repair and modify overburdened arrays at the base of the tower's crowning crystal. The team must continue to work even when the monastery falls under attack. When confronted, the team defends the array, using part of the apparatus as a weapon. The characters must disrupt the machine and the dragon powering it.

Tactical Encounter: "Radiant Array," page 134.

Area 3: Chasm

Once a conduit for psychic energy generated by githzerai monks, a 100-foot chasm in the center of the Chamber of Meditation's floor now courses with radiant energy. Characters who try to descend the chasm without disrupting the radiant array will likely be disintegrated by radiant energy.

Area 4: Lower Chamber

Before Astridaria's arrival, the resonance crystal at the center of the lower chamber amplified psychic energy from the monks and channeled that energy through the arcane array to the crystal that crowns the tower. Astridaria uses the chamber in the same way, breathing radiant energy into the crystal to create an amplified stream. Her intent is to create a weapon with which to attack the Elemental Chaos.

Tactical Encounter: "Agent of Prophecy," page 136.

Area 5: Hoard Room

This cave houses the monastery's sacred memory crystals—and now also Astridaria's hoard. It contains at least eight treasure parcels of your choosing. Guarding this place are a pair of hoard guardian sentinels (see "Agent of Prophecy," page 136).

JASON A. ENGLE

Rage of Angels

Encounter Level 23 (26,500 XP)

Setup

1 angel of authority (A)
10 angels of light (L)
2 angels of vengeance (V)

If the characters used the teleportation circle, the angels have heard the sound of the gong. Otherwise, heroes who can beat the passive Perception of the angels of light with Stealth can surprise them.

The angels are dutifully waiting here until Astridaria unleashes the next part of her plan while waiting for the naga and the angels above at the radiant array to finish making repairs to its mechanisms.

When the PCs enter the Chamber of Meditation, read:

A chamber spans the length, width, and height of the tower. An altar at the far side juts toward a pillar of radiant energy at the center. The energy flows up from below the chamber to a platform and an arcane array. A spiral staircase curls up around the radiant pillar, connecting the chamber's ground floor to the platform. Angelic figures—and one figure dark and serpentine—move about on the platform.

If the PCs arrived by the teleportation circle, add:

On the ground floor, more than a dozen angels, most the size of humans but others of giants' stature, move toward you.

If the angels do not know that the PCs approach, add the following instead:

On the ground floor lounge more than a dozen angels, most the size of humans but others of giants' stature. They watch the work on the array, practice with their weapons, or kneel in meditation.

Tactics

When the angels spot the characters, they rush to stop them from disrupting the work on the platform.

The angels of light lead the advance.

The angel of authority follows the angels of light. It looses a *lightning bolt* and then closes with the characters to use *majestic rally*. It repeats *majestic rally* whenever the power recharges.

Angels of vengeance use *sign of vengeance* to teleport next to controllers, leaders, and ranged-weapon users and harass them throughout combat.

Although the angels work to repel any intrusion into the monastery, their chief concern is stopping the intruders from disrupting the work being done on the radiant array.

Angel of Authority (A) — Level 22 Controller (Leader)
Large immortal humanoid (angel) — XP 4,150 each

Initiative +17 **Senses** Perception +18
HP 20; **Bloodied** 101
AC 36; **Fortitude** 32, **Reflex** 34, **Will** 35
Immune fear; **Resist** 15 radiant
Speed 8, fly 12 (hover)

⊕ **Quarterstaff** (standard; at-will) ✦ **Radiant, Weapon**
Reach 2; +27 vs. AC; 1d10 + 8 damage plus 1d10 radiant damage.

↗ **Lightning Bolt** (standard; at-will) ✦ **Lightning**
Ranged 10; +26 vs. Fortitude; 2d10 + 8 lightning damage, and the target is dazed until the end of the angel of authority's next turn.

↞ **Majestic Rally** (standard; recharge ⚄ ⚅) ✦ **Radiant, Thunder**
Close burst 5; targets enemies; +26 vs. Will; 1d10 + 8 radiant damage plus 1d10 thunder damage, and the target is weakened (save ends). *Miss:* Half damage. *Effect:* Each angel within the burst gains a +2 bonus to attack rolls until the end of the angel of authority's next turn.

Angelic Presence (while not bloodied)
Any attack against the angel of authority takes a -2 penalty to the attack roll.

Alignment Unaligned **Languages** Supernal
Skills Insight +23, Religion +23
Str 20 (+16) **Dex** 22 (+17) **Wis** 25 (+18)
Con 19 (+15) **Int** 24 (+18) **Cha** 27 (+19)
Equipment plate armor, quarterstaff

---

10 Angels of Light (L) — Level 23 Minion Skirmisher
Medium immortal humanoid (angel) — XP 1,275 each

Initiative +19 **Senses** Perception +19
HP 1; a missed attack never damages a minion; see also *death burst.*
AC 37; **Fortitude** 34, **Reflex** 34, **Will** 36
Immune fear; **Resist** 15 radiant
Speed 8, fly 12 (hover)

⊕ **Angelic Glaive** (standard; at-will) ✦ **Weapon**
Reach 2; +28 vs. AC; 10 damage.

↞ **Death Burst** (when the angel of light drops to 0 hit points) ✦ **Radiant**
The angel of light explodes in a burst of radiant light: close burst 10; targets enemies; +26 vs. Fortitude; 10 radiant damage. *Effect:* Each angel in the burst gains 10 temporary hit points.

Alignment Unaligned **Languages** Supernal
Str 18 (+15) **Dex** 23 (+17) **Wis** 27 (+19)
Con 23 (+17) **Int** 15 (+13) **Cha** 23 (+17)
Equipment glaive

Features of the Area

Illumination: The crowning crystal at the top of the monastery brightly illuminates the entire chamber.

Ceiling: The ceiling over this area is 220 feet high at the zenith (the crowning crystal).

Platform: The array platform is 120 feet above the floor of this chamber.

Altar: A creature that starts its turn on an altar square gains a +2 bonus to Will and a +5 bonus to saving throws against any effect that deals ongoing psychic damage or that dazes, dominates, or stuns. These bonuses last until the end of the creature's next turn.

2 Angels of Vengeance (V)	**Level 19 Elite Brute**
Large immortal humanoid (angel)	XP 4,800 each

Initiative +13   **Senses** Perception +16
HP 446; **Bloodied** 223
AC 34; **Fortitude** 33, **Reflex** 29, **Will** 33; see also *cloak of vengeance*
Immune disease, fear; **Resist** 15 cold, 15 fire, 15 radiant; see also *coldfire pillar*
Saving Throws +2
Speed 8, fly 12 (hover); see also *sign of vengeance*
Action Points 1

⊕ **Longsword** (standard; at-will) ✦ **Cold, Fire, Weapon**
    Reach 2; +25 vs. AC; 1d10 + 9 damage plus 1d8 fire damage plus 1d8 cold damage.

✝ **Double Attack** (standard; at-will)
    The angel of vengeance makes two longsword attacks.

➵ **Sign of Vengeance** (minor; encounter) ✦ **Teleportation**
    Ranged sight; the angel of vengeance places an invisible sign upon the target. Until the end of the encounter, as a move action, the angel of vengeance can teleport adjacent to the target.

⟵ **Coldfire Pillar** (free, when first bloodied; encounter) ✦ **Cold, Fire, Polymorph**
    The angel of vengeance transforms into a 30-foot-high pillar of blue flame. Close burst 2; +23 vs. Reflex; 1d8 + 9 cold damage plus 1d8 + 9 fire damage. The angel of vengeance is immune to all damage until the start of its next turn.

Cloak of Vengeance (until bloodied) ✦ **Cold, Fire**
    Any character attacking the angel of vengeance takes a -2 penalty until the angel is bloodied. While *cloak of vengeance* is in effect, a creature that makes a successful melee attack against the angel of vengeance takes 1d8 fire damage and 1d8 cold damage.

Alignment Unaligned	**Languages** Supernal	
Skills Insight +21, Intimidate +22		
Str 27 (+17)	**Dex** 18 (+13)	**Wis** 25 (+16)
Con 23 (+15)	**Int** 19 (+13)	**Cha** 26 (+17)

Equipment plate armor, 2 longswords

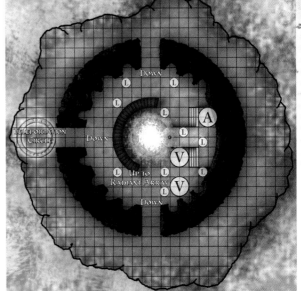

Energy Pillar: The radiant energy comprising the pillar has the consistency of water and clings to creatures in contact with it. It flows from beneath the chamber floor up through the platform array to the crowning crystal. A creature entering the pillar or starting its turn within the pillar takes 20 radiant damage and slides 2 squares in the direction of the current (upward). With a DC 20 Athletics check, a creature within the pillar can swim down the current as if in water.

Spiral Stairs: This steep flight of stairs winds its way around the energy pillar upward to the platform and the radiant array. The stairs are difficult terrain.

SCALING FLYING MONSTERS

Many of the monsters in this lair have a fly speed and can hover. Although at epic tier there is a greater possibility that characters have powers or magic items that grant them flight, their ability to fly is by no means certain. Even when they do have flight powers, most are either encounter or daily in frequency, and a procession of encounters with flying enemies that outmaneuver the characters and keep just out of reach of attacks can become frustrating very quickly.

When you run flying monsters, it's critical that you keep your character's fly powers in mind, and cater your monsters' movement tactics accordingly. This doesn't mean you have to make your flying monsters walk into battle. Having flying creatures dive bomb the characters with flying charges, or use their flight to bypass difficult terrain, are fun ways to showcase their fly speed without slowing the encounter to a maddening slog. Have your brute, soldier, and skirmisher fliers hover 1 square off the ground within melee reach of their foes; although this tactic has few mechanical differences from a ground assault, it can grant a tad more maneuverability when the monster is surrounded, and creates an interesting visual. Flying controllers and artillery can hover higher up, but not so high that they are out of reach of the controllers and ranged strikers among the characters. This type of flying will often open interesting options for cover and concealment, especially in a terrain-rich encounter environment.

If the PCs have a number of flight powers at their disposal, and are using them with great frequency in a given encounter, take off the kid gloves. Having the occasional frantic aerial battle that utilizes all three dimensions is one of the fun features of epic-level play.

STEPHEN RADNEY MACFARLAND

RADIANT ARRAY
Encounter Level 24 (30,000 XP)

SETUP

3 angels of the sigil and word (A)
Galzaik, dark naga (G)

While the battle rages on the ground floor, 120 feet below this place, three angels and Galzaik, the dark naga, work to repair the overloaded radiant array. They continue to work on the array until the characters approach.

When the PCs reach the platform, read:
In the middle of the platform, an array studded with crystal controls, strange levers, and eldritch diodes crackles every few moments with unstable bursts of radiant energy. A dark naga and three angels turn from their work on it to face you.

The naga hisses, "You are out of your depth here. Leave now, or perish."

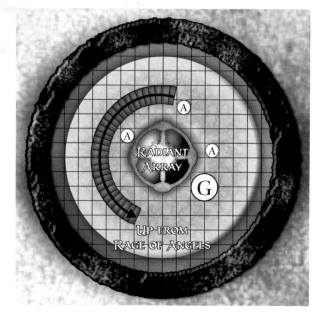

3 Angels of the Sigil and Word (A)		Level 23 Soldier
Medium immortal humanoid (angel)		XP 5,100 each

Initiative +18   **Senses** Perception +23
HP 217; **Bloodied** 108
AC 39; **Fortitude** 35, **Reflex** 35, **Will** 35
Speed 6, fly 10 (hover)
⊕ **Radiant Sword** (standard; at-will) ✦ **Radiant, Weapon**
+29 vs. AC; 2d10 + 8 radiant damage, and the target is under the effect of *angelic sigil* (save ends).
↩ **Dominating Word** (minor 1/round; encounter) ✦ **Charm**
Close burst 5; targets one creature under the effect of *angelic sigil*; +25 vs. Will; the target is dominated (save ends).
↩ **Repelling Word** (minor 1/round; at-will) ✦ **Force**
Close burst 5; targets one creature under the effect of *angelic sigil*; +25 vs. Fortitude; the angel pushes the target 4 squares, and the target is knocked prone.
Angelic Presence (while not bloodied)
Any attack against the angel takes a -2 penalty to the attack roll.
Angelic Sigil
Each creature under the effect of *angelic sigil* is marked by the angel and takes a -5 penalty to saving throws.
Alignment Unaligned   **Languages** Supernal
Skills Arcana +22, Thievery +23
Str 22 (+17)   **Dex** 24 (+18)   **Wis** 24 (+18)
Con 25 (+18)   **Int** 22 (+17)   **Cha** 25 (+18)
Equipment plate armor, radiant sword

Galzaik (G)	Level 21 Elite Controller
Large immortal magical beast (reptile)	XP 6,400

Initiative +14   **Senses** Perception +21; darkvision
HP 404; **Bloodied** 202
AC 35; **Fortitude** 33, **Reflex** 31, **Will** 35
Saving Throws +2
Speed 8
Action Points 1
⊕ **Tail Sting** (standard; at-will) ✦ **Poison**
Reach 2; +24 vs. AC; 2d6 + 8 poison damage (3d6 + 8 poison damage against a dazed target), and the target is slowed (save ends).
↩ **Lure** (minor; at-will) ✦ **Charm**
Close burst 5; targets enemies; +25 vs. Will; the target is pulled 1 square and dazed (save ends).
↩ **Psychic Miasma** (standard; recharge ⚄ ⚅) ✦ **Psychic**
Close burst 3; +26 vs. Will; 3d6 + 10 psychic damage, and the target is dazed (save ends). *First Failed Saving Throw:* The target is stunned (save ends).
Alignment Evil   **Languages** Common, Draconic, Supernal
Skills History +22, Insight +21, Stealth +19
Str 26 (+18)   **Dex** 18 (+14)   **Wis** 22 (+16)
Con 26 (+18)   **Int** 24 (+17)   **Cha** 30 (+20)

TACTICS

Angels of the sigil and word use their radiant swords to place *angelic sigils* on characters and then push those characters off the platform. If some of the characters have powers that enable them to push at will (such as fighters who have *tide of iron*), the angels target those characters with *dominating word* and have those characters knock other characters off the platform.

Galzaik uses *lure* and *psychic miasma* in concert with the angels' powers. He pulls and then dazes or stuns characters for the angels to push or dominate.

STEPHEN RADNEY MACFARLAND

Features of the Area

Illumination: The crowning crystal at the top of the monastery brightly illuminates the entire area.

Ceiling: The ceiling is 100 feet above the platform, ending at the crowning crystal.

Spiral Stairs: This steep flight of stairs winds its way around the energy pillar downward to the Chamber of Meditation. The stairs are difficult terrain.

Platform Floor: The platform floor consists of a translucent blue, glasslike material as hard as steel.

Array: Creatures adjacent to the array can manipulate it to make the following attacks.

⤹ Radiant Ray (standard; recharge ⚄ ⚅) ✦ **Radiant**
Ranged 10; +25 vs. Reflex; 2d12 + 8 radiant damage, and ongoing 10 radiant damage (save ends).

⤺ Radiant Blast (standard; recharge ⚅) ✦ **Radiant**
Close burst 5; +23 vs. Fortitude; 2d8 + 8 radiant damage, and the target is pushed 5 squares.

Each of the recharges is for the radiant array, and not the creature using the power. The angels and Galzaik know how to manipulate the array to make both of these attacks, but if another creature wants to make these attacks, it must succeed on a DC 31 Arcana or Thievery check as a minor action to determine how to manipulate the radiant array to make the attacks. A successful check allows the creature to make these attacks for the remainder of the expedition into Vyc Zaleeth.

Disabling the Array

Once the characters have defeated the angels and the dark naga, their next task is to disrupt the array so they can reach the psychic resonance crystal at the bottom of Vyc Zaleeth. If the players have a hard time figuring this out, have them discover documents in the possession of one of the angels notes that include a side view map of the monastery.

Setup: To disable the array, characters must determine what makes it work, to the extent that they can switch it off or disconnect a vital mechanism.

Level: 22.

XP: 8,300.

Complexity: 2 (requires 6 successes before 3 failures).

Primary Skills: Arcana, Athletics, Thievery.

Arcana (DC 17, standard action): The character tries to determine which of the controls manipulate the streams of radiant energy. A successful check, in addition to counting as 1 success in the challenge, provides a +2 bonus to the next Thievery check made by an ally in this skill challenge. This skill can be used to gain a maxmum of 3 successes in the challenge.

Athletics (DC 24, standard action): The character uses brute force guided by the skill of his or her fellow party members to detach large chunks of the array. This skill can be used to gain a maximum of 2 successes in the challenge, but Athletics checks can be attempted only after the characters have already gained 3 successes in the challenge by using other skills.

Thievery (DC 28, standard action): The character attempts to disable part of the array. On a failed check, the array erupts, dealing 20 radiant damage to the character and to each creature within 5 squares of him or her.

Secondary Skills: Acrobatics, Endurance.

Acrobatics (DC 28, immediate interrupt, when the array erupts; at-will): The character shifts 4 squares to avoid the discharged energy. A successful check does not count as a success in the challenge.

Endurance (DC 17, immediate interrupt, when the array erupts; at-will): A character can shield an adjacent creature from the effect of the eruption. On a successful check, the shielded character takes no radiant damage. A successful check does not count as a success in the challenge.

Success: The radiant energy stream is disrupted. The chasm in the floor becomes a simple 100-foot shaft with sheer walls that require a DC 22 Athletics check to scale.

Partial Success: If the characters accrue at least 2 successes before getting 3 failures, the radiant energy stream is partially disrupted. A creature that enters the sputtering energy stream or starts its turn there takes 15 radiant damage instead of 20.

Failure: The radiant energy stream continues to flow freely. The characters can repeat the challenge, but all the DCs increase by 4.

AGENT OF PROPHECY

Encounter Level 25 (40,600 XP)

SETUP

Astridaria, elder mithral dragon (A)
2 hoard guardian sentinels

If the characters did not disrupt the radiant energy stream, they can surprise Astridaria and engage her before her *breath weapon* recharges. Otherwise, the disruption of the stream alerts Astridaria, at which

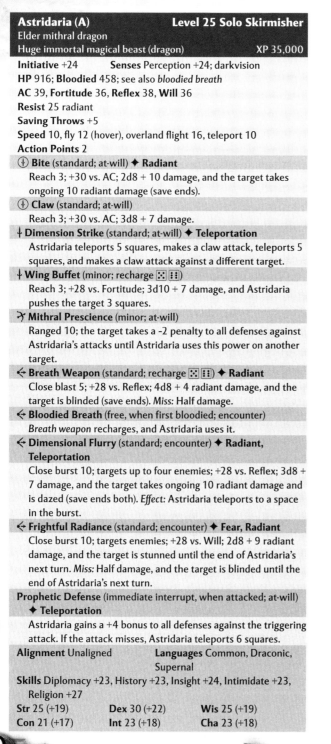

Astridaria (A)	Level 25 Solo Skirmisher
Elder mithral dragon	
Huge immortal magical beast (dragon)	XP 35,000

Initiative +24   **Senses** Perception +24; darkvision
HP 916; **Bloodied** 458; see also *bloodied breath*
AC 39, **Fortitude** 36, **Reflex** 38, **Will** 36
Resist 25 radiant
Saving Throws +5
Speed 10, fly 12 (hover), overland flight 16, teleport 10
Action Points 2

⊕ **Bite** (standard; at-will) ✦ **Radiant**
　Reach 3; +30 vs. AC; 2d8 + 10 damage, and the target takes ongoing 10 radiant damage (save ends).

⊕ **Claw** (standard; at-will)
　Reach 3; +30 vs. AC; 3d8 + 7 damage.

↯ **Dimension Strike** (standard; at-will) ✦ **Teleportation**
　Astridaria teleports 5 squares, makes a claw attack, teleports 5 squares, and makes a claw attack against a different target.

↯ **Wing Buffet** (minor; recharge ⚄ ⚅)
　Reach 3; +28 vs. Fortitude; 3d10 + 7 damage, and Astridaria pushes the target 3 squares.

⤳ **Mithral Prescience** (minor; at-will)
　Ranged 10; the target takes a -2 penalty to all defenses against Astridaria's attacks until Astridaria uses this power on another target.

↤ **Breath Weapon** (standard; recharge ⚄ ⚅) ✦ **Radiant**
　Close blast 5; +28 vs. Reflex; 4d8 + 4 radiant damage, and the target is blinded (save ends). *Miss:* Half damage.

↤ **Bloodied Breath** (free, when first bloodied; encounter)
　Breath weapon recharges, and Astridaria uses it.

↤ **Dimensional Flurry** (standard; encounter) ✦ **Radiant, Teleportation**
　Close burst 10; targets up to four enemies; +28 vs. Reflex; 3d8 + 7 damage, and the target takes ongoing 10 radiant damage and is dazed (save ends both). *Effect:* Astridaria teleports to a space in the burst.

↤ **Frightful Radiance** (standard; encounter) ✦ **Fear, Radiant**
　Close burst 10; targets enemies; +28 vs. Will; 2d8 + 9 radiant damage, and the target is stunned until the end of Astridaria's next turn. *Miss:* Half damage, and the target is blinded until the end of Astridaria's next turn.

Prophetic Defense (immediate interrupt, when attacked; at-will) ✦ **Teleportation**
　Astridaria gains a +4 bonus to all defenses against the triggering attack. If the attack misses, Astridaria teleports 6 squares.

Alignment Unaligned   **Languages** Common, Draconic, Supernal
Skills Diplomacy +23, History +23, Insight +24, Intimidate +23, Religion +27
Str 25 (+19)   **Dex** 30 (+22)   **Wis** 25 (+19)
Con 21 (+17)   **Int** 23 (+18)   **Cha** 23 (+18)

point she teleports to a ledge overlooking the chamber and lies in wait for the characters.

If the PCs have disrupted the energy pillar before entering the chamber, read:
At the center of this chamber, a crystal similar to the one crowning the monastery's tower, though much smaller, hums and sputters with radiant energy.

If the PCs have not disrupted the energy pillar, or have only partially disrupted it, read:
At the center of this chamber, a crystal similar to the one crowning the monastery's tower, though much smaller, glows intensely and beams the stream of radiant energy skyward.

If Astridaria is not prepared for the PCs, add:
Next to the crystal is a massive mithral dragon, long and snakelike. As you look on, she uses her breath weapon on the crystal.

TACTICS

Even if the adventurers surprise Astridaria, she uses the ledge as a staging area for her attacks. When flanked, she teleports to the ledge and then charges or swoops back down to loose her *breath weapon*.

Throughout the fight, Astridaria talks to herself about being the agent of prophecy and about her urgent need to restart the war between the Astral Sea and the Elemental Chaos. Even without an Insight check, the characters can tell she is insane.

Astridaria fights until bloodied, at which point she flees to her hoard room in the hope that one or both of her guardians (see below) remain to fight the characters. If confronted again, she fights until reduced to

---

ASTRIDARIA'S RAMBLINGS

Astridaria is a chatty foe. She constantly quips and pontificates during her battle with the characters. Here are a few bits of dialogue for you to use during the battle.

"You all are just the sickness of the universe made manifest. Crawling maggots trying to eat away and corrode the function that must occur."

"Please, this must be done. It is only through the crucible of this war that the universe can take on its true and just existence."

"The Chained One knew this to be true, but used the wrong implement to achieve the proper ends. It's not darkness that will bring everlasting harmony, but light!"

"Small-minded fools! You will see the light!" (Usually uttered just before Astridaria uses her *breath weapon* against the characters).

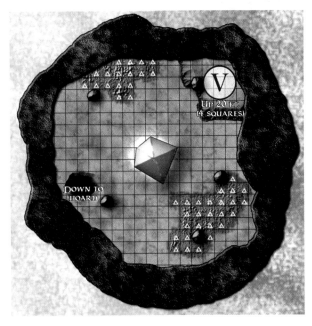

2 Hoard Guardian Sentinels	Level 20 Soldier
Large natural animate (construct)	XP 2,800 each

Initiative +15   **Senses** Perception +19, darkvision
HP 186; **Bloodied** 93
AC 34; **Fortitude** 32, **Reflex** 30, **Will** 28
Immune disease, poison, sleep
Speed 8

⊕ **Slam** (standard; at-will)
     Reach 2; +23 vs. AC; 2d8 + 5 damage, and the sentinel marks
     the target (save ends) and pulls it 1 square.

↯ **No Escape** (immediate interrupt, when an enemy leaves an
     adjacent square; at-will)
     +25 vs. Reflex; the target doesn't leave the square, and its
     movement ends.

↞ **Concussive Breath** (standard; recharge ⚄ ⚅) ✦ Force
     Close blast 5; +23 vs. Reflex; 2d10 + 5 force damage, and the
     sentinel slides the target 3 squares.

↗ **Petrifying Eyes** (standard; recharge when no creature is
     affected by this power) ✦ Cold, Gaze
     Ranged 5; +21 vs. Fortitude; 2d10 + 5 damage, and the target
     is dazed and slowed (save ends both). *First Failed Saving Throw:*
     The target is immobilized instead of dazed and slowed (save
     ends). *Second Failed Saving Throw:* The target becomes a statue
     of mithral and is petrified.

Alignment Unaligned		**Languages** –
Str 24 (+15)	**Dex** 17 (+11)	**Wis** 19 (+12)
Con 18 (+12)	**Int** 14 (+10)	**Cha** 4 (+5)

one-quarter of her hit points (229), at which point she flees again. If cornered, she fights to the death.

FEATURES OF THE AREA

Walls: The rugged stone of the walls is the same stone that comprises the outer walls of the monastery.

Ledge: The ledge consists of the same steel-hard, glasslike material as the floor of the array platform in the Chamber of Meditation. It is 20 feet high.

Ceiling: The ceiling is 60 feet high at the edges and 80 feet high toward the middle of the chamber. At the very center of the chamber, over the crystal, the monastery's chasm reaches skyward to the Chamber of Meditation.

Stalagmites: Stalagmites are blocking terrain and cover the entirety of their squares.

Rubble: Rubble is difficult terrain.

Crystal: The crystal is blocking terrain. Any creature touching it takes 50 radiant damage. If the crystal is within an area-of-effect attack that deals radiant damage, it flares up after that attack and makes the following attack.

↞ **Radiant Feedback** (standard; recharge ⚄ ⚅) ✦ Radiant
     Close burst 4; +25 vs. Fortitude; the target takes ongoing 15
     radiant damage and is dazed (save ends both). Astridaria is
     immune to this effect.

THE HOARD ROOM

The cave just below this chamber is the site of Astridaria's hoard room. Guarding her hoard is a pair of constructs known as hoard guardians.

TACTICS

If Astridaria is fighting with the sentinels, the pair form a defensive barrier between the characters and the mithral dragon, giving their mistress a degree of protection while she makes *dimensional strike* forays against soft targets.

Whether or not they are fighting in concert with Astridaria, the sentinels start their attack with *petrifying eyes* and then follow up with *concussive breath*. They use their slam attack only when their other powers are not available.

CONCLUSION

Among Astridaria's hoard and the monastery's numerous memory crystals is a strange gray crystal. Though this gray crystal is also a memory crystal, it is not of githzerai make. It takes a DC 30 Arcana check to access its information, which is a jumble of fragmented memories and strange quotations in the Supernal language. By succeeding on the Arcana check, a character can learn that the crystal was constructed by Astridaria herself, and it details how she believes she could have succeeded in unifying the universe. It also explains a method for locating a wandering artifact called the *Crystal of the Ebon Flame* and a ritual to convert the artifact into an object of pure radiant energy, which was her next goal after reigniting the war between the Elemental Chaos and the Astral Sea.

Gold dragon lair for five 24th-level adventurers

In the Shadowfell, dark clouds tumble across the leaden skies over the Plain of Sighing Stones, but they bring no rain. Cerulean lightning lances between heaven and earth, scorching parched earth while thunder echoes for miles around. Legends tell of an angry god that lives in these clouds, a deity that betrayed its kin to bring comfort to death's scions, those giants that quit the mortal world to forge an empire in its dark reflection.

No god dwells in the perpetual storm, though. The clouds and lightning manifest a mighty dragon's suffering. Cursed with madness and condemned to live out its days as a prisoner of its own disinterest, compromising its once noble ideals to extend its existence in the company of those it detests, the dragon known as the Golden Architect is the doom of heaven, the fallen beast, and the scourge of the Shadowfell.

BACKGROUND

Arcana or History DC 16: Nearly a thousand years gone, and the Golden Architect's Citadel still roams the skies above the Plain of Sighing Stones, a grim testament to the evils worked in the lands it passes over. Ages ago, giants from the mortal world abandoned their holds to erect a new kingdom, a sprawling empire to immortalize their avarice and arrogance for all time. It was here, on this parched landscape, that some raised a great city, a walled monstrosity more massive than any city yet created by mortal hands. Its construction leached all the resources from the plain, turning it into the barren wasteland that it is today.

History DC 20: Though they were fully capable of constructing the city, the giants concerned themselves with combating the Shadowfell's influence and so left the work to their slaves. Cursed dark ones, shadowborn humans whose descendants still roam these lands, and others toiled endlessly to raise the death giants' city. Perhaps they might have fled, might have failed, but they could never falter—because always watching their progress was Golgorax the Golden Architect, a vile beast imprisoned in the floating Citadel, who designed the city and orchestrated its builders.

History DC 27: The Golden Architect was not always a cruel tyrant and was once counted among the most virtuous of his kind. Long had the dragon fought against Tiamat's servants, leading dragonborn against abishai, chromatic dragons, and dragonspawn. But each defeat and failure added to the dragon's bitterness, until one day—overcome with grief—the dragon fled the natural world to find the oblivion promised by the Shadowfell.

Not long after his arrival, the Shadowfell ran afoul of the death giants. Too weakened to fight, the dragon surrendered and swore oaths to his new masters, promising to build the city they desired. Though the dragon was already bound by his vows, the giants imprisoned the wyrm in a floating fortress so he could oversee the work and instruct their slaves. Confined in the structure and consumed with despair, the dragon went mad, and with his insanity came cruelty, callousness, and evil.

History DC 30: The dragon completed his task and the city was built. The giants did not dwell there long, however, because they proved unable to withstand the Shadowfell's influence. To buttress themselves against the approaching dissolution, they drained the souls from their thralls, which became horrific things trapped between life and death. Dark magic and darker deeds caused the city to crumble away. And after a generation, the once-grand city tumbled down to rubble and dust.

The dragon lived on even as the giants scattered, and he has languished in his fortress for centuries. Although the Citadel is more lair than prison now, the Golden Architect's broken spirit keeps him from leaving. A few death giants remain, captors turned servants. The dragon devours prisoners they capture while the giants consume their souls. They have persisted, but the magic in the Citadel is failing, and the denizens require more souls, more lives to continue their wretched existence. If they fail, they will find the oblivion they fear.

ENVIRONMENT

The fortress is expertly crafted, assembled from sandstone blocks each as long and wide as a human is tall. Its great age and the Shadowfell's decaying influence have erased much of its splendor. The once-grand draconic images now look sinister and malformed, retaining only the barest suggestion of dragons festooning the exterior. Inside, the place is a collection of passages and chambers arranged as if by a madman. It stands as testament to Golgorax's state of mind as he added to its original structure.

Most of the place is dark, stained by wicked deeds. Light sources brought into its corridors and rooms seem dulled, deadened even though the range of their light is unchanged. Periodically, one can hear the high-pitched cackle of the mad dragon echoing through the passages, bouncing off the walls to distort in an unnerving manner.

From a distance, the Citadel is indistinguishable from a large, black cluster of cumulus clouds, and so it's easily mistaken for a storm. It is an error abetted by the bolts of lightning blasting the land below—those same bolts had been used to shatter sandstone for the craftsmen to carve into bricks for the giants' city long ago. Reaching the Citadel is impossible unless a character has a way to fly or has patience enough to wait for the cloud to descend just before the death giants emerge to snatch up their next batch of victims. Flying characters can slip inside through the Eye in area 1 or through any of the gaps in the Citadel's floor.

The Citadel rises from the clouds, suspended in the air by ancient magic bound into the stones by the slaves' blood spilled when the structure was built. As presented, the Citadel is a freestanding structure, with other sections having long ago fallen or crumbled away. But you can expand the complex, adding extra levels below through which the adventurers must pass to reach the dragon in its lair.

The clouds supporting the Citadel are not natural phenomena but are instead warped souls trapped in the Shadowfell by death giant magic. Flying through them are all sorts of insubstantial undead, including wraiths, specters, and worse. Moving through the clouds does not draw the attention of these haunts, but those who linger might run into trouble in the form of five dread wraiths (*MM* 267).

Illumination: Unless otherwise noted, all rooms are dark.

Ceiling: Rooms and passages have ceilings 50 feet high, except where otherwise noted.

Doors: Stone doors are all closed and always open toward the west or south. Their size and weight require a DC 24 Strength check to open them, even when they are not locked.

Gaps: In places, the floor has fallen away. A creature that slips through the floor falls hundreds of feet until it lands on the Plain of Sighing Stones, likely taking 20d10 damage as a result.

GOLGORAX, THE GOLDEN ARCHITECT

Golgorax is an emaciated gold dragon, a once-proud and mighty beast brought low by ennui and self-loathing. The Golden Architect can no longer muster the will to escape the Shadowfell and contents himself with inane conversation with the death giant attendants and those imagined ghosts from the dragon's past. Exposure to the Shadowfell and his soul's slow siphoning have weakened the Golden Architect, so now he is but a pale shadow of his former greatness.

The dragon rarely stirs from his lair, but his needs are considerable, and he and his death giant lackeys scour the Plain of Sighing Stones for chattel—those savage humanoids that inherited the lands wasted by the giants ages ago. As the cloudborne fortress skims the powdery landscape, giants disembark to round up victims, and feed their bodies to the dragon while keeping their souls for themselves.

AREA 1: THE DRAGON'S EYE

A massive round chamber, this area features the Eye, an opening in the floor. In ancient days, Golgorax monitored his workers by peering through the opening.

To protect this chamber from unwanted guests, the death giants placed a number of sentinels to watch over the opening.

Tactical Encounter: "Mute Sentinels," page 142.

AREA 2: HALL OF CURSES

This hall tells the Golden Architect's tale in the paintings adorning its walls.

When the PCs can see into this room, read:
Painted figures cover the walls in this long hallway. Two sets of stairs lead to exits. The stairs to the west are steep and end at massive stone doors, and the stairs to the north lead up to darkness. Part of the floor is missing here, and through the gap you can see dark clouds.

Ordinarily this chamber is empty, but from time to time the death giants come here to check up on the undead in area 1.

Western Doors: Stone doors block passage to area 5. The doors are sealed, protected by a sturdy lock set in the center between each door. Opening the doors requires four successful Thievery checks before three failures against DC 29. If a character fails to open the door, it can thereafter be opened only by force (break DC 29, AC 4, Fortitude 12, Reflex 4, hp 80). Breaking open the doors automatically alerts all creatures in the complex.

AREA 3: THE PORTAL ROOM

Once he had destroyed most of the death giants, Golgorax constructed this chamber as an escape route to the natural world. Malaise bred by long years spent in the Shadowfell has kept the dragon from using it. This fact has not prevented the dragon from protecting the room by setting a couple of traps and posting death giants nearby to prevent intrusion or escape.

Recently, a nightwalker has been roaming the complex, and it is puzzling over the traps in hopes of expanding its malign influence into the mortal world.

Tactical Encounter: "Night Haunt," page 144.

AREA 4: STAIRS

The numerous staircases found in this chamber reveal the gold dragon's brimming madness. Death giant guards often linger here to escape the dragon's rages.

When the PCs can see this room, read:
Staircases and landings fill this high-ceilinged chamber, constructed as if by a mad architect. Unfinished stairs extend out from walls painted with images of alcoves that seemingly serve no purpose. The southernmost staircase leads to an archway carved to resemble a dragon's maw.

If the characters avoided facing the death giants during the "Night Haunt" encounter described on page 144, the giants make their stand here.

AREA 5: LOST GLORY
The hallways here lead to different areas in the dungeon.

When the PCs can see this area, read:
A tarnished copper statue in the center of this area captures a proud dragon's likeness. It wrought to depict the dragon in flight, wings extended out to either side and balanced on a long tail.

Four hallways extend away from the intersection. To the north, a short hall ends at descending stairs. The eastern and western halls end at doors. The southern hall extends for a bit before turning west.

AREA 6: STOREROOM
This storeroom holds barrels, boxes, crates, and empty shelves. All containers are empty and dry, though stains suggest they once held food, drink, and other supplies. No one in the complex comes here anymore; therefore, the characters, provided they are not fleeing from any of the Citadel's denizens, can take an extended rest in this room.

AREA 7: SLAVE QUARTERS
Long ago, dark ones, shadowborn humans, and other slaves languished in this room. Now the room holds only ghosts, figments from another time.

When the PCs can see into this room, read:
Rotten, infested wood and brittle tangles of old bedding litter this chamber. Flitting about near the ceiling are ghostly forms.

Phantoms: About a dozen or so harmless phantoms move about the ceiling. They do not respond to conversation.

Secret Door: The slaves built a secret passage in the wall (the door is visible with a DC 24 Perception check) to lead to the ovens so they could supplement their gruel with more substantial meals.

AREA 8: DEATH CHAMBERS
Part barracks, part torture chambers, the death giants quarter here when not raiding for fresh victims or attending the Golden Architect in his sanctum.

When the PCs can see these chambers, read:
A macabre scene stretches before you as you take in these chambers. The room near the doors is clearly a torture chamber, replete with a variety of implements used for inflicting pain.

Across the room is a short hall that opens into living quarters. There you see beds, chests, and a table, all sized for giants.

These rooms are normally empty. The equipment here no longer functions, rusted or broken from hard use. The chamber beyond holds old furniture that has been equally abused. Blood stains the floor and is spattered on the walls. Nothing of value can be found in either chamber.

AREA 9: OVENS
Once serving as a kitchen for the living inhabitants, this room now serves to rid the complex of offal, bones, and other detritus.

When the PCs enter this room, read:
Lining the northern and southern walls are two rows of black ovens. Crimson light shines through their grates and the fires fill the room with uncomfortable heat. Bits of rotten flesh, stains, and broken bones litter the floor.

Ovens: Creatures touching the doors take 10 fire damage. Opening an oven door requires a DC 24 Strength check. A creature pushed or placed inside an oven takes 4d10 fire damage and ongoing 15 fire damage (save ends). A target cannot save against the ongoing damage if it ends its turn inside an oven.

AREA 10: LAIR OF THE GOLDEN ARCHITECT
Formerly a sumptuous chamber designed to house the dragon in comfort, long years of frustration and idle destruction have brought much of this room to ruin. The Golden Architect spends his time amid the wreckage, lamenting his fate and giving in to the insidious influence and malaise pervading the plane. Golgorax's attendants endure his insults and condemnations characterizing the long stretches between meals, and they shuffle about the room, tossing debris through the hole in the floor to keep the chamber free of rubble.

Tactical Encounter: "Gold Madness," page 146.

TREASURE
The lair contains four treasure parcels. Consider including two magic item parcels and two monetary parcels. You can place the treasure with the dragon or spread it around the Citadel. Here is sample treasure for a 24th-level party:

Parcel 1: Level 28 magic item from the players' wish lists.

Parcel 2: Level 27 magic item from the players' wish lists.

Parcel 6: 1,000 pp, a statue of a gold dragon carved from astral fire (worth 50,000 gp), a manuscript describing the lost arts of necromancy penned by Vecna (worth 50,000 gp), and a wooden coffer containing 10 emeralds (worth 5,000 gp each).

Parcel 9: A loose pile of 90,000 gp.

One square = 5 feet

MUTE SENTINELS

Encounter Level 24 (34,800 XP)

SETUP

2 death giant soulfire hurlers (D)
4 giant mummies (M)

Positioned around the opening in the floor are four giant mummies, each the remains of a death giant that angered the Golden Architect. They stand here mutely, watchful for intruders as they stare through the opening at the nothing beyond.

Most of the time, the giant mummies are left alone, but when the characters enter the complex, a pair of death giant soulfire hurlers has come to check on them.

When the PCs enter area 1, read:
A ledge extends out around the opening in the floor's center ending at the curved walls forming the room. Four hulking figures, each wrapped in fabric, stir with unlife. Green eyes flicker at your intrusion. You see a pair of doors behind one giant mummy. Beyond another, where a set of stairs climbs, you spy two coal-gray giants wreathed in ghostly shapes of what can only be souls.

Place the miniatures where shown on the tactical map, and have the players place their miniatures in squares adjacent to the Eye. The creatures roll for initiative and attack when the first intruder enters. If the characters come to this room through area 2 or from some other direction, the mummies attack only if they or the death giants are first attacked.

TACTICS

The giant mummies each attack a different intruder to cast the widest net with their *despair* auras. On the first round, the giant mummies make bull rush attacks (+16 vs. Fortitude) against the characters to push them out over the opening in the floor. If one of the heroes attacks with a radiant power, all the giant mummies converge on that character and make *rotting slam* attacks until the character falls.

Given the somewhat cramped quarters in this room, the giant mummies likely catch one or more allies in their *dust of blinding death* attacks. The death giants are aware of this attack and try to keep at least

---

2 Death Giant Soulfire Hurlers (D)	Level 27 Artillery
Large shadow humanoid (giant)	XP 11,000 each

Initiative +22 **Senses** Perception +23; darkvision
Soulsnatcher aura 10; enemies within the aura take 5 necrotic damage and a -2 penalty to attack rolls and all defenses; a creature that dies within the aura bestows one soul shard to the death giant; see also *soul shroud*.
HP 180; **Bloodied** 90
AC 41; **Fortitude** 39, **Reflex** 41, **Will** 37
Resist 15 necrotic
Speed 7
⊕ **Greataxe** (standard; at-will) ✦ **Weapon**
  Reach 2; +34 vs. AC; 2d6 + 11 damage (crit 6d6 + 18), and the target is pushed 1 square.
❊ **Hurled Soulfire** (standard; at-will) ✦ **Necrotic**
  Area burst 1 within 10; +32 vs. Reflex; 2d8 + 9 necrotic damage. The death giant can expend one soul shard to increase the power's damage to 4d8 + 9.
Consume Soul Shard (minor; at-will) ✦ **Healing**
  The death giant expends one soul shard and regains 20 hit points.
Soul Shroud
  The *soul shroud* contains soul shards that swirl around the death giant to protect and empower it. At the beginning of an encounter, the *soul shroud* contains four soul shards. When the *soul shroud* is depleted of soul shards, the death giant takes a -2 penalty to attack rolls.
Alignment Evil **Languages** Giant, Draconic
Skills Intimidate +22
Str 24 (+20) **Dex** 29 (+22) **Wis** 21 (+18)
Con 23 (+19) **Int** 12 (+14) **Cha** 18 (+17)
Equipment chainmail, greataxe

---

4 Giant Mummies (M)	Level 21 Brute
Large natural humanoid (undead)	XP 3,200 each

Initiative +12 **Senses** Perception +16; darkvision
Despair (Fear) aura 5; enemies within the aura take a -2 penalty to attack rolls against the giant mummy.
HP 240; **Bloodied** 120; see also *dust of death*
Regeneration 10 (if the giant mummy takes radiant damage, regeneration doesn't function on its next turn)
AC 33; **Fortitude** 34, **Reflex** 30, **Will** 31; see also *despair* above
Immune disease, poison; **Resist** 10 necrotic; **Vulnerable** 10 fire
Speed 6
⊕ **Rotting Slam** (standard; at-will) ✦ **Disease, Necrotic**
  +24 vs. AC; 3d8 + 6 necrotic damage, and the target contracts level 21 mummy rot (see below).
↤ **Dust of Blinding Death** (when first bloodied and again when reduced to 0 hit points) ✦ **Acid**
  The giant mummy releases a cloud of corrosive dust: close burst 2; +22 vs. Fortitude; 1d8 + 7 acid damage, and the target takes ongoing 10 acid damage and is blinded (save ends both).
Alignment Unaligned **Languages** Giant
Str 22 (+16) **Dex** 14 (+12) **Wis** 12 (+11)
Con 24 (+17) **Int** 6 (+8) **Cha** 16 (+13)

Mummy Rot	Level 21 Disease	Endurance improve DC 29, maintain DC 24, worsen DC 23 or lower

| ◁ The target is cured | ◁ **Initial Effect:** The target regains only half the normal number of hit points from healing effects. | ◁▷ The target regains only half the normal number of hit points from healing effects. In addition, the target takes 10 necrotic damage, which cannot be healed until the target is cured of the disease. | ▷ The target dies. |

ONE SQUARE = 5 FEET

FEATURES OF THE AREA

Illumination: Darkness.

Doors: Two sets of doors are set in the western walls, one off area 1 and the other leading from area 2. The doors off area 1 are unlocked and bear bas-reliefs of the death giant city, a jumble of towers, bridges, and steep walls. The doors leading from area 2 are described on page 139.

Stairs: A steep set of stairs climbs to area 2. Each space containing these stairs costs 3 squares of movement to enter. Both sets of stairs in area 2 also are steep and require 3 squares of movement to enter.

Eye: A 35-foot-diameter opening occupies the center of area 1. A character falling through the opening drops away to land on the Plain of Sighing Stones. The distance the character falls depends on how high the Citadel is flying (typically 200 feet).

Damaged Floor: The floor in area 2 is damaged. Any creature entering a space containing the damaged floor must succeed on a saving throw or fall through the crack to plummet to the plain as described on page 139.

Statues: Two statues flank the western doors in area 1. Each statue depicts a towering winged humanoid dressed in robes. In place of a head, each has a skull with green fire burning in the eye sockets. These statues contain necrotic power, and any undead creature starting its turn in a space adjacent to a statue gains 10 temporary hit points. Any living creature in a space adjacent to the statue regains only half its healing surge value when spending a healing surge.

A character can topple a statue with a DC 24 Strength check and cause any creature in the statue's path to be targeted by the following attack: reach 2; +24 vs. Reflex; 2d12 + 8 damage, and the target is knocked prone and is immobilized (save ends). A toppled statue loses its necrotic qualities. A statue has AC 4, Fortitude 10, Reflex 4, and 80 hit points. A DC 16 Athletics check is required to climb a statue.

Hieroglyphics: The walls throughout both rooms are painted in complex pictograms recounting the rise and fall of the death giant city. A character capable of reading the Davek or Supernal scripts can make out enough of their meaning to piece together the dragon's history as described in the "Background" entries on page 138.

2 squares between them and their undead allies. If a giant mummy becomes blinded, it shifts in a random direction each round and attacks the closest creature it notices until it succeeds on a saving throw. The giant mummies fight until destroyed.

The death giant soulfire hurlers hang back in area 2 and use *hurled soulfire* against controllers and leaders lurking behind defenders. They use this tactic, falling back deeper into their room if needed, until they exhaust their soul shards. When they can't use their area attacks, they draw their greataxes and engage the lead characters in melee, slaying fallen characters to harvest new soul shards when possible.

The death giants fight until reduced to 44 or fewer hit points. One flees to enlist the death giants in area 4, while the other moves to area 10 to warn the gold dragon.

Night Haunt

Encounter Level 24 (32,450 XP)

Setup

1 that which should not be trap (W)
1 entropic collapse trap (E)
Askaran-Rus (A)
3 death giants (G)

Askaran-Rus was once a mortal necromancer, but when his time ran out and his soul drifted to the Shadowfell, he refused to surrender to fate and instead gathered the stuff of shadow to construct a new body for himself—an obscene thing filled with cruelty, spite, and endless malice.

It was an accident that Askaran-Rus wound up in the Citadel. He, like others before him, sought to enslave the indigenous people wandering the Plain of Sighing Stones and was swept up with the rest when the Citadel descended. Neither the death giants nor the dragon has much interest in the nightwalker, and Askaran-Rus has little interest in them. What he seeks is escape, and he believes he has found it in the portal shining in this room.

This encounter can occur if the characters enter area 3 or area 4. See page 139 for details on area 4.

When the PCs can see into area 3, read:
Beyond the doors, you see what looks to be a shrine of sorts. Strange pillars stretch fifty feet to the ceiling overhead, and a pale stone basin holds a bubbling noxious black slime. At the north end of the room, a shimmering window shines with blue light. You also see a towering figure of a black giant, composed of inky darkness except for its eyes, which burn with white light.

Tactics

Askaran-Rus goes on the offensive when he notices the characters. He makes a slam attack against any creature that comes within his reach and uses *void gaze* to rid himself of any defenders or melee strikers. He moves deeper into the room when possible, hoping to lure the adventurers into the area of entropic collapse or push them into *that which should not be*. He reserves *finger of death* for the character who annoys him the most. Askaran-Rus has no intention of dying today—or any other day. If he thinks he might lose, he'll look for an opportunity to escape.

The death giants respond to sounds of combat, starting on the second round, and move from their starting positions to investigate. Once the death giants join the fight, the nightwalker switches tactics. He uses *void gaze* to push enemies into squares adjacent to the death giants, so the giants can burn the

adventurers with their burst attacks. The death giants rely on greataxe attacks until two or more enemies are in range of *soulfire burst*. The death giants fight until destroyed.

Askaran-Rus (A)		Level 24 Elite Brute (Leader)
Large shadow humanoid (undead), nightwalker		XP 12,100

Initiative +18   **Senses** Perception +17; darkvision
Void Chill (Cold, Necrotic) aura 5; each enemy that starts its turn in the aura takes 5 cold and necrotic damage and grants combat advantage until the start of the enemy's next turn.
HP 548; **Bloodied** 274
AC 35; **Fortitude** 37, **Reflex** 35, **Will** 37
Immune disease, poison; **Resist** 20 cold, 20 necrotic; **Vulnerable** 20 radiant
Saving Throws +2
Speed 8
Action Points 1
⊕ **Slam** (standard; at-will) ✦ **Cold, Necrotic**
   Reach 2; +27 vs. AC; 1d8 + 8 damage plus 2d8 cold and necrotic damage, and the target is dazed until the end of Askaran-Rus's next turn.
↗ **Finger of Death** (standard; encounter) ✦ **Gaze, Necrotic**
   Ranged 5; targets a bloodied creature; +25 vs. Fortitude; the target drops to 0 hit points. (Resistance to necrotic damage doesn't affect this power.)
↤ **Void Gaze** (minor 1/round; at-will) ✦ **Gaze, Necrotic**
   Close blast 5; +25 vs. Will; 2d10 + 8 necrotic damage, Askan-Rus pushes the target 4 squares, and the target takes a -2 penalty to all defenses (save ends).
Alignment Evil   **Languages** Common, telepathy 20
Skills Stealth +23
Str 26 (+20)   **Dex** 22 (+18)   **Wis** 20 (+17)
Con 24 (+19)   **Int** 16 (+15)   **Cha** 26 (+20)

---

3 Death Giants (G)		Level 22 Brute
Large shadow humanoid (giant)		XP 4,150 each

Initiative +16   **Senses** Perception +19; darkvision
Soulcatcher aura 5; a creature that dies within the aura bestows one soul shard to the death giant (see *soul shroud*).
HP 255; **Bloodied** 127
AC 34; **Fortitude** 37, **Reflex** 33, **Will** 31
Resist 15 necrotic
Speed 7
⊕ **Greataxe** (standard; at-will) ✦ **Weapon**
   Reach 2; +25 vs. AC; 4d6 + 9 damage (crit 4d6 + 33).
↤ **Soulfire Burst** (standard; at-will) ✦ **Necrotic**
   Close burst 1; +23 vs. Reflex; 2d8 + 5 necrotic damage. The death giant must expend one soul shard to use this power.
Consume Soul Shard (minor; at-will) ✦ **Healing**
   The death giant expends one soul shard and regains 20 hit points.
Soul Shroud
   The *soul shroud* contains soul shards that swirl around the death giant to protect and empower it. At the beginning of an encounter, the *soul shroud* contains four soul shards. While the *soul shroud* is depleted of soul shards, the death giant takes a -2 penalty to attack rolls.
Alignment Evil   **Languages** Giant
Skills Intimidate +18
Str 28 (+20)   **Dex** 20 (+16)   **Wis** 16 (+14)
Con 25 (+18)   **Int** 12 (+12)   **Cha** 15 (+13)
Equipment chainmail, greataxe

Entropic Collapse (E) — Level 23 Warder
Trap — XP 5,100

This chamber swirls with dust, as though no one has disturbed the place in a long, long time.

Trap: Golgorax relishes the idea of sharing his madness with creatures that would dare enter his Citadel. He had set his entropic collapse to release as soon as any creature—magical or not—comes within 2 squares of the portal. It creates a temporary unweaving of the strands of time. Although reality reasserts itself a few moments later, the damage to the psyches of those that glimpse beyond time takes longer to heal.

Perception
✦ DC 29: The character notices that the swirling dust appears to glow with faint luminescence.

Additional Skill: Arcana
✦ DC 24: The character notices and identifies the telltale dust glow that often presages entropic collapse.

Trigger
When a character moves into a square within 2 squares of the portal, or when a character 3 or fewer squares away uses an arcane power, the trap attacks.

Attack ✦ Psychic
Opportunity Action   **Close** burst 3
Target: Each creature in burst
Attack: +29 vs. Will
Hit: 5d6 + 8 psychic damage, and the target is dazed (save ends).
Miss: Half damage, and the target is dazed (save ends).
Special: Immortals, animates, and undead are immune to the effects of an entropic collapse.

FEATURES OF THE AREA

Illumination: Light from the portal provides area 3 with dim light.

Pillars: Four 50-foot-tall pillars support the ceiling in area 3. Each pillar has AC 4, Fortitude 10, Reflex 4, and 80 hit points. Destroying a pillar causes it to create a zone of difficult terrain in a close burst 1 centered on the pillar that lasts until cleared. If three or more pillars fall, the ceiling starts to collapse. At the end of each round, make an attack against each creature in the room: +24 vs. Reflex; 2d6 + 7 damage, and the target is knocked prone. On a critical hit, the target is knocked prone and restrained (save ends). After 3 rounds of this, the entire ceiling collapses, automatically burying all creatures in the

That Which Should Not Be (W) — Level 20 Blaster
Trap — XP 2,800

A black soupy morass fills the basin and when a living creature draws near, it stirs into action.

Trap: The basin ooze is a little touchy, and the trap springs as soon a living creature moves adjacent to it.

Perception
✦ DC 16: The character notices the foulness in the basin.
✦ DC 24: The character notices the fluids twitch and writhe.

Initiative +24

Trigger
When a character ends its movement in a space adjacent to the basin, the hazard rolls initiative and attacks on its turn.

Attack ✦ Necrotic
Standard Action   **Melee** 5
Target: One creature
Attack: +23 vs. Reflex
Hit: 2d6 + 7 necrotic damage, and the target is grabbed. It takes a -5 penalty to attempts to escape the grab. The creature takes ongoing 10 necrotic damage as long as it is grabbed by that which should not be.
Miss: Half damage, and the target is knocked prone.
Special: That which should not be can have up to four creatures grabbed at once.

Countermeasures
✦ A creature can attack that which should not be with a fire attack (AC 32, other defenses 30). If that which should not be is hit with two fire attacks, it is disabled.
✦ With a DC 27 Strength check, a creature can knock the basin to the floor, spilling the ooze and disabling the trap.

room. All creatures take 3d10 + 5 damage and are trapped. It takes a DC 26 Athletics check to crawl out of the rubble.

Statues: Two statues that depict fused bodies and faces trapped in stasis stand near the middle of area 3. Characters standing in spaces adjacent to these statues grant combat advantage to all enemies. Each statue has AC 4, Fortitude 10, Reflex 4, and 40 hit points. Reducing a statue to 0 hit points causes the statue to make the following attack: close burst 2: +24 vs. Will, and the target is pushed 3 squares and dazed (save ends).

Permanent Portal: The portal opens onto the natural world to a location of your choosing. A creature that moves through it passes to the natural world instantly, and the portal becomes inactive until the start of the next round.

Stairs: Characters climbing the stairs in area 4 must spend 3 squares of movement to enter their spaces.

ONE SQUARE = 5 FEET

Gold Madness

Encounter Level 26 (54,352 XP)

Setup

Golgorax, the Golden Architect (G)
1 death titan (T)
2 voidsoul specters (V)
4 death thrall attendants (D)

The Golden Architect coils around his treasure on the ledge overlooking the room, tossing insults and making impossible demands of his servants.

When the PCs can see into this area, read:
Although this massive chamber stands in shambles, you can still see what this room once was. Walls bear gold leaf in strips. Intricate carvings evoke draconic imagery, wisdom, and architectural wonders—all captured in the complex pictographic patterns still visible in some places. The ceiling has largely given away, revealing ledges tens of feet in the air.

As you take in the scene, you notice shapes stirring in the room's shadows. Four large, shadowy humanoids turn eyes toward you, while n even larger one rises from its place to confront you from behind the bronze death mask concealing its features.

As the tension spikes, a shrill laugh sounds from above, and you see tarnished gold scales reflecting light dully from the draconic visage peering over the lip of the room's highest ledge.

Perception Check
DC 34 *You see pale figures swirling around inside the yawning hole in the floor.*

Tactics

The battle here erupts swiftly. The giants and dragon converge on the adventurers in rage that their inner sanctum has been breached. The gold dragon descends from his ledge, using *fearsome presence* to daze the characters, and then he uses his *breath weapon*, not caring whether it catches his allies. The dragon maneuvers to keep allies inside his aura.

When the death titan exhausts its soul shards, the dragon uses *confer soul shard* to boost its ally's attacks. The death titan uses *soul devourer* against the lead character and then moves and spends its action point to make a melee or *soulfire burst* attack.

The death titan keeps moving to keep the largest number of adventurers inside its aura and fights alongside the thrall attendants so it can scoop up their soul shards when they are slain.

The voidsoul specters creep behind the characters' front lines to attack leaders, ranged strikers, and controllers. They avoid divine characters when possible, turning invisible to escape their notice. All the monsters fight until destroyed.

Golgorax (G)	Level 28 Elite Controller (Leader)
Elder gold dragon	
Huge natural magical beast (dragon, shapechanger)	XP 26,000

Initiative +21 **Senses** Perception +23; darkvision
Emboldening Flames (Fire) aura 3; each ally within the aura deals 5 extra fire damage on its melee and ranged attacks.
HP 522; **Bloodied** 261; see also *bloodied breath*
AC 42; **Fortitude** 39, **Reflex** 42, **Will** 41
Resist 25 fire
Saving Throws +2
Speed 8, fly 12 (hover), overland flight 15
Action Points 1

ⓘ **Bite** (standard; at-will) ✦ **Fire**
Reach 3; +33 vs. AC; 2d8 + 9 damage plus 2d8 fire damage.

ⓘ **Claw** (standard; at-will)
Reach 3; +33 vs. AC; 2d8 + 9 damage.

✦ **Double Attack** (standard; at-will)
The dragon makes two claw attacks.

↶ **Breath Weapon** (standard; encounter) ✦ **Fire**
Close blast 5; +30 vs. Reflex; 5d8 + 9 fire damage, and the target is weakened (save ends). *Miss:* Half damage.

↶ **Bloodied Breath** (immediate reaction, when first bloodied; encounter)
Golgorax's *breath weapon* recharges, and the dragon uses it immediately.

↶ **Fearsome Presence** (standard; encounter) ✦ **Fear**
Close burst 10; targets enemies; +30 vs. Will; the target is dazed until the end of Golgorax's next turn. *Aftereffect:* The target takes a -2 penalty to attack rolls (save ends).

↶ **Fiery Rebuke** (immediate reaction, when hit by an attack; at-will) ✦ **Fire**
Close burst 5; +30 vs. Fortitude; the target is pushed 5 squares and takes ongoing 10 fire damage (save ends).

↶ **Shadow Gloom** (minor; recharge ⚄ ⚅) ✦ **Necrotic**
Close burst 3; targets enemies; +30 vs. Will; the target slides 3 squares and is blinded (save ends).

↗ **Confer Soul Shard** (minor; encounter) ✦ **Necrotic**
The dragon donates part of his soul to a death giant: Ranged 5; targets death giants or death titans; the target gains one soul shard, and the dragon grants combat advantage until the start of his next turn.

Change Shape (minor; encounter) ✦ **Polymorph**
The dragon can alter its physical form to take on the appearance of any Medium humanoid or beast (see Change Shape, MM 280).

Alignment Evil	**Languages** Common, Draconic, Giant

Skills Arcana +30, Athletics +28, Diplomacy +29, History +30, Insight +23, Intimidate +29, Religion +30

Str 28 (+23)	**Dex** 24 (+21)	**Wis** 19 (+18)
Con 29 (+23)	**Int** 32 (+25)	**Cha** 30 (+24)

Features of the Area

Illumination: Darkness.

Ceiling: A domed ceiling rises 100 feet overhead.

Ledges: The two ledges in this room are remnants of the multiple levels that made up this chamber. The northern ledge is 30 feet overhead, and the southern one is 60 feet above the floor. The lower ledge is unstable. Any Medium or larger creature that ends its movement there is subject to an attack: +30 vs. Reflex; the floor gives way, dropping the target to the floor below for 3d10 damage.

Doors: Unlocked stone doors lead into this room. Because of their size and weight, they require a DC 24 Strength check to open.

Death Titan (T)
Level 25 Elite Brute

Huge shadow humanoid (giant) — XP 14,000

Initiative +18   **Senses** Perception +20; darkvision

Soulburner aura 5; enemies in the aura take a -2 penalty to attack rolls and defenses; a creature that dies within the aura bestows one soul shard to the death titan (see *soul shroud*).

HP 574; **Bloodied** 287

AC 39; **Fortitude** 42, **Reflex** 38, **Will** 35

Resist 30 necrotic

Saving Throws +2

Speed 8

Action Points 1

⊕ **Greataxe** (standard; at-will) ✦ **Weapon**

   Reach 3; +28 vs. AC; 2d8 + 10 damage (crit 6d8 + 26).

↯ **Double Attack** (standard; at-will)

   The death titan makes two greataxe attacks.

⤢ **Soul Devourer** (standard; recharge ⚅⚅) ✦ **Necrotic**

   Ranged 5; +28 vs. Fortitude; the target loses a healing surge, and the death titan's soul shroud gains one soul shard. A target without healing surges takes damage equal to half its total hit points.

⤜ **Soulfire Burst** (standard; at-will) ✦ **Necrotic**

   Close burst 1; +26 vs. Reflex; 2d12 + 6 necrotic damage. The death titan must expend one soul shard to use this power.

Consume Soul Shard (minor; at-will) ✦ **Healing**

   The death titan expends one soul shard and regains 20 hit points.

Soul Shroud

   The *soul shroud* contains soul shards that swirl around the death titan to protect and empower it. At the beginning of an encounter, the *soul shroud* contains four soul shards. While the *soul shroud* is depleted of soul shards, the death titan takes a -2 penalty to attack rolls.

Alignment Evil   **Languages** Giant

Skills Intimidate +20

Str 31 (+22)	**Dex** 23 (+18)	**Wis** 17 (+15)
Con 27 (+20)	**Int** 12 (+13)	**Cha** 16 (+15)

Equipment plate armor, greataxe

Statues: Four obsidian statues depicting the likeness of the gold dragon flank each set of doors. These statues radiate malice, and fear attacks against creatures in spaces adjacent to the statues gain a +2 bonus to the attack rolls.

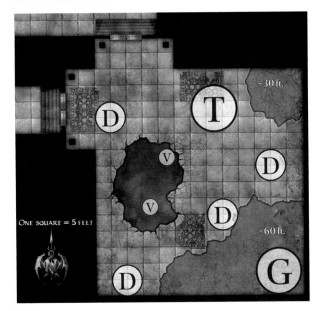

One square = 5 feet

---

2 Voidsoul Specters (V)
Level 23 Lurker

Medium shadow humanoid (undead) — XP 5,100 each

Initiative +23   **Senses** Perception +16; darkvision

Spectral Cold (Cold) aura 1; each enemy that starts its turn within the aura takes 10 cold damage and takes a -2 penalty to all defenses until the start of its next turn.

HP 115; **Bloodied** 57

AC 35; **Fortitude** 32, **Reflex** 35, **Will** 34

Immune disease, poison; **Resist** 30 necrotic, insubstantial; **Vulnerable** 10 radiant

Speed fly 8 (hover); phasing

⊕ **Spectral Touch** (standard; at-will) ✦ **Necrotic**

   +25 vs. Reflex; 2d12 + 6 necrotic damage.

⤢ **Life Siphon** (standard; encounter) ✦ **Healing, Necrotic**

   Close blast 5; +25 vs. Fortitude; 2d12 + 6 necrotic damage, and the voidsoul specter regains 5 hit points for every creature damaged by the attack.

Invisibility (minor 1/round; at-will) ✦ **Illusion**

   The voidsoul specter becomes invisible until it attacks or until it is hit by an attack. It remains invisible while using *life siphon*.

Alignment Chaotic evil   **Languages** Common

Skills Stealth +24

Str 12 (+12)	**Dex** 26 (+19)	**Wis** 10 (+11)
Con 19 (+15)	**Int** 11 (+11)	**Cha** 23 (+17)

---

4 Death Thrall Attendants (D)
Level 22 Minion Brute

Large shadow humanoid (giant) — XP 1,038 each

Initiative +16   **Senses** Perception +19; darkvision

HP 1; a missed attack never damages a minion.

AC 34; **Fortitude** 36, **Reflex** 33, **Will** 32

Resist 15 necrotic

Speed 7

⊕ **Greataxe** (standard; at-will) ✦ **Weapon**

   Reach 2; +25 vs. AC; 11 damage (crit 21 damage).

⤜ **Soulfire Explosion** (when reduced to 0 hit points) ✦ **Necrotic**

   Close burst 1; +23 vs. Reflex; 5 damage and the target loses a healing surge. If the target doesn't have a healing surge available, it takes damage equal to its healing surge value.

Soul Thrall

   An attendant gains a +2 bonus to attack rolls while in a death giant's or death titan's aura.

Alignment Evil   **Languages** Giant

Str 28 (+20)	**Dex** 20 (+16)	**Wis** 16 (+14)
Con 25 (+18)	**Int** 12 (+12)	**Cha** 15 (+13)

Equipment chainmail, greataxe

Each statue has AC 4, Fortitude 10, Reflex 4, and 80 hit points. If a statue is destroyed, the gold dragon becomes enraged and will spend his action point during his next turn.

Gap: A hole in the floor drops away to open air. A character falling through the opening lands on the Plain of Sighing Stones. The distance the character falls depends on how high the citadel is flying (typically 200 feet).

Damaged Floor: Each space adjacent to the gap is considered damaged. Any creature that enters a space containing damaged floor must succeed on a saving throw or fall through the crack to plummet to the Plain.

Mercury dragon lair for five 26th-level adventurers

Throughout the tempestuous realms of the Elemental Chaos, massive "earthbergs" float through seas of water or magma, and even through the smoke and the empty skies. Some are tiny, mere rocks defying gravity; others are the size of great islands. These are often inhabited by great elementals, by demons, by slaads, by archons, and, yes, by dragons.

One of these, a great inverted mountain called the Earthen Dagger, is perhaps among the most dangerous—not just because it is the home of an amoral dragon of ancient age and mercenary temperament, not merely due to the potent elementals that guard him, not even because of the molten flows and poisonous fumes that rise from the hollows of the mountain as though fed by eternal springs. No, the Earthen Dagger poses such a threat because, thanks to planar magics that infuse its every rock, its orbit carries the earthberg—at seemingly random but all too frequent intervals—from the Elemental Chaos to the clouded skies of the world.

BACKGROUND

Arcana or History DC 17: There's no telling who or what might have occupied the Earthen Dagger in epochs past. Maybe the mountain occurred naturally in the turbulent Elemental Chaos, or perhaps it was ripped away from a larger landmass and deliberately set afloat. Doubtless, it played home to a wide variety of creatures throughout the years, and it surely spent many more years bereft of inhabitants as it passed through realms of poison, ice, and fire. During its sporadic visits to the mortal realm, powerful wizards and lesser dragons established lairs in its caverns only to find themselves assailed by dangers for which they were woefully unprepared when the mountain returned to its home plane. And then it was found, during one of its mortal world excursions, by the mercury dragon Tananzinaen.

History DC 22: A young dragon at the time, Tananzinaen had worked alongside several other dragons, both metallic and chromatic. Rather than compete for his own treasure and territory, Tananzinaen elected to help other dragons establish their territories, in exchange for hunting rights and a small percentage of their collected hoards. At one point, two rival dragons learned that Tananzinaen had hired himself out to both of them, and they expressed their displeasure with him violently. Escaping with nothing more than his life—and only barely that—the mercury dragon stumbled upon the Earthen Dagger and took shelter in its crags, hoping its movements

would take him beyond his enemies' territories. Like so many before him, he was swept along when it returned to the Elemental Chaos—but unlike those before him, Tananzinaen was rugged enough to survive the new environment.

History DC 28: The ever-pragmatic dragon immediately recognized the value of such a lair. A sanctum that would, on a regular and (after long-term observation) predictable basis, take him to another world where his enemies could not follow was worth a great deal. Tananzinaen made himself at home and continued to hire out his services—as soldier, scout, courier, enforcer, or assassin—to other dragons as well as to mortal kings, emperors, priests, and criminals. He made certain to never again hire himself out to both sides of a conflict, and he swiftly found himself rolling in riches with contacts amid the rich and powerful across the world.

History DC 31: As he grew older and became powerful enough that hiding and secrecy were no longer of great concern, Tananzinaen began accepting contracts from creatures of the Elemental Chaos. At times, he worked for various sorts of elementals, but his most frequent employer became the Caliph Ma'mun, a political rival of the efreet Sultan of the City of Brass. As part of his payment, Tananzinaen demanded that the caliph supply him with guards, loyal soldiers that would protect his treasures and his lair when he was away.

And thus it stands today: A mercenary dragon, ancient and powerful, lairs within a floating isle that takes him from the mortal world to the Elemental Chaos and back, keeping him mostly out of reach of the many parties he has wronged. Only the greatest of heroes can hope to reach the Earthen Dagger, let alone fight their way through Tananzinaen's elemental guards and finally end the threat of the ancient dragon.

ENVIRONMENT

There's nothing remotely normal about the Earthen Dagger and its environs. The inverted mountain floats through the skies of both the mortal realm and the Elemental Chaos. You might decide to give the characters a break and have the winds and weather remain relatively clear. Or you might buffet them with powerful storms or, in the Elemental Chaos, gusts of fire and toxic rains.

The outside slope of the mountain requires a DC 30 Athletics check to climb—in part because of its rough stone and the movement of the mountain, and in part because anyone scaling the mountain must contend with the outward angle of the slope.

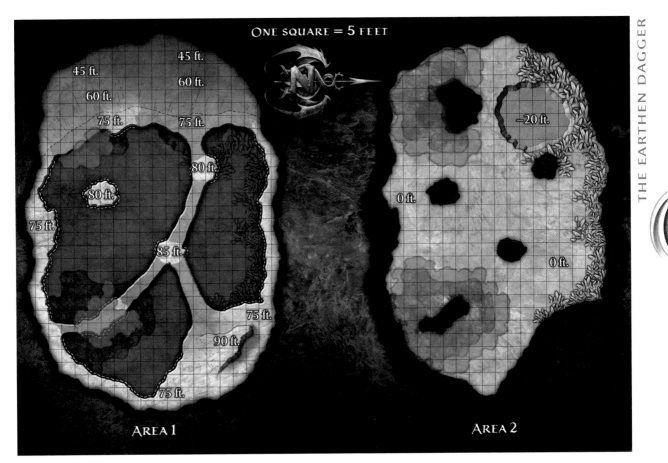

ONE SQUARE = 5 FEET

45 ft.
45 ft.
60 ft.
60 ft.
75 ft.   75 ft.
80 ft.
80 ft.
75 ft.
85 ft.
75 ft.
90 ft.
75 ft.

AREA 1

−20 ft.
0 ft.
0 ft.

AREA 2

The mountain is cloaked in a faint haze, toxic and uncomfortably hot. In addition to its combat effects (defined in the tactical encounters), it has a long-term impact on creatures. This is considered an environmental danger (*DMG* 158) consisting of pervasive smoke, requiring characters to make DC 26 Endurance checks when they enter this area for the first time (or when they reenter it after leaving). Anyone who fails this check loses a healing surge. This danger comes from a combination of the toxic haze and the heat, neither of which is nearly as dangerous on its own. Any creature immune to either fire or poison is not harmed by the haze.

When you run these encounters, decide how high off the ground the mountain is flying. It is important to establish the earthberg's flying height because creatures might find themselves pushed off the edges of area 1 or into the hole and down the slope providing egress from area 2.

The map shows only two levels of the mountain, but others could continue below these, either extensions of Tananzinaen's lair or home to something else of which even the dragon is unaware.

As the PCs approach the floating isle, read:
You see an enormous mass of stone hanging in the sky. It's in the shape of a great mountain, but it is widest on top and tapers to a twisted point hundreds of feet lower. A shimmering haze hovers above its surface, and thick plumes of dark smoke rise from caverns deep within.

AREA 1: THE UPPER LEVEL

This topmost level of the earthberg is a rugged stone surface, replete with numerous gaping craters that provide access to the level (or levels, if you choose) below. A broad plateau of stone on the southern end rises higher than its surroundings. The efreet guards dwell in a separate area, but most spend their waking hours here.

Tactical Encounter: "Fire at Will," page 150, and possibly "Poisoned Pit," page 152.

AREA 2: THE LOWER LEVEL

This is the lair of Tananzinaen. The efreets do not come here unless in pursuit of invaders. The dragon is guarded by strange creatures formed of toxic haze called venomous remnants, formed by means of an ancient ritual around the escaping essences of those slain by the poisonous smoke. Tananzinaen does not take kindly to intrusion into his lair, and if the characters make it this far without being politely escorted out by the efreets, he assumes that they are enemies.

Tactical Encounter: "Fire at Will," page 150, and "Poisoned Pit," page 152.

TREASURE

Hidden in the lower level—within the areas of liquid stone, necrotic crystal, and/or toxic smoke—the characters might find wealth and magic items equivalent to two level 28 treasure parcels.

JASON A. ENGLE

Fire at Will

Encounter Level 26 (53,300 XP)

Setup

3 efreet flamestriders (F)
1 efreet karadjin (K)
1 efreet pyresinger (P)
1 thunderblast cyclone (C)

The efreets that stand watch over Tananzinaen's lair, as part of his long-term payment from the Caliph Ma'mun, are vicious combatants, and they take their responsibility as sentries seriously. If any strangers—such as the characters—set foot upon the dragon's isle, the efreet karadjin challenges them, demanding to know their purpose. If they don't answer properly—if they do not swiftly convince it that they have come to hire the dragon for some great purpose—the karadjin demands they leave and immediately moves to attack.

When the PCs first set foot on the earthberg, read:

As you set foot on the floating isle, you can feel the heat radiating from the stone surface. An array of ledges and narrow bridges overlook a deep chasm shrouded in dense haze. You can't see what lies below.

A thunderous voice, with an undertone of roiling flame, calls through the haze.

If any of the PCs speak or understand Draconic, continue:

"You have trespassed upon the sovereign domain of the mighty and blessed Tananzinaen, He of the Quicksilver Hide. Explain yourselves swiftly, lest you burn."

When the efreets attack, read:

Several forms appear in the haze. They have flames flickering across their flesh. One is taller than an ogre and carries a blazing scimitar. The others are slender and move about in the distance. Atop the eastern mesa, you see a whirling cyclone that seems to have lights reminiscent of eyes inside its shapeless form. As you take in this scene, two more efreets rise on columns of fire through the haze below.

Arcana Check

DC 26 *The smoke that wafts up from below is particularly noxious, leading you to the conclusion that exposure to it would increase your susceptibility to poison.*

Tactics

The efreet karadjin and the flamestriders close to melee, while the pyresinger and the thunderblast cyclone remain at range, flying back and forth between areas or hovering off the edge of the earthberg to prevent characters from drawing near.

---

3 Efreet Flamestriders (F) — **Level 23 Skirmisher**
Large elemental humanoid (fire) — XP 5,100 each

Initiative +20 **Senses** Perception +15
Blazing Soul (Fire) aura 1; each creature within the aura that is taking ongoing fire damage takes 5 extra ongoing fire damage.
HP 217; **Bloodied** 108
AC 37; **Fortitude** 36, **Reflex** 35, **Will** 34
Immune fire
Speed 6, fly 8 (hover); see also *fiery teleport*
⊕ **Scimitar** (standard; at-will) ✦ **Fire, Weapon**
  Reach 2; +28 vs. AC; 2d10 + 8 damage (crit 6d10 + 28), and ongoing 5 fire damage (save ends).
➷ **Fiery Grasp** (standard; at-will) ✦ **Fire**
  Ranged 20; a fiery hand appears and grabs the target; +25 vs. Reflex; 1d6 + 8 fire damage, and the target takes ongoing 10 fire damage and is immobilized (save ends both).
Fiery Teleport (move; at-will) ✦ **Teleportion**
  The flamestrider can teleport 20 squares, reappearing in a puff of smoke; its destination must be adjacent to a fire creature or a fire.
Alignment Evil **Languages** Primordial
Skills Bluff +22, Insight +20, Intimidate +20
Str 27 (+19) **Dex** 24 (+18) **Wis** 18 (+15)
Con 25 (+18) **Int** 16 (+14) **Cha** 22 (+17)
Equipment scimitar

Efreet Karadjin (K) — **Level 28 Soldier (Leader)**
Large elemental humanoid (fire) — XP 13,000

Initiative +23 **Senses** Perception +23
HP 260; **Bloodied** 130
AC 44; **Fortitude** 45, **Reflex** 42, **Will** 42
Immune fire
Speed 6, fly 8 (hover)
⊕ **Scimitar of Horrendous Flame** (standard; at-will) ✦ **Fire, Weapon**
  Reach 2; +35 vs. AC; 2d10 + 9 damage (crit 6d10 + 29) plus 1d10 fire damage, and the target takes ongoing 15 fire damage and is immobilized (save ends both). *Aftereffect:* Ongoing 15 fire damage (save ends). Saving throws against this power take a -2 penalty.
↯ **Fiery Vendetta** (immediate reaction, when an enemy within reach attacks one of the efreet karadjin's allies; at-will) ✦ **Fire, Weapon**
  The efreet karadjin makes a melee basic attack against the triggering enemy.
Elemental Command (minor; at-will)
  One allied elemental creature within 10 squares of the efreet karadjin (and within its line of sight) shifts.
Alignment Evil **Languages** Draconic, Primordial
Skills Arcana +25, Bluff +26, Insight +23, Intimidate +26
Str 28 (+23) **Dex** 25 (+21) **Wis** 18 (+18)
Con 30 (+24) **Int** 22 (+20) **Cha** 25 (+21)
Equipment scimitar

The melee combatants favor pushing characters off edges or the bridge if circumstances allow, since they can easily follow using flight or teleportation. All the creatures fight to the death.

Efreet Pyresinger (P) — Level 25 Controller
Large elemental humanoid (fire) — XP 7,000

Initiative +20   **Senses** Perception +16

Fiery Soul (Fire) aura 1; each creature that enters the aura or starts its turn there takes 10 fire damage; each creature within the aura that is taking ongoing fire damage takes 5 extra ongoing fire damage.

HP 233; **Bloodied** 116

AC 40; **Fortitude** 37, **Reflex** 36, **Will** 36

Immune fire

Speed 6, fly 8 (hover)

⊕ **Scimitar** (standard; at-will) ✦ **Fire, Weapon**

  Reach 2; +30 vs. AC; 2d10 + 9 damage (crit 6d10 + 29), and ongoing 5 fire damage (save ends).

↗ **Fire Bolt** (standard; at-will) ✦ **Fire, Weapon**

  Ranged 10; +31 vs. AC; 3d6 + 8 fire damage, and ongoing 5 fire damage (save ends).

↗ **Fiery Chains** (standard; recharge ⚄ ⚅ ⚄) ✦ **Fire**

  Ranged 10; +28 vs. Reflex; 2d8 + 7 fire damage, and the target takes ongoing 20 fire damage and is restrained (save ends both). As a move action, the efreet pyresinger can slide a target wrapped in *fiery chains* 1 square.

※ **Sheets of Flame** (standard; recharge ⚄ ⚅ ⚄) ✦ **Fire, Zone**

  Area burst 3 within 20; the pyresinger fills the area with 20-foot-high sheets of roaring flame. Any creature that enters the area or begins its turn in it or adjacent to it takes 10 fire damage. The sheets of flame block line of sight and last until the end of the pyresinger's next turn.

Alignment Evil   **Languages** Draconic, Primordial

Skills Arcana +22, Bluff +25, Diplomacy +25, Insight +21, Intimidate +25

Str 29 (+21)	**Dex** 26 (+20)	**Wis** 18 (+16)
Con 25 (+19)	**Int** 20 (+17)	**Cha** 26 (+20)

Equipment scimitar, scepter

Thunderblast Cyclone (C) — Level 26 Elite Artillery
Huge elemental magical beast (air, water) — XP 18,000

Initiative +24   **Senses** Perception +16

HP 382; **Bloodied** 191

AC 42; **Fortitude** 40, **Reflex** 42, **Will** 35

Immune disease, poison; **Resist** 30 lightning, 30 thunder

Saving Throws +2

Speed fly 10 (hover)

Action Points 1

⊕ **Lightning Arc** (standard; at-will) ✦ **Lightning**

  Reach 3; +29 vs. Reflex; 2d8 + 11 lightning damage.

⊙ **Lightning Bolt** (standard; at-will) ✦ **Lightning**

  Ranged 10; +29 vs. Reflex; 2d8 + 11 lightning damage.

⬅ **Thunderclap** (standard; at-will) ✦ **Thunder**

  Close burst 2; +28 vs. Fortitude; 2d10 + 9 thunder damage.

⬅ **Charged Mist** (standard; recharge ⚄ ⚅) ✦ **Lightning**

  Close burst 3; no attack roll; 1d10 + 9 lightning damage, and the thunderblast cyclone becomes insubstantial until the end of its next turn.

※ **Lightning Storm** (standard; begins uncharged; recharges when the fireburst cyclone uses *charged mist*) ✦ **Lightning, Thunder**

  Area burst 3 within 20; +29 vs. Reflex; 6d8 + 9 lightning and thunder damage. *Miss:* Half damage.

Alignment Unaligned   **Languages** Primordial

Str 25 (+20)	**Dex** 32 (+24)	**Wis** 17 (+16)
Con 29 (+22)	**Int** 8 (+12)	**Cha** 15 (+15)

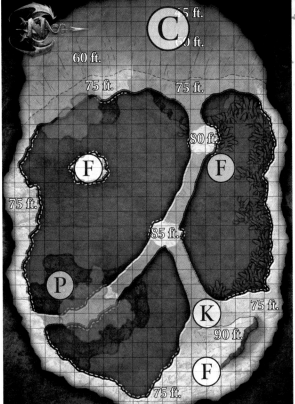

ONE SQUARE = 5 FEET

FEATURES OF THE AREA

Illumination: Bright light.

Bridges: The bridges run above the interior of the Earthen Dagger, which is represented in the "Poisoned Pit" encounter on the following page.

Elevation: The elevation numbers on the map indicate the distance above the floor of the poisoned pit.

Ledges: The dashed lines on the map represent places where a ledge drops off from area 1 into area 2. These vertical surfaces require a DC 28 Athletics check to climb.

Pervasive Haze: The entire earthberg is cocooned in a faint haze. Creatures treat all squares more than 5 squares away as lightly obscured. The area below the bridges is heavily obscured, meaning creatures can't see down into the poisoned pit.

Slopes: A slope counts as difficult terrain for creatures moving up, but not down. A creature that is pushed or that slides down a slope moves 1 extra square, and a character that falls prone on a slope slides 1 square in the direction of lower elevation.

Toxic Smoke: The purple blotches on one of the bridges and on the western edge of the largest hole represent toxic smoke billowing up from below. The smoke is also present in the squares on either side of the bridge and those adjacent to the western ledge. A creature that begins its turn in toxic smoke gains vulnerable 10 poison until the end of its next turn.

POISONED PIT

Encounter Level 29 (88,500 XP)

SETUP

Tananzinaen, ancient mercury dragon (T)
6 venomous remnants (V)

The lower level of the earthberg is Tananzinaen's lair,
where he basks in the warmth and the toxic fumes
of the isle's molten pools. Whether he remained
unaware of the combat above or chose to allow his
guards to handle it, he did not emerge during the initial combat—but once the characters reach the lower
level, he deems them a true threat.

When the PCs enter the lowest level, read:
*The flickering of molten rock, roiling clouds of toxic fumes,
and thick shadows transform the cavern into an echo of the
deepest hells.*

**If the PCs arrive more than 10 squares away
from the dragon, continue with:**
*The air here is so thick with fumes that you can barely
make out the features in front of you.*

**If the PCs arrive or move to within 5 squares of
any venomous remnant, continue with:**
*Here and there, a thick pocket of haze seems to be moving.
Tendrils of smoke form coiling, winding arms, and burning
embers slowly blink, revealing themselves as eyes.*

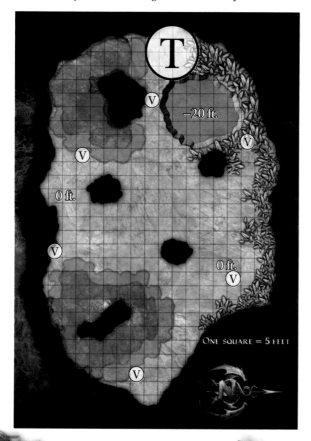

One square = 5 feet

Tananzinaen (T)	Level 29 Solo Lurker
Ancient mercury dragon	
Gargantuan natural magical beast	XP 75,000
(dragon, shapechanger)	

Initiative +28   **Senses** Perception +22; darkvision
HP 1,044; **Bloodied** 522; see also *bloodied breath*
AC 43; **Fortitude** 42, **Reflex** 43, **Will** 39
Resist 10 fire, 30 poison
Saving Throws +5
Speed 9, fly 8 (hover), overland flight 15
Action Points 2

⊕ **Claw** (standard; at-will)
  Reach 4; +32 vs. AC; 2d8 + 12 damage.

↯ **Bite** (standard; at-will)
  Reach 4; +32 vs. AC; 2d10 + 12 damage.

↯ **Draconic Fury** (standard; at-will)
  The dragon makes two claw attacks and one bite attack.

↯ **Quick Snap** (immediate interrupt, when an enemy moves
  adjacent to the dragon; at-will)
  Tananzinaen makes a bite attack against the triggering
  enemy. On a hit, the target also grants combat advantage to
  Tananzinaen (save ends).

↞ **Breath Weapon** (standard; recharge ⚃ ⚅) ✦ **Poison**
  Close blast 5; +32 vs. Fortitude; 4d8 + 8 poison damage, and
  the target takes ongoing 15 poison damage and treats the
  mercury dragon as invisible (save ends both). *Miss:* Half damage.

↞ **Bloodied Breath** (free, when first bloodied; encounter)
  Breath weapon recharges, and Tananzinaen uses it.

↞ **Frightful Presence** (standard; encounter) ✦ **Fear**
  Close burst 10; targets enemies; +32 vs. Will; the target is
  stunned until the end of the dragon's next turn. *Aftereffect:* The
  target takes a -2 penalty to attack rolls (save ends).

↞ **Caliph's Reward** (minor; usable only while bloodied; encounter)
  ✦ **Fire**
  Close burst 10; targets enemies; +30 vs. Reflex; the target takes
  ongoing 15 fire damage and a -2 penalty to all defenses (save
  ends both).

Fluid Shape (immediate interrupt; when an enemy targets the
  dragon; requires a creature be adjacent to the dragon; recharge
  ⚃ ⚅) ✦ **Polymorph**
  The triggering attack targets a different creature adjacent to
  Tananzinaen.

Quicksilver Form (move action; encounter) ✦ **Polymorph**
  Tananzinaen becomes a liquid wave of quicksilver and shifts
  8 squares. He remains in quicksilver form until the end of his
  next turn. While in quicksilver form, Tananzinaen can't attack
  or fly, but gains a climb speed of 6, ignores difficult terrain, and
  doesn't provoke opportunity attacks. He can squeeze through
  any aperture a Tiny creature could fit through. Tananzinaen can
  return to his normal form as a free action on his turn. When
  he returns to normal, each creature within 2 squares grants
  combat advantage to him until the end of his next turn. *Sustain
  Minor:* The quicksilver form persists.

Change Shape (minor; at-will) ✦ **Polymorph**
  Tananzinaen can alter his physical form to appear as any
  Medium or Large humanoid, including a unique individual (see
  "Change Shape," MM2 216).

Combat Advantage
  Tananzinaen deals 3d6 extra damage against a target granting
  combat advantage to him.

Alignment Unaligned   **Languages** Common, Draconic
Skills Acrobatics +29, Bluff +26, Stealth +29
Str 26 (+22)   **Dex** 31 (+24)   **Wis** 17 (+17)
Con 21 (+19)   **Int** 15 (+16)   **Cha** 24 (+21)

If the PCs arrive or move to within 10 squares of the dragon, continue with:

In the darkest reaches of the cave, something stirs, something impossibly huge. It blends with the smoke, but you can see that its hide shimmers like liquid in the flickering light of the magma nearby.

6 Venomous Remnants (V)	Level 26 Minion Artillery
Medium elemental animate	XP 2,250 each

Initiative +19 **Senses** Perception +18; darkvision
Choking Aura (Poison) aura 2; each living creature that enters the aura or starts its turn there takes 5 poison damage.
HP 1; a missed attack never damages a minion.
AC 38; **Fortitude** 37, **Reflex** 36, **Will** 39
Immune disease, poison
Speed fly 7 (hover)
⊕ **Toxic Touch** (standard; at-will) ✦ **Poison**
   +31 vs. Reflex; 8 poison damage.
⊙ **Toxic Breath** (standard; at-will) ✦ **Poison**
   Ranged 20; +33 vs. Fortitude; 12 poison damage.
�֎ **Venomous Rain** (standard; encounter) ✦ **Poison**
   Area burst 3 within 20; targets enemies; +33 vs. Fortitude; the target loses any resistance to poison until the end of the venomous remnant's next turn and takes 10 poison damage.
   Effect: Each venomous remnant in the area gains a +5 bonus to defenses until the end of the triggering remnant's next turn.
Alignment Unaligned **Languages** Abyssal, Draconic
Str 16 (+16) **Dex** 22 (+19) **Wis** 20 (+18)
Con 25 (+20) **Int** 14 (+15) **Cha** 28 (+22)

TACTICS

When combat begins, the venomous remnants approach from multiple directions, possibly even departing the floor of the area and returning from another angle, rather than clumping up to offer characters the opportunity to take them down with a single area effect. They prefer to fight either in the toxic smoke or above the molten squares, because their ability to hover and their poison immunity grant them great tactical advantage in those areas. They take turns using *venomous rain* to make their and Tananzinaen's attacks more effective and to prolong their lives. Venomous remnants fight until destroyed.

Tananzinaen begins combat with his *breath weapon*, if doing so is tactically sound. Otherwise, he focuses an array of melee attacks against a single foe. In any case, Tananzinaen rarely engages in battle for more than a round or two at a time. By using *frightful presence*, his *breath weapon*'s invisibility, *quicksilver form*, or simple shift-and-move tactics, he moves away from melee after a round or two and departs the level. He either reenters with Stealth (keep in mind the concealment offered by the haze and smoke) or entices the characters to come after him—whatever it takes to become hidden or gain combat advantage.

Tananzinaen is a patient fighter, and he's quite content to force the characters to chase him up and down the two levels of the mountain as he watches for opportunities to ambush them (or possibly push them off the edges). He does not, however, grant

them an opportunity for a rest; if it appears they aren't going to follow him after a minute or two, he reappears, engages in combat for a round or two, and retreats once more. Like the venomous remnants, he prefers to fight in the toxic smoke—or at least against foes that are in it.

This is Tananzinaen's lair, his treasure, and his place of business. Although he might seem to retreat, as described above, he never departs. He fights to the death to defend his home.

FEATURES OF THE AREA

Illumination: Dim light.
Ceiling: Much of the lower level is open to the sky. In the east, the ceiling slopes, from as high as 70 feet to as low as 30 feet.
Pervasive Haze: The entire lower area of the earthberg is cocooned in a thick haze. Creatures treat all squares more than 5 squares away as lightly obscured and all squares more than 10 squares away as heavily obscured.
Hole: The hole drops roughly 20 feet straight down before turning into a steep slope that runs for another 40 feet to the southeast, leading to an exit from the mountain (not shown on the map). It requires a DC 28 Athletics check to climb.
Walls and Pillars: The various vertical surfaces here require a DC 28 Athletics check to climb.
Molten Rock: A creature that enters or starts its turn in a square of molten rock (the red areas) takes 10 fire damage and is slowed until the start of its next turn.
Necrotic Crystal: This deep violet crystal radiates necrotic magic. Any attack against a creature standing in a patch of necrotic crystal scores a critical hit on a roll of 18-20. On such a critical hit, half the damage is necrotic rather than the attack's normal damage type. (Flying creatures are unaffected, unless they land in such a square.)
Toxic Smoke: The smoke in the areas represented by purple blotches rises from the molten rock. A creature that begins its turn in this toxic smoke gains vulnerable 10 poison until the end of its next turn.

CHAPTER 4

NEW MONSTERS

THE FIVE varieties of metallic dragon introduced in *Monster Manual 2*—the adamantine, iron, copper, silver, and gold—are the most common kinds. Many other metallic dragons roam the world and the planes beyond. Fiery brass dragons soar over the desert skies, fierce cobalt dragons lurk amid the cold mists of the Shadowfell, and shapechanging steel dragons roam the crowded cities of humankind in the guises of male and female humanoids.

Like the more commonly known metallic dragons, the members of these varieties run the gamut of alignment, motivation, and personality. Some are noble champions of good, while others are merciless tyrants or self-serving plunderers. Even the most benevolent and reasonable of metallic dragons are proud and inflexible creatures, rarely willing to alter their course at the urging of humans or their kind; more than a few societies have found that a "benevolent" dragon's ambitions signal disaster for lesser beings in the area. Few creatures in the world have the power to act for good or evil as dragons do.

Many creatures can trace their origins to metallic dragons, or claim some kinship with them. The fierce magical warriors known as draconians hatch from corrupted metallic dragon eggs, while vulture drakes and liondrakes are both distant cousins of dragons. Metallic dragons also attract servants and create constructs for their defense. Kobolds, known for their devotion to chromatic dragons, sometimes serve metallic dragons too.

In this chapter, you'll find the following:

✦ Descriptions of the rarer metallic dragons—brass, bronze, cobalt, mercury, mithral, orium, and steel.

✦ Wyrmlings of each metallic dragon variety.

✦ Creatures made from metallic dragons, including the evil race of draconians and hollow dragon constructs.

✦ Monsters that have draconic heritage or associations, such as couatls and liondrakes.

✦ Legendary metallic dragons of the world, and the god Bahamut, the Platinum Dragon.

✦ Methods of customization, including alternative powers and a method for making solo dragons into elites.

LARS GRANT-WEST

Adamantine, iron, copper, silver, and gold dragons are the most common and well-known metallic dragons (see *Monster Manual 2*). However, other varieties exist, including brass, bronze, cobalt, mercury, mithral, orium, and steel dragons.

BRASS DRAGON

FIRE-BREATHING MONSTERS haunting deserts and other dry lands, brass dragons tend to be callous, violent, and selfish. The best are honorable mercenaries, brave and loyal if paid well. The worst are brigands that plunder any travelers who venture into their territory.

BRASS DRAGON LORE

Nature DC 12: Brass dragons favor deserts and arid badlands. Their breath takes the form of a fiery blast that can force nearby foes to give ground or a jet of flame that can burn an enemy and all others around it.

Nature DC 17: Brass dragons have a pronounced mercenary streak and often strike bargains with neighboring monsters to fight on their behalf in exchange for treasure. They ally with azers, dragonborn, efreets, hill giants, humans, and yuan-ti.

BRASS DRAGON TACTICS

Brass dragons fight on the wing. They make good use of their hover ability to remain airborne and out of the reach of ground-bound enemies, scouring foes with blasts of fire—both their *breath weapon* and *fire stream* attacks. Once its foes are scattered, a brass dragon singles out the foe who poses the most dangerous threat at range and lands to attack. Normally the dragon lands next to its intended victim, attacks with *dragon ire*, and then spends an action point to stun its foes momentarily with *frightful presence* so that it can take to the air again before its enemies can threaten it on the ground.

An elder or ancient brass dragon usually waits to use *ignite* until after it hits multiple targets with its breath weapon.

ENCOUNTER GROUPS

Brass dragons ally with well-organized humanoid bands that can meet their price (usually, the lion's share of any treasure they take). They prefer to hang back and provide devastating ranged fire, while their brute and soldier allies press the attack.

Level 6 Encounter (XP 1,325)
- ✦ 3 human guards (level 3 soldier, MM 162)
- ✦ 1 young brass dragon (level 4 solo artillery)

Level 13 Encounter (XP 4,000)
- ✦ 1 adult brass dragon (level 11 solo artillery)
- ✦ 2 minotaur warriors (level 10 soldier, MM 190)

Young Brass Dragon		**Level 4 Solo Artillery**
Large natural magical beast (dragon)		XP 875

Initiative +5   **Senses** Perception +9; darkvision
HP 232; **Bloodied** 116; see also *bloodied breath*
AC 17; **Fortitude** 17, **Reflex** 16, **Will** 15
Resist 15 fire
Saving Throws +5
Speed 8, fly 10 (hover), overland flight 12
Action Points 2

⊕ **Bite** (standard; at-will) ✦ **Fire**
  Reach 2; +11 vs. AC; 1d8 + 3 damage plus 1d6 fire damage.
⊕ **Claw** (standard; at-will)
  Reach 2; +11 vs. AC; 1d6 + 3 damage.
✦ **Dragon Ire** (standard; at-will)
  The dragon makes two claw attacks or one bite attack, and then shifts 1 square.
✦ **Wing Buffet** (immediate reaction, when an enemy enters or leaves an adjacent square)
  Targets the triggering enemy; +9 vs. Fortitude; 1d8 + 3 damage, the target is knocked prone, and the dragon shifts 2 squares.
⬅ **Breath Weapon** (standard; recharge ⚄ ⚅) ✦ **Fire**
  Close blast 5; +9 vs. Reflex; 3d6 + 3 fire damage, and the dragon pushes the target 3 squares. *Miss:* Half damage.
⬅ **Bloodied Breath** (free, when first bloodied; encounter)
  Breath weapon recharges, and the dragon uses it.
➢ **Fire Stream** (standard; at-will) ✦ **Fire**
  Ranged 5; +9 vs. Reflex; 1d8 + 5 fire damage. *Effect:* Each creature adjacent to the target takes 1d8 fire damage.
⬅ **Frightful Presence** (standard; encounter) ✦ **Fear**
  Close burst 5; targets enemies; +9 vs. Will; the target is stunned until the end of the dragon's next turn. *Aftereffect:* The target takes a –2 penalty to attack rolls (save ends).
Alignment Unaligned   **Languages** Common, Draconic
Skills Athletics +10, Insight +9, Intimidate +8
Str 17 (+5)	**Dex** 16 (+5)	**Wis** 15 (+4)
Con 18 (+6)	**Int** 13 (+3)	**Cha** 12 (+3)

Adult Brass Dragon		**Level 11 Solo Artillery**
Large natural magical beast (dragon)		XP 3,000

Initiative +9   **Senses** Perception +13; darkvision
HP 464; **Bloodied** 232; see also *bloodied breath*
AC 24; **Fortitude** 24, **Reflex** 23, **Will** 22
Resist 20 fire
Saving Throws +5
Speed 8, fly 10 (hover), overland flight 12
Action Points 2

⊕ **Bite** (standard; at-will) ✦ **Fire**
  Reach 2; +18 vs. AC; 1d10 + 5 damage plus 1d6 fire damage.
⊕ **Claw** (standard; at-will)
  Reach 2; +18 vs. AC; 1d8 + 5 damage.
✦ **Dragon Ire** (standard; at-will)
  The dragon makes two claw attacks or one bite attack, and then shifts 1 square.
✦ **Wing Buffet** (immediate reaction, when an enemy enters or leaves an adjacent square)
  Targets the triggering enemy; +16 vs. Fortitude; 1d10 + 5 damage, the target is knocked prone, and the dragon shifts 2 squares.

⬿ **Breath Weapon** (standard; recharge ⚅ ⚅) ✦ **Fire**

Close blast 5; +16 vs. Reflex; 3d8 + 5 fire damage, and the dragon pushes the target 3 squares. *Miss:* Half damage.

⬿ **Bloodied Breath** (free, when first bloodied; encounter)

Breath weapon recharges, and the dragon uses it. If the dragon is flying, it can shift up to 5 squares before making this attack.

↗ **Fire Stream** (standard; at-will) ✦ **Fire**

Ranged 10; +16 vs. Reflex; 2d6 + 5 fire damage. *Effect:* Each creature adjacent to the target takes 2d6 fire damage.

⬿ **Frightful Presence** (standard; encounter) ✦ **Fear**

Close burst 5; targets enemies; +16 vs. Will; the target is stunned until the end of the dragon's next turn. *Aftereffect:* The target takes a -2 penalty to attack rolls (save ends).

Alignment Unaligned	**Languages** Common, Draconic
Skills Athletics +14, Insight +13, Intimidate +11	
Str 19 (+9)	**Dex** 18 (+9)	**Wis** 16 (+8)
Con 20 (+10)	**Int** 15 (+7)	**Cha** 13 (+6)

Elder Brass Dragon	**Level 18 Solo Artillery**
Huge natural magical beast (dragon)	XP 10,000

Initiative +14   **Senses** Perception +18; darkvision

HP 704; **Bloodied** 352; see also *bloodied breath*

AC 31; **Fortitude** 31, **Reflex** 30, **Will** 29

Resist 25 fire

Saving Throws +5

Speed 8, fly 10 (hover), overland flight 15

Action Points 2

⊕ **Bite** (standard; at-will) ✦ **Fire**

Reach 3; +25 vs. AC; 2d6 + 7 damage plus 1d12 fire damage.

⊕ **Claw** (standard; at-will)

Reach 3; +25 vs. AC; 1d10 + 7 damage.

⬦ **Dragon Ire** (standard; at-will)

The dragon makes two claw attacks or one bite attack, and then shifts 1 square.

⬦ **Wing Buffet** (immediate reaction, when an enemy moves enters or leaves an adjacent square)

Targets the triggering enemy; +23 vs. Fortitude; 2d8 + 7 damage, the target is knocked prone, and the dragon shifts 2 squares.

⬿ **Breath Weapon** (standard; recharge ⚅ ⚅) ✦ **Fire**

Close blast 5; +23 vs. Reflex; 4d10 + 7 fire damage, and the dragon pushes the target 3 squares. *Miss:* Half damage.

⬿ **Bloodied Breath** (free, when first bloodied; encounter)

Breath weapon recharges, and the dragon uses it. If the dragon is flying, it can shift 10 squares before making this attack.

↗ **Fire Stream** (standard; at-will) ✦ **Fire**

Ranged 15; +23 vs. Reflex; 2d8 + 7 fire damage. *Effect:* Each creature adjacent to the target takes 2d8 fire damage.

⬿ **Frightful Presence** (standard; encounter) ✦ **Fear**

Close burst 10; targets enemies; +23 vs. Will; the target is stunned until the end of the dragon's next turn. *Aftereffect:* The target takes a -2 penalty to attack rolls (save ends).

Ignite (free, after using *breath weapon* or *fire stream*; encounter) ✦ **Fire**

Any creature hit by the triggering attack also takes ongoing 10 fire damage and is dazed (save ends both).

Alignment Unaligned	**Languages** Common, Draconic
Skills Athletics +20, Insight +18, Intimidate +16, Nature +18	
Str 23 (+15)	**Dex** 20 (+14)	**Wis** 18 (+13)
Con 24 (+16)	**Int** 17 (+12)	**Cha** 15 (+11)

CHRIS SEAMAN

Ancient Brass Dragon — Level 26 Solo Artillery
Gargantuan natural magical beast (dragon) — XP 45,000

Initiative +20   **Senses** Perception +23; darkvision
HP 968; **Bloodied** 484; see also *bloodied breath*
AC 39; **Fortitude** 39, **Reflex** 38, **Will** 37
Resist 30 fire
Saving Throws +5
Speed 8, fly 12 (hover), overland flight 15
Action Points 2

ⓟ **Bite** (standard; at-will) ✦ **Fire**
Reach 4; +33 vs. AC; 2d8 + 9 damage plus 2d8 fire damage.

ⓟ **Claw** (standard; at-will)
Reach 4; +33 vs. AC; 2d8 + 9 damage.

✦ **Dragon Ire** (standard; at-will)
The dragon makes two claw attacks or one bite attack, and then shifts 2 squares.

✦ **Wing Buffet** (immediate reaction, when an enemy enters or leaves an adjacent square)
Targets the triggering enemy; +31 vs. Fortitude; 2d10 + 9 damage, the target is knocked prone, and the dragon shifts 2 squares.

↞ **Breath Weapon** (standard; recharge ⚄ ⚅) ✦ **Fire**
Close blast 7; +31 vs. Reflex; 5d10 + 9 fire damage, and the target is knocked prone. *Miss:* Half damage.

↞ **Bloodied Breath** (free, when first bloodied; encounter)
Breath weapon recharges, and the dragon uses it. If the dragon is flying, it can shift 12 squares before making this attack.

⤳ **Fire Stream** (standard; at-will) ✦ **Fire**
Ranged 20; +31 vs. Reflex; 3d8 + 9 fire damage. *Effect:* Each creature adjacent to the target takes 3d8 fire damage.

✳ **Fiery Strafe** (standard; recharge ⚅) ✦ **Fire, Zone**
The dragon flies up to 12 squares and creates a wall of fire 1 square high on the ground directly beneath its path; area wall 12 within 10 (only in squares the dragon flew over); any creature that starts its turn in the wall's space or moves into it takes 25 fire damage. The wall lasts until the end of the dragon's next turn.

↞ **Frightful Presence** (standard; encounter) ✦ **Fear**
Close burst 10; targets enemies; +31 vs. Will; the target is stunned until the end of the dragon's next turn. *Aftereffect:* The target takes a -2 penalty to attack rolls (save ends).

Ignite (free, after using *breath weapon* or *fire stream*; encounter) ✦ **Fire**
Any creature hit by the triggering attack also takes ongoing 15 fire damage and is dazed (save ends both).

Alignment Unaligned   **Languages** Common, Draconic
Skills Athletics +26, Insight +23, Intimidate +21, Nature +23

Str 27 (+21)	Dex 24 (+20)	Wis 20 (+18)
Con 26 (+21)	Int 19 (+17)	Cha 17 (+16)

BRONZE DRAGON

ORDER'S SWORN SERVANTS, bronze dragons can seem arrogant and haughty, with an inflated sense of self, a tendency that can put them at odds with those they meet. In rare cases, this self-righteousness grows into something far more sinister, and the bronze dragon takes over what it sees as lesser races, ruling as a cruel tyrant that demands worship and subservience from its subjects. Bronze dragons claim coastlines, inlets, and islands as their own, constructing lairs in coastal caves that have access to the sea. More aggressive bronze dragons purposely choose lairs near shipping lanes so they can claim tribute from merchant vessels as those craft pass by. All bronze dragons share a deep and abiding hatred for blue dragons, and they are vigilant in protecting their homes from these despised interlopers.

BRONZE DRAGON LORE

Nature DC 14: Bronze dragons live in coastal areas, especially in places where they can collect tribute from other creatures. In combat, a bronze dragon dives directly into melee.

Nature DC 19: Arrogant and haughty, bronze dragons sometimes become tyrants over members of lesser races. Bronzes breathe lightning that blasts opponents back, then arcs off to hit others.

BRONZE DRAGON TACTICS

A bronze dragon is an unsubtle opponent that engages its enemies in close combat, when its attacks are the most effective. The dragon starts combat by moving to a position where it can catch two or more enemies with its *breath weapon*. It uses *frightful presence* to soften up the opposition, and then it spends an action point to use its *breath weapon*, blasting the close targets and then punishing cowards hiding in the back, as lightning arcs from one enemy to the next.

ENCOUNTER GROUPS

A bronze dragon rarely keeps the company of other creatures, tolerating only those that show it the respect and honor it believes it is due.

Level 16 Encounter (XP 7,000)
✦ 1 adult bronze dragon (level 14 solo brute)
✦ 8 cyclops guards (level 14 minion, *MM* 46)

Level 24 Encounter (XP 33,550)
✦ 1 elder bronze dragon (level 21 solo brute)
✦ 1 storm devil (level 23 artillery, *Manual of the Planes* 127)
✦ 3 war devils (level 22 brute, *MM* 67)

Young Bronze Dragon — Level 7 Solo Brute
Large natural magical beast (aquatic, dragon) XP 1,500

Initiative +6 **Senses** Perception +8; darkvision
HP 296; **Bloodied** 148; see also *bloodied breath*
AC 19; **Fortitude** 21, **Reflex** 18, **Will** 18
Resist 15 lightning
Saving Throws +5
Speed 6, fly 8 (hover), overland flight 10, swim 6
Action Points 2

⊕ **Bite** (standard; at-will) ✦ **Lightning**
   Reach 2; +10 vs. AC; 1d10 + 6 damage plus 2d6 lightning damage.
⊕ **Claw** (standard; at-will)
   Reach 2; +10 vs. AC; 2d6 + 8 damage.
⫟ **Double Attack** (standard; at-will)
   The dragon makes two claw attacks.
⫟ **Wing Smash** (immediate reaction, when an enemy moves to a
   space where it flanks the dragon; at-will)
   +8 vs. Fortitude; 1d12 + 6 damage, and the dragon pushes the
   target 1 square.
⇐ **Breath Weapon** (standard; recharge ⚄ ⚅) ✦ **Lightning**
   Close blast 3; +8 vs. Reflex; 2d8 + 4 lightning damage, and the
   dragon pushes the target 2 squares. If the attack hit at least one
   target, the dragon makes a secondary attack against a creature
   within 10 squares that was not a target of the primary attack.
   Miss: Half damage. *Secondary Attack:* +8 vs. Reflex; 2d8 + 4
   lightning damage, and the dragon pushes the target 1 square.
⇐ **Bloodied Breath** (free, when first bloodied; encounter)
   Breath weapon recharges, and the dragon uses it.
⇐ **Frightful Presence** (standard; encounter) ✦ **Fear**
   Close burst 5; targets enemies; +8 vs. Will; the target is stunned
   until the end of the dragon's next turn. *Aftereffect:* The target
   takes a -2 penalty to attack rolls (save ends).
Restorative Dive (minor; while bloodied and completely
   submerged in water; encounter) ✦ **Healing**
   The dragon regains 74 hit points and gains a +2 bonus to attack
   rolls until the end of its next turn.

Alignment Unaligned **Languages** Common, Draconic
Str 23 (+9)	**Dex** 17 (+6)	**Wis** 11 (+3)
Con 18 (+7)	**Int** 11 (+3)	**Cha** 16 (+6)

Adult Bronze Dragon — Level 14 Solo Brute
Large natural magical beast (aquatic, dragon) XP 5,000

Initiative +12 **Senses** Perception +13; darkvision
HP 507; **Bloodied** 253; see also *bloodied breath*
AC 26; **Fortitude** 28, **Reflex** 25, **Will** 25
Resist 20 lightning
Saving Throws +5
Speed 6, fly 8 (hover), overland flight 10, swim 6
Action Points 2

⊕ **Bite** (standard; at-will) ✦ **Lightning**
   Reach 2; +17 vs. AC; 2d8 + 8 damage plus 3d6 lightning damage.
⊕ **Claw** (standard; at-will)
   Reach 2; +17 vs. AC; 2d8 + 10 damage.
⫟ **Double Attack** (standard; at-will)
   The dragon makes two claw attacks.
⫟ **Wing Smash** (immediate reaction, when an enemy moves to a
   space where it flanks the dragon; at-will)
   +15 vs. Fortitude; 2d12 + 6 damage, and the dragon pushes the
   target 2 squares.
⇐ **Breath Weapon** (standard; recharge ⚄ ⚅) ✦ **Lightning**
   Close blast 3; +15 vs. Reflex; 3d8 + 5 lightning damage, and the
   dragon pushes the target 2 squares. If the attack hit at least one
   target, the dragon makes a secondary attack against a creature
   within 10 squares that was not a target of the primary attack.
   Miss: Half damage. *Secondary Attack:* +15 vs. Reflex; 2d10 + 5
   lightning damage, and the dragon pushes the target 1 square.

⇐ **Bloodied Breath** (free, when first bloodied; encounter)
   Breath weapon recharges, and the dragon uses it.
⇐ **Frightful Presence** (standard; encounter) ✦ **Fear**
   Close burst 5; targets enemies; +13 vs. Will; the target is
   stunned until the end of the dragon's next turn. *Aftereffect:* The
   target takes a -2 penalty to attack rolls (save ends).
Restorative Dive (minor; while bloodied and completely
   submerged in water; encounter) ✦ **Healing**
   The dragon regains 126 hit points and gains a +2 bonus to
   attack rolls until the end of its next turn.

Alignment Unaligned **Languages** Common, Draconic
Skills History +13, Intimidate +16
Str 26 (+15)	**Dex** 21 (+12)	**Wis** 13 (+8)
Con 21 (+12)	**Int** 12 (+8)	**Cha** 20 (+12)

Elder Bronze Dragon — Level 21 Solo Brute
Huge natural magical beast (aquatic, dragon) XP 16,000

Initiative +17 **Senses** Perception +17; darkvision
HP 723; **Bloodied** 361; see also *bloodied breath*
AC 33; **Fortitude** 35, **Reflex** 32, **Will** 32
Resist 25 lightning
Saving Throws +5
Speed 8, fly 10 (hover), overland flight 12, swim 8
Action Points 2

⊕ **Bite** (standard; at-will) ✦ **Lightning**
   Reach 3; +24 vs. AC; 3d10 + 10 damage plus 4d6 lightning
   damage.
⊕ **Claw** (standard; at-will)
   Reach 3; +24 vs. AC; 2d10 + 12 damage.
⫟ **Double Attack** (standard; at-will)
   The dragon makes two claw attacks.
⫟ **Wing Smash** (immediate reaction, when an enemy moves to a
   space where it flanks the dragon; at-will)
   +22 vs. Fortitude; 3d12 + 8 damage, and the dragon pushes the
   target 3 squares.
⫟ **Pinning Claw** (immediate reaction, when an adjacent enemy
   moves or shifts; at-will)
   +24 vs. AC; 2d10 + 12 damage, and the dragon grabs the target.
   If the dragon uses *double attack* while grabbing a target, it must
   target a grabbed creature with at least one attack if it is able.
⇐ **Breath Weapon** (standard; recharge ⚄ ⚅) ✦ **Lightning**
   Close blast 3; +22 vs. Reflex; 3d10 + 8 lightning damage, and
   the dragon pushes the target 4 squares. If the attack hit at least
   one target, the dragon makes a secondary attack against a
   creature within 10 squares that was not a target of the primary
   attack. *Miss:* Half damage. *Secondary Attack:* +22 vs. Reflex;
   2d12 + 7 lightning damage, and the dragon pushes the target 2
   squares.
⇐ **Bloodied Breath** (free, when first bloodied; encounter)
   Breath weapon recharges, and the dragon uses it.
⇐ **Frightful Presence** (standard; encounter) ✦ **Fear**
   Close burst 10; targets enemies; +22 vs. Will; the target is
   stunned until the end of the dragon's next turn. *Aftereffect:* The
   target takes a -2 penalty to attack rolls (save ends).
Restorative Dive (minor; while bloodied and completely
   submerged in water; encounter) ✦ **Healing**
   The dragon regains 180 hit points and gains a +2 bonus to
   attack rolls until the end of its next turn.

Alignment Unaligned **Languages** Common, Draconic
Skills History +17, Intimidate +21
Str 30 (+20)	**Dex** 24 (+17)	**Wis** 14 (+12)
Con 25 (+17)	**Int** 14 (+12)	**Cha** 22 (+16)

Ancient Bronze Dragon — Level 29 Solo Brute
Gargantuan natural magical beast (aquatic, dragon)   XP 75,000

Initiative +23   **Senses** Perception +23; darkvision
Living Tempest (Lightning) aura 5; each creature that starts its turn within the aura takes 15 lightning damage.
HP 968; **Bloodied** 484; see also *bloodied breath*
AC 41; **Fortitude** 43, **Reflex** 40, **Will** 40
Saving Throws +5
Speed 10, fly 12 (hover), overland flight 15, swim 10
Action Points 2

⊕ **Bite** (standard; at-will) ✦ **Lightning**
Reach 4; +32 vs. AC; 2d12 + 13 damage plus 6d8 lightning damage.

⊕ **Claw** (standard; at-will)
Reach 4; +32 vs. AC; 3d12 + 10 damage.

✦ **Double Attack** (standard; at-will)
The dragon makes two claw attacks.

✦ **Wing Smash** (immediate reaction, when an enemy moves to a space where it flanks the dragon; at-will)
+30 vs. Fortitude; 3d12 + 13 damage, and the dragon pushes the target 3 squares.

✦ **Pinning Claw** (immediate reaction, when an adjacent enemy moves or shifts; at-will)
+32 vs. AC; 3d12 + 10 damage, and the dragon grabs the target. If the dragon uses *double attack* while grabbing a target, it must target a grabbed creature with at least one attack if it is able.

↩ **Breath Weapon** (standard; recharge ⚄ ⚅) ✦ **Lightning**
Close blast 3; +30 vs. Reflex; 4d10 + 10 lightning damage, and the dragon pushes the target 4 squares. If the attack hit at least one target, the dragon makes a secondary attack against a creature within 10 squares that was not a target of the primary attack. *Miss:* Half damage. *Secondary Attack:* +22 vs. Reflex; 3d12 + 9 lightning damage, and the dragon pushes the target 2 squares.

↩ **Bloodied Breath** (free, when first bloodied; encounter)
Breath weapon recharges, and the dragon uses it.

↩ **Frightful Presence** (standard; encounter) ✦ **Fear**
Close burst 10; targets enemies; +30 vs. Will; the target is stunned until the end of the dragon's next turn. *Aftereffect:* The target takes a -2 penalty to attack rolls (save ends).

Restorative Dive (minor; while bloodied and completely submerged in water; encounter) ✦ **Healing**
The dragon regains 242 hit points and gains a +2 bonus to attack rolls until the end of its next turn.

Alignment Unaligned   **Languages** Common, Draconic
Skills History +22, Intimidate +27
Str 34 (+26)   **Dex** 29 (+23)   **Wis** 19 (+18)
Con 29 (+23)   **Int** 17 (+17)   **Cha** 27 (+22)

LARS GRANT-WEST

COBALT DRAGON

Brooding and distrustful, cobalt dragons respect only strength. They breathe bitterly cold clouds of vapor that freeze their victims in thick ice.

Cobalt dragons are usually found in frigid, gloomy lands, such as the forests of the far north or the mist-bound vales of the Shadowfell. They measure their power by the quality and quantity of lesser creatures they can subjugate; most cobalts take pride in the martial spirit and abilities of their minions, but the worst are brutal, bullying tyrants who demand fealty and tribute. This trait makes it dangerous for travelers to venture into lands claimed by cobalt dragons, since the dragons might attack passing travelers to establish their own strength. Good-aligned cobalt dragons are likely to accept a foe's surrender after a suitable show of force and allow them to go their way after a judicious bribe or promise of tribute. Wicked cobalt dragons are inclined to fall on travelers and simply devour them if the lesser creatures can't offer any worthwhile ransom for their lives.

Young Cobalt Dragon	Level 5 Solo Controller
Large natural magical beast (dragon)	XP 1,000

Initiative +4   **Senses** Perception +9; darkvision
HP 268; **Bloodied** 134; see also *bloodied breath*
AC 20; **Fortitude** 18, **Reflex** 16, **Will** 16
Resist 15 cold

Saving Throws +5
Speed 6 (ice walk), fly 8 (hover), overland flight 10
Action Points 2

ⓐ **Bite** (standard; at-will) ✦ **Cold**
Reach 2; +11 vs. AC; 1d8 + 4 cold damage, and the target is slowed (save ends).

ⓐ **Claw** (standard; at-will)
Reach 2; +11 vs. AC; 1d6 + 4 damage.

⫘ **Dragon's Pounce** (standard; at-will)
The dragon makes a bite attack, shifts 2 squares, and then makes two claw attacks against a different target.

⟵ **Wing Flurry** (immediate reaction, when an enemy misses the dragon with a melee or close attack; at-will)
Close burst 2; +7 vs. Fortitude; 1d6 + 4 damage, and the target is pushed 2 squares.

⟵ **Savage Mauling** (standard; recharges when first bloodied)
Close burst 2; targets slowed or restrained creatures; +11 vs. AC; 2d6 + 5 damage, the dragon pushes the target 3 squares, and the target is knocked prone. This forced movement can affect a creature restrained by the dragon's own breath weapon.

⟵ **Breath Weapon** (standard; recharge ⚄ ⚅) ✦ **Cold**
Close blast 5; +9 vs. Fortitude; 1d6 + 4 cold damage, and the target is restrained (save ends). *Aftereffect:* The target is slowed (save ends). *Miss:* Half damage.

⟵ **Bloodied Breath** (free, when first bloodied; encounter)
Breath weapon recharges, and the dragon uses it.

⟵ **Frightful Presence** (standard; encounter) ✦ **Fear**
Close burst 5; targets enemies; +7 vs. Will; the target is stunned until the end of the dragon's next turn. *Aftereffect:* The target takes a -2 penalty to attack rolls (save ends).

Alignment Unaligned   **Languages** Common, Draconic
Skills Athletics +11, Endurance +11, Intimidate +9
| **Str** 18 (+6) | **Dex** 14 (+4) | **Wis** 14 (+4) |
| **Con** 19 (+6) | **Int** 11 (+2) | **Cha** 15 (+4) |

HOWARD LYON

Adult Cobalt Dragon — Level 12 Solo Controller
Large natural magical beast (dragon)   XP 3,500

Initiative +9   **Senses** Perception +14; darkvision
HP 500; **Bloodied** 250; see also *bloodied breath*
AC 27; **Fortitude** 26, **Reflex** 23, **Will** 24
Resist 20 cold
Saving Throws +5
Speed 6 (ice walk), fly 8 (hover), overland flight 12
Action Points 2

⊕ **Bite** (standard; at-will) ✦ **Cold**
Reach 2; +18 vs. AC; 2d6 + 6 cold damage, and the target is slowed (save ends).

⊕ **Claw** (standard; at-will)
Reach 2; +18 vs. AC; 1d8 + 6 damage.

↯ **Dragon's Pounce** (standard; at-will)
The dragon makes a bite attack, shifts 2 squares, and then makes two claw attacks against a different target.

↯ **Wing Flurry** (immediate reaction, when an enemy misses the dragon with a melee or close attack; at-will)
Close burst 2; +14 vs. Fortitude; 1d8 + 6 damage, and the dragon pushes the target 2 squares.

↩ **Savage Mauling** (standard; recharges when first bloodied)
Close burst 2; targets slowed or restrained creatures; +15 vs. AC; 2d8 + 6 damage, the dragon pushes the target 3 squares, and the target is knocked prone. This forced movement can affect a creature restrained by the dragon's own breath weapon.

↩ **Breath Weapon** (standard; recharge ⚄ ⚅) ✦ **Cold**
Close blast 5; +15 vs. Fortitude; 2d8 + 6 cold damage, and the target is restrained (save ends). *Aftereffect:* The target is slowed (save ends). *Miss:* Half damage.

↩ **Bloodied Breath** (free, when first bloodied; encounter)
Breath weapon recharges, and the dragon uses it.

↩ **Frightful Presence** (standard; encounter) ✦ **Fear**
Close burst 5; targets enemies; +14 vs. Will; the target is stunned until the end of the dragon's next turn. *Aftereffect:* The target takes a –2 penalty to attack rolls (save ends).

Alignment Unaligned   **Languages** Common, Draconic
Skills Athletics +17, Endurance +16, Intimidate +14
Str 22 (+12)   **Dex** 16 (+9)   **Wis** 16 (+9)
Con 21 (+11)   **Int** 13 (+7)   **Cha** 17 (+9)

Elder Cobalt Dragon — Level 19 Solo Controller
Huge natural magical beast (dragon)   XP 12,000

Initiative +12   **Senses** Perception +17; darkvision
Aura of Chill Mist (Cold) aura 2; each creature that enters the aura or starts its turn there takes 10 cold damage. The ground is coated with ice and becomes difficult terrain, and the squares of the aura are lightly obscured.
HP 736; **Bloodied** 368; see also *bloodied breath*
AC 33; **Fortitude** 33, **Reflex** 29, **Will** 31
Resist 25 cold
Saving Throws +5
Speed 8 (ice walk), fly 10 (hover), overland flight 15
Action Points 2

⊕ **Bite** (standard; at-will) ✦ **Cold**
Reach 3; +25 vs. AC; 2d8 + 8 cold damage, and the target is slowed (save ends).

⊕ **Claw** (standard; at-will)
Reach 3; +25 vs. AC; 1d10 + 8 damage.

↯ **Dragon's Pounce** (standard; at-will)
The dragon makes a bite attack, shifts 3 squares, and then makes two claw attacks against a different target.

↯ **Wing Flurry** (immediate reaction, when an enemy misses the dragon with a melee or close attack; at-will)
Close burst 3; +22 vs. Fortitude; 1d10 + 8 damage, and the dragon pushes the target 3 squares.

↩ **Savage Mauling** (standard; recharges when first bloodied)
Close burst 3; targets slowed or restrained creatures; +22 vs. AC; 3d8 + 8 damage, the dragon pushes the target 3 squares, and the target is knocked prone. This forced movement can affect a creature restrained by the dragon's own breath weapon.

↩ **Breath Weapon** (standard; recharge ⚄ ⚅) ✦ **Cold**
Close blast 5; +22 vs. Fortitude; 3d8 + 8 cold damage, and the target is restrained (save ends). *Aftereffect:* The target is slowed (save ends). *Miss:* Half damage.

↩ **Bloodied Breath** (free, when first bloodied; encounter)
Breath weapon recharges, and the dragon uses it.

↩ **Frightful Presence** (standard; encounter) ✦ **Fear**
Close burst 10; targets enemies; +21 vs. Will; the target is stunned until the end of the dragon's next turn. *Aftereffect:* The target takes a –2 penalty to attack rolls (save ends).

Alignment Unaligned   **Languages** Common, Draconic
Skills Athletics +21, Endurance +21, Intimidate +19
Str 25 (+16)   **Dex** 17 (+12)   **Wis** 17 (+12)
Con 24 (+16)   **Int** 14 (+11)   **Cha** 21 (+14)

Ancient Cobalt Dragon — Level 27 Solo Controller
Gargantuan natural magical beast (dragon)   XP 55,000

Initiative +18   **Senses** Perception +22; darkvision
Aura of Chill Mist (Cold) aura 5; each creature that enters the aura or starts its turn there takes 20 cold damage. The ground is coated with ice and becomes difficult terrain, and the squares of the aura are lightly obscured.
HP 1,004; **Bloodied** 502; see also *bloodied breath*
AC 41; **Fortitude** 41, **Reflex** 37, **Will** 39
Resist 30 cold
Saving Throws +5
Speed 8 (ice walk), fly 12 (hover), overland flight 15
Action Points 2

⊕ **Bite** (standard; at-will) ✦ **Cold**
Reach 4; +33 vs. AC; 3d6 + 9 cold damage, and the target is slowed (save ends).

⊕ **Claw** (standard; at-will)
Reach 4; +33 vs. AC; 2d8 + 9 damage.

↯ **Dragon's Pounce** (standard; at-will)
The dragon makes a bite attack, shifts 3 squares, and then makes two claw attacks against a different target.

↯ **Wing Flurry** (immediate reaction, when an enemy misses the dragon with a melee or close attack; at-will)
Close burst 4; +28 vs. Fortitude; 2d8 + 9 damage, and the dragon pushes the target 3 squares.

↩ **Savage Mauling** (standard; recharges when first bloodied)
Close burst 4; targets slowed or restrained creatures; +30 vs. AC; 4d8 + 9 damage, the dragon pushes the target 3 squares, and the target is knocked prone. This forced movement can affect a creature restrained by the dragon's own breath weapon.

↩ **Breath Weapon** (standard; recharge ⚄ ⚅) ✦ **Cold**
Close blast 5; +28 vs. Fortitude; 3d10 + 9 cold damage, and the target is restrained (save ends). *Aftereffect:* The target is slowed (save ends). *Miss:* Half damage.

↩ **Bloodied Breath** (free, when first bloodied; encounter)
Breath weapon recharges, and the dragon uses it.

❄ **Rimedeath Fog** (standard; recharge ⚄ ⚅) ✦ **Cold, Zone**
Area burst 3 within 20; +30 vs. Fortitude; 2d10 + 9 cold damage, and the target is slowed and weakened (save ends both). *Miss:* Half damage. *Effect:* The burst becomes a zone of freezing fog. It is difficult terrain and the squares within it are heavily obscured. The zone persists until the dragon uses this power again or until the end of the encounter.

↺ **Frightful Presence** (standard; encounter) ✦ **Fear**
Close burst 10; targets enemies; +28 vs. Will; the target is stunned until the end of the dragon's next turn. *Aftereffect:* The target takes a -2 penalty to attack rolls (save ends).

Alignment Unaligned		Languages Common, Draconic
Skills Athletics +27, Endurance +26, Intimidate +25		
Str 28 (+22)	Dex 20 (+18)	Wis 19 (+17)
Con 27 (+21)	Int 16 (+16)	Cha 24 (+20)

COBALT DRAGON LORE

Nature DC 12: Cobalt dragons typically haunt cold lands or the borders of the Shadowfell. Their breath is a deadly cold fog that congeals around victims, imprisoning them in ice.

Nature DC 17: Cobalt dragons are savage and suspicious. They despise weaklings and respect little aside from strength. They often dominate nearby tribes of barbaric dwarves, humans, orcs, ogres, or giants. The best cobalt dragons are fierce protectors of their chosen people, but others tyrannize their minions as bloodthirsty and vindictive gods.

COBALT DRAGON TACTICS

Cobalt dragons are fierce in battle, throwing themselves into the midst of their foes with abandon. They are not strong fliers and prefer to stay on the ground, using their *breath weapon* and bite to restrain or slow foes, and *dragon's pounce* to attack multiple targets while their foes are slowed. Cobalt dragons often spend an action point to use *savage mauling* immediately after a successful breath weapon attack. They usually save *frightful presence* for stunning enemies when closely pressed, then move out into open ground again.

Older cobalt dragons are fond of pushing enemies right to the feet of their allies and minions. They rarely take any great care to protect their minions—in their eyes, followers that prove weak in battle are unworthy.

ENCOUNTER GROUPS

Cobalt dragons often rule over tribes of savage or barbaric folk. Their minions are anxious to impress their draconic masters by careening recklessly into battle.

Level 7 Encounter (XP 1,525)
✦ 3 human berserkers (level 4 brute, *MM* 163)
✦ 1 young cobalt dragon (level 5 solo controller)

Level 14 Encounter (XP 5,150)
✦ 1 adult cobalt dragon (level 12 solo controller)
✦ 3 ogre thugs (level 11 minion, *MM* 198)
✦ 1 ogre warhulk (level 11 elite brute, *MM* 199)

Level 21 Encounter (XP 16,800)
✦ 1 elder cobalt dragon (level 19 solo controller)
✦ 3 frost giants (level 17 brute, *Monster Manual 2* 122)

MERCURY DRAGON

SKILLED SCOUTS, EMISSARIES, AND ASSASSINS, mercury dragons are capable of shapechanging tricks that other dragons can't match. The breath of a mercury dragon poisons the body and the mind, rendering its victims unable to see the mercury dragon escape or circle around for a killing blow. A mercury dragon craves variety and new experiences.

Young Mercury Dragon		Level 6 Solo Lurker
Large natural magical beast (dragon, shapechanger)		XP 1,250

Initiative +12   **Senses** Perception +8; darkvision
HP 288; **Bloodied** 144; see also *bloodied breath*
AC 20; **Fortitude** 17, **Reflex** 19, **Will** 18
Resist 15 poison
Saving Throws +5
Speed 6, fly 6 (hover), overland flight 10
Action Points 2

⊕ **Bite** (standard; at-will)
Reach 2; +11 vs. AC; 1d10 + 6 damage.

⊕ **Claw** (standard; at-will)
Reach 2; +11 vs. AC; 1d8 + 6 damage.

‡ **Draconic Fury** (standard; at-will)
The dragon makes two claw attacks and one bite attack.

‡ **Quick Snap** (immediate interrupt, when an enemy moves adjacent to the dragon; at-will)
The dragon makes a bite attack against the triggering enemy. On a hit, the target also grants combat advantage to the dragon (save ends).

↺ **Breath Weapon** (standard; recharge ⚅ ⚅) ✦ **Poison**
Close blast 5; +9 vs. Fortitude; 1d12 + 4 poison damage, and the target takes ongoing 5 poison damage and treats the dragon as invisible (save ends both). *Miss:* Half damage.

↺ **Bloodied Breath** (free, when first bloodied; encounter)
Breath weapon recharges, and the dragon uses it.

↺ **Frightful Presence** (standard; encounter) ✦ **Fear**
Close burst 5; targets enemies; +9 vs. Will; the target is stunned until the end of the dragon's next turn. *Aftereffect:* The target takes a -2 penalty to attack rolls (save ends).

Quicksilver Form (move action; encounter) ✦ **Polymorph**
The dragon becomes a liquid wave of quicksilver and shifts 4 squares. It remains in quicksilver form until the end of its next turn. While in quicksilver form, the dragon can't attack or fly, but it gains a climb speed of 6, ignores difficult terrain, and doesn't provoke opportunity attacks. It can squeeze through any aperture a Tiny creature could fit through. The dragon can return to its normal form as a free action on its turn. When it returns to normal, each creature within 2 squares grants combat advantage to the dragon until the end of the dragon's next turn. *Sustain Minor:* The quicksilver form persists.

Combat Advantage
The dragon deals 1d6 extra damage against a target granting combat advantage to it.

Alignment Unaligned		Languages Common, Draconic
Skills Acrobatics +13, Bluff +12, Stealth +13		
Str 16 (+6)	Dex 21 (+8)	Wis 11 (+3)
Con 16 (+6)	Int 13 (+4)	Cha 19 (+7)

Adult Mercury Dragon — Level 13 Solo Lurker

Large natural magical beast (dragon, shapechanger) — XP 4,000

Initiative +16 **Senses** Perception +11; darkvision
HP 516; **Bloodied** 258; see also *bloodied breath*
AC 27; **Fortitude** 26, **Reflex** 27, **Will** 23
Resist 20 poison
Saving Throws +5
Speed 7, fly 7 (hover), overland flight 10
Action Points 2

⊕ **Bite** (standard; at-will)
  Reach 2; +18 vs. AC; 1d12 + 7 damage.
⊕ **Claw** (standard; at-will)
  Reach 2; +18 vs. AC; 1d10 + 7 damage.
↯ **Draconic Fury** (standard; at-will)
  The dragon makes two claw attacks and one bite attack.
↯ **Quick Snap** (immediate interrupt, when an enemy moves adjacent to the dragon; at-will)
  The dragon makes a bite attack against the triggering enemy. On a hit, the target also grants combat advantage to the dragon (save ends).
⟵ **Breath Weapon** (standard; recharge ⚅ ⚅) ✦ **Poison**
  Close blast 5; +16 vs. Fortitude; 2d8 + 4 poison damage, and the target takes ongoing 5 poison damage and treats the dragon as invisible (save ends both). *Miss:* Half damage.
⟵ **Bloodied Breath** (free, when first bloodied; encounter)
  Breath weapon recharges, and the dragon uses it.
⟵ **Frightful Presence** (standard; encounter) ✦ **Fear**
  Close burst 5; targets enemies; +16 vs. Will; the target is stunned until the end of the dragon's next turn. *Aftereffect:* The target takes a -2 penalty to attack rolls (save ends).
Quicksilver Form (move action; encounter) ✦ **Polymorph**
  The dragon becomes a liquid wave of quicksilver and shifts 4 squares. It remains in quicksilver form until the end of its next turn. While in quicksilver form, the dragon can't attack or fly, but it gains a climb speed of 6, ignores difficult terrain, and doesn't provoke opportunity attacks. It can squeeze through any aperture a Tiny creature could fit through. The dragon can return to its normal form as a free action on its turn. When it returns to normal, each creature within 2 squares grants combat advantage to the dragon until the end of the dragon's next turn. *Sustain Minor:* The quicksilver form persists.
Change Shape (minor; at-will) ✦ **Polymorph**
  The dragon can alter its physical form to appear as any Medium or Large humanoid, including a unique individual (see "Change Shape," MM2 216).
Combat Advantage
  The dragon deals 2d6 extra damage against a target granting combat advantage to it.

Alignment Unaligned **Languages** Common, Draconic
Skills Acrobatics +17, Bluff +16, Stealth +17
Str 19 (+10) **Dex** 23 (+12) **Wis** 11 (+6)
Con 17 (+9) **Int** 13 (+7) **Cha** 20 (+11)

ZOLTAN BOROS & GABOR SZIKSZAI

Elder Mercury Dragon — Level 21 Solo Lurker
Huge natural magical beast (dragon, shapechanger)   XP 16,000

Initiative +22   **Senses** Perception +16; darkvision
HP 780; **Bloodied** 390; see also *bloodied breath*
AC 35; **Fortitude** 34, **Reflex** 35, **Will** 31
Resist 25 poison
Saving Throws +5
Speed 8, fly 8 (hover), overland flight 12
Action Points 2

⊕ **Bite** (standard; at-will)
   Reach 3; +26 vs. AC; 2d6 + 9 damage.

⊕ **Claw** (standard; at-will)
   Reach 3; +26 vs. AC; 1d12 + 9 damage.

↯ **Draconic Fury** (standard; at-will)
   The dragon makes two claw attacks and one bite attack.

↯ **Quick Snap** (immediate interrupt, when an enemy moves
   adjacent to the dragon; at-will)
   The dragon makes a bite attack against the triggering enemy.
   On a hit, the target also grants combat advantage to the dragon
   (save ends).

↞ **Breath Weapon** (standard; recharge ⚄ ⚅) ✦ **Poison**
   Close blast 5; +24 vs. Fortitude; 3d8 + 6 poison damage, and
   the target takes ongoing 10 poison damage and treats the
   dragon as invisible (save ends both). *Miss:* Half damage.

↞ **Bloodied Breath** (free, when first bloodied; encounter)
   Breath weapon recharges, and the dragon uses it.

↞ **Frightful Presence** (standard; encounter) ✦ **Fear**
   Close burst 10; targets enemies; +24 vs. Will; the target is
   stunned until the end of the dragon's next turn. *Aftereffect:* The
   target takes a -2 penalty to attack rolls (save ends).

Quicksilver Form (move action; encounter) ✦ **Polymorph**
   The dragon becomes a liquid wave of quicksilver and shifts 6
   squares. It remains in quicksilver form until the end of its next
   turn. While in quicksilver form, the dragon can't attack or fly,
   but it gains a climb speed of 6, ignores difficult terrain, and
   doesn't provoke opportunity attacks. It can squeeze through
   any aperture a Tiny creature could fit through. The dragon can
   return to its normal form as a free action on its turn. When
   it returns to normal, each creature within 2 squares grants
   combat advantage to the dragon until the end of the dragon's
   next turn. *Sustain Minor:* The quicksilver form persists.

Change Shape (minor; at-will) ✦ **Polymorph**
   The dragon can alter its physical form to appear as any Medium
   or Large humanoid, including a unique individual (see "Change
   Shape," *MM2* 216).

Combat Advantage
   The dragon deals 3d6 extra damage against a target granting
   combat advantage to it.

Alignment Unaligned   **Languages** Common, Draconic
Skills Acrobatics +23, Bluff +21, Stealth +23
Str 21 (+15)   **Dex** 26 (+18)   **Wis** 13 (+11)
Con 19 (+14)   **Int** 13 (+11)   **Cha** 22 (+16)

Ancient Mercury Dragon — Level 28 Solo Lurker
Gargantuan natural magical beast   XP 65,000
(dragon, shapechanger)

Initiative +28   **Senses** Perception +21; darkvision
HP 1,012; **Bloodied** 506; see also *bloodied breath*
AC 42; **Fortitude** 41, **Reflex** 42, **Will** 38
Resist 30 poison
Saving Throws +5
Speed 9, fly 8 (hover), overland flight 15
Action Points 2

⊕ **Bite** (standard; at-will)
   Reach 4; +33 vs. AC; 2d10 + 11 damage.

⊕ **Claw** (standard; at-will)
   Reach 4; +33 vs. AC; 2d8 + 11 damage.

↯ **Draconic Fury** (standard; at-will)
   The dragon makes two claw attacks and one bite attack.

↯ **Quick Snap** (immediate interrupt, when an enemy moves
   adjacent to the dragon; at-will)
   The dragon makes a bite attack against the triggering enemy.
   On a hit, the target also grants combat advantage to the dragon
   (save ends).

↞ **Breath Weapon** (standard; recharge ⚄ ⚅) ✦ **Poison**
   Close blast 5; +31 vs. Fortitude; 4d8 + 7 poison damage, and
   the target takes ongoing 15 poison damage and treats the
   dragon as invisible (save ends both). *Miss:* Half damage.

↞ **Bloodied Breath** (free, when first bloodied; encounter)
   Breath weapon recharges, and the dragon uses it.

↞ **Frightful Presence** (standard; encounter) ✦ **Fear**
   Close burst 10; targets enemies; +31 vs. Will; the target is
   stunned until the end of the dragon's next turn. *Aftereffect:* The
   target takes a -2 penalty to attack rolls (save ends).

Fluid Shape (immediate interrupt, when an enemy attacks the
   dragon; recharge ⚄ ⚅) ✦ **Polymorph**
   The triggering attack instead targets a different creature
   adjacent to the dragon.

Quicksilver Form (move action; encounter) ✦ **Polymorph**
   The dragon becomes a liquid wave of quicksilver and shifts 8
   squares. It remains in quicksilver form until the end of its next
   turn. While in quicksilver form, the dragon can't attack or fly,
   but it gains a climb speed of 6, ignores difficult terrain, and
   doesn't provoke opportunity attacks. It can squeeze through
   any aperture a Tiny creature could fit through. The dragon can
   return to its normal form as a free action on its turn. When
   it returns to normal, each creature within 2 squares grants
   combat advantage to the dragon until the end of the dragon's
   next turn. *Sustain Minor:* The quicksilver form persists.

Change Shape (minor; at-will) ✦ **Polymorph**
   The dragon can alter its physical form to appear as any Medium
   or Large humanoid, including a unique individual (see "Change
   Shape," *MM2* 216).

Combat Advantage
   The dragon deals 3d6 extra damage against a target granting
   combat advantage to it.

Alignment Unaligned   **Languages** Common, Draconic
Skills Acrobatics +29, Bluff +26, Stealth +29
Str 25 (+21)   **Dex** 30 (+24)   **Wis** 15 (+16)
Con 21 (+19)   **Int** 15 (+16)   **Cha** 24 (+21)

MERCURY DRAGON LORE

Nature DC 12: Mercury dragons often make
their homes in volcanoes, mountain peaks, and the
Elemental Chaos. But these born travelers sometimes
spend months away from their lairs.

Nature DC 17: The poison breath of a mercury dragon can render creatures unable to see the dragon for several seconds. And because the poisoned creature can see everything else, the dragon's enemy might not realize that the dragon is effectively invisible. When threatened, a mercury dragon can turn its body into a liquid pool of quicksilver that moves like an ooze.

Mercury Dragon Tactics

A mercury dragon is stealthy and prefers to observe its quarry for a time before attacking when terrain or timing gives it an advantage. It breathes on its enemies as soon as it can, then attacks those who can't see it. It often uses *frightful presence* in the second round of a fight if its *breath weapon* missed some of its foes, or if some were out of range.

A mercury dragon uses *quicksilver form* either to escape or to move to advantageous terrain, such as a place its adversaries cannot reach. Then it resumes its normal form and alternates between its *breath weapon* and *draconic fury* attacks.

When most enemies shake off the poison breath, the mercury dragon breathes again if the breath weapon has recharged, or the dragon moves away to encourage a foe to move adjacent and thus trigger *quicksilver form*.

An ancient mercury dragon's shapechanging is so effective that it can use *fluid shape* to entice one enemy into attacking another. An older mercury dragon can adopt a humanoid shape and disguise itself as a member of a "lesser" race. Mercury dragons don't have a steel dragon's affinity for civilization, however, and often spoil their disguises by demonstrating their ignorance of customs or manners.

Encounter Groups

Unlike many other dragons, mercury dragons don't crave social dominance for its own sake. Many a mercury dragon is happier serving as a ruler's grandmaster assassin, special emissary, or mysterious spy than it would be if it had to rule from its lair. With the ability to change shape and use *quicksilver form* to reach places other creatures cannot go, mercury dragons make peerless thieves and scouts as well.

Level 16 Encounter (XP 7,000)
+ 1 adult mercury dragon (level 13 solo lurker)
+ 1 drow priest (level 15 controller, *MM* 95)
+ 3 drow warriors (level 11 lurker, *MM* 94)

Level 23 Encounter (XP 29,400)
+ 1 elder mercury dragon (level 21 solo lurker)
+ 1 efreet cinderlord (level 23 artillery, *MM* 98)
+ 2 efreet fireblades (level 22 soldier, *MM* 98)

MITHRAL DRAGON

THE MYSTERIOUS MITHRAL DRAGONS can glimpse the future. Devoted to causes and deities, these dragons involve themselves in the affairs of the faithful, appearing to a select few and then disappearing suddenly. Single-minded in pursuit of its cause, a mithral can be an implacable foe or an unflinching ally.

Mithral Dragon Lore

Religion DC 16: Mithral dragons work for causes, particularly religious ones, and are natives of the Astral Sea. In battle, they attack only when it's advantageous for them to do so, even if a fight drags on.

Religion DC 21: Mithral dragons can see into the future and teleport. A mithral might abandon its faith without notice at the behest of a higher calling. Mithral dragons breathe streams of radiant energy.

Mithral Dragon Tactics

Mithral dragons fight only on battlefields of their choosing. They prefer areas that feature obstructions and difficult terrain, to capitalize on their teleportation abilities and to limit the mobility of earthbound foes.

A mithral dragon spreads its attacks around, herding enemies into a group before unleashing its *breath weapon* or using *dimensional flurry*. It uses *dimension strike* to appear suddenly in the midst of ranged attackers.

Elder and ancient mithrals have *mithral prescience*, which forces slivers of their foresight into their enemies' minds and causes strange draconic visions to overlay their senses. A dragon reserves that attack for formidable foes that prove resilient to its other attacks.

Young Mithral Dragon	Level 11 Solo Skirmisher
Large immortal magical beast (dragon)	XP 3,000

Initiative +13   **Senses** Perception +14; darkvision
HP 444; **Bloodied** 222; see also *bloodied breath*
AC 25; **Fortitude** 23, **Reflex** 25, **Will** 23
Resist 15 radiant
Saving Throws +5
Speed 8, fly 10 (hover), overland flight 12, teleport 10
Action Points 2

⊕ **Bite** (standard; at-will) ✦ **Radiant**
 Reach 2; +16 vs. AC; 2d8 + 4 damage, and the target takes ongoing 5 radiant damage (save ends).

⊕ **Claw** (standard; at-will)
 Reach 2; +16 vs. AC; 2d8 + 4 damage.

† **Dimension Strike** (standard; at-will) ✦ **Teleportation**
 The dragon teleports 5 squares, makes a claw attack, teleports 5 squares, and makes a claw attack against a different target.

† **Wing Buffet** (minor; recharge ⚄ ⚅)
 Reach 2; +14 vs. Fortitude; 2d8 + 6 damage, and the dragon pushes the target 3 squares.

↞ **Breath Weapon** (standard; recharge ⚄ ⚅) ✦ **Radiant**
 Close blast 5; +14 vs. Reflex; 2d6 + 4 radiant damage, and the target is blinded (save ends). *Miss:* Half damage.

↺ Bloodied Breath (free, when first bloodied; encounter)
Breath weapon recharges, and the dragon uses it.

↺ Dimensional Flurry (standard; encounter) ✦ **Radiant, Teleportation**
Close burst 10; targets up to four enemies; +14 vs. Reflex; 2d8 + 4 damage, and the target takes ongoing 5 radiant damage and is dazed (save ends both). *Effect:* The dragon teleports to a space in the burst.

↺ Frightful Presence (standard; encounter) ✦ **Fear**
Close burst 5; targets enemies; +14 vs. Will; the target is stunned until the end of the dragon's next turn. *Aftereffect:* The target takes a –2 penalty to attack rolls (save ends).

Prophetic Defense (immediate interrupt, when the dragon is hit by an attack; at-will) ✦ **Teleportation**
The dragon gains a +4 bonus to all defenses against the triggering attack. If the attack misses, the dragon teleports 6 squares.

Alignment Unaligned	**Languages** Common, Draconic, Supernal	
Skills Diplomacy +13, History +13, Insight +14, Intimidate +13, Religion +13		
Str 18 (+9)	**Dex** 23 (+11)	**Wis** 18 (+9)
Con 15 (+7)	**Int** 16 (+8)	**Cha** 16 (+8)

Adult Mithral Dragon	**Level 18 Solo Skirmisher**
Large immortal magical beast (dragon)	XP 10,000

Initiative +19　　**Senses** Perception +20; darkvision
HP 684; **Bloodied** 342; see also *bloodied breath*
AC 32; **Fortitude** 29, **Reflex** 31, **Will** 29
Resist 20 radiant
Saving Throws +5
Speed 8, fly 10 (hover), overland flight 12, teleport 10
Action Points 2

⊕ Bite (standard; at-will) ✦ **Radiant**
Reach 2; +23 vs. AC; 2d8 + 7 damage, and the target takes ongoing 5 radiant damage (save ends).

⊕ Claw (standard; at-will)
Reach 2; +23 vs. AC; 2d8 + 7 damage.

♯ Dimension Strike (standard; at-will) ✦ **Teleportation**
The dragon teleports 5 squares, makes a claw attack, teleports 5 squares, and makes a claw attack against a different target.

♯ Wing Buffet (minor; recharge ⚄ ⚅)
Reach 2; +21 vs. Fortitude; 3d8 + 6 damage, and the dragon pushes the target 3 squares.

↺ Breath Weapon (standard; recharge ⚄ ⚅) ✦ **Radiant**
Close blast 5; +21 vs. Reflex; 3d8 + 4 radiant damage, and the target is blinded (save ends). *Miss:* Half damage.

↺ Bloodied Breath (free, when first bloodied; encounter)
Breath weapon recharges, and the dragon uses it.

↺ Dimensional Flurry (standard; encounter) ✦ **Radiant, Teleportation**
Close burst 10; targets up to four enemies; +14 vs. Reflex; 2d8 + 7 damage, and the target takes ongoing 5 radiant damage and is dazed (save ends both). *Effect:* The dragon teleports to a space in the burst.

↺ Frightful Presence (standard; encounter) ✦ **Fear**
Close burst 5; targets enemies; +21 vs. Will; the target is stunned until the end of the dragon's next turn. *Aftereffect:* The target takes a –2 penalty to attack rolls (save ends).

Prophetic Defense (immediate interrupt, when the dragon is hit by an attack; at-will) ✦ **Teleportation**
The dragon gains a +4 bonus to all defenses against the triggering attack. If the attack misses, the dragon teleports 6 squares.

Alignment Unaligned	**Languages** Common, Draconic, Supernal	
Skills Diplomacy +19, History +19, Insight +20, Intimidate +19, Religion +19		
Str 22 (+15)	**Dex** 27 (+17)	**Wis** 22 (+15)
Con 19 (+13)	**Int** 20 (+14)	**Cha** 20 (+14)

Elder Mithral Dragon	**Level 25 Solo Skirmisher**
Huge immortal magical beast (dragon)	XP 35,000

Initiative +24　　**Senses** Perception +24; darkvision
HP 916; **Bloodied** 458; see also *bloodied breath*
AC 39, **Fortitude** 36, **Reflex** 38, **Will** 36
Resist 25 radiant
Saving Throws +5
Speed 10, fly 12 (hover), overland flight 16, teleport 10
Action Points 2

⊕ Bite (standard; at-will) ✦ **Radiant**
Reach 3; +30 vs. AC; 2d8 + 10 damage, and the target takes ongoing 10 radiant damage (save ends).

⊕ Claw (standard; at-will)
Reach 3; +30 vs. AC; 3d8 + 7 damage.

♯ Dimension Strike (standard; at-will) ✦ **Teleportation**
The dragon teleports 5 squares, makes a claw attack, teleports 5 squares, and makes a claw attack against a different target.

♯ Wing Buffet (minor; recharge ⚄ ⚅)
Reach 3; +28 vs. Fortitude; 3d10 + 7 damage, and the dragon pushes the target 3 squares.

↗ Mithral Prescience (minor; at-will)
Ranged 10; the target takes a –2 penalty to all defenses against the dragon's attacks until the dragon uses this power on another target.

↺ Breath Weapon (standard; recharge ⚄ ⚅) ✦ **Radiant**
Close blast 5; +28 vs. Reflex; 4d8 + 4 radiant damage, and the target is blinded (save ends). *Miss:* Half damage.

↺ Bloodied Breath (free, when first bloodied; encounter)
Breath weapon recharges, and the dragon uses it.

↺ Dimensional Flurry (standard; encounter) ✦ **Radiant, Teleportation**
Close burst 10; targets up to four enemies; +28 vs. Reflex; 3d8 + 7 damage, and the target takes ongoing 10 radiant damage and is dazed (save ends both). *Effect:* The dragon teleports to a space in the burst.

↺ Frightful Presence (standard; encounter) ✦ **Fear**
Close burst 10; targets enemies; +28 vs. Will; the target is stunned until the end of the dragon's next turn. *Aftereffect:* The target takes a –2 penalty to attack rolls (save ends).

Prophetic Defense (immediate interrupt, when the dragon is hit by an attack; at-will) ✦ **Teleportation**
The dragon gains a +4 bonus to all defenses against the triggering attack. If the attack misses, the dragon teleports 6 squares.

Alignment Unaligned	**Languages** Common, Draconic, Supernal	
Skills Diplomacy +23, History +23, Insight +24, Intimidate +23, Religion +23		
Str 25 (+19)	**Dex** 30 (+22)	**Wis** 25 (+19)
Con 21 (+17)	**Int** 23 (+18)	**Cha** 23 (+18)

IMMORTAL DRAGONS

Unlike other creatures of the immortal origin, immortal dragons age. However, they do not diminish in old age. An immortal dragon never moves into the twilight stage of dragon development (see page 15).

Ancient Mithral Dragon — Level 31 Solo Skirmisher

Gargantuan immortal magical beast (dragon) — XP 115,000

Initiative +28   **Senses** Perception +29; darkvision
HP 1,120; **Bloodied** 560; see also *bloodied breath*
AC 45, **Fortitude** 42, **Reflex** 44, **Will** 42
Resist 30 radiant
Saving Throws +5
Speed 12, fly 14 (hover), overland flight 18, teleport 10
Action Points 2

① **Bite** (standard; at-will) ✦ **Radiant**
    Reach 4; +36 vs. AC; 2d8 + 12 damage, and the target takes ongoing 15 radiant damage (save ends).

① **Claw** (standard; at-will)
    Reach 4; +36 vs. AC; 3d8 + 10 damage.

✦ **Dimension Strike** (standard; at-will) ✦ **Teleportation**
    The dragon teleports 5 squares, makes a claw attack, teleports 5 squares, and makes a claw attack against a different target.

✦ **Wing Buffet** (minor; recharge ⚄ ⚅)
    Reach 4; +34 vs. Fortitude; 4d10 + 7 damage, and the dragon pushes the target 3 squares.

⟐ **Mithral Prescience** (minor; at-will)
    Ranged 10; the target takes a -2 penalty to all defenses against the dragon's attacks until the dragon uses this power on another target.

⟐ **Breath Weapon** (standard; recharge ⚄ ⚅) ✦ **Radiant**
    Close blast 5; +34 vs. Reflex; 4d10 + 5 radiant damage, and the target is blinded (save ends). *Miss:* Half damage.

⟐ **Bloodied Breath** (free, when first bloodied; encounter)
    Breath weapon recharges, and the dragon uses it.

⟐ **Dimensional Flurry** (standard; encounter) ✦ **Radiant, Teleportation**
    Close burst 10; targets up to four enemies; +34 vs. Reflex; 4d8 + 5 damage, and the target takes ongoing 15 radiant damage and is dazed (save ends both). *Effect:* The dragon teleports to a space in the burst.

⟐ **Frightful Presence** (standard; encounter) ✦ **Fear**
    Close burst 10; targets enemies; +34 vs. Will; the target is stunned until the end of the dragon's next turn. *Aftereffect:* The target takes a -2 penalty to attack rolls (save ends).

Prophetic Defense (immediate interrupt, when the dragon is hit by an attack; at-will) ✦ **Teleportation**
    The dragon gains a +4 bonus to all defenses against the triggering attack. If the attack misses, the dragon teleports 6 squares.

Alignment Unaligned   **Languages** Common, Draconic, Supernal
Skills Diplomacy +28, History +28, Insight +29, Intimidate +28, Religion +28

Str 28 (+24)	**Dex** 33 (+26)	**Wis** 28 (+24)
Con 24 (+22)	**Int** 26 (+23)	**Cha** 26 (+23)

Encounter Groups

On the rare occasions when mithral dragons team up with other creatures, they fight alongside soldiers or brutes—allies that fight toe-to-toe with enemies and free the dragon to teleport in and out of combat.

Level 14 Encounter (XP 5,000)
✦ 1 young mithral dragon (level 11 solo skirmisher)
✦ 4 dragonborn gladiators (level 10 soldier, MM 86)

Level 30 Encounter (XP 95,000)
✦ 1 elder mithral dragon (level 25 solo skirmisher)
✦ 2 godforged colossi (level 29 elite brute, MM 44)

KEREM BEYIT

ORIUM DRAGON

ORIUM DRAGONS LIVE AMONG RUINS of ancient civilizations, commanding lesser creatures to rebuild the glories of yesteryear and recapture the magic of fallen empires. To those under its protection, an orium dragon is a wise but sometimes harsh monarch. Those who threaten the dragon's dreams of renewed empire find themselves choking on its corrosive breath—while they watch the vapor coalesce into a smoky serpent that attacks at the dragon's command.

ORIUM DRAGON LORE

Nature DC 14: Orium dragons make their lairs in ancient ruins, especially those in jungles and other warm environments. They gather and guard the treasure and lore they salvage from the ruins.

Nature DC 19: Unlike most breath weapons, an orium dragon's acidic breath doesn't disperse. It collapses in on itself, creating a serpent of magic vapor that attacks the dragon's enemies.

ORIUM DRAGON TACTICS

The orium dragon's *breath weapon* stands out as its most potent and most versatile ability. It deals damage as other breath weapons do, but then transforms into a vaporous serpent that can move and attack right after the dragon's turn. The *breath weapon* recharges when the minion is destroyed. (Give the players a visual cue when this happens, so they know the consequences of destroying the minion—though the minion also deals enough damage to make it dangerous if it sticks around).

Elder and ancient orium dragons have unusually long tails, which they can coil around an enemy. They use *tail coil* against the first enemy to move adjacent to them, then continue to squeeze every round. If dangerous terrain is nearby, an orium dragon can move a grabbed target, making a Strength attack against the target's Fortitude. If the dragon hits, it can move at half speed and pull the target behind it. Being grabbed by an ancient orium is particularly dangerous if the target is moved inside the dragon's *corrosive fumes* aura.

ENCOUNTER GROUPS

The typical orium dragon lives in jungle ruins, surrounded by a tribe of monsters that treat it like a god.

Level 9 Encounter (XP 2,400)
✦ 1 young orium dragon (level 8 solo soldier)
✦ 2 greenscale darters (level 5 lurker, *MM* 178)
✦ 1 greenscale marsh mystic (level 6 controller, *MM* 179)

Level 16 Encounter (XP 7,000)
✦ 1 adult orium dragon (level 13 solo soldier)
✦ 3 medusa archers (level 10 elite controller, *MM* 186)

HOWARD LYON

Young Orium Dragon — Level 8 Solo Soldier
Large natural magical beast (dragon)   XP 1,750

Initiative +9   **Senses** Perception +9; darkvision
HP 360; **Bloodied** 180; see also *bloodied breath*
AC 24; **Fortitude** 22, **Reflex** 20, **Will** 19
Resist 15 acid
Saving Throws +5
Speed 6, fly 8 (hover), overland flight 12
Action Points 2

⊕ **Bite** (standard; at-will) ✦ Acid
Reach 2; +15 vs. AC; 1d10 + 6 damage plus 1d6 acid damage.

⊕ **Claw** (standard; at-will)
Reach 2; +15 vs. AC; 1d8 + 6 damage, and the target is marked until the end of the dragon's next turn.

✦ **Draconic Fury** (standard; at-will)
The dragon makes two claw attacks and one bite attack.

⟵ **Breath Weapon** (standard; recharges when one of the dragon's vaporous spirits is reduced to 0 hit points) ✦ Acid
Close blast 5; +13 vs. Fortitude; 2d8 + 4 acid damage, and a young vaporous serpent minion (see below) appears in any single unoccupied square in the blast. It acts just after the dragon in the initiative order.

⟵ **Bloodied Breath** (free, when first bloodied; encounter)
Breath weapon recharges, and the dragon uses it.

⟵ **Frightful Presence** (standard; encounter) ✦ Fear
Close burst 5; targets enemies; +13 vs. Will; the target is stunned until the end of the dragon's next turn. *Aftereffect:* The target takes a -2 penalty to attack rolls (save ends).

Alignment Unaligned   **Languages** Common, Draconic
Skills History +10, Insight +9, Intimidate +11
Str 20 (+9)   **Dex** 16 (+7)   **Wis** 11 (+4)
Con 18 (+8)   **Int** 12 (+5)   **Cha** 15 (+6)

Young Vaporous Serpent — Level 8 Minion Brute
Medium elemental beast   XP —

Initiative as dragon   **Senses** Perception +1
HP 1; a missed attack never damages a minion.
AC 21; **Fortitude** 20, **Reflex** 19, **Will** 18
Resist 15 acid
Speed 6

⊕ **Bite** (standard; at-will) ✦ Acid
+13 vs. AC; 10 acid damage.

Alignment Unaligned   **Languages** —
Str 17 (+7)   **Dex** 10 (+4)   **Wis** 4 (+1)
Con 12 (+5)   **Int** 4 (+1)   **Cha** 4 (+1)

Adult Orium Dragon — Level 13 Solo Soldier
Large natural magical beast (dragon)   XP 4,000

Initiative +13   **Senses** Perception +12; darkvision
HP 532; **Bloodied** 266; see also *bloodied breath*
AC 29; **Fortitude** 27, **Reflex** 25, **Will** 24
Resist 20 acid
Saving Throws +5
Speed 6, fly 8 (hover), overland flight 12
Action Points 2

⊕ **Bite** (standard; at-will) ✦ Acid
Reach 2; +20 vs. AC; 1d10 + 6 damage plus 2d6 acid damage.

⊕ **Claw** (standard; at-will)
Reach 2; +20 vs. AC; 1d12 + 6 damage, and the target is marked until the end of the dragon's next turn.

✦ **Draconic Fury** (standard; at-will)
The dragon makes two claw attacks and one bite attack.

⟵ **Breath Weapon** (standard; recharges when one of the dragon's vaporous spirits is reduced to 0 hit points) ✦ Acid
Close blast 5; +16 vs. Fortitude; 2d8 + 4 acid damage, and an adult vaporous serpent minion (see below) appears in any single unoccupied square in the blast. It acts just after the dragon in the initiative order.

⟵ **Bloodied Breath** (free, when first bloodied; encounter)
Breath weapon recharges, and the dragon uses it.

⟵ **Frightful Presence** (standard; encounter) ✦ Fear
Close burst 5; targets enemies; +15 vs. Will; the target is stunned until the end of the dragon's next turn. *Aftereffect:* The target takes a -2 penalty to attack rolls (save ends).

Alignment Unaligned   **Languages** Common, Draconic
Skills History +13, Insight +12, Intimidate +14
Str 23 (+12)   **Dex** 20 (+11)   **Wis** 13 (+7)
Con 21 (+11)   **Int** 14 (+8)   **Cha** 17 (+9)

Adult Vaporous Serpent — Level 13 Minion Brute
Medium elemental beast   XP —

Initiative as dragon   **Senses** Perception +3
HP 1; a missed attack never damages a minion.
AC 26; **Fortitude** 25, **Reflex** 24, **Will** 23
Resist 20 acid
Speed 6

⊕ **Bite** (standard; at-will) ✦ Acid
+18 vs. AC; 13 acid damage.

Alignment Unaligned   **Languages** —
Str 20 (+11)   **Dex** 12 (+7)   **Wis** 4 (+3)
Con 15 (+8)   **Int** 4 (+3)   **Cha** 4 (+3)

Elder Orium Dragon — Level 20 Solo Soldier
Huge natural magical beast (dragon)   XP 14,000

Initiative +18   **Senses** Perception +17; darkvision
HP 768; **Bloodied** 384; see also *bloodied breath*
AC 36; **Fortitude** 34, **Reflex** 32, **Will** 30
Resist 25 acid
Saving Throws +5
Speed 8, fly 10 (hover), overland flight 15
Action Points 2

⊕ **Bite** (standard; at-will) ✦ Acid
Reach 3; +26 vs. AC; 2d6 + 7 damage plus 2d6 acid damage.

⊕ **Claw** (standard; at-will)
Reach 3; +26 vs. AC; 2d6 + 7 damage, and the target is marked until the end of the dragon's next turn.

✦ **Draconic Fury** (standard; at-will)
The dragon makes two claw attacks and one bite attack.

✦ **Tail Coil** (immediate reaction, when an enemy moves into an adjacent square; at-will)
Targets the triggering enemy; +24 vs. Reflex; 3d6+7 damage, and the target is grabbed. A creature grabbed by this attack takes 15 damage at the start of each of its turns. The dragon can grab only one creature with *tail coil* at a time.

BEHIND THE SCREEN: VAPOROUS SERPENT MINIONS

The minions created by an orium dragon's breath are designed to be more powerful than standard minions. They deal more damage, effectively acting as an extra attack for the dragon. They aren't meant to be used on their own or dropped into other encounters.

↩ **Breath Weapon** (standard; recharges when one of the dragon's vaporous spirits is reduced to 0 hit points) ✦ **Acid**
Close blast 5; +21 vs. Fortitude; 3d6 + 6 acid damage, and an elder vaporous serpent minion (see below) appears in any single unoccupied square in the blast. It acts just after the dragon in the initiative order.

↩ **Bloodied Breath** (free, when first bloodied; encounter)
Breath weapon recharges, and the dragon uses it.

↩ **Frightful Presence** (standard; encounter) ✦ **Fear**
Close burst 10; targets enemies; +19 vs. Will; the target is stunned until the end of the dragon's next turn. *Aftereffect:* The target takes a -2 penalty to attack rolls (save ends).

Alignment Unaligned	**Languages** Common, Draconic

Skills History +18, Insight +17, Intimidate +19

Str 26 (+18)	**Dex** 23 (+16)	**Wis** 14 (+12)
Con 24 (+17)	**Int** 16 (+13)	**Cha** 18 (+14)

Elder Vaporous Serpent	**Level 20 Minion Brute**
Medium elemental beast	XP —

Initiative as dragon **Senses** Perception +7
HP 1; a missed attack never damages a minion.
AC 33; **Fortitude** 32, **Reflex** 31, **Will** 30
Resist 25 acid
Speed 6

⊕ **Bite** (standard; at-will) ✦ **Acid**
+25 vs. AC; 17 acid damage.

Alignment Unaligned	**Languages** —

Str 23 (+16)	**Dex** 15 (+12)	**Wis** 4 (+7)
Con 18 (+14)	**Int** 4 (+7)	**Cha** 4 (+7)

Ancient Orium Dragon	**Level 28 Solo Soldier**
Gargantuan natural magical beast (dragon)	XP 65,000

Initiative +24 **Senses** Perception +22; darkvision
Corrosive Fumes (Acid) aura 3; any creature that enters the aura or starts its turn there takes 20 acid damage.
HP 1,040; **Bloodied** 520; see also *bloodied breath*
AC 44; **Fortitude** 42, **Reflex** 40, **Will** 38
Resist 30 acid
Saving Throws +5
Speed 12, fly 12 (hover), overland flight 15
Action Points 2

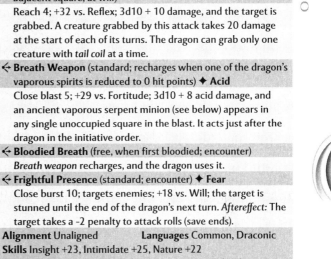

⊕ **Bite** (standard; at-will) ✦ **Acid**
Reach 4; +37 vs. AC; 2d10 + 10 damage plus 4d6 acid damage.

⊕ **Claw** (standard; at-will)
Reach 4; +34 vs. AC; 2d10 + 10 damage, and the target is marked until the end of the dragon's next turn.

✦ **Draconic Fury** (standard; at-will)
The dragon makes two claw attacks and one bite attack.

✦ **Tail Coil** (immediate reaction, when an enemy moves into an adjacent square; at-will)
Reach 4; +32 vs. Reflex; 3d10 + 10 damage, and the target is grabbed. A creature grabbed by this attack takes 20 damage at the start of each of its turns. The dragon can grab only one creature with *tail coil* at a time.

↩ **Breath Weapon** (standard; recharges when one of the dragon's vaporous spirits is reduced to 0 hit points) ✦ **Acid**
Close blast 5; +29 vs. Fortitude; 3d10 + 8 acid damage, and an ancient vaporous serpent minion (see below) appears in any single unoccupied square in the blast. It acts just after the dragon in the initiative order.

↩ **Bloodied Breath** (free, when first bloodied; encounter)
Breath weapon recharges, and the dragon uses it.

↩ **Frightful Presence** (standard; encounter) ✦ **Fear**
Close burst 10; targets enemies; +18 vs. Will; the target is stunned until the end of the dragon's next turn. *Aftereffect:* The target takes a -2 penalty to attack rolls (save ends).

Alignment Unaligned	**Languages** Common, Draconic

Skills Insight +23, Intimidate +25, Nature +22

Str 30 (+24)	**Dex** 27 (+22)	**Wis** 17 (+17)
Con 28 (+23)	**Int** 19 (+18)	**Cha** 22 (+20)

Ancient Vaporous Serpent	**Level 28 Minion Brute**
Medium elemental beast	XP —

Initiative as dragon **Senses** Perception +12
HP 1; a missed attack never damages a minion.
AC 41; **Fortitude** 40, **Reflex** 39, **Will** 38
Resist 30 acid
Speed 6

⊕ **Bite** (standard; at-will) ✦ **Acid**
+33 vs. AC; 20 acid damage.

Alignment Unaligned	**Languages** —

Str 29 (+24)	**Dex** 18 (+19)	**Wis** 4 (+12)
Con 22 (+21)	**Int** 4 (+12)	**Cha** 4 (+12)

THE SECRETS OF ORIUM

Though seldom used today, the red-gold metal orium figures prominently in ancient lore. Many adventurers, and their enemies, look for relics created with this metal.

Uses: When prepared properly, using long-lost crafting methods, orium greatly increases the power of magic channeled through it. Most often, ancient crafters used orium to make implements. Some tales, though, describe other magic items made from the metal. A popular legend describes a cabal of ancient wizards who carried spellbooks made up of hundreds of thin sheets of orium. The metal is too soft for weapons or armor, but those items can have orium studs or gilding to enhance their magic.

History: Evidence indicates that orium originated in the Feywild, smelted in the workshops of the cyclopses from ore found deep in the Feywild's Underdark. In time, eladrin stole the secret of crafting orium and brought it

back to their cities, and eventually to the world. It's said empires as recent as Bael Turath still held the secret, but most extant orium items date from more ancient times.

Orium's Poison: The ability to craft orium never entirely disappeared. In fact, smelting it is simple. But unless the crafter purifies the ore during smelting, using the secret techniques of the ancients, the resulting orium is highly poisonous. Even the greatest precautions prove ineffective against unpurified orium, because its subtle, magical emanations contaminate the body and mind over prolonged use. Only the most ambitious spellcasters (especially liches) use implements or magic items made with this substance. Since an orium dragon's breath draws its poison from the metal infused in the dragon's blood, some dragons explore ruins in search of the purified form of the metal. They hope to transfer its secret—and its power—to their own bodies.

In humanoid cities, steel dragons conceal their identities by adopting humanoid forms. In battle, steel dragons are quick and employ a wide array of attacks.

STEEL DRAGON LORE

Nature DC 14: Steel dragons take humanoid form, retaining some evidence of their coloration—gray hair, gray eyes, or steel jewelry. A steel dragon might take any role from a noble to a favored servant of a powerful and charismatic master. Steel dragons work within their communities to promote freedom and undermine authoritarian forces.

Nature DC 19: Steel dragons have difficulty with all kinds of absolute authority, even authority that has the best of intentions. Because other kinds of metallic dragons—especially gold dragons—use their power and experience to justify their actions, steel dragons dislike them.

STEEL DRAGON TACTICS

Steel dragons try to avoid being cornered. When drawn into combat, they keep to areas that offer plenty of maneuvering room.

A steel dragon uses its *breath weapon* to knock foes senseless, then skirts the battlefield's edges. It bites to give itself space and strikes with its claws to bring enemies down. Elder and ancient steel dragons can weave loose bits of energy from their *breath weapons* to ensnare enemies in prisons of crushing force. If a steel dragon is outmatched, it uses *change shape* to hide in crowds of humanoids or to surround itself with innocent bystanders.

ENCOUNTER GROUPS

Steel dragons primarily keep the company of humans. They join adventuring groups, serve powerful wizards, or ally with revolutionaries.

Level 8 Encounter (XP 1,800)
✦ 1 young steel dragon (level 7 solo skirmisher)
✦ 4 human lackeys (level 7 minion, *MM* 162)

Level 22 Encounter (XP 20,800)
✦ 1 elder steel dragon (level 21 solo skirmisher)
✦ 3 rakshasa assassins (level 17 skirmisher, *MM* 217)

Young Steel Dragon	Level 7 Solo Controller
Large natural magical beast (dragon, shapechanger)	XP 1,500

Initiative +5 — **Senses** Perception +11; darkvision
HP 324; **Bloodied** 162; see also *bloodied breath*
AC 22; **Fortitude** 19, **Reflex** 17, **Will** 20
Resist 15 force
Saving Throws +5
Speed 8, fly 10 (hover), overland flight 12
Action Points 2

⊕ **Bite** (standard; at-will) ✦ **Force**
Reach 2; +12 vs. AC; 2d8 + 4 damage plus 1d8 force damage, and the dragon slides the target 1 square.

⊕ **Claw** (standard; at-will)
Reach 2; +12 vs. AC; 2d6 + 4 damage.

↯ **Double Attack** (standard; at-will)
The dragon makes two claw attacks.

↯ **Wing Scatter** (immediate reaction, when an enemy moves into an adjacent square; at-will)
Targets the triggering enemy; +11 vs. Fortitude; 1d8 + 4 damage, and the target is knocked prone. *Effect:* The dragon shifts 1 square and flies 3 squares.

↯ **Dragon's Suggestion** (minor 1/round; at-will) ✦ **Charm**
+9 vs. Will; the dragon slides the target 1 square, and the target grants combat advantage until the end of the dragon's next turn. *Effect:* The dragon shifts 1 square.

⬳ **Breath Weapon** (standard; recharge ⚄ ⚅) ✦ **Force**
Close blast 5; +11 vs. Fortitude; 2d10 + 4 force damage, and the target is dazed (save ends). *Miss:* Half damage.

⬳ **Bloodied Breath** (free, when first bloodied; encounter)
Breath weapon recharges, and the dragon uses it.

⬳ **Frightful Presence** (standard; encounter) ✦ **Fear**
Close burst 5; targets enemies; +11 vs. Will; the target is stunned until the end of the dragon's next turn. *Aftereffect:* The target takes a -2 penalty to attack rolls (save ends).

Change Shape (minor; at-will) ✦ **Polymorph**
The dragon can alter its physical form to appear as a unique human (see "Change Shape," *MM2* 216).

Alignment Unaligned   **Languages** Common, Draconic
Skills Bluff +13, Diplomacy +13, Insight +11

Str 19 (+7)	**Dex** 14 (+5)	**Wis** 16 (+6)
Con 17 (+6)	**Int** 13 (+4)	**Cha** 21 (+8)

Adult Steel Dragon	Level 14 Solo Controller
Large natural magical beast (dragon, shapechanger)	XP 5,000

Initiative +11   **Senses** Perception +16; darkvision
HP 560; **Bloodied** 280; see also *bloodied breath*
AC 29; **Fortitude** 26, **Reflex** 24, **Will** 27
Resist 20 force
Saving Throws +5
Speed 8, fly 10 (hover), overland flight 12
Action Points 2

⊕ **Bite** (standard; at-will) ✦ **Force**
Reach 2; +19 vs. AC; 2d8 + 6 damage plus 1d10 force damage, and the dragon slides the target 2 squares.

⊕ **Claw** (standard; at-will)
Reach 2; +19 vs. AC; 2d8 + 6 damage.

↯ **Double Attack** (standard; at-will)
The dragon makes two claw attacks.

↯ **Wing Scatter** (immediate reaction, when an enemy moves into an adjacent square; at-will)
Targets the triggering enemy; +18 vs. Fortitude; 2d8 + 6 damage, and the target is knocked prone. *Effect:* The dragon shifts 1 square and flies 3 squares.

↯ **Dragon's Suggestion** (minor 1/round; at-will) ✦ **Charm**
+16 vs. Will; the dragon slides the target 1 square, and the target grants combat advantage until the end of the dragon's next turn. *Effect:* The dragon shifts 1 square.

⬳ **Breath Weapon** (standard; recharge ⚄ ⚅) ✦ **Force**
Close blast 5; +18 vs. Fortitude; 4d6 + 6 force damage, and the target is dazed (save ends). *Miss:* Half damage.

⬳ **Bloodied Breath** (free, when first bloodied; encounter) ✦ **Force**
Breath weapon recharges, and the dragon uses it.

⤢ Frightful Presence (standard; encounter) ✦ **Fear**

Close burst 5; targets enemies; +18 vs. Will; the target is stunned until the end of the dragon's next turn. *Aftereffect:* The target takes a -2 penalty to attack rolls (save ends).

Change Shape (minor; at-will) ✦ **Polymorph**

The dragon can alter its physical form to appear as a unique human (see "Change Shape," *MM2* 216).

Alignment Unaligned	Languages Common, Draconic

Skills Bluff +19, Diplomacy +19, Insight +16

Str 22 (+13)	Dex 18 (+11)	Wis 19 (+11)
Con 20 (+12)	Int 15 (+9)	Cha 24 (+14)

Elder Steel Dragon — Level 21 Solo Controller

Huge natural magical beast (dragon, shapechanger)   XP 16,000

Initiative +17	**Senses** Perception +20; darkvision

HP 800; **Bloodied** 400; see also *bloodied breath*

AC 36; **Fortitude** 33, **Reflex** 32, **Will** 34

Resist 25 force

Saving Throws +5

Speed 10, fly 12 (hover), overland flight 15

Action Points 2

⊕ Bite (standard; at-will) ✦ **Force**

Reach 3; +26 vs. AC; 3d6 + 8 damage plus 2d6 force damage, and the dragon slides the target 2 squares.

⊕ Claw (standard; at-will)

Reach 3; +26 vs. AC; 3d6 + 8 damage.

⸸ Double Attack (standard; at-will)

The dragon makes two claw attacks.

⸸ Wing Scatter (immediate reaction, when an enemy moves into an adjacent square; at-will)

Targets the triggering enemy; +24 vs. Fortitude; 3d6 + 8 damage, and the target is knocked prone. *Effect:* The dragon shifts 1 square and flies 3 squares.

⸸ Dragon's Suggestion (minor 1/round; at-will) ✦ **Charm**

+23 vs. Will; the dragon slides the target 2 squares, and the target grants combat advantage until the end of the dragon's next turn. *Effect:* The dragon shifts 1 square.

⤢ Breath Weapon (standard; recharge ⚄ ⚅) ✦ **Force**

Close blast 5; +25 vs. Fortitude; 4d8 + 8 force damage, and the target is dazed (save ends). *Miss:* Half damage.

⤢ Bloodied Breath (free, when first bloodied; encounter) ✦ **Force**

Breath weapon recharges, and the dragon uses it.

⤢ Frightful Presence (standard; encounter) ✦ **Fear**

Close burst 10; targets enemies; +25 vs. Will; the target is stunned until the end of the dragon's next turn. *Aftereffect:* The target takes a -2 penalty to attack rolls (save ends).

❈ Force Prison (standard; recharges when the dragon uses *breath weapon*) ✦ **Force, Zone**

Area burst 1 within 10; +25 vs. Reflex; 3d10 + 8 force damage. *Effect:* The burst becomes a zone of force until the end of the dragon's next turn. A creature within the zone can't leave it.

Change Shape (minor; at-will) ✦ **Polymorph**

The dragon can alter its physical form to appear as a unique human (see "Change Shape," *MM2* 216).

Alignment Unaligned	Languages Common, Draconic

Skills Bluff +24, Diplomacy +24, Insight +20

Str 26 (+18)	Dex 24 (+17)	Wis 21 (+15)
Con 24 (+17)	Int 17 (+13)	Cha 28 (+19)

CHRIS SEAMAN

Ancient Steel Dragon	Level 29 Solo Controller
Gargantuan natural magical beast (dragon, shapechanger)	XP 75,000

Initiative +23   **Senses** Perception +26; darkvision
HP 1,072; **Bloodied** 536; see also *bloodied breath*
AC 44; **Fortitude** 41, **Reflex** 40, **Will** 42
Resist 30 force
Saving Throws +5
Speed 12, fly 14 (hover), overland flight 20
Action Points 2

⊕ **Bite** (standard; at-will) ✦ **Force**
   Reach 4; +34 vs. AC; 3d8 + 11 damage plus 3d8 force damage, and the target slides 3 squares.

⊕ **Claw** (standard; at-will)
   Reach 4; +34 vs. AC; 3d6 + 11 damage.

† **Double Attack** (standard; at-will)
   The dragon makes two claw attacks.

† **Wing Scatter** (immediate reaction, when an enemy moves into an adjacent square; at-will)
   Targets the triggering enemy; +32 vs. Fortitude; 3d6 + 11 damage, and the target is knocked prone. *Effect:* The dragon shifts 1 square and flies 3 squares.

† **Dragon's Suggestion** (minor 1/round; at-will) ✦ **Charm**
   +31 vs. Will; the dragon slides the target 3 squares, and the target grants combat advantage until the end of the dragon's next turn. *Effect:* The dragon shifts 1 square.

↞ **Breath Weapon** (standard; recharge ⚅ ⚅) ✦ **Force**
   Close blast 5; +33 vs. Fortitude; 5d8 + 9 force damage, and the target is dazed (save ends). *Miss:* Half damage.

↞ **Bloodied Breath** (free, when first bloodied; encounter) ✦ **Force**
   Breath weapon recharges, and the dragon uses it.

↞ **Frightful Presence** (standard; encounter) ✦ **Fear**
   Close burst 10; targets enemies; +33 vs. Will; the target is stunned until the end of the dragon's next turn. *Aftereffect:* The target takes a –2 penalty to attack rolls (save ends).

✳ **Force Prison** (standard; recharges when the dragon uses *breath weapon*) ✦ **Force, Zone**
   Area burst 1 within 10; +33 vs. Reflex; 4d8 + 9 force damage. *Effect:* The burst becomes a zone of force until the end of the dragon's next turn. A creature within the zone can't leave it.

Hidden Steel (minor; encounter) ✦ **Charm**
   The dragon becomes invisible until the end of its next turn or until it attacks. *Sustain Minor:* The effect persists.

Change Shape (minor; at-will) ✦ **Polymorph**
   The dragon can alter its physical form to appear as a unique human (see "Change Shape," MM2 216).

Alignment Unaligned   **Languages** Common, Draconic
Skills Bluff +30, Diplomacy +30, Insight +26
Str 31 (+24)   **Dex** 28 (+23)   **Wis** 25 (+21)
Con 28 (+23)   **Int** 21 (+19)   **Cha** 32 (+25)

METALLIC WYRMLINGS

Even immediately after hatching, dragons are powerful creatures, capable of unleashing formidable bite, claw, and *breath weapon* attacks. An impetuous or bored wyrmling still having the curiosity and playfulness of youth can be extremely dangerous.

ADAMANTINE DRAGON WYRMLING

ADAMANTINE WYRMLINGS ARE BORN STARVING, and they swiftly set out to hunt for food. Dependent on darkness and shadows to hide from larger predators, these creatures might not see light for the first months or years of life. They quickly develop the territoriality and temper of their parents, and this aspect of their nature occasionally results in adamantine wyrmlings killing one another.

These wyrmlings are a dark, dull gray. Their scales are already heavy, but they lie flat, rather than forming overlapping edges as they do on older dragons.

Adamantine Dragon Wyrmling	Level 5 Elite Soldier
Medium natural magical beast (dragon)	XP 400

Initiative +6   **Senses** Perception +3; darkvision
HP 126; **Bloodied** 63
AC 21; **Fortitude** 20, **Reflex** 18, **Will** 17
Resist 5 thunder
Saving Throws +2
Speed 5, fly 6 (hover), overland flight 8
Action Points 1

⊕ **Bite** (standard; at-will) ✦ **Thunder**
   +10 vs. Reflex; 1d6 + 5 damage plus 1d6 thunder damage.

⊕ **Claw** (standard; at-will)
   +10 vs. Reflex; 1d8 + 5 damage.

† **Double Attack** (standard; at-will)
   The dragon makes two claw attacks.

↞ **Breath Weapon** (standard; recharges when first bloodied) ✦ **Thunder**
   Close blast 4; +8 vs. Fortitude; 3d6 + 4 thunder damage.

Alignment Unaligned   **Languages** Draconic
Skills Insight +8
Str 18 (+6)   **Dex** 15 (+4)   **Wis** 13 (+3)
Con 15 (+4)   **Int** 10 (+2)   **Cha** 10 (+2)

ADAMANTINE DRAGON WYRMLING LORE

Nature DC 12: Adamantine wyrmlings hatch underground and often do not see light for months. Their scales are already remarkably tough.

ADAMANTINE WYRMLING TACTICS

An adamantine wyrmling focuses on a single foe, chewing and chewing on its target until it drops and only then moving on to the next one. It blasts all its foes with its *breath weapon* when it can.

Top: Cobalt wyrmling. Below, left to right: Bronze, brass, and adamantine wyrmlings

ENCOUNTER GROUPS

When they don't remain in family groups, adamantine dragon wyrmlings are found in the company of creatures they can bully or creatures that have stolen and coerced them.

Level 5 Encounter (XP 1,200)

✦ 1 adamantine dragon wyrmling (level 5 elite soldier)
✦ 1 troglodyte impaler (level 7 artillery, *MM* 252)
✦ 2 troglodyte maulers (level 6 soldier, *MM* 252)

BRASS DRAGON WYRMLING

MOST BRASS DRAGON WYRMLINGS LIVE in the dry lands in which they are born. Though they have extremely deadly ranged breath weapons, they are more fragile than other dragons. As a result, they make alliances with small groups of intelligent creatures, such as tribes of nomadic dragonborn. To creatures other than their allies, brass dragons are belligerent bullies with a strong territorial instinct.

At birth, a brass dragon wyrmling's scales are a dull matte brown. As the dragon ages, new metallic scales replace the matte scales.

Brass Dragon Wyrmling	Level 2 Elite Artillery
Medium natural magical beast (dragon)	XP 250

Initiative +3   **Senses** Perception +7; darkvision
HP 68; **Bloodied** 34
AC 16; **Fortitude** 16, **Reflex** 15, **Will** 14
Resist 5 fire
Saving Throws +2
Speed 6, fly 8 (hover), overland flight 10
Action Points 1

⊕ **Bite** (standard; at-will) ✦ **Fire**
    +9 vs. AC; 1d8 + 2 damage plus 1d6 fire damage.

⊕ **Claw** (standard; at-will)
    +9 vs. AC; 1d6 + 2 damage.

↯ **Dragon Ire** (standard; at-will)
    The wyrmling makes two claw attacks, and then shifts 1 square.

⬳ **Breath Weapon** (standard; recharges when first bloodied) ✦ **Fire**
    Close blast 4; +5 vs. Reflex; 3d6 + 2 fire damage, and the wyrmling pushes the target 1 square. *Miss:* Half damage.

↗ **Fire Stream** (standard; at-will) ✦ **Fire**
    Ranged 20; +7 vs. Reflex; 1d8 + 4 fire damage, and any creature adjacent to the target takes 1d6 fire damage.

Alignment Unaligned   **Languages** Draconic
Skills Athletics +8, Insight +7, Intimidate +6
| **Str** 15 (+3) | **Dex** 14 (+3) | **Wis** 13 (+2) |
| **Con** 16 (+4) | **Int** 11 (+1) | **Cha** 10 (+1) |

FRANZ VOHWINKEL

BRASS DRAGON WYRMLING LORE

Nature DC 10: A brass dragon lays its eggs in caves hidden in arid, rocky outcroppings or desert hills. These caves are usually close to civilized areas, and brass dragon wyrmlings often become leaders of mercenary bands. Brass dragon wyrmlings have powerful breath weapons they can use at a distance, but are weak in close combat.

BRASS DRAGON WYRMLING TACTICS

When compared to other wyrmlings, the brass dragon wyrmling is relatively fragile. It uses tougher allies as a defense from melee combatants. A brass dragon wyrmling attacks foes from a distance using *fire stream*. It uses its *breath weapon* once it is in melee, and then retreats from foes. Once forced into melee, the dragon fights with its bite attack and *dragon ire*.

ENCOUNTER GROUPS

At such a young age, a brass dragon wyrmling seeks out other intelligent creatures for protection, especially those that see the benefit of an alliance with a dragon. Dragonborn and humans are common allies.

Level 2 Encounter (XP 650)
+ 2 human bandits (level 2 skirmisher)
+ 1 human guard (level 3 soldier)
+ 1 brass dragon wyrmling (level 2 elite artillery)

BRONZE DRAGON WYRMLING

ALTHOUGH IT MUST STILL LEARN the precepts of duty from a parent, a bronze wyrmling has a strong sense of responsibility from the moment it leaves the egg—one that causes it to seek out purpose as thoroughly as it hunts for sustenance. Although this is normally fine, it occasionally causes a bronze wyrmling to "fall in with a bad crowd."

Bronze dragon wyrmlings are bright in color when born, easily mistaken for copper dragons. Their scales swiftly darken, however, and before they reach the young stage, they are unmistakably bronze.

BRONZE DRAGON WYRMLING LORE

Nature DC 12: Bronze dragons lay their eggs near the coast, in dark caves or buried in wet sand. They occasionally compete for territory with blue dragons, which obliterate bronze nests when they find them—or steal the eggs and raise the wyrmlings as servants.

BRONZE DRAGON WYRMLING TACTICS

A bronze wyrmling acts as though it were already far older and larger when it moves and engages its

Bronze Dragon Wyrmling	Level 5 Elite Brute
Medium natural magical beast (dragon)	XP 400

Initiative +3 — Senses Perception +2; darkvision
HP 152; **Bloodied** 76
AC 17; **Fortitude** 19, **Reflex** 16, **Will** 16
Resist 5 lightning
Saving Throws +2
Speed 6, fly 6 (hover), swim 6, overland flight 8
Action Points 1

⊕ **Bite** (standard; at-will) ✦ **Lightning**
+8 vs. AC; 2d8 + 4 lightning damage.

⊕ **Claw** (standard; at-will)
+8 vs. AC; 2d6 + 6 damage.

↯ **Bronze Flurry** (standard; at-will)
The wyrmling makes a bite attack and a wing attack. If both hit the same target, the target is also knocked prone.

↩ **Breath Weapon** (standard; recharges when first bloodied) ✦ **Lightning**
Close blast 3; +6 vs. Reflex; 2d6 + 6 lightning damage. If the attack hit at least one creature, the wyrmling makes a secondary attack against a creature within 5 squares that was not a target of the primary attack. *Secondary Attack:* +6 vs. Reflex; 1d6 + 6 lightning damage, and the target is pushed 1 square.

Alignment Unaligned — **Languages** Draconic
Skills Athletics +11
Str 18 (+6) — **Dex** 13 (+3) — **Wis** 10 (+2)
Con 16 (+5) — **Int** 10 (+2) — **Cha** 12 (+3)

enemy. It leads off with its *breath weapon* unless foes are too spread out to make it rewarding. Even when hard-pressed, the wyrmling probably won't flee, since it hasn't yet learned to balance its innate senses of purpose and self-preservation.

ENCOUNTER GROUPS

Bronze wyrmlings rarely leave the family, but they occasionally work with other creatures—either when learning the basics of service, while watched over by their parents, or when forced into servitude.

Level 5 Encounter (XP 1,100)
+ 2 blue wyrmlings (level 4 elite artillery, *Draconomicon: Chromatic Dragons*, page 180)
+ 1 bronze wyrmling (level 5 elite brute)

COBALT DRAGON WYRMLING

BORN FROM NESTS CARVED IN GLACIERS near snowy taiga terrain or in shallow underground caves hidden in the Shadowfell, cobalt dragon wyrmlings are vicious savages. A cobalt dragon's hunting grounds lie anywhere prey collects within its territory, such as melting glaciers or cold mountain springs. Although normally isolated, cobalt wyrmlings do form hunting parties when food is scarce or when a more powerful threat appears (such as the encroachment of civilization or the appearance of a hungry young white or black dragon).

Its scales are a reflective, metallic blue that blends in with the dragon's arctic surroundings, allowing the wyrmling to escape or to ambush opponents.

Cobalt Dragon Wyrmling	Level 3 Elite Controller
Medium natural magical beast (dragon)	XP 300

Initiative +2   **Senses** Perception +7; darkvision
HP 98; **Bloodied** 49
AC 18; **Fortitude** 16, **Reflex** 14, **Will** 14
Resist 5 cold
Saving Throws +2
Speed 6 (ice walk), fly 6, overland flight 8
Action Points 1

ⓐ **Bite** (standard; at-will) ✦ **Cold**
   +8 vs. AC; 1d10 + 4 cold damage, and the target is slowed (save ends).

ⓐ **Claw** (standard; at-will)
   +8 vs. AC; 1d6 + 5 damage.

⌁ **Dragon's Pounce** (standard; at-will)
   The wyrmling makes a bite attack, shifts 2 squares, and makes a claw attack against a different target.

⟿ **Savage Mauling** (standard; encounter)
   Close burst 1; targets slowed or restrained creatures; +9 vs. AC; 3d6 + 3 damage, and the wyrmling pushes the target 3 squares and knocks it prone. This forced movement can affect a creature restrained by the wyrmling's own breath weapon.

⟿ **Breath Weapon** (standard; recharges when first bloodied) ✦ **Cold**
   Close blast 4; +7 vs. Fortitude; 1d6 + 3 cold damage, and the target is restrained (save ends). *Aftereffect:* The target is slowed (save ends).

Alignment Unaligned	**Languages** Draconic

Skills Athletics +9, Endurance +9, Intimidate +7, Stealth +7

Str 16 (+4)	**Dex** 12 (+2)	**Wis** 12 (+2)
Con 17 (+4)	**Int** 10 (+1)	**Cha** 13 (+2)

COBALT DRAGON WYRMLING LORE

Nature DC 10: Cobalt dragons nest in cold, forested areas, especially near glaciers or deep in the Shadowfell. Shortly after hatching, cobalt dragon wyrmlings are abandoned to fend for themselves.

COBALT DRAGON WYRMLING TACTICS

A cobalt dragon wyrmling hides in wait and ambushes unsuspecting foes. It restrains as many enemies as possible with its *breath weapon* before following up with its *savage mauling* attack, and might spend its action point to do both in the same round. If quickly overpowered by superior strength and firepower, the wyrmling might be impressed by such a victory and surrender, pledging to help those that defeated it.

ENCOUNTER GROUPS

Even at a young age, a cobalt dragon wyrmling might be found in charge of a small group of savages. Occasionally, a cobalt wyrmling is subjugated by tougher foes, such as a band of hobgoblin mercenaries. In the Shadowfell, cobalt dragon wyrmlings can be found with undead, especially chillborn zombies.

Level 3 Encounter (XP 750)
✦ 1 cobalt dragon wyrmling (level 3 elite controller)
✦ 1 hobgoblin archer (level 3 artillery, *MM* 139)
✦ 2 hobgoblin soldiers (level 3 soldier, *MM* 139)

COPPER DRAGON WYRMLING

COPPER WYRMLINGS PREFER to dwell in, and hunt from, the safety of rocky terrain that features great crags and protrusions. This environment allows them to hide from threats or to mimic the tactics of older coppers when attacking prey. They develop their covetous nature early, and some copper parents encourage this by rewarding one offspring in view of the others, stoking jealousy and–they believe–the urge to perform better for greater reward.

Unlike many other dragons, copper dragons don't dramatically change in color or shape as they age. Their scales are a lustrous copper at birth, and their wings are fully developed.

Copper Dragon Wyrmling	Level 4 Elite Skirmisher
Medium natural magical beast (dragon)	XP 350

Initiative +8   **Senses** Perception +3; darkvision
HP 112; **Bloodied** 56
AC 18; **Fortitude** 16, **Reflex** 17, **Will** 14
Resist 5 acid
Saving Throws +2
Speed 8, fly 10 (hover), overland flight 10
Action Points 1

ⓐ **Bite** (standard; at-will) ✦ **Acid**
   The wyrmling shifts 2 squares before and after making the attack: +9 vs. AC; 1d6 + 4 damage plus 1d4 acid damage.

ⓐ **Claw** (standard; at-will)
   +9 vs. AC; 1d8 + 4 damage.

⌁ **Double Attack** (standard; at-will)
   The wyrmling makes two claw attacks and then shifts 2 squares.

⌁ **Flyby Attack** (standard; at-will)
   The wyrmling flies up to 8 squares and makes one melee basic attack at any point during that movement. The wyrmling doesn't provoke opportunity attacks when moving away from the target.

⟿ **Breath Weapon** (standard; recharges when first bloodied) ✦ **Acid**
   Close blast 4; +7 vs. Reflex; 1d8 + 4 acid damage, and the target is slowed (save ends).

Alignment Unaligned	**Languages** Draconic

Skills Acrobatics +11, Bluff +9

Str 14 (+4)	**Dex** 18 (+6)	**Wis** 14 (+4)
Con 16 (+5)	**Int** 11 (+2)	**Cha** 12 (+3)

COPPER DRAGON WYRMLING LORE

Nature DC 15: Copper dragons lay their eggs in caves or narrow ravines among mountains, rocky hills, or badlands. The hatchlings often hide among the various crags, cracks, and crevices. Hatchlings

Left to right: Mercury, copper, gold, and iron wyrmlings

eventually leave the nest when their growing covetousness begins to compete with their parents'. They can sometimes be lured away by promises of treasure they can hide from the family.

COPPER DRAGON WYRMLING TACTICS

A copper wyrmling imitates its elders, making frequent use of *flyby attack* and saving its *breath weapon* for enemies that clump together. It uses *double attack*—an undeveloped form of the copper dragon's various mobility powers—against lone targets.

ENCOUNTER GROUPS

Copper wyrmlings work with other creatures any time they are likely to receive higher rewards for the risk and as long as they aren't required to do anything too distasteful.

Level 5 Encounter (XP 1,100)
+ 1 copper dragon wyrmling (level 4 elite skirmisher)
+ 2 dwarf bolters (level 4 artillery, *MM* 97)
+ 2 dwarf hammerers (level 5 soldier, *MM* 97)

GOLD DRAGON WYRMLING

AS BEFITS THE MIGHTY (and perhaps arrogant) race of gold dragons, their wyrmlings are born with a wide suite of abilities, including fully functional wings and breath weapons. Gold wyrmlings often challenge one another in games. They take such activities seriously, competing for small territories and prizes (such as prime prey). These efforts help train them for adulthood so that they will be capable—and worthy—of ruling true domains. A gold wyrmling is torn between a burning desire to prove itself to its parents and an innate belief that it is already superior—or destined to be so—to all other creatures it encounters.

A gold wyrmling's scales are dull, almost sand-hued, and grow brighter as the dragon ages.

GOLD DRAGON WYRMLING LORE

Nature DC 15: Gold dragon eggs are found in caves deep in the hills alongside rolling plains or in the foothills of larger mountain ranges. Gold wyrmlings grow up in the presence of great riches and magic. Even at only a few days old, gold wyrmlings have a strong sense of self and try to command other creatures (including, at times, their siblings).

JASON A. ENGLE

Gold Dragon Wyrmling	Level 7 Elite Controller
Medium natural magical beast (dragon)	XP 600

Initiative +4   **Senses** Perception +5; darkvision

HP 156; **Bloodied** 78; see also *breath weapon*

AC 21; **Fortitude** 19, **Reflex** 21, **Will** 19

Resist 5 fire

Saving Throws +2

Speed 7, fly 9 (hover), overland flight 14

Action Points 1

(+) **Bite** (standard; at-will) ✦ **Fire**
     +12 vs. AC; 1d6 + 5 damage plus 1d6 fire damage.

(+) **Claw** (standard; at will)
     +12 vs. AC; 1d10 + 4 damage.

+ **Double Attack** (standard; at-will)
     The wyrmling makes two claw attacks.

← **Breath Weapon** (standard; recharges when first bloodied) ✦ **Fire**
     Close blast 4; +11 vs. Reflex; 2d6 + 5 fire damage, and the target is weakened until the end of the wyrmling's next turn.

Alignment Unaligned   **Languages** Common, Draconic

Skills Athletics +11, Insight +10, Intimidate +11

Str 16 (+6)	**Dex** 12 (+4)	**Wis** 14 (+5)
Con 14 (+5)	**Int** 20 (+8)	**Cha** 17 (+6)

GOLD DRAGON WYRMLING TACTICS

A gold wyrmling seeks to control a battle from the moment it begins, initiating combat with its *breath weapon* and then moving in to engage foes that have been weakened. A gold wyrmling rarely retreats unless severely injured. The notion of another creature proving superior is alien to the dragon's instincts, even if it can intellectually understand the possibility.

ENCOUNTER GROUPS

Gold wyrmlings associate with creatures they can boss around (though they would call it "learning how to command").

Level 4 Encounter (XP 900)
✦ 1 gold wyrmling (level 7 elite controller)
✦ 1 griffon (level 7 brute, *MM* 147)

IRON DRAGON WYRMLING

IRON WYRMLINGS ARE SOME OF THE WEAKEST wyrmlings, but they are born in larger clutches and have a stronger tendency toward social behavior when first hatched. They rarely come out of hiding, except to swiftly strike at the prey they are learning to hunt before diving back into the shadows. They prefer caves but are almost as comfortable hiding beneath the underbrush and dead leaves on the forest floor. They emerge to attack only if they greatly outsize or outnumber their target, and they try to avoid prolonged battles.

An iron wyrmling's scales are a dark rust color that flakes off in a sort of molting as the dragon approaches the young stage of its development.

Iron Dragon Wyrmling	Level 3 Elite Skirmisher
Medium natural magical beast (dragon)	XP 300

Initiative +4   **Senses** Perception +3; darkvision

HP 96; **Bloodied** 48

AC 17; **Fortitude** 17, **Reflex** 15, **Will** 14

Resist 5 lightning

Saving Throws +2

Speed 6, fly 8 (hover), overland flight 7

Action Points 1

(+) **Bite** (standard; at-will) ✦ **Lightning**
     +8 vs. AC; 2d6 + 3 damage plus 1d6 lightning damage.

(+) **Claw** (standard; at will)
     +8 vs. AC; 1d10 + 3 damage.

+ **Swift Claws** (standard; at-will)
     The wyrmling makes two claw attacks and shifts 2 squares.

← **Breath Weapon** (standard; recharges when first bloodied) ✦ **Lightning**
     Close blast 4; +6 vs. Reflex; 2d6 + 2 lightning damage, and the wyrmling pulls the target 1 square.

Alignment Unaligned   **Languages** Draconic

Skills Stealth +9

Str 18 (+6)	**Dex** 15 (+4)	**Wis** 13 (+3)
Con 16 (+5)	**Int** 10 (+2)	**Cha** 10 (+2)

IRON DRAGON WYRMLING LORE

Nature DC 10: Iron dragons hide their eggs in caves or darkened woods. Sometimes, the wyrmlings spend their first few days of life without ever emerging into the open. Iron dragons are born in larger clutches than most other varieties of dragons, and they hunt in packs until they grow strong enough to survive on their own. Iron wyrmlings are instinctive ambush predators.

IRON DRAGON WYRMLING TACTICS

An iron wyrmling bursts from concealment and attacks quickly before retreating back to a safer position. It flees immediately if the attack proves ineffective. Otherwise, it takes advantage of the maneuverability provided by *swift claws* and its fast fly speed to circle its prey and make opportunistic strikes.

ENCOUNTER GROUPS

Iron wyrmlings hunt in teams or alongside creatures pressed into service by their parents.

Level 5 Encounter (XP 1,150)
✦ 3 iron wyrmlings (level 3 elite skirmisher)
✦ 2 kobold dragonshields (level 2 soldier, *MM* 168)

MERCURY DRAGON WYRMLING

THE NESTS OF MERCURY DRAGONS are found near poisonous volcanic vents and noxious sulfurous springs. These inhospitable conditions require mercury wyrmlings to travel great distances to hunt for food, instilling a desire to explore the world at an extremely young age. As a result, a mercury dragon wyrmling can often be found a great distance from its home.

A mercury dragon wyrmling's form is incredibly fluid, and its reflective appearance makes it difficult to spot in areas that have homogeneous surroundings.

Mercury Dragon Wyrmling	Level 4 Elite Lurker
Medium natural magical beast (dragon, shapechanger)	XP 350

Initiative +10   **Senses** Perception +2; darkvision
HP 90; **Bloodied** 45
AC 18; **Fortitude** 15, **Reflex** 17, **Will** 16
Resist 5 poison
Saving Throws +2
Speed 6, fly 6 (hover), overland flight 8
Action Points 1

⊕ **Claw** (standard; at-will)
+9 vs. AC; 1d8 + 5 damage.

⨪ **Double Attack** (standard; at-will)
The wyrmling makes two claw attacks.

⟻ **Breath Weapon** (standard; recharges when first bloodied) ✦ **Poison**
Close blast 4; +7 vs. Fortitude; 1d12 + 3 poison damage, and the target takes ongoing 5 poison damage and treats the wyrmling as invisible (save ends both).

Combat Advantage
The wyrmling deals 1d6 extra damage against a target granting combat advantage to it.

Quicksilver Form (move; encounter) ✦ **Polymorph**
The wyrmling becomes a liquid wave of quicksilver and shifts 4 squares. It remains in quicksilver form until the end of its next turn. While in quicksilver form, the wyrmling can't attack or fly, but gains a climb speed of 6, ignores difficult terrain, and doesn't provoke opportunity attacks. It can squeeze through any aperture a Tiny creature could fit through. The wyrmling can return to its normal form as a free action on its turn. When it returns to normal, each creature within 2 squares grants combat advantage to the wyrmling until the end of the wyrmling's next turn.

Alignment Unaligned   **Languages** Draconic
Skills Acrobatics +11, Bluff +10, Stealth +11
Str 15 (+4)	**Dex** 18 (+6)	**Wis** 11 (+2)
Con 15 (+4)	**Int** 12 (+3)	**Cha** 16 (+5)

MERCURY DRAGON WYRMLING LORE

DC 12: A mercury dragon wyrmling's lair has many small tunnels and narrow passageways filled with noxious gases from deep underground. Since these lairs are usually found near inhospitable lands, a mercury dragon hunts across a large area. A wyrmling's bite isn't developed at such a young age, but its vicious claws can quickly tear apart its enemies, especially when those enemies are caught unaware. A mercury dragon wyrmling can turn into a swiftly moving wave of liquid metal.

MERCURY DRAGON WYRMLING TACTICS

Those battling a mercury wyrmling within its lair find themselves at a disadvantage. These volcanic caves are typically pocked with smaller caves that only Tiny creatures can access, enabling the wyrmling to take on *quicksilver form* and escape aggressors. Then it flows out of some other seemingly unconnected hole, takes on its normal form, and gains combat advantage against its foes.

ENCOUNTER GROUPS

A mercury dragon wyrmling nurtures its underlings so they will protect its lair while it's out exploring. Powerful thieves sometimes steal mercury dragon eggs, planning to raise the wyrmling to be an expert spy or assassin.

Level 3 Encounter (XP 750)
✦ 1 mercury dragon wyrmling (level 4 elite lurker)
✦ 2 needlefang drake swarms (level 2 soldier, MM 90)
✦ 1 spitting drake (level 3 artillery, MM 91)

Level 4 Encounter (XP 900)
✦ 1 mercury dragon wyrmling (level 4 elite lurker)
✦ 2 doppelganger sneaks (level 3 skirmisher, MM 71)
✦ 1 halfling prowler (level 6 lurker, MM 153)

MITHRAL DRAGON WYRMLING

THE RARE OCCASION when a mithral dragon wyrmling leaves the Astral Sea signifies the beginning of a time of change. The wyrmling has seen the importance of the moment and has come to guide the world through a chaotic time. A mithral wyrmling's horns are short, as is the ridge of spikes that runs the length of its neck. The ridge stands out only when the wyrmling is angered.

MITHRAL DRAGON WYRMLING LORE

Nature DC 15: Mithral dragon wyrmlings hatch in the Astral Sea and rarely visit the world. A mithral dragon wyrmling can teleport but cannot attack with its wings. Its *breath weapon* blinds foes with radiant light.

Left to right: Orium, steel, mithral, and silver wyrmlings

Mithral Dragon Wyrmling	Level 9 Elite Skirmisher
Medium immortal magical beast (dragon)	XP 800

Initiative +11   **Senses** Perception +7; darkvision
HP 186; **Bloodied** 93
AC 23; **Fortitude** 21, **Reflex** 23, **Will** 21
Resist 5 radiant
Saving Throws +2
Speed 8, fly 8 (hover), overland flight 10, teleport 5
Action Points 1

⊕ **Bite** (standard; at-will) ✦ **Radiant**
    +14 vs. AC; 2d6 + 4 damage, and the target takes ongoing 5 radiant damage (save ends).

⊕ **Claw** (standard; at-will)
    +14 vs. AC; 2d6 + 4 damage.

⥋ **Dimension Strike** (standard; at-will) ✦ **Teleportation**
    The wyrmling teleports half its speed, makes a claw attack, teleports half its speed, and makes a claw attack against a different target.

↢ **Breath Weapon** (standard; recharges when first bloodied) ✦ **Radiant**
    Close blast 4; +12 vs. Reflex; 2d6 + 2 radiant damage, and the target is blinded (save ends).

Alignment Unaligned   **Languages** Common, Draconic, Supernal
Skills Insight +12, Intimidate +11, Religion +11

Str 17 (+7)	Dex 21 (+9)	Wis 17 (+7)
Con 13 (+5)	Int 14 (+6)	Cha 14 (+6)

MITHRAL DRAGON WYRMLING TACTICS

An extremely mobile fighter, a mithral dragon wyrmling incapacitates enemies with its *breath weapon* and then focuses attacks upon enemies that are still able to see. A favorite tactic is to use *dimension strike* against two targets and then teleport out of reach.

ENCOUNTER GROUPS

Mithral dragon wyrmlings fight with allies that allow them their full range of mobility, such as soldiers and controllers that have the ability to slow enemies.

Level 8 Encounter (XP 1,850)
✦ 1 mithral dragon wyrmling (level 9 elite skirmisher)
✦ 2 angels of valor (level 8 soldier, *MM* 16)
✦ 1 eladrin twilight incanter (level 8 controller, *MM* 102)

Level 11 Encounter (XP 3,100)
✦ 1 mithral dragon wyrmling (level 9 elite skirmisher)
✦ 1 githyanki mindslicer (level 13 artillery, *MM* 128)
✦ 2 githyanki warriors (level 12 soldier, *MM* 128)

HOWARD LYON

ORIUM DRAGON WYRMLING

As ORIUM DRAGONS ACCUMULATE KNOWLEDGE, they discover the locations of additional crumbling ruins. Not having the time to investigate each potential site, a dragon sends its children to investigate and potentially create their own lairs.

Orium dragon wyrmlings are surprisingly mature for their age. Unlike other wyrmlings, they act cautiously and methodically. They won't fight until threatened, but they believe that threats to their lairs are just as dangerous as threats to themselves.

Orium Dragon Wyrmling	Level 6 Elite Soldier
Medium natural magical beast (dragon)	XP 500

Initiative +7   **Senses** Perception +3; darkvision
HP 146; **Bloodied** 73
AC 22; **Fortitude** 20, **Reflex** 18, **Will** 17
Resist 5 acid
Saving Throws +2
Speed 6, fly 8 (hover), overland flight 10
Action Points 1
⊕ **Bite** (standard; at-will) ✦ **Acid**
    +13 vs. AC; 1d8 + 6 damage plus 1d6 acid damage.
⊕ **Claw** (standard; at-will)
    +13 vs. AC; 1d6 + 6 damage, and the target is marked until the end of the wyrmling's next turn.
† **Draconic Fury** (standard; at-will)
    The wyrmling makes two claw attacks and one bite attack.
⇐ **Breath Weapon** (standard; recharges when first bloodied) ✦ **Acid**
    Close blast 3; +11 vs. Fortitude; 2d6 + 3 acid damage, and a wyrmling vaporous serpent minion (see below) appears in any single unoccupied square in the blast. It acts just after the wyrmling in the initiative order.
Alignment Unaligned   **Languages** Draconic
Skills History +8, Insight +8, Intimidate +9
Str 19 (+7)   **Dex** 15 (+5)   **Wis** 10 (+3)
Con 17 (+6)   **Int** 10 (+3)   **Cha** 13 (+4)

Wyrmling Vaporous Serpent	Level 6 Minion Brute
Medium elemental beast	XP —

Initiative as wyrmling   **Senses** Perception +0
HP 1; a missed attack never damages a minion.
AC 19; **Fortitude** 18, **Reflex** 17, **Will** 16
Resist 10 acid
Speed 6
⊕ **Bite** (standard; at-will) ✦ **Acid**
    +11 vs. AC; 6 acid damage.
Alignment Unaligned   **Languages** —
Str 16 (+6)   **Dex** 10 (+3)   **Wis** 4 (+0)
Con 12 (+4)   **Int** 4 (+0)   **Cha** 4 (+0)

ORIUM DRAGON WYRMLING TACTICS

An orium dragon wyrmling uses its *breath weapon* as soon as it's possible to catch multiple foes in the area of effect, then flanks with its vaporous serpent and makes a *double attack*.

ORIUM DRAGON WYRMLING LORE

Nature DC 15: Orium dragon wyrmlings prize knowledge and are found near areas of archaeological significance, such as ancient temples or decayed ruins of lost civilizations. At a young age, orium wyrmlings are extremely protective over their unexplored lairs. Orium dragon wyrmlings do not have the physical strength that older versions have, but their breath weapons are fully developed.

ENCOUNTER GROUPS

The lairs of orium dragon wyrmlings have spent centuries hidden away in the wilderness, so they are filled with dangerous wild animals. In ruins formed when civilizations were lost to the Feywild, orium dragons find fey allies. A wyrmling might awe a tribe of intelligent savages into worshiping it.

Level 6 Encounter (XP 1,250)
✦ 1 orium dragon wyrmling (level 6 elite soldier)
✦ 1 dire boar (level 6 brute, *MM* 35)
✦ 1 greenscale marsh mystic (level 6 controller, *MM* 179)
✦ 1 blackscale bruiser (level 6 brute, *MM* 179)

Level 7 Encounter (XP 1,600)
✦ 1 orium dragon wyrmling (level 6 elite soldier)
✦ 1 vine horror spellfiend (level 7 artillery, *MM* 260)
✦ 2 unicorns (level 9 skirmisher, *MM* 257)

SILVER DRAGON WYRMLING

FROM BIRTH, SILVER WYRMLINGS LEARN the importance of forthrightness and righteous combat. They and their siblings engage in vicious mock battles that rarely result in lasting injury. Silver dragon parents take their responsibilities more seriously than other dragon parents do, but still encourage their offspring to spend time in the world.

Silver Dragon Wyrmling	Level 5 Elite Brute
Medium natural magical beast (dragon)	XP 400

Initiative +4   **Senses** Perception +3; darkvision
HP 152; **Bloodied** 76
AC 17; **Fortitude** 19, **Reflex** 16, **Will** 15
Resist 5 cold
Saving Throws +2
Speed 5, fly 6 (clumsy), overland flight 8
Action Points 1

⊕ **Bite** (standard; at-will)
+8 vs. AC; 2d8 + 4 damage.

⊕ **Claw** (standard; at-will)
+8 vs. AC; 1d6 + 4 damage.

✦ **Dragon Onslaught** (standard; at-will)
The wyrmling makes a claw attack against each enemy adjacent to it.

↞ **Breath Weapon** (standard; recharges when first bloodied) ✦ **Cold**
Close blast 4; +6 vs. Reflex; 1d6 + 5 cold damage, and the target gains vulnerable 5 to all damage (save ends).

Alignment Unaligned	**Languages** Common, Draconic

Skills Athletics +12

Str 20 (+7)	**Dex** 15 (+4)	**Wis** 12 (+3)
Con 16 (+5)	**Int** 11 (+2)	**Cha** 13 (+3)

SILVER DRAGON WYRMLING LORE

Nature DC 12: Silver dragons hide their eggs in frozen caves, buried in snow. Hatchlings venture from the nest as soon as they can walk. A silver dragon wyrmling uses its *breath weapon* in melee combat, fighting on the ground when possible.

SILVER DRAGON WYRMLING TACTICS

A silver dragon wymling lands in the midst of enemies and uses *wing slice*. It prefers to fight with allies that can slow or immobilize foes, so the dragon can use *wing slice* and *breath weapon* most effectively.

ENCOUNTER GROUPS

Silver dragon wyrmlings ally with other creatures to learn combat tactics and to defeat more potent dangers than they can face alone.

Level 5 Encounter (XP 1,200)

✦ 1 silver dragon wyrmling (level 5 elite brute)
✦ 3 human guards (level 3 soldier, MM 162)
✦ 2 human mages (level 4 artillery, MM 163)

STEEL DRAGON WYRMLING

STEEL DRAGON PARENTS, entrenched in human affairs, hide their wyrmlings and instruct them secretly until the wyrmlings' shapechanging powers develop. However, a wyrmling's intense curiosity tempts it to escape a watchful parent's eye to hunt and to cause mischief.

A steel wyrmling is extremely slender. The spines on its head are shorter than those of a full-grown steel.

Steel Dragon Wyrmling	Level 5 Elite Controller
Medium natural magical beast (dragon)	XP 400

Initiative +3   **Senses** Perception +9; darkvision
HP 126; **Bloodied** 63
AC 20; **Fortitude** 17, **Reflex** 15, **Will** 18
Resist 5 force
Saving Throws +2
Speed 6, fly 8 (hover), overland flight 10
Action Points 1

⊕ **Bite** (standard; at-will) ✦ **Force**
+10 vs. AC; 1d8 + 4 damage plus 1d6 force damage, and the wyrmling slides the target 1 square.

⊕ **Claw** (standard; at-will)
+10 vs. AC; 1d10 + 3 damage.

✦ **Double Attack** (standard; at-will)
The wyrmling makes two claw attacks.

✦ **Dragon's Suggestion** (minor 1/round; at-will) ✦ **Charm**
+9 vs. Will; the wyrmling slides the target 1 square, and the target grants combat advantage until the end of the wyrmling's next turn.

↞ **Breath Weapon** (standard; recharges when first bloodied) ✦ **Force**
Close blast 5; +9 vs. Fortitude; 2d10 + 2 force damage, and the target is dazed (save ends).

Alignment Unaligned	**Languages** Common, Draconic

Skills Bluff +11, Diplomacy +11, Insight +9

Str 17 (+5)	**Dex** 12 (+3)	**Wis** 14 (+4)
Con 15 (+4)	**Int** 11 (+2)	**Cha** 19 (+6)

STEEL DRAGON WYRMLING LORE

Nature DC 12: Steel dragon wyrmlings cannot change shape. Wyrmlings hatched in civilization are hidden until they learn to blend in with the local population. Steel dragon wyrmlings fight carefully, so they don't harm their allies.

STEEL DRAGON WYRMLING TACTICS

A steel dragon wyrmling relishes teamwork in combat. It uses *dragon's suggestion* to slide enemies into flanked positions. When it uses its *breath weapon*, it avoids hurting allies.

ENCOUNTER GROUPS

A steel dragon wyrmling relies on a tight group of associates, possibly a group of bandits and thieves. If far from society, a steel wyrmling befriends the closest group of intelligent humanoids.

Level 4 Encounter (XP 824)

✦ 1 steel dragon wyrmling (level 5 elite controller)
✦ 1 doppelganger sneak (level 3 skirmisher, MM 71)
✦ 4 human rabble (level 2 minion, MM 162)
✦ 1 wererat (level 3 skirmisher, MM 180)

Level 5 Encounter (XP 1,050)

✦ 1 steel dragon wyrmling (level 5 elite controller)
✦ 1 bugbear strangler (level 6 lurker, MM 136)
✦ 2 bugbear warriors (level 5 brute, MM 135)

HOLLOW DRAGONS

A METALLIC DRAGON CAN BECOME A CONSTRUCT called a hollow dragon: an empty shell of the dragon's scales and hide animated by powerful magic and the dragon's essence. Unlike evil chromatic dragons, which turn to the magic of shadow and undeath to prolong their existence (see the dracoliches in the *Monster Manual* and other undead dragons in *Draconomicon: Chromatic Dragons*), metallic dragons use elemental magic to become eternal guardians of great treasures, ancient artifacts, and holy sites.

A hollow dragon lacks bones and organs. Draconic essence and elemental power leak, glowing, from its mouth and eyes, from between its scales, and from runes carved into its scales. The flesh might wither, but the magic, the draconic essence, and the scales endure.

A hollow dragon's attacks have a damage type based on the kind of dragon it was when alive. For instance, gold hollow dragons have fire-based attacks, but those of a steel hollow dragon would be force-based.

Gold Hollow Dragon		Level 16 Solo Brute
Huge natural magical beast (construct, dragon)		XP 7,000

Initiative +12 **Senses** Perception +17; darkvision
Manifest Essence (Fire) aura 3; each creature that starts its turn in the aura takes 5 fire damage. The damage increases to 10 while the dragon is bloodied.
HP 640; **Bloodied** 320; see also *bloodied fury*
AC 28; **Fortitude** 29, **Reflex** 27, **Will** 28
Immune disease, poison; **Resist** 30 fire
Saving Throws +5
Speed 6, fly 10 (clumsy)
Action Points 2
⊕ **Bite** (standard; at-will) ✦ **Fire**
   Reach 3; +19 vs. AC; 1d8 + 7 damage, and ongoing 10 fire damage (save ends).
↓ **Tail Slap** (minor; at-will)
   Reach 3; +18 vs. AC; 3d8 + 7 damage.
↓ **Bloodied Fury** (free, when first bloodied; encounter)
   The dragon makes a bite attack and two *tail slaps*.
↢ **Breath of Power** (standard; recharge ⚄ ⚅) ✦ **Fire**
   Close blast 5; +17 vs. Reflex; 2d10 + 7 fire damage, and the target takes ongoing 10 fire damage and is dazed (save ends both). *Miss:* Half damage.
↢ **Burst of Essence** (immediate reaction, when an enemy hits the dragon with a melee or ranged attack; at-will) ✦ **Fire**
   The dragon's skin ruptures, releasing a gout of its essence: close blast 3; +17 vs. Reflex; 3d8 + 7 fire damage.
↢ **Essence Explosion** (when reduced to 0 hit points; encounter) ✦ **Fire**
   Close burst 5; +17 vs. Reflex; 2d10 + 7 fire damage, and the target is knocked prone. *Miss:* Half damage.
Alignment Unaligned **Languages** Common, Draconic
Skills Arcana +16, Insight +17, Intimidate +18
| **Str** 22 (+14) | **Dex** 19 (+12) | **Wis** 18 (+12) |
| **Con** 24 (+15) | **Int** 17 (+11) | **Cha** 21 (+13) |

Gold Hollow Wyrm		Level 24 Solo Soldier
Gargantuan natural magical beast (construct, dragon)		XP 30,250

Initiative +21 **Senses** Perception +23; darkvision
Manifest Essence (Fire) aura 3; each creature that starts its turn in the aura takes 10 fire damage. The damage increases to 15 while the wyrm is bloodied.
HP 904; **Bloodied** 452; see also *bloodied fury*
AC 39; **Fortitude** 37, **Reflex** 36, **Will** 36
Immune disease, poison; **Resist** 35 fire
Saving Throws +5
Speed 8, fly 12 (clumsy)
Action Points 2
⊕ **Bite** (standard; at-will) ✦ **Fire**
   Reach 4; +31 vs. AC; 2d6 + 9 fire damage, and ongoing 10 fire damage (save ends).
↓ **Tail Slap** (minor; at-will)
   Reach 4; +29 vs. AC; 4d6 + 8 damage.
↓ **Bloodied Fury** (free, when first bloodied; encounter)
   The dragon makes a bite attack and two *tail slaps*.
↓ **Consume** (standard; recharge ⚄ ⚅) ✦ **Fire**
   The wyrm traps an enemy inside itself: reach 4; +29 vs. Reflex; 3d8 + 9 damage, and the target is swallowed. While the target is swallowed, it is dazed and restrained, and it takes 20 fire damage at the start of the wyrm's turn. The target has line of sight and line of effect only to the wyrm, and no creature has line of sight or line of effect to the target. The swallowed creature can make only melee or close basic attacks. The wyrm's aura does not affect the target.
   As a move action, the target can escape with an Athletics check vs. Fortitude or an Acrobatics check vs. Reflex. If the target escapes this way, it appears in a space adjacent to the wyrm. The target also escapes when the wyrm uses *breath of power*, appearing in a space within the blast after the attack. When the wyrm dies, the target is no longer swallowed and can escape as a move action, appearing in the wyrm's former space.
↢ **Breath of Power** (standard; recharge ⚄ ⚅) ✦ **Fire**
   Close blast 7; +29 vs. Reflex; 4d6 + 9 fire damage, and the target takes ongoing 15 fire damage and is dazed (save ends both). *Miss:* Half damage.
↢ **Burst of Essence** (immediate reaction, when an enemy hits the dragon with a melee or ranged attack; at-will) ✦ **Fire**
   The dragon's skin ruptures, releasing a gout of its essence: close blast 3; +29 vs. Reflex; 4d8 + 9 fire damage.
↢ **Essence Explosion** (when reduced to 0 hit points; encounter) ✦ **Fire**
   Close burst 5; +29 vs. Reflex; 3d10 + 7 fire damage, and the target is knocked prone. *Miss:* Half damage.
Alignment Unaligned **Languages** Common, Draconic
Skills Arcana +21, Insight +23, Intimidate +24
| **Str** 28 (+21) | **Dex** 23 (+19) | **Wis** 23 (+18) |
| **Con** 26 (+20) | **Int** 19 (+16) | **Cha** 25 (+19) |

HOLLOW DRAGON LORE

Arcana or Nature DC 20: The essence of a formerly living dragon animates the otherwise empty hide of a hollow dragon. Dragons that seek immortality but do not want to become dracoliches become hollow dragons. Only a few spellcasters and worshipers of draconic deities know the process to create hollow dragons and hollow wyrms.

Arcana or Nature DC 25: Hollow dragons keep to themselves. Though they do not need to eat, old or evil ones might become so far removed from the living that they lose all empathy and become violent predators.

Hollow Dragon Tactics

A hollow dragon fights up close, allowing enemies to surround it so that it has many targets. It makes multiple melee attacks each round and uses *breath of power* as soon as it can catch several foes with it. It mauls targets with bites and *tail slaps* and then launches *breath of power* in the same round by spending an action point. When bloodied, it spends a second action point and fights to the death.

A hollow wyrm fights like a hollow dragon, with the addition of the *consume* power. It uses *breath of power* even if it has a foe swallowed, unless it has a limited number of targets nearby.

Encounter Groups

Hollow dragons enjoy their solitude but might accompany other guardians.

Level 19 Encounter (XP 12,200)
+ 1 hollow dragon (level 16 solo brute)
+ 1 cambion hellfire magus (level 18 artillery, *MM* 39)
+ 1 stone golem (level 17 elite soldier, *MM* 142)

Level 26 Encounter (XP 50,350)
+ 1 hollow wyrm (level 24 solo soldier)
+ 1 angel of authority (level 22 controller, *MM2* 8)
+ 6 angels of light (level 23 minion skirmisher, *MM2* 9)
+ 2 marut executioners (level 22 brute, *MM2* 162)

THE HOLLOW TRANSFORMATION

Becoming a hollow dragon requires a ritual that unbinds the elemental energy present in a dragon. If performed correctly, it reshapes the subject into an eternal channel for energy funneled directly from the Elemental Chaos. The particulars of the ritual of transformation are widespread among metallic dragons, but known to few others.

Physical Effects: When a dragon transforms into a hollow dragon, it lets its internal elemental forces consume its entire body. It endures tremendous pain as every bit of its flesh disintegrates, leaving only a core of vibrant energy contained within a shell of metal scales. Dragons in twilight might be the most desperate to prolong their lives, but also run the greatest risk. The transformation can rend a weaker dragon, causing the creature to explode in a flash of elemental energy. Though the dragon retains much of its former knowledge and personality, it no longer has

the magical attributes of its former body. A hollow dragon can no longer shapeshift, nor can a formerly agile dragon move as quickly as it could in life. The transformation even robs the dragon of its *frightful presence*.

Mental Repercussions: Few metallic dragons are willing to become hollow dragons, partly because the practice of transformation has a bad reputation. The number of stories of dragons driven mad by the pain of transformation or rent asunder by the force of the process itself are too numerous. Still, the transformation is less risky than transforming into a dracolich. Even those who make it through find their personalities change over time. They grow less and less familiar with the mindset of the living. Without needing to eat, sleep, mate, or fulfill other biological needs, hollow dragons develop a different sense of time, and become inscrutable to normal mortals.

OTHER CREATURES

This section covers a selection of creatures that might ally with metallic dragons.

COUATL

ALL BUT A FEW COUATLS fight for the forces of good. Evil couatls, perhaps jaded by endless battles, find the allure of power too difficult to resist.

Couatl Rogue Serpent	Level 14 Skirmisher
Large immortal magical beast	XP 1,000

Initiative +14   **Senses** Perception +8
HP 134; **Bloodied** 67
AC 28; **Fortitude** 24, **Reflex** 26, **Will** 24
Speed 8, fly 10 (hover)

ⓐ **Bite** (standard; at-will) ✦ **Poison, Radiant**
> +19 vs. AC; 2d6 + 5 damage, and the target takes ongoing 5 poison and radiant damage and takes 5 poison and radiant damage each time it makes an opportunity attack (save ends both).

✝ **Passing Bites** (standard; recharge ⚄ ⚅)
> The couatl rogue serpent makes a bite attack, shifts its speed, and makes another bite attack.

Venomous Teleport (move; recharge ⚄ ⚅) ✦ **Teleportation**
> The couatl rogue serpent swaps positions with a creature within 10 squares of it that is taking ongoing poison and radiant damage.

Radiant Absorption ✦ **Radiant**
> If a couatl rogue serpent takes radiant damage, its attacks deal 5 extra radiant damage until the end of its next turn.

Twist Free
> A couatl makes saving throws against immobilizing or restraining effects at the start of its turn as well as at the end of its turn. In addition, a couatl can make saving throws against immobilizing or restraining effects that do not allow saving throws and would normally end at the end of its turn or at the end of an enemy's turn.

Alignment Evil   **Languages** Supernal
Skills Bluff +15, Diplomacy +15, Nature +13, Stealth +17
| **Str** 19 (+10) | **Dex** 22 (+12) | **Wis** 15 (+8) |
| **Con** 14 (+8) | **Int** 18 (+10) | **Cha** 19 (+10) |

COUATL ROGUE SERPENT TACTICS

A couatl rogue serpent tries to bite as many enemies as possible with its venom, so it can use *venomous teleport*. Its bite allows it to move away safely. It uses *passing bites* to damage two enemies, and might follow up with *venomous teleport* to put them closer together.

Couatl Redeemer	Level 24 Artillery
Large immortal magical beast	XP 6,050

Initiative +16   **Senses** Perception +19
HP 174; **Bloodied** 87
AC 37; **Fortitude** 33, **Reflex** 36, **Will** 36
Speed 8, fly 8 (hover)

ⓐ **Bite** (standard; at-will) ✦ **Poison, Radiant**
> +30 vs. AC; 2d6 + 5 damage, the target is immobilized until the end of the couatl redeemer's next turn, and the target takes ongoing 10 poison and radiant damage (save ends).

ⓡ **Brilliant Beam** (standard; at-will) ✦ **Radiant**
> Ranged 20; +29 vs. Reflex; 2d10 + 10 radiant damage.

✳ **Soul Sear** (standard; encounter) ✦ **Poison, Radiant**
> Area burst 2 within 20; +27 vs. Fortitude; 2d6 + 5 poison and radiant damage, the target is weakened, and the target takes ongoing 10 poison and radiant damage (save ends both). *Miss:* Half damage, and the target takes ongoing 5 poison and radiant damage (save ends).

✳ **Whirlwind** (standard; encounter)
> Area burst 2 within 20; +27 vs. Reflex; 3d10 + 5 damage, and the target is immobilized in a whirlwind (save ends).

Radiant Absorption ✦ **Radiant**
> If a couatl redeemer takes radiant damage, its attacks deal 5 extra radiant damage until the end of its next turn.

Twist Free
> A couatl makes saving throws against immobilizing or restraining effects at the start of its turn as well as at the end of its turn. In addition, a couatl can make saving throws against immobilizing or restraining effects that do not allow saving throws and would normally end at the end of its turn or at the end of an enemy's turn.

Alignment Unaligned   **Languages** Supernal
Skills Arcana +26, Bluff +20, Diplomacy +20, Insight +24
| **Str** 18 (+16) | **Dex** 19 (+16) | **Wis** 24 (+19) |
| **Con** 24 (+19) | **Int** 28 (+21) | **Cha** 17 (+15) |

COUATL REDEEMER TACTICS

A couatl redeemer engages enemies at maximum range, opening with *soul sear* on a cluster of enemies and falling back with *brilliant beam*. It uses *whirlwind* when enemies approach or to help its allies. When forced to enter melee, it immobilizes its foe with a bite and then withdraws.

COUATL LORE

Religion DC 18: A couatl rogue serpent can switch places with any creature suffering from a couatl's venom, and it injects a magic venom that burns more strongly when the couatl's allies are endangered.

Religion DC 24: Couatl redeemers can see into other creatures' hearts and know their intentions. Their venom is especially virulent. They can manipulate wind, holding foes in columns of air.

ENCOUNTER GROUPS

Couatls mistrust other creatures; however, they value potent allies. Couatls lair near powerful creatures, such as dragons, that view interlopers as hostile. Couatls might band with creatures that want to procure the same secrets, treasure, or information that the couatls seek. Couatls ally with less intelligent creatures for greater ease in keeping secrets.

Level 15 Encounter (XP 6,000)
+ 1 adult orium dragon (level 13 solo soldier)
+ 2 couatl rogue serpents (level 14 skirmisher)

Level 25 Encounter (XP 36,300)
+ 2 couatl redeemers (level 24 artillery)
+ 2 angels of supremacy (level 24 soldier, *MM2* 10)
+ 2 fell wyverns (level 24 skirmisher, *MM* 268)

COUATL THEMES

Metallic dragons and couatls share some similar attributes, including the single-minded pursuit of their goals and a tendency to be benevolent. Couatls ally with dragons that guard ancient sites, and you can create themed encounters or adventures around these areas.

Jungle Ruins: Orium dragons and couatl rogue serpents or star serpents (see *Monster Manual 2*) guard cyclopean ruins deep within steaming jungles. The mammoth stone ziggurats hold secrets from ancient times. The characters might come to the ruins to seek artifacts they need and find themselves opposed by the dragon and the couatls. Or the creatures might call on the characters for assistance to drive out yuan-ti, demons, or undead that dwell in the tunnels beneath the ruins.

Domains of Light: To guard their astral lairs as they meditate, mithral dragons employ couatl allies. These couatls (usually redeemers) believe ardently that the visions of a mithral dragon foretell good fortune, so they aggressively guard the dominions these dragons call home. The characters might run across guardian couatls while sailing through the Astral Sea, and defeating them could draw a mithral dragon's wrath. If the characters merely seek the dragon's help—even if they're invited to an audience—the couatls might try to fight them off to keep the master's reverie unbroken.

Golden Serpents: Imperious gold dragons sometimes take couatls on as trusted lords or advisors. To give a sense of prosperity to its domain, a gold might commission beautiful architecture adorned with precious metals, rare pigments, and gems. The couatls also help keep up this appearance (whether deserved or artificial), as the dragon sends out the magnificent serpents to strike awe into its subjects. The characters might have a gold dragon patron that lives in such a domain, or might discover that the place is a facade that masks the misery and starvation of the people.

FRANZ VOHWINKEL

DRACONIAN

EVIL SPELLCASTERS AND PRIESTS create cruel servitors known as draconians by using a ritual that corrupts metallic dragon eggs. The kind of draconian depends on the egg it hatched from. For instance, a gold dragon egg produces a small number of the prized aurak draconians, and a bronze dragon egg can spawn up to a dozen bozak draconians.

The transformation that changes a dragon into a draconian causes the energy transference between the dragon's heart and fundamentum to become unstable. While the draconian lives, the pumping heart keeps a dragon's elemental energy in check, but once the heart stops, the energy exponentially increases and alters the draconian's corpse. Some undergo a minor transformation, such as turning to stone, but in others the elemental forces grow so immense that they cause an explosive overload of destructive energy.

DRACONIANS AND METALLIC DRAGON EGGS

Draconian Kind	Corrupted Egg
Adamaaz	Adamantine
Aurak	Gold
Baaz	Brass
Bozak	Bronze
Ferak	Iron
Kapak	Copper
Kobaaz	Cobalt
Sivak	Silver

ADAMAAZ DRACONIAN

ADAMAAZ DRACONIANS ARE FIERCE CREATURES that relish ambushes and melee combat. They stalk their prey in the dead of night, wearing pitch-black armor that complements their dark adamantine scales.

ADAMAAZ DRACONIAN LORE

Nature DC 12: Although they are extremely indirect and evasive outside combat, adamaaz draconians are well-trained soldiers once a battle starts. They ambush foes, then bring them down using brute force.

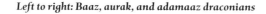

Left to right: Baaz, aurak, and adamaaz draconians

WAYNE ENGLAND

Adamaaz Draconian	Level 6 Soldier
Medium natural humanoid (reptile)	XP 250

Initiative +9   **Senses** Perception +5; darkvision
HP 74; **Bloodied** 37; see also *thunderous throe*
AC 22; **Fortitude** 19, **Reflex** 19, **Will** 17
Speed 5, fly 5 (clumsy)

⊕ **Falchion** (standard; at-will) ✦ **Weapon**
   +13 vs. AC; 2d4 + 5 damage (crit 2d4 + 12).

↩ **Thunderous Throes** (when the draconian drops to 0 hit points)
   ✦ **Thunder**
   Close burst 2; +11 vs. Fortitude; 2d8 + 3 thunder damage, the
   target is knocked prone, and the target is deafened (save ends).

Marauding Step (immediate reaction, when an adjacent enemy
   shifts; at-will)
   The draconian shifts 1 square and makes a melee basic attack
   against the triggering enemy.

Alignment Evil	**Languages** Common, Draconic

Skills Athletics +12, Intimidate +10, Stealth +12

Str 19 (+7)	**Dex** 18 (+7)	**Wis** 14 (+5)
Con 18 (+7)	**Int** 13 (+4)	**Cha** 15 (+5)

Equipment plate armor, falchion

Nature DC 17: When an adamaaz draconian is slain, elemental energy is released in a thunderous explosion that deafens and knocks down nearby creatures.

ADAMAAZ DRACONIAN TACTICS

Surprisingly quick and nimble, an adamaaz draconian prefers to ambush its foes from higher ground—typically a cliff edge or rooftop. A gutsy combatant, it lands in the middle of its foes. It then ducks and weaves through the fray, reacting to its enemy's attacks with *marauding step*, and cutting them down with its powerful falchion.

AURAK DRACONIAN

MASTERS OF THE MIND, aurak draconians assault their foes with psychic urgings and twisting thoughts. Aurak draconians are wingless, but they can teleport short distances.

Aurak draconians are also incredibly hard to kill. Before dying, an aurak draconian immolates itself in green flames and flies into a burning, bloody frenzy. It strikes its enemy with savage claws before finally falling.

AURAK DRACONIAN LORE

Nature DC 14: Aurak draconians are rare. They are masters of magic that can twist the mind of a foe to do their bidding.

Nature DC 19: When an aurak draconian is killed, it is consumed by a frenzy that transforms the creature into a terrifying, fiery horror. It fights until it burns out or a particularly powerful blow finally downs the creature.

Aurak Draconian	Level 8 Controller (Leader)
Medium natural humanoid (reptile)	XP 350

Initiative +5   **Senses** Perception +9; darkvision
Fiery Frenzy (Fire) aura 1; only when the aurak draconian drops
   to 0 hit points; each enemy that starts its turn within the aura
   takes 5 fire damage. See also *death frenzy*.
HP 70; **Bloodied** 35; see also *death frenzy*
AC 22; **Fortitude** 19, **Reflex** 21, **Will** 21
Speed 6

⊕ **Claw** (standard; at-will)
   +13 vs. AC; 2d6 + 5 damage.

⊛ **Fiery Blast** (standard; at-will) ✦ **Fire**
   Ranged 5; +12 vs. Reflex; 1d10 + 7 fire damage.

↗ **Mindbend** (standard; encounter) ✦ **Charm, Psychic**
   Ranged 10; +12 vs. Will; 1d6 + 5 psychic damage, and the
   target is dominated (save ends).

Death Frenzy (when the draconian drops to 0 hit points)
   The draconian does not fall dead, but instead flies into a savage
   and fiery rage. Its *fiery frenzy* aura is activated. The draconian
   can make only melee basic attacks, but it deals 1d6 extra
   damage on those attacks. At the end of each of its turns, the
   draconian makes a saving throw. If it fails, it dies. It also dies if
   an enemy scores a critical hit against it.

Dimensional Step (move; recharge ⚅⚅) ✦ **Teleportation**
   The aurak draconian teleports 5 squares.

Defend Me! (minor; at-will)
   One ally within 5 squares shifts 1 square.

Change Shape (minor; encounter) ✦ **Polymorph**
   An aurak draconian can alter its physical form to appear as any
   Medium humanoid (see "Change Shape," MM2 216).

Alignment Evil	**Languages** Common, Draconic

Skills Diplomacy +13, Insight +14

Str 13 (+5)	**Dex** 13 (+5)	**Wis** 20 (+9)
Con 17 (+7)	**Int** 20 (+9)	**Cha** 18 (+8)

Equipment robes

AURAK DRACONIAN TACTICS

Arrogant to the extreme, an aurak draconian guides its allies to build a defensive barrier between it and its foes. The aurak then tries to dominate the most powerful enemy, while striking at others with its *fiery blasts*. It constantly moves nearby allies to defensive and offensive positions with its *defend me!* power, while using *dimensional step* to gain a better spot on the battlefield from which to pepper enemies with fiery death.

Once it enters its *death frenzy*, any notion of subtle tactics leaves the aurak. It spends its last actions wreaking as much havoc as possible against as many enemies as it can.

BAAZ DRACONIAN

BAAZ DRACONIANS SERVE AS RANK-AND-FILE troopers of draconian armies. Although lacking the intelligence of other draconians, they are not without guile. Hiding under heavy masks and cloaks, baaz draconians slip into civilized areas to further the draconian cause.

Bozak draconian

Baaz Draconian Foot Soldier — Level 8 Minion Soldier
Medium natural humanoid (reptile) — XP 88

Initiative +9   **Senses** Perception +4; darkvision
HP 1; a missed attack never damages a minion; see also *stone dead*.
AC 24; **Fortitude** 22, **Reflex** 20, **Will** 19
Speed 5, fly 5 (clumsy)

⊕ **Longsword** (standard; at-will) ✦ **Weapon**
    +15 vs. AC; 6 damage, and the target is marked until the end of the draconian's next turn.

† **Stone Dead** (when the draconian drops to 0 hit points) ✦ **Polymorph**
    The draconian turns into a statue, and the square it occupies becomes difficult terrain that provides cover. If the draconian was reduced to 0 hit points by a melee attack using a weapon, it makes the following attack against that weapon's wielder: +12 vs. Reflex; the target is disarmed, and the weapon is stuck partially inside the statue. An adjacent creature can yank out the weapon by spending a standard action. The statue crumbles to dust at the end of the encounter.

Alignment Evil   **Languages** Common, Draconic
Skills Athletics +11, Bluff +11, Intimidate +11

Str 15 (+6)	**Dex** 16 (+7)	**Wis** 10 (+4)
Con 20 (+9)	**Int** 9 (+3)	**Cha** 15 (+6)

Equipment scale armor, longsword

Baaz Draconian Lore

Nature DC 10: Baaz draconians are the most common draconian variety, and they serve as foot soldiers in a draconian army.

Nature DC 15: A slain baaz draconian instantly transforms into a rocky statue. This transformation happens so quickly that the creature can trap the weapon that killed it.

Baaz Draconian Tactics

Baaz draconians rely on strength in numbers. A group pins down a single opponent, usually a striker, to allow more mobility for the baaz draconians' allies. Baaz draconians do not hesitate to attack enemies that have been disarmed.

Bozak Draconian

THE INTELLIGENT BOZAK DRACONIANS become gifted sorcerers and cunning warriors. They hold respected positions in draconian society.

Bozak Draconian Lore

Nature DC 12: Bozak draconians are natural leaders and accomplished in the arcane arts. They can fire bolts of lightning.

Nature DC 20: When a bozak draconian is slain, its scaly skin shrivels, revealing a bleached skeleton that explodes in a shower of razor-sharp bone shards.

Bozak Draconian Tactics

Bozak draconians attack from a distance, relying on allies to tie up enemies. They use *lightning lash* to break apart clustered enemies and *lightning burst* if their foes insist on staying in a close group. When

Baaz Draconian — Level 2 Soldier
Medium natural humanoid (reptile) — XP 125

Initiative +5   **Senses** Perception +2; darkvision
HP 41; **Bloodied** 20; see also *stone dead*
AC 18; **Fortitude** 15, **Reflex** 14, **Will** 13
Speed 5, fly 5 (clumsy)

⊕ **Longsword** (standard; at-will) ✦ **Weapon**
    +9 vs. AC; 1d8 + 5 damage, and the target is marked until the end of the draconian's next turn.

† **Leaping Charge** (standard; at-will) ✦ **Weapon**
    The draconian makes a charge attack, ignoring difficult terrain; +10 vs. AC; 2d8 + 5 damage, and the target is marked until the end of the draconian's next turn.

† **Stone Dead** (when the draconian drops to 0 hit points) ✦ **Polymorph**
    The draconian turns into a statue, and the square it occupies becomes difficult terrain that provides cover. If the draconian was reduced to 0 hit points by a melee attack using a weapon, it makes the following attack against that weapon's wielder: +7 vs. Reflex; the target is disarmed, and the weapon is stuck partially inside the statue. An adjacent creature can yank out the weapon as a standard action. The statue crumbles to dust at the end of the encounter.

Alignment Evil   **Languages** Common, Draconic
Skills Athletics +7, Bluff +7, Intimidate +7

Str 13 (+2)	**Dex** 14 (+3)	**Wis** 12 (+2)
Con 17 (+4)	**Int** 8 (+0)	**Cha** 13 (+2)

Equipment scale armor, longsword

WAYNE ENGLAND

Bozak Draconian — Level 5 Artillery

Bozak Draconian	Level 5 Artillery
Medium natural humanoid (reptile)	XP 200

Initiative +4   **Senses** Perception +6; darkvision
HP 51; **Bloodied** 25; see also *shrapnel skeleton*
AC 17; **Fortitude** 16, **Reflex** 17, **Will** 18
Speed 6, fly 6 (clumsy)

⊕ **Short Sword** (standard; at-will) ✦ **Weapon**
+10 vs. AC; 1d6 + 7 damage.

⊗ **Lightning Lash** (standard; at-will) ✦ **Lightning**
Ranged 10; +10 vs. Reflex; 1d8 + 4 lightning damage, and all creatures adjacent to the target slide 1 square and take 5 lightning damage.

↤ **Shrapnel Skeleton** (when the draconian drops to 0 hit points)
The draconian's flesh crumbles to dust, revealing a skeleton that explodes in a shower of bone shards: close burst 2; +10 vs. Reflex; 2d10 + 4 damage. *Miss:* Half damage.

⁘ **Lightning Burst** (standard; encounter) ✦ **Lightning**
Area burst 2 within 20; +10 vs. Reflex; 2d8 + 4 lightning damage. *Miss:* Half damage.

Alignment Evil   **Languages** Common, Draconic
Skills Diplomacy +9, Insight +11
Str 14 (+4)   **Dex** 15 (+4)   **Wis** 18 (+6)
Con 15 (+4)   **Int** 17 (+5)   **Cha** 14 (+4)
Equipment leather armor, short sword

it faces imminent death, a bozak draconian moves closer to its enemies, so it can hit creatures with *shrapnel skeleton*.

FERAK DRACONIAN

FERAK DRACONIANS REVEL in brutal hand-to-hand combat, and use jagged short swords. Highly aggressive but less intelligent than other draconians, they are used as rank-and-file troops.

Ferak Draconian — Level 3 Brute

Ferak Draconian	Level 3 Brute
Medium natural humanoid (reptile)	XP 150

Initiative +1   **Senses** Perception +3; darkvision
HP 55; **Bloodied** 27; see also *rust cloud*
AC 15; **Fortitude** 17, **Reflex** 13, **Will** 15
Speed 7, fly 7 (clumsy)

⊕ **Short Sword** (standard; at-will) ✦ **Weapon**
+6 vs. AC; 1d6 + 4 damage.

‡ **Double Slash** (standard; at-will)
The draconian makes two short sword attacks.

↤ **Rust Cloud** (when the draconian drops to 0 hit points) ✦ **Zone**
The draconian explodes into a cloud of rust: close burst 2; +4 vs. Fortitude; 2d6 + 3 damage. *Effect:* The draconian's square and all squares in the burst become a zone of lightly obscured squares until the end of the encounter.

Alignment Evil   **Languages** Common, Draconic
Skills Athletics +10, Intimidate +5, Stealth +6
Str 18 (+5)   **Dex** 11 (+1)   **Wis** 15 (+3)
Con 15 (+3)   **Int** 7 (−1)   **Cha** 8 (+0)
Equipment hide armor, 2 short swords

FERAK DRACONIAN LORE

Nature DC 10: Ferak draconians are brutal fighters that relish close combat. They are the shock troops of the draconian armies, used to bring about the most casualties possible.

Nature DC 15: When a ferak draconian dies, its body bursts into a cloud of rust that hangs in the air.

FERAK DRACONIAN TACTICS

Ferak draconians are not subtle fighters. They ambush enemies by gliding down out of trees or other high structures and landing in the middle of a group of foes, next to fragile targets such as controllers or strikers.

KAPAK DRACONIAN

KAPAK DRACONIANS SERVE IN DRACONIAN ARMIES as stealthy infiltrators and ranged infantry. Their expertise in stealth, and their poisonous saliva, makes them sought-after assassins.

KAPAK DRACONIAN LORE

Nature DC 12: Kapak draconians have soft, padded feet that allow them to move quietly. They exude poisonous saliva; when a kapak draconian licks its weapon, it intends to kill.

Ferak draconian

TOMÁS GIORELLO

Kapak Draconian — Level 4 Lurker
Medium natural humanoid (reptile) — XP 175

Initiative +10   **Senses** Perception +3; darkvision
HP 45; **Bloodied** 22; see also *acid pool*
AC 18; **Fortitude** 15, **Reflex** 17, **Will** 15
Speed 6, fly 6 (clumsy)

⊕ **Short Sword** (standard; at-will) ✦ **Weapon**
+9 vs. AC; 1d6 + 4 damage.

⊕ **Shortbow** (standard; at-will) ✦ **Weapon**
Ranged 15/30; +9 vs. AC; 1d8 + 4 damage.

↩ **Acid Pool** (when the draconian drops to 0 hit points) ✦ **Acid, Zone**
The draconian dissolves into a pool of acid: close burst 1; +7 vs. Reflex; 2d8 + 4 acid damage. *Effect:* The draconian's square and all squares in the burst become a zone that lasts until the end of the encounter. Any creature that enters the zone or starts its turn there takes 5 acid damage.

Apply Poison (standard, at-will) ✦ **Poison**
The draconian gains a +4 bonus to all defenses and to Stealth checks until the start of its next turn, and it applies poison to its short sword or shortbow by licking the weapon. The next attack with that weapon deals 2d6 extra poison damage.

Draconian Sniper
A hidden kapak draconian that misses with a ranged attack remains hidden.

Alignment Evil   **Languages** Common, Draconic
Skills Stealth +11
Str 14 (+4)   **Dex** 19 (+6)   **Wis** 14 (+4)
Con 15 (+4)   **Int** 10 (+2)   **Cha** 12 (+3)
Equipment leather armor, short sword, shortbow with 20 arrows

Nature DC 17: A kapak draconian transforms into a pool of acid when it is slain, spraying acid on nearby creatures.

KAPAK DRACONIAN TACTICS

At first, a kapak draconian engages enemies from a distance, attacking with poisoned arrows. After using a poisoned arrow, it uses *apply poison*, then moves to hide. If it ends up in melee, it uses *apply poison* to increase its defenses, then moves out of the combat.

KOBAAZ DRACONIAN

KOBAAZ DRACONIANS HAVE A SERIOUS TEMPERAMENT that makes them perfect troops. Wielding their sharp glaives, kobaaz draconians are terrifying fighters trained in combating crowds of foes. Kobaaz draconians are uncommon, and more capable than the majority of other draconians variants, so they are afforded better training and equipment.

KOBAAZ DRACONIAN LORE

Nature DC 12: Whenever a draconian army needs reliable warriors, the duty falls to the kobaaz draconians. Their expertise with the glaive can keep even the most vicious foes back.

Nature DC 17: When a kobaaz draconian is slain, the elemental energy held within it transforms its body into a statue made of ice.

Kobaaz Draconian — Level 4 Controller
Medium natural humanoid (reptile) — XP 175

Initiative +4   **Senses** Perception +3; darkvision
HP 57; **Bloodied** 28; see also *ice statue*
AC 18; **Fortitude** 17, **Reflex** 15, **Will** 14
Speed 5, fly 5 (clumsy)

⊕ **Glaive** (standard; at-will) ✦ **Weapon**
Reach 2; +9 vs. AC; 2d4 + 4 damage, and the target slides 3 squares.

† **Arching Blade** (standard; encounter)
The kobaaz draconian makes a *glaive* attack against each enemy within reach. If an attack hits, the target is also knocked prone. After these attacks are made, the draconian can shift 1 square.

↩ **Ice Statue** (when the kobaaz draconian drops to 0 hit points) ✦ **Cold, Polymorph**
The kobaaz draconian crystallizes into an icy statue. It becomes blocking terrain, and any creature that starts its turn within 2 squares of the statue takes 5 cold damage and is slowed until the end of its current turn.

Threatening Reach
A kobaaz draconian can make opportunity attacks against all enemies within its weapon's reach.

Alignment Evil   **Languages** Common, Draconic
Skills Athletics +11
Str 18 (+6)   **Dex** 14 (+4)   **Wis** 12 (+3)
Con 17 (+5)   **Int** 11 (+2)   **Cha** 11 (+2)
Equipment scale armor, glaive

KOBAAZ DRACONIAN TACTICS

A kobaaz draconian wades into the middle of combat, supporting other melee combatants with its versatile attacks and keeping enemies from moving within its reach.

SIVAK DRACONIAN

SIVAK DRACONIANS ARE THE LARGEST and most physically imposing draconians. Due to their large wings, sivaks are the only draconians that can truly fly. Their ability to transform into creatures they have slain makes them useful spies in civilized society.

Sivak Draconian — Level 8 Skirmisher
Large natural humanoid (reptile) — XP 350

Initiative +11   **Senses** Perception +7; darkvision
HP 90; **Bloodied** 45; see also *death mask*
AC 22; **Fortitude** 20, **Reflex** 21, **Will** 19
Speed 7, fly 7

⊕ **Greatsword** (standard; at-will) ✦ **Weapon**
Reach 2; +13 vs. AC; 1d12 + 6 damage.

† **Leaping Strike** (standard; recharge ⚄ ⚅) ✦ **Weapon**
The draconian shifts 3 squares and makes an attack: reach 2; +13 vs. AC; 2d12 + 6 damage.

Death Mask (when the draconian drops to 0 hit points; targets the creature that reduced the draconian to 0 hit points) ✦ **Fear, Psychic, Polymorph**
The draconian dies, and changes its form to that of the creature that killed it; +9 vs. Will; 2d6 + 5 psychic damage, and the target is dazed until the end of its next turn. The draconian's body decomposes into dust after three days.

Flying Charge
When it is charging, a draconian can charge to any unoccupied space adjacent to the target, instead of just the closest space.

Steal Appearance (immediate reaction, when the sivak draconian kills a humanoid; at-will) ✦ **Polymorph**
The draconian alters its physical form to appear as the slain creature (see "Change Shape," *MM2* 216). The draconian can end the transformation as a minor action.

Alignment Evil	**Languages** Common, Draconic	
Skills Bluff +10, Streetwise +10		
Str 18 (+8)	**Dex** 20 (+9)	**Wis** 16 (+7)
Con 18 (+8)	**Int** 12 (+5)	**Cha** 12 (+5)
Equipment plate armor, greatsword		

SIVAK DRACONIAN LORE

Nature DC 14: Sivak draconians are surprisingly agile flyers, able to quickly shift their center of mass and charge foes in a manner hard to predict. They can on the appearance of people they slay, making them excellent infiltrators.

Nature DC 19: When killed, a sivak draconian transforms into the appearance of the person that slew it. This can shock and unsettle the killer.

SIVAK DRACONIAN TACTICS

Sivak draconians charge over opponents and drop into flanking positions, giving them better chances to hit with their serrated greatswords. When surrounded, a sivak draconian makes a short *leaping strike* to free itself.

ENCOUNTER GROUPS

Draconians are most often encountered with their own kind. Due to their military background, they also associate with other martial races, such as hobgoblins. They frequently work for chromatic dragons. Only the most evil among metallic dragons would ever work alongside draconians.

Level 3 Encounter (XP 752)
✦ 2 baaz draconians (level 2 soldier)
✦ 1 bozak draconian (level 5 artillery)
✦ 4 hobgoblin grunts (level 3 minion, *MM* 138)
✦ 1 hobgoblin soldier (level 3 soldier, *MM* 139)

Level 7 Encounter (XP 1,550)
✦ 2 adamaaz draconians (level 6 soldier)
✦ 1 aurak draconian (level 8 elite controller)
✦ 1 sivak draconian (level 8 skirmisher)

Level 9 Encounter (XP 2,202)
✦ 4 baaz draconian foot soldiers (level 8 minion soldier)
✦ 1 sivak draconian (level 8 skirmisher)
✦ 1 young red dragon (level 7 solo soldier, *MM* 82)

Left to right: Kapak, kobaaz, and sivak draconians

WAYNE ENGLAND

DRAKE

DRAKES ARE SMALLER AND LESS POWERFUL than dragons, but the larger ones are far easier to train to use as mounts. Metallic dragons often train these creatures and either give them to their humanoid servants or use them to guard hoards, lairs, or strongholds.

LIONDRAKE

Liondrakes are fierce, intelligent desert hunters that blend the characteristics of a brass dragon and a great lion. They are fast, powerful adversaries armed with a devastating roar.

Though liondrakes understand Draconic and can manage a few words of Common, they rarely speak.

Liondrake		Level 12 Skirmisher
Large natural magical beast (mount, reptile)		XP 700

Initiative +12 **Senses** Perception +14; darkvision
HP 122; **Bloodied** 61
AC 26; **Fortitude** 26, **Reflex** 24, **Will** 23
Speed 7, fly 10 (clumsy)
⊕ **Bite** (standard; at-will)
  Reach 2; +17 vs. AC; 2d6 + 6 damage.
⊕ **Claw** (standard; at-will)
  Reach 2; +17 vs. AC; 1d8 + 3 damage.
⊣ **Battle Leap** (standard; at-will)
  The liondrake shifts 4 squares and makes two claw attacks or a bite attack.
↞ **Terrifying Roar** (standard; recharge ⚄ ⚅) ✦ **Fear, Thunder**
  Close burst 5; targets enemies; +13 vs. Fortitude; 2d8 + 4 thunder damage, and the target is dazed (save ends).
Fierce Steed (while mounted by a friendly rider of 12th level or higher) ✦ **Mount, Thunder**
  When it makes charge attacks, the liondrake and its rider gain a +4 to defense against opportunity attacks.
Alignment Unaligned   **Languages** Common, Draconic
Skills Athletics +17
Str 22 (+12)   **Dex** 19 (+10)   **Wis** 16 (+9)
Con 18 (+10)   **Int** 6 (+4)   **Cha** 11 (+6)

LIONDRAKE TACTICS

A liondrake's wings are not strong, and it is a poor flier. Therefore, it prefers to fight on the ground. However, a drake is capable of great wing-assisted leaps. A liondrake begins a battle by rushing into the middle of its foes with *battle leap* and then using *terrifying roar*. It fights a highly mobile battle, using *battle leap* to keep from being surrounded. The drake follows *battle leap* with a move action if it needs to completely disengage.

LIONDRAKE LORE

Nature DC 16: Liondrakes are related to dragons, but only distantly. They favor warm, arid environs, especially deserts. They have a largely undeserved reputation for devouring hapless travelers lost in the wastelands.

Nature DC 21: Liondrakes are the product of magical experimentation by wizards of a long-lost kingdom. These mages infused lions with the essence of brass dragons in an effort to create powerful steeds and guard beasts for their overlord. The drakes have bred true in the centuries since.

VULTURE DRAKE

Vulture drakes were originally natural creatures of the world, but they have been corrupted by the dark energy of the Shadowfell. Cunning scavengers that love the taste of carrion, they are favored flying mounts of the shadar-kai and other creatures in the service of the Raven Queen.

A vulture drake is gaunt and menacing, with long, cumbersome wings. Its skin stretches taut on its skeletal frame.

Vulture Drake		Level 9 Brute
Large natural beast (mount, reptile)		XP 400

Initiative +7   **Senses** Perception +12
HP 119; **Bloodied** 59
AC 21; **Fortitude** 22, **Reflex** 21, **Will** 21
Resist 10 necrotic
Speed 6, fly 8 (clumsy)
⊕ **Bite** (standard; at-will) ✦ **Necrotic**
  +12 vs. AC; 1d8 + 5 damage, and ongoing 5 necrotic damage (save ends).
⊕ **Claw** (standard; at-will)
  +12 vs. AC; 1d6 + 5 damage.
⊣ **Swooping Charge** (standard; at-will)
  The vulture drake makes a charge attack, starting in the air and ending on the ground. It can make two claw attacks against the target it charges, instead of making one melee basic attack. If both attacks hit, the target is knocked prone.
↞ **Death Shriek** (immediate reaction, when first damaged; encounter) ✦ **Fear, Necrotic, Thunder**
  Close blast 5; +10 vs. Will; 2d8 + 5 thunder damage, and the target takes ongoing 5 necrotic damage and a –2 penalty to attack rolls and saving throws (save ends both).

DAVE ALLSOP

Death Scent		
Creatures taking ongoing necrotic damage gain no benefit from concealment or total concealment when they are attacked by a vulture drake.		
Shadow Mount (when mounted by a friendly rider of 7th level or higher; at-will)		
The vulture drake grants its rider resist 10 necrotic and a +4 bonus to saving throws against fear effects.		
Alignment Unaligned		**Languages** –
Str 18 (+8)	**Dex** 16 (+7)	**Wis** 16 (+7)
Con 19 (+8)	**Int** 3 (-1)	**Cha** 10 (+4)

VULTURE DRAKE TACTICS

A vulture drake charges directly into combat from the air, making use of its *swooping charge* and deliberately setting itself up to be hit so that it can use its *death shriek*. It focuses its attacks on a single target, and then takes off to charge another enemy once the first one is no longer a threat.

VULTURE DRAKE LORE

Nature DC 14: Vulture drakes are also known as deathwings. They are common in areas of the Shadowfell, and it is believed that when one is sighted in the world, it portends great ill.

Nature DC 19: A cabal of cobalt dragons known as the Conclave of the Black Frost first bred vulture drakes in the Shadowfell. The conclave eventually came into conflict with the Raven Queen, and her

shadowsworn agents eradicated them. Those same agents spared the vulture drakes, seeing them as useful in the Raven Queen's war against the powers of undeath.

ENCOUNTER GROUPS

Aggressive, intelligent, and territorial, liondrakes are highly valued guardians. They sometimes agree to serve worthy champions as steeds.

Vulture drakes are often found as mounts of the shadar-kai and other creatures that follow the Raven Queen.

Level 10 Encounter (XP 2,950)
✦ 3 shadar-kai warriors (level 8 soldier, *MM* 231)
✦ 1 shadar-kai witch (level 7 controller, *MM* 231)
✦ 4 vulture drakes (level 9 brute)

Level 12 Encounter (XP 3,900)
✦ 1 human wizard lich (level 14 elite controller, *MM* 176)
✦ 1 liondrake (level 12 skirmisher)
✦ 2 mezzodemons (level 11 soldier, *MM* 58)

KEREM BEYIT

DRAKKENSTEEDS ARE FIERCE, remarkably cunning reptilian predators. A drakkensteed's broad, sharp wings and long neck evoke flying predators of bygone epochs, yet its four-legged stance—complete with dagger-sharp claws—and its fanged snout are clearly draconic in nature. From their lairs in high peaks and caves, families of drakkensteeds claim a wide region as their own hunting ground, tolerating no competition.

Drakkensteed eggs and young are worth more than their weight in gold, since drakkensteeds can be trained to serve as mounts for particularly strong-willed riders.

Drakkensteed	Level 16 Skirmisher
Large natural magical beast (mount, reptile)	XP 1,400

Initiative +15   **Senses** Perception +12; low-light vision
HP 157; **Bloodied** 78
AC 30; **Fortitude** 29, **Reflex** 27, **Will** 26
Speed 8, fly 10, overland flight 15
⊕ **Claw** (standard; at-will)
    +21 vs. AC; 2d8 + 7 damage.
⊕ **Wing Swipe** (standard; at-will)
    +21 vs. AC; 1d6 + 7 damage.
✦ **Flyby Attack** (standard; at-will)
    The drakkensteed flies up to 10 squares and makes one claw attack, or two wing swipes against different creatures, at any point during that movement. The drakkensteed doesn't provoke opportunity attacks when moving away from the targets of the attacks.
↤ **Fearsome Roar** (standard; encounter) ✦ **Fear**
    Close burst 3; targets enemies; +19 vs. Fortitude; the target is dazed (save ends).
Drakkensteed Action (while mounted by a friendly rider of 16th level or higher; encounter) ✦ **Fear, Mount**
    When the rider spends an action point to take an extra action, the drakkensteed's *fearsome roar* recharges, and the drakkensteed uses it as a free action.
Alignment Unaligned   **Languages** —
Str 24 (+15)   **Dex** 21 (+13)   **Wis** 19 (+12)
Con 21 (+13)   **Int** 3 (+4)   **Cha** 10 (+8)

DRAKKENSTEED TACTICS

Drakkensteeds initiate combat with a *fearsome roar*, hoping to cripple foes early, and then follow with a *flyby attack*. Drakkensteeds fight on the ground if circumstances warrant, but they prefer to keep to the air and rely on hit-and-run tactics.

DRAKKENSTEEDS OF A DIFFERENT BREED

The cobalt dragon-bred drakkensteed described here is just one variety of this creature. These drakkensteeds can be "bred" from the blood of almost any kind of dragon. Those created from other dragons tend to have a simple breath weapon keyed to the damage type of the parent dragon and resistances that mirror the dragon of their origin.

Grave-Born Drakkensteed	Level 21 Artillery
Large natural magical beast (mount, undead)	XP 3,200

Initiative +16   **Senses** Perception +15; darkvision
HP 155; **Bloodied** 77
AC 33; **Fortitude** 34, **Reflex** 32, **Will** 31
Immune disease, poison; **Resist** 15 necrotic
Speed 6, fly 8, overland flight 14
⊕ **Claw** (standard; at-will) ✦ **Necrotic**
    +26 vs. AC; 1d6 + 7 damage, and ongoing 10 necrotic damage (save ends).
↗ **Eyes of the Grave** (standard; at-will) ✦ **Fear, Gaze, Necrotic**
    Ranged 10; +26 vs. Fortitude; 3d6 + 8 necrotic damage, and the target takes a –2 penalty to attack rolls made against the drakkensteed or its rider until the end of the drakkensteed's next turn.
↤ **Breath of the Grave** (standard; encounter) ✦ **Necrotic**
    Close blast 4; +26 vs. Fortitude; 3d8 + 8 necrotic damage, and the target is weakened (save ends).
Gift of the Grave (while mounted by a friendly rider of 21st level or higher; encounter) ✦ **Fear, Gaze, Necrotic, Mount**
    When the rider spends an action point to take an extra action, the drakkensteed's *breath of the grave* recharges, and the drakkensteed uses it as a free action.
Grave Resistance (while mounted by a friendly rider of 21st level or higher) ✦ **Mount**
    The mounted rider gains resist 15 necrotic and resist 15 poison.
Alignment Unaligned   **Languages** —
Str 26 (+18)   **Dex** 23 (+16)   **Wis** 21 (+15)
Con 23 (+16)   **Int** 2 (+6)   **Cha** 7 (+8)

GRAVE-BORN DRAKKENSTEED TACTICS

Grave-born drakkensteeds retain their instincts to protect and cooperate with their riders. They fight from a distance, making use of *eyes of the grave* and *breath of the grave*, engaging in melee only when commanded or forced to do so. Since they are already dead, they fight until destroyed unless commanded otherwise.

Cobalt Dragon-Bred Drakkensteed	Level 26 Skirmisher
Large natural magical beast (dragon, mount)	XP 9,000

Initiative +23   **Senses** Perception +19; darkvision
HP 240; **Bloodied** 120
AC 38; **Fortitude** 39, **Reflex** 38, **Will** 36
Resist 15 cold
Speed 8, fly 10, overland flight 15
⊕ **Claw** (standard; at-will) ✦ **Cold**
    +31 vs. AC; 2d6 + 8 damage plus 1d6 cold damage.
⊕ **Wing Swipe** (standard; at-will) ✦ **Cold**
    +31 vs. AC; 1d6 + 8 damage plus 1d6 cold damage.
✦ **Flyby Attack** (standard; at-will)
    The drakkensteed flies up to 10 squares and makes one claw attack, or two wing swipes against different creatures, at any point during that movement. The drakkensteed doesn't provoke opportunity attacks when moving away from the targets of the attacks.

DAVE ALLSOP

↩ Breath Weapon (standard; encounter) ✦ **Cold**
Close blast 6; +29 vs. Reflex; 4d12 + 6 cold damage.

↩ Fearsome Roar (standard; encounter) ✦ **Fear**
Close burst 4; deafened creatures are immune; +29 vs. Fortitude; the target is dazed (save ends). A friendly rider of 22nd level or higher is immune.

Gift of the Dragon (while mounted by a friendly rider of 22nd level or higher; encounter) ✦ **Mount**
When the mounted rider spends an action point to take an extra action, the drakkensteed's *fearsome roar* or *breath weapon* recharges (rider's choice), and the drakkensteed uses it as a free action.

Draconic Resistance (while mounted by a friendly rider of 22nd level or higher) ✦ **Mount**
The mounted rider gains resist 15 cold.

Alignment Unaligned		Languages Draconic
Str 28 (+22)	Dex 26 (+21)	Wis 23 (+19)
Con 24 (+20)	Int 7 (+11)	Cha 13 (+14)

DRAGON-BRED DRAKKENSTEED TACTICS

Dragon-bred drakkensteeds follow a *fearsome roar* with a *breath weapon* attack if their foes are sufficiently clumped together. They then rely on *flyby attacks*, fighting like standard drakkensteeds.

DRAKKENSTEED LORE

Nature DC 20: Drakkensteeds are reptilian creatures, somewhat akin to drakes. They are believed to have diverged from the same line that produced wyverns and other modern drakes, but much farther back during their development. Although not especially intelligent, they are cunning and, if their innate stubbornness can be overcome, trainable as mounts. They can be trained to understand a spoken language—normally Common or Draconic—even though they cannot speak. A drakkensteed egg can be worth as much as 6,000 gp to the right buyer (a level 17 treasure parcel).

Nature DC 27: A few powerful spellcasters have developed a ritual to reanimate drakkensteeds as a particular form of undead. These undead creatures generate internal necrotic energy and retain many of the instincts that make drakkensteeds such coveted mounts.

Not bred, but rather created through a secret process in which the egg of a drakkensteed is infused with the blood of a metallic dragon, dragon-bred drakkensteeds are more dangerous and more intelligent than their mundane kin, but they remain highly trainable. Some serve their creators, although others live in the wild and breed true. A dragon-bred drakkensteed egg can be worth up to 90,000 gp (a level 27 treasure parcel.)

ENCOUNTER GROUPS

Wild drakkensteeds fight only in family groups, but when trained, they fight alongside their riders and any creatures they are commanded to accompany.

Level 17 Encounter (XP 8,600)
✦ 3 drakkensteeds (level 16 skirmisher)
✦ 2 yuan-ti malison disciples of Zehir (level 17 controller, MM 270)
✦ 1 yuan-ti malison incanter (level 15 artillery, MM 269)

Level 25 Encounter (XP 36,000)
✦ 2 cobalt dragon-bred drakkensteeds (level 26 skirmisher)
✦ 2 dragonborn champions (level 26 soldier, MM 87)

Most kobolds revere chromatic dragons. Relatively few kobolds get along with or serve metallic dragons, but those that do are often a cut above the rabble that sides with the chromatics. Such kobolds are not common fodder, monsters that run when an ally falls in combat. They are encountered along with metallic dragon masters or powerful servitors of those masters. When they team up with other kobolds, they usually lead their inferiors.

DRAGONKIN KOBOLD

A DRAGONKIN KOBOLD BINDS itself to the service of a dragon, sealing its allegiance by grafting one of its master's discarded scales into the flesh of its chest. It gains powers tied to its master's elemental energy, but surrenders its individuality and free will.

Dragonkin kobolds were introduced in *Draconomicon: Chromatic Dragons*. The kobolds presented here are suitable for an iron or bronze dragon. You can customize dragonkin kobolds by changing the energy they wield to match the breath weapon of the dragon they serve.

Dragonkin Channeler	Level 5 Controller
Small natural humanoid, kobold (reptile)	XP 200

Initiative +5   **Senses** Perception +4; darkvision
HP 61; **Bloodied** 30
AC 19; **Fortitude** 16, **Reflex** 18, **Will** 17
Resist 5 lightning
Speed 6
ⓐ **Shocking Staff** (standard; at-will) ✦ **Lightning**
    +9 vs. Reflex; 1d6 + 3 lightning damage, and the target is dazed until the end of the kobold's next turn.
↝ **Channel Lightning** (immediate reaction, when attacked with a lightning power; at-will) ✦ **Lightning**
    The channeler uses the lightning around it to charge its *shocking staff* and make an attack: ranged 10; +9 vs. Reflex; 3d6 + 3 lightning damage.
✴ **Electrify** (standard; recharge ▣ ▦) ✦ **Lightning, Zone**
    Area burst 2 within 10; +9 vs. Reflex; 1d6 + 3 lightning damage, and the target is dazed (save ends). *Effect:* The area becomes a zone of difficult terrain until the start of the channeler's next turn. Each creature that enters the zone takes 5 lightning damage.
Shifty (minor; at-will)
    The kobold shifts 1 square.
Trap Sense
    A kobold gains a +2 bonus to all defenses against traps.
Alignment Unaligned   **Languages** Common, Draconic
Str 10 (+2)   **Dex** 17 (+5)   **Wis** 15 (+4)
Con 13 (+3)   **Int** 10 (+2)   **Cha** 14 (+4)
Equipment leather armor, staff

DRAGONKIN CHANNELER TACTICS

A channeler wields its draconic master's elemental energy through a mystic connection. In battle, the dragonkin stays near its master's enemies, hoping to be caught in a *breath weapon* attack that will allow it to use *channel lightning*. Otherwise, it uses *electrify* to guard its master's flanks or enters melee if it has nothing else to do.

Dragonkin Zealot	Level 5 Lurker
Small natural humanoid, kobold (reptile)	XP 200

Initiative +10   **Senses** Perception +8; darkvision
HP 49; **Bloodied** 24
AC 20; **Fortitude** 16, **Reflex** 19, **Will** 16
Resist 5 lightning
Speed 6
ⓐ **Dagger** (standard; at-will)
    +11 vs. AC; 2d4 + 4 damage.
↝ **Shuriken** (standard; at-will)
    Ranged 6/12; +10 vs. AC; 1d6 + 6 damage.
Run Away and Hide (immediate reaction, when the dragonkin zealot takes damage; recharges when the zealot uses *electric zeal*)
    The dragonkin zealot shifts its speed. If it reaches a square where it has cover or concealment, it can make a Stealth check to become hidden.
Electric Zeal (minor; recharges when the zealot uses *run away and hide*) ✦ **Lightning**
    The dragonkin zealot deals 3d6 extra lightning damage on melee attacks until the start of its next turn.
Shifty (minor; at-will)
    The kobold shifts 1 square.
Trap Sense
    A kobold gains a +2 bonus to all defenses against traps.
Alignment Unaligned   **Languages** Common, Draconic
Skills Stealth +11
Str 10 (+2)   **Dex** 19 (+6)   **Wis** 13 (+3)
Con 13 (+3)   **Int** 8 (+1)   **Cha** 10 (+2)
Equipment leather armor, dagger, 5 shuriken

DRAGONKIN ZEALOT TACTICS

The zealot spies on intruders in a dragon's territory, trailing them in secret until it is time for an assault. The dragonkin zealot enters battle near cover or concealment so it can use *electric zeal* to empower its attack before dashing away and hiding.

Dragonkin Champion	Level 7 Brute
Small natural humanoid, kobold (reptile)	XP 300

Initiative +6   **Senses** Perception +5; darkvision
HP 94; **Bloodied** 47
AC 18; **Fortitude** 19, **Reflex** 18, **Will** 17
Resist 5 lightning
Speed 6
ⓐ **Spear** (standard; at-will) ✦ **Weapon**
    +10 vs. AC; 2d6 + 6 damage.
╪ **Shocking Spear** (standard; recharges when the kobold's draconic master uses *breath weapon*) ✦ **Lightning, Weapon**
    The kobold makes two attacks: reach 2; +10 vs. AC; 3d6 + 6 lightning damage.
Draconic Inspiration
    A kobold deals 1d6 extra lightning damage against any creature adjacent to one of the kobold's dragon allies.

KOBOLD

ENCOUNTER GROUPS

Dragonkin kobolds live only to serve their masters' wishes.

Level 8 Encounter (XP 1,900)
- ✦ 3 dragonkin kobold champions (level 7 brute)
- ✦ 1 young cobalt dragon (level 5 solo controller)

Level 9 Encounter (XP 2,100)
- ✦ 1 dragonkin kobold channeler (level 5 controller)
- ✦ 2 dragonkin kobold zealots (level 5 lurker)
- ✦ 1 young bronze dragon (level 7 solo brute)

WYRMGUARD KOBOLD

BRAVE AND TRUSTWORTHY (by kobold standards), wyrmguard kobolds guard their dragon masters zealously. Wyrmguards single out one creature or object—usually a dragon, one of the dragon's lieutenants, or one of its prized possessions—to protect, forcing enemies to take care of them before harming those they guard.

Wyrmguard kobolds wear armor decorated with runes of warding. Their gear is a combination of mundane items and magic tools—all wyrmguards practice some amount of magic.

Wyrmguard Sentinel	Level 7 Soldier
Small natural humanoid, kobold (reptile)	XP 300

Initiative +8   **Senses** Perception +6; darkvision
HP 80; **Bloodied** 40
AC 23; **Fortitude** 20, **Reflex** 19, **Will** 19
Speed 6
ⓘ **Dragontooth Spear** (standard; at-will) ✦ **Weapon**
  +14 vs. AC; 2d8 + 2 damage, and the target is marked until the end of the sentinel's next turn.
Sentinel's Ward (minor; at-will)
  The wyrmguard sentinel designates an ally or object within 10 squares as its ward, and any creature it was already warding is no longer its ward. The ward takes half damage from creatures marked by the sentinel.
Combat Superiority
  A sentinel has a +3 bonus to attack rolls on opportunity attacks. If a move provoked the attack, an enemy struck by the wyrmguard's opportunity attack stops moving. If it still has actions remaining, the enemy can use them to resume moving.
Shifty (minor; at-will)
  The sentinel shifts 1 square.
Trap Sense
  A sentinel gains a +2 bonus to all defenses against traps.

Alignment Unaligned		**Languages** Common, Draconic
Str 19 (+7)	**Dex** 16 (+6)	**Wis** 16 (+6)
Con 16 (+6)	**Int** 10 (+3)	**Cha** 13 (+4)

Equipment scale armor, dragontooth spear

WYRMGUARD SENTINEL TACTICS

A wyrmguard sentinel stands tireless guard or walks regular patrols near a place or object it protects. It attempts to keep foes nearby using *combat superiority*. *Sentinel's ward* allows a sentinel to protect one ally at a time. Frequently, wyrmguard sentinels are grouped

Shifty (minor; at-will)
The kobold shifts 1 square.
Trap Sense
A kobold gains a +2 bonus to all defenses against traps.

Alignment Unaligned		**Languages** Common, Draconic
Str 19 (+7)	**Dex** 17 (+6)	**Wis** 16 (+5)
Con 14 (+5)	**Int** 12 (+4)	**Cha** 10 (+3)

Equipment spear

DRAGONKIN CHAMPION TACTICS

Dragonkin champions fight poorly when caught away from their draconic masters. When in their preferred circumstances, dragonkin champions fight more shrewdly than most brutes, waiting until their masters have pressed the enemy before engaging in melee. They use *shifty* to avoid becoming trapped, knowing that the longer they survive, the more harm they'll be able to inflict on their master's enemies.

DRAGONKIN KOBOLD LORE

Nature DC 12: Dragonkin kobolds protect the lairs and interests of dragons. Each kobold has a scale from its master permanently embedded in its chest. A dragonkin kobold is fanatically loyal and thinks nothing of sacrificing itself for its master's sake.

DAVE ALLSOP

with leaders, who keep them alive in exchange for the protection they provide.

Wyrmguard Scout	Level 9 Artillery
Small natural humanoid, kobold (reptile)	XP 400

Initiative +11   **Senses** Perception +12; darkvision
HP 75; **Bloodied** 37
AC 21; **Fortitude** 19, **Reflex** 22, **Will** 20
Speed 6

⊕ **Dagger** (standard; at-will) ✦ **Weapon**
     +16 vs. AC; 2d4 + 3 damage.

⊗ **Dragon Bolt** (standard; at-will) ✦ **Poison**
     Ranged 20; +14 vs. Reflex; 2d6 + 5 poison damage.

✳ **Dragon Clash** (standard; targets enemies; recharges when the scout's ward is damaged by an enemy) ✦ **Poison**
     Area burst 1 within 20; +12 vs. Fortitude; 3d6 + 5 poison damage.

Scout's Ward (minor; at-will)
     The wyrmguard sentinel designates an ally or object within 10 squares as its ward, and any creature it was already warding is no longer its ward. The scout deals 2d6 extra damage against the enemy nearest to its ward.

Shifty (minor; at-will)
     The scout shifts 1 square.

Trap Sense
     A scout gains a +2 bonus to all defenses against traps.

Alignment Unaligned		**Languages** Common, Draconic
Str 10 (+4)	**Dex** 20 (+9)	**Wis** 17 (+7)
Con 15 (+6)	**Int** 12 (+5)	**Cha** 15 (+6)

Equipment leather armor, dagger

WYRMGUARD SCOUT TACTICS

Scouts prefer to remain at the outer edge of their range, usually on ledges or other high terrain, sniping at foes while their allies move in closer. They choose wards as early as possible, and then concentrate on protecting their wards using *dragon clash* when possible (even if they can hit only one target) and *dragon bolt* the rest of the time.

Different scouts use different damage types. The example scout's damage type is based on using it with a mercury dragon, but it can change to fit alongside other dragons.

WYRMGUARD LORE

Arcana or Nature DC 14: Wyrmguard kobolds are normally used as bodyguards for their creators or assigned to guard a specific location, individual, or treasure. Some have been assigned to guard a dragon's clutch of eggs.

Arcana or Nature DC 19: Wyrmguard kobolds guard those they admire and learn minor magic that lets them place protective wards. When they are without dragons or leaders to guard, they guard each other effectively. Most wyrmguard kobolds serve dragons, and might be encountered alongside them.

ENCOUNTER GROUPS

Wyrmguards are usually found in mixed groups of creatures, all loyal to the same dragon. It's rare to find more than a couple of wyrmguards in a single group of monsters—and they aggravate players if too many appear in the same encounter.

Level 7 Encounter (XP 1,600)
✦ 2 wyrmguard sentinels (level 7 soldier)
✦ 1 young cobalt dragon (level 5 solo controller)

Level 9 Encounter (XP 2,300)
✦ 2 dragonborn gladiators (level 10 soldier, *MM* 86)
✦ 1 portal drake (level 10 controller, *Draconomicon: Chromatic Dragons*, page 223)
✦ 2 wyrmguard scouts (level 9 artillery)

DAVE ALLSOP

THREE-TOOTH

Though kobolds that could reasonably be called "heroes" are few and far between, Three-Tooth has made herself known by attacking the people of the bigger, tougher races and surviving, often with the help of her dragon ally.

Three-Tooth	Level 10 Elite Artillery
Small natural humanoid, kobold (reptile)	XP 1,000

Initiative +11 **Senses** Perception +8; darkvision
HP 176; **Bloodied** 88
AC 22; **Fortitude** 19, **Reflex** 21, **Will** 22
Saving Throws +2
Speed 6
Action Points 1
⊕ **Dagger** (standard; at-will) ✦ **Weapon**
 +17 vs. AC; 2d4 + 5 damage.
⊗ **Venom Bolt** (standard; at-will) ✦ **Implement, Poison**
 Ranged 20; three attacks against up to three different targets; +15 vs. Reflex; 1d8 + 5 poison damage, and Three-Tooth pushes the target 3 squares.
�֎ **Resonating Orb** (standard; recharge ⚄ ⚅) ✦ **Force, Implement**
 Area burst 2 within 20; +15 vs. Reflex; 2d8 + 5 force damage, and the target is knocked prone. Damage from this attack ignores temporary hit points.
Kobold Sorcery
 When Three-Tooth rolls an even number on an attack roll with an implement power (whether the attack hits or misses), she slides the target 1 square after the attack.
Blinking Shifty (minor; at-will) ✦ **Healing, Teleportation**
 Three-Tooth teleports 2 squares and regains 3 hit points.
Teleport Escape (move; encounter) ✦ **Teleportation**
 Three-Tooth teleports 10 squares.
Trap Sense
 Three-Tooth gains a +2 bonus to all defenses against traps.
Alignment Unaligned **Languages** Common, Draconic
Str 14 (+7) **Dex** 22 (+11) **Wis** 16 (+8)
Con 19 (+9) **Int** 14 (+7) **Cha** 24 (+12)
Equipment dagger

THREE-TOOTH'S TACTICS

Three-Tooth makes a great recurring villain or rival. She isn't particularly bloodthirsty, just extremely good at pushing enemies away from things she wants and teleporting away from danger to prepared escape positions. Thanks to her *blinking shifty* power, she's both more mobile and more resilient than most spellslinging artillery.

THREE-TOOTH LORE

Arcana or Nature DC 16: Three-Tooth, a great kobold hero—or villain, depending on her mood—is reputed to be the only survivor of a kobold nest that adopted a mercury wyrmling. The other kobolds died in battle or in the dragon's jaws, but Three-Tooth lived to become a powerful magician. She sometimes travels alongside her mercury dragon friend, which stays shapeshifted into a kobold form.

Arcana or Nature DC 21: Three-Tooth garners great respect from other kobolds, and her legend is deeper and larger than most realize. In fact, many of her adventures are attributed to previous aliases, such as Four-Tooth and Six-Tooth. She tends to pick fights, and brutal beatings at the hands of tough monsters have necessitated several name changes.

ENCOUNTER GROUPS

Three-Tooth takes work as a mercenary, usually accompanied by her mercury dragon ally, Drokona. The characters might run into Three-Tooth while she's fighting a monstrous enemy, and then end up in a chaotic battle between three forces.

Level 8 Encounter (XP 1,500)
✦ Drokona, elite young mercury dragon (level 6 elite lurker; see the young mercury dragon on page 163 and the material on elite dragons on page 218)
✦ Three-Tooth (level 10 elite artillery)

SPAWN OF RINGING EGGS

Once in a while, a kobold lays an extremely rare egg that rings like metal when struck with a claw. The tribe keeps its special eggs hidden until they hatch. The kobolds that emerge from metal eggs grow up to become the strongest kobolds of their generation. Often, they become champions in the service of a metallic dragons, as if that was their destiny.

Kobolds never speak publicly about the "ringing eggs." It's a secret that is referred to only by euphemisms, even in a well-known kobold folk tale, in which a kobold champion in the service of a gold dragon returns to slay all her relatives and crèche mates. Some kobolds consider this story a good reason to track down and destroy anyone else's ringing eggs, but the selfish creatures wouldn't think of destroying their own.

Chromatic dragons that know of ringing eggs do what they can to find and destroy them. They seldom find enough suspect eggs to make it worth their trouble. Few metallic dragons admit to caring about an oddity of kobold reproduction, but that doesn't mean they haven't noticed the situation and sought a way to exploit it. Explanations for the magic behind the phenomenon range from a hidden blessing of Bahamut to a curse by an ancient archmage.

Few dragons are truly anonymous. Any dragon that survives to adulthood becomes a figure of local fame (or notoriety), at the least. However, some dragons earn truly legendary reputations that extend for hundreds, sometimes thousands, of miles beyond their homelands. The waking of an ancient dragon is an event that stirs fearful gossip in taverns and alehouses across half a continent. Here, then, are a few dragons whose reputations precede them.

ANDRAEMOS

MANY DRAGONS ACHIEVE a certain level of fame—or infamy—for terrorizing a local populace and demanding or seizing its wealth. These relationships, between a dragon and a fearful region, are the subjects of countless stories told in scores of inns. Many dragons are content to make a name for themselves in just a township or two. But others have larger plans.

Andraemos's ambitions began at a young age. Legend tells that he was one of four hatchlings in a brood, but he outlived each of his siblings, stealing their food behind the back of their mother. It wasn't long before he had learned everything he thought he could from his parent and set off into his harsh desert home to make his own way.

But Andraemos wasn't done with his mother yet. She had seen the quiet ambition in his eyes and knew about the theft of food that enabled him to grow strong at the expense of his siblings. Such is the way of the desert, she knew, so she let it lie. But before Andraemos could escape her desert territory, she decided she did not relish the thought of a competitor

dragon—especially one so hungry for power—lairing near her. She attacked, so the stories say, and caught the young dragon by surprise. But Andraemos was cleverer than even his mother had given him credit for being, and when their battle led into a narrow ravine filled with fragile, towering spires of rock, Andraemos finally found his advantage. He spun in mid-flight and fired a blast of fire at a precarious boulder perched atop a delicate spire of stone. The spire splintered and collapsed, and with perfect timing, the boulder fell on Andraemos's mother, crushing her skull and driving her body to the ravine floor below.

Andraemos	Level 15 Solo Artillery
Adult brass dragon	
Large natural magical beast (dragon)	XP 6,000

Initiative +12   **Senses** Perception +15; darkvision
HP 600; **Bloodied** 300; see also *bloodied breath*
AC 28; **Fortitude** 28, **Reflex** 27, **Will** 26
Resist 20 fire
Saving Throws +5
Speed 8, fly 10 (hover), overland flight 12
Action Points 2

⊕ **Bite** (standard; at-will) ✦ **Fire**
     Reach 2; +22 vs. AC; 1d10 + 7 damage plus 1d6 fire damage.

⊕ **Claw** (standard; at-will)
     Reach 2; +22 vs. AC; 1d8 + 7 damage.

↯ **Dragon Ire** (standard; at-will)
     Andraemos makes two claw attacks or one bite attack, and then shifts 1 square.

↯ **Wing Buffet** (immediate reaction, when an enemy enters or leaves an adjacent square)
     Targets the triggering enemy; +20 vs. Fortitude; 1d10 + 7 damage, the target is knocked prone, and Andraemos shifts 2 squares.

↞ **Breath Weapon** (standard; recharge ⚄ ⚅) ✦ **Fire**
     Close blast 5; +20 vs. Reflex; 3d8 + 7 fire damage, and the target is knocked prone. *Miss:* Half damage.

ZOLTAN BOROS & GABOR SZIKSZAI

↩ **Bloodied Breath** (free, when first bloodied; encounter) ✦ Fire
Breath weapon recharges, and Andraemos uses it. If he is flying, he can shift 5 squares before making this attack.

⌁ **Fire Stream** (standard; at-will) ✦ Fire
Ranged 10; +20 vs. Reflex; 3d6 + 6 fire damage, and any creature adjacent to the target takes 2d10 fire damage.

↩ **Frightful Presence** (standard; encounter) ✦ Fear
Close burst 5; targets enemies; +20 vs. Will; the target is stunned until the end of the dragon's next turn. *Aftereffect:* The target takes a -2 penalty to attack rolls (save ends).

Mark of Death
Andraemos's attacks deal 1d6 extra damage to any target marked by one of his allies.

Alignment Unaligned	**Languages** Common, Draconic

Skills Arcana +16, Athletics +17, Insight +15, Intimidate +16

Str 21 (+12)	**Dex** 20 (+12)	**Wis** 16 (+10)
Con 22 (+13)	**Int** 18 (+11)	**Cha** 19 (+11)

ANDRAEMOS LORE

Nature DC 18: The brass dragon Andraemos rules a large swath of the desert. His domain is bordered on several sides by trade routes. He collects tribute from several of the towns on these routes, content to claim their money rather than destroy them outright.

Andraemos has established himself as a powerful force to be reckoned with in the region. During a scouting trip around his territory, he noticed a group of desert nomads. They were in the process of capturing a caravan that had been passing through the area, and Andraemos was captivated by their fighting style, which involved redirecting an enemy's attacks against the enemy and its allies. Curious about their presence, Andraemos landed and demanded that they give him the tribute he deserved as master of the desert. But the bandits—a group of eladrin—were unimpressed. They had recently come to the desert through a portal from the Feywild, and they had braved many dangers to make it to Andraemos's desert. Confronted with the dragon, they were prepared to die trying to survive.

Thinking quickly, the dragon recognized the value in employing the services of the clever and morally ambiguous eladrin, and their partnership endures to this day. Calling them the Sand Knives, he began to use them to enforce his will across the region. The eladrin have brought in more of their kind from the Feywild portal—which Andraemos now controls—and his territory has expanded tremendously.

Nature DC 23: The dragon has cowed a large tribe of goblins into a truce. Andraemos eventually plans to bring the goblins under his rule, but he is content to let them bribe him with tribute until he feels secure enough in his enlarged territory to destroy their leaders and take over leadership of the tribe.

Perhaps the dragon's biggest coup, however, was the capture of the desert city of Kashtaph. A corrupt merchant elected from an even more corrupt council ran the city. When this leader—a female human named Azril Illaenon—sent her eldest daughter to woo the son of a prince in a neighboring city-state, Andraemos's eladrin brigands captured her. In exchange for sparing her daughter's life, Andraemos wanted the city gates opened to his eladrin and the names and addresses of each member of the merchant council.

A bloody night followed Azril's capitulation to the dragon's demands, and the woman now rules the city in Andraemos's name, sending him a healthy cut of all the city's lucrative business ventures. Most of the citizens have no clue that their city is now run by a dragon, and Andraemos prefers it that way—for now.

Nature DC 28: It is whispered that Andraemos's mother once captured one of the fabled *Broken Blades of Banatruul*. He discovered the artifact in her hoard years after her death. He has sent his Sand Knives out into the world over many years, trying to find the matching blade, and rumor has it that one of them recently returned with it after being away for nearly three years.

Sand Knives Bandit	**Level 13 Minion Soldier**
Medium fey humanoid, eladrin	XP 200

Initiative +15	**Senses** Perception +8; low-light vision

HP 1; a missed attack never damages a minion.
AC 29; **Fortitude** 24, **Reflex** 27, **Will** 23
Saving Throws +5 against charm effects
Speed 6

⊕ **Scimitar** (standard; at-will) ✦ Weapon
+20 vs. AC; 6 damage (crit 9).

⊙ **Longbow** (standard; at-will) ✦ Weapon
Ranged 20/40; +20 vs. AC; 6 damage.

⤡ **Mark of Knives** (minor; at-will)
Melee 1; the target is marked until the end of its next turn.

Fey Step (move; encounter) ✦ Teleportation
The bandit teleports 5 squares.

Alignment Unaligned	**Languages** Common, Elven

Str 18 (+10)	**Dex** 25 (+13)	**Wis** 14 (+8)
Con 16 (+9)	**Int** 15 (+8)	**Cha** 17 (+9)

Equipment leather armor, scimitar, longbow with 20 arrows

ANDRAEMOS'S TACTICS

Andraemos is nearly always within hailing distance of a group of his Sand Knives. Nevertheless, he does make regular excursions to the limits of his domain, so it is possible to catch him alone. In battle, the dragon prefers to fight from a distance. He uses his *breath weapon* at the first opportunity, then *frightful presence* to incapacitate as many enemies as possible. He reserves *fire stream* for a particularly pesky foe.

ENCOUNTER GROUPS

Andraemos is most likely encountered with a group of Sand Knives.

Level 17 Encounter (XP 8,800)
✦ Andraemos (level 15 solo artillery)
✦ 2 eladrin bladesingers (level 11 skirmisher, MM2 97)
✦ 8 sand knives bandits (level 13 minion soldier)

THE GOD OF HONOR, JUSTICE AND NOBILITY, Bahamut is known as the Grandfather of Dragons or Lawbringer, but most often called the Platinum Dragon. Though the deity can appear in many forms, he is usually portrayed as a powerful dragon with platinum scales, the form he takes on when he goes to battle.

Adventurers often worship Bahamut, who is called to protect the weak, fight evildoers, and defend outposts of justice and civilization across the world. Paladins in particular often bear his heraldry—a platinum dragon head in profile—on their shields or as a holy symbol. And although not all metallic dragons show obeisance to the Platinum Dragon, those working at cross-purposes are careful to avoid the attention of Bahamut or the legions of crusading dragons and worshipers at his command.

BAHAMUT LORE

Arcana or Religion DC 5: Bahamut is the lawful god of justice and honor. Those who worship the Platinum Dragon seek to emulate him by defending the weak and ensuring that the guilty receive fair and immediate punishment.

Many metallic dragons, even if they don't worship Bahamut outright, regard him as the most revered elder among the ancient dragons. Many dragonborn bend their knee in fealty to Bahamut, as do paladins of all races.

Arcana or Religion DC 15: Bahamut holds court in a shining castle on the slopes of Mount Mertion, one of the seven mystic mountains in the domain of Celestia, amid the Astral Sea. Some powerful paladins and clerics make pilgrimages there in hopes of receiving a powerful blessing from the Platinum Dragon.

Arcana or Religion DC 20: Over the centuries, folk tales have persisted of Bahamut walking the world while magically disguised as a sage or hermit. He travels with seven trained canaries, which transform into gold dragons if anyone is foolish enough to threaten the docile old man.

The folk tale is well known enough among Bahamut's faithful that priests sometimes undertake pilgrimages in the company of trained canaries, seeking to emulate their god.

Bahamut sometimes tests the worthiness of his champions by directly engaging in battle with them. Bahamut doesn't pull any punches, and the battle ends when the champions are bloodied or when Bahamut yields. Powerful healers are on hand in case Bahamut's zeal for testing his champions overcomes their defenses.

Arcana or Religion DC 25: A council of seven ancient metallic dragons advises Bahamut on matters of honor and acts as a jury when Bahamut sits in direct judgment of an evildoer—often one apprehended by his champions. Because Bahamut walks the world in disguise, he has less need for exarchs than most deities. The best-known of his few exarchs is Kuyutha, Bahamut's emissary to dragonborn clans everywhere.

THE OLD MAN WITH THE CANARIES

WHEN HE'S NOT HOLDING COURT in his shining castle, Bahamut walks the natural world in the most unassuming of disguises: an elderly man accompanied by seven trained canaries. This old man, variously called a sage or a hermit in folklore, travels from place to place with no apparent purpose. He's quick to offer advice, information, or assistance to other travelers.

One folk tale in particular is told with a hundred variations: The sage with the canaries shares a campfire with roadside travelers, offering mysterious advice that borders on prophecy. Still, the travelers would have regarded the old man as nothing more than a curiosity if it weren't for the monsters that attacked

SEEKING WORTHINESS

Few folk tales reveal why Bahamut disguises himself in the way he does—they're more concerned with the plot twist when the old man with the canaries becomes something much more. Bahamut sometimes travels the world in disguise to assist his followers directly, especially if one of Tiamat's insidious plots needs to be thwarted. But more often, he walks the natural world to seek out "worthiness"—a subject he waxes philosophical about, and the topic of much of the sage advice he dispenses to those he meets.

When Bahamut walks the world, he tries to discern the worthiness of everything he encounters—"worthiness" viewed through a lens of justice, nobility, and honor. Consequently, he uses his deific power to help others fight, rather than just turning into his platinum dragon form and tearing through enemies in the blink of an eye. Bahamut wants to assess the worthiness of those he's fighting alongside, and so he blesses and heals his fellow travelers but does little direct fighting.

It's possible that Bahamut wants to assess the worthiness of the characters, but you can also make a meeting with Bahamut a chance encounter. Bahamut might be assessing the worthiness of other travelers, of the route itself, or of the dangers along the way.

the camp. Were they ever surprised when the old man started throwing around unfathomably powerful magic and turning his canaries into gold dragons.

ENCOUNTERS WITH THE OLD MAN

The folk tale of a disguised Bahamut is the quintessential encounter with the deity, and you can bring the kernel of that story to life in your game. The "sage with the canaries" can meet the characters during an adventure, act mysterious and inscrutable, and then reveal his true nature when the heroes must face monsters they could never hope to defeat without a god's aid.

If the characters have befriended Bahamut, he'll fight alongside them in his old man form, turning what would otherwise be a merciless slaughter of the characters into a fair fight. A group of characters plus Bahamut should be able to take on opponents of around ten levels higher than the characters.

Note what Bahamut does and doesn't do well in this form. He can effortlessly heal multiple characters, purge harmful effects, and improve the characters' attacks so they can hit and damage monsters that would otherwise be almost invulnerable, but Bahamut doesn't directly improve defenses or hit points, so the heroes are going to feel the full brunt of powerful monster attacks. That's when the drama occurs: The characters are not only doing much more than they're ordinarily capable of, they're taking the worst beating of their lives.

A fight against Bahamut tests the players' tactical acumen: Can they focus their attacks on specific enemies while preventing the monsters from focusing their attacks in the same way? If a character dies while in Bahamut's company, it's often because that character was wiped out in a single round by multiple monster attacks before Bahamut could respond with his powerful healing magic.

Although a fight against Bahamut while he is at the characters' side is a good tactical test, it's not worth the full XP award for an encounter ten levels higher. The presence of a full-blown god does level the playing field. When the encounter is over, award the characters one-quarter of the usual experience award (the value for a fight two levels higher than the party). If Bahamut sticks around for more than an encounter or two, choose treasure parcels appropriate for the characters at the level they are, not ones typical of the tough monsters they're facing.

Encounters using Bahamut work best when the characters, perhaps unsure exactly what's up with the old man, take the battle seriously and fight with their usual vigor. If the characters realize that they have a god in their midst, they might not take the battle seriously. Bahamut can (and probably will) use the Raise Dead ritual on any characters who fall in battle, after all. The heroes need Bahamut to win the battles you have planned, but Bahamut doesn't need them. In these battles, Bahamut isn't at risk, but for reasons of his own, he remains in the guise of an old man and lets the characters do most of the fighting.

You can try to conceal Bahamut's nature, making the characters unsure whether they're faced with Bahamut, an aspect of Bahamut, or a mysterious-but-powerful spellcaster of some sort. Longtime D&D players will recognize the canaries—they were part

THE SEVEN GOLD WYRMS

Bahamut's closest servants are seven gold dragons that guard his palace and sometimes travel with him disguised as canaries. For important tasks that aren't quite important enough to demand his personal attention, Bahamut dispatches one of these dragons. Each works on specific tasks, and no one knows if there's any sort of hierarchy among these servants. These are the current wyrms in Bahamut's inner circle; many have died and been replaced over time.

Borkadd the Claw: Compulsive and obstinate, Borkadd represents Bahamut as the hand of justice. He chronicles the laws of many lands, as well as Bahamut's personal code. He's more than a glorified secretary, though: Borkadd enforces Bahamut's law against those who can't be stopped by other means.

Kuria the Eye: This sleek, serpentine dragon remains aloof—sometimes threatening—even to those she knows well. Her tasks require secrecy, taking advantage of her suspicious nature.

Sonngrad the Wing: Bahamut's messenger, Sonngrad, has powerful wings that let her fly at great speed. She is the most commonly encountered of the seven dragons. Though focused and businesslike while on a mission, she's also a curious thrill-seeker. Bahamut usually gives her a bit of time after each task she completes to explore the places she's visiting.

Gruemar the Voice: The slender Gruemar is a master negotiator, sent out to settle disputes and prevent bloodshed. Though his speech sounds tranquil and warm, it never reveals a hint of weakness.

Marroshok the Tail: Massive and genial, Marroshok is the closest thing Bahamut has to a bodyguard. Though he's usually friendly, he's merciless in combat.

Troannaxia the Presence: A magnificent, shining creature, Troannaxia is sent to cow the proud into submission using the majesty of her presence. Unlike Gruemar, she intimidates instead of conversing. Bahamut sends her out when he encounters obstinate resistance that requires a blunt approach.

Urgala the Fang: When Bahamut musters a great army, Urgala leads them. Her knowledge of tactics is unsurpassed, and she flies over the battlefield to scout and command. Normally proud and uncompromising, Urgala sometimes becomes stubborn or rude when she is in a bad mood.

of Bahamut's backstory in the 1st Edition *Monster Manual*—but you can change the trappings of the old man to make his disguise less obvious.

TACTICS

When Bahamut is disguised as the old man with the canaries, his priorities are to level the playing field between the characters and the monsters. In his first two or three turns, he uses *Bahamut's blessing* on attacking characters, then a combination of *Bahamut's cleansing* and *Bahamut's mercy* on the most wounded characters. If possible, have Bahamut use *blessing* and *cleansing/mercy* on different individuals so no player thinks Bahamut is ignoring him or her. Using *Bahamut's blessing* twice is a good way for Bahamut to spend his first action point; heroes will have a hard time hitting the monsters without the *blessing* in place.

Once the characters have all received *Bahamut's blessing*, Bahamut uses *Bahamut's mercy* once or twice per turn, and releases one of his seven canaries—at which point it turns into a gold dragon. He can use a canary in two ways. *Gold dragon rescue* moves a nearly dead character out of harm's way. The gold dragon swoops down, stuns nearby assailants so they can't make opportunity attacks—and then the character can fly away during his next turn. If the characters aren't dealing enough damage to the monster or they're being outflanked, Bahamut uses *summon gold dragon* in whatever place is most inconvenient for the monsters. That's the closest Bahamut comes to attacking the monsters directly. He prefers to use his own melee attack only for opportunity attacks.

The Old Man with the Canaries	Level 36 Solo Soldier (Leader)
Medium immortal humanoid	XP —

Initiative +24 **Senses** Perception +32
HP 1,645; **Bloodied** 822; see also *discorporation*
AC 52; **Fortitude** 47, **Reflex** 45, **Will** 47
Resist 20 cold, 20 fire
Saving Throws +5; whenever an attack causes an effect on Bahamut that a save can end, he immediately makes a saving throw. Bahamut also makes saving throws at the end of his turn as normal.
Speed 8, teleport 5
Action Points 2

⊕ **Unarmed Attack** (standard; at-will) ✦ **Weapon**
  +41 vs. AC; 1d12 + 20 damage, and the target is dazed until the end of its next turn.

�֍ **Gold Dragon Rescue** (standard; uses one canary)
  Area burst 1 within 30, centered on ally; +41 vs. AC; the target is stunned (save ends). *Effect:* The ally in the origin square gains fly 10 until the end of its next turn.

↗ **Summon Gold Dragon** (standard; uses one canary) ✦ **Summoning**
  Ranged 20; Bahamut summons a Large gold dragon in an unoccupied space within range. The dragon has speed 8, fly 10 (hover) and, unlike a typical summoned creature, has its own defenses and hit points (all defenses 34; hp 120).
  Minor Action: +27 vs. AC; 1d12 + 10 damage.
  Opportunity Attack: +27 vs. AC; 1d12 + 10 damage.

Bahamut's Blessing (standard; at-will)
  Ranged 30; two targets; each target gains a +10 bonus to attack rolls, a +10 bonus to skill checks, and a +10 bonus to damage rolls.

Bahamut's Cleansing (minor; at-will)
  Ranged 30; two targets; each target can end one effect a save can end.

Bahamut's Mercy (minor; at-will) ✦ **Healing**
  Ranged 30; two targets; each target can spend a healing surge and regain an additional 25 hit points.

DISCORPORATION

When a deity is bloodied, the deity's mind leaves its body and the deity is unable to assume physical form for some time. The discorporation usually lasts at least a few months, but it can sometimes take several years before the deity can resume its form. During this time, the deity's power is weaker, but it is far from negligible. If characters wish to truly kill a deity, they must fulfill one or more conditions specific to that deity. This could require destroying the deity's most prominent temple, or finding an artifact that can deliver the killing blow. If the specific conditions are satisfied, the deity cannot discorporate and instead becomes bloodied as normal. Here are some sample quests the characters could undertake (if they, for some reason, need to kill Bahamut) or thwart (if evil forces are attempting to destroy the Platinum Dragon).

The Corrupted Ritual: Bahamut offers his protection when ritually called by high priests of his faith, manifesting in his draconic form. Sinister forces could alter key parts of that ritual, obtain access to one of Bahamut's grand temples to perform it, then battle the summoned Bahamut to the death.

The Prodigal Son: There's a reason Bahamut is called the Grandfather of Dragons and not the Father of Dragons. It is whispered that Bahamut has a son—somewhere among the planes—who has rebelled against his father, for reasons unknown. That child, if found, could face down his father in battle and claim his birthright, taking Bahamut's place among the deities. But thus far, even the most powerful evil soothsayers have been unable to learn the name or location of Bahamut's son. Their ritual divinations continue, however, and agents of Tiamat are alert for rumors about this child.

Dishonor and Trickery: Bahamut regards himself as honor, virtue, and justice coalesced into a living form. If Bahamut could be tricked into doing something inherently and irrevocably dishonorable, he would have no choice but to cast off his mantle of godhood lest the very concept of honor be forever tainted. Once bereft of godhood, the mortal shell of Bahamut could be destroyed as easily as any ancient dragon.

Bahamut Runs Rampant (standard; encounter) ✦ **Polymorph**
    Bahamut assumes his draconic form (described below).
Seven Canaries
    Bahamut has seven trained canaries, which he can transform
    into gold dragons. Some of his powers use up these canaries. All
    the canaries return during a short rest.
Discorporation (when bloodied)
    When Bahamut becomes bloodied, he discorporates and is
    unable to take physical form for a time.

Alignment Lawful good	**Languages** Supernal

Skills Arcana +31, Athletics +33, Diplomacy +32, Endurance +34,
    Heal +32, History +31, Insight +32, Intimidate +32, Religion +31

Str 31 (+28)	**Dex** 23 (+24)	**Wis** 28 (+27)
Con 33 (+29)	**Int** 27 (+26)	**Cha** 29 (+27)

Equipment robe

Bahamut's Dragon Form

Although his magically disguised form is the most likely way that the characters will experience Bahamut, epic-tier characters could encounter Bahamut in his full glory. His battle form is a magnificent dragon, shimmering with platinum scales tougher than any shield. If the characters encounter Bahamut in his court (where he might be in any form, including his draconic form) or otherwise meet in friendship, it's unlikely that a fight is going to break out—unless Bahamut wants to test their worthiness in direct combat.

Because Bahamut is a 36th-level solo, he represents a fundamentally unfair fight for all but the most powerful D&D characters. A test of worthiness might make a satisfying final hurdle for characters about to achieve the immortality feature of their epic destiny, for example.

When Bahamut fights a character, he explains ahead of time that he won't attack bloodied characters, but those individuals would dishonor themselves and their comrades if they continue to fight while bloodied. And Bahamut will yield before he discorporates, because discorporation would give Tiamat and other villains a few months or weeks of free rein without an active god of justice and honor to oppose them.

Tactics

For all his power, Bahamut in his dragon shape fights much like any dragon. He uses his breath weapons as often as he can, choosing *polar breath* when beset by multiple melee adversaries, *misty breath* if he's intentionally being merciful or there are noncombatants among his enemies, and *disintegration breath* when he wants to deal a lot of damage.

Bahamut uses *frightful majesty* if he finds himself in a disadvantageous position and none of his breath weapons is available. Whenever he can, he uses *Bahamut's clutches* against a defender or a melee striker. His bite attack deals damage and steals healing surges, and can quickly deplete the health of even an epic defender. And although Bahamut is honorable, he's cunning enough to move with a grabbed enemy, flying upward before releasing that enemy for a painful (but nonfatal) plummet.

ZOLTAN BOROS & GABOR SZIKSZAI

Bahamut	Level 36 Solo Soldier (Leader)
Huge immortal magical beast (dragon)	XP 275,000

Initiative +24   **Senses** Perception +32; darkvision
HP 1,316; **Bloodied** 658; see also *bloodied breath* and
    discorporation
AC 52; **Fortitude** 47, **Reflex** 45, **Will** 47
Immune attacks by creatures of lower than 20th level
Resist 20 cold, 20 fire
Saving Throws +5; whenever an attack causes an effect on
    Bahamut that a save can end, he immediately makes a saving
    throw against that effect. Bahamut also makes saving throws at
    the end of his turn as normal.
Speed 10, fly 15 (hover), teleport 10
Action Points 2
⊕ **Bite** (standard; at-will)
    Reach 3; +42 vs. AC; 3d12 + 10 damage, and the target loses
    two healing surges.
⊕ **Claw** (standard; at-will)
    Reach 3; +41 vs. AC; 2d12 + 10 damage.
† **Bahamut's Clutches** (immediate interrupt; when an enemy
    moves into a square adjacent to Bahamut; at-will)
    +41 vs. Reflex; 2d12 + 10 damage, and the target is grabbed.
    Failed Escape Attempt: Bahamut automatically hits the target
    with his bite attack.
↩ **Polar Breath** (minor; recharge ⚄ ⚅; all breath weapons share
    one recharge roll) ✦ **Cold**
    Close blast 10; +40 vs. Reflex; 4d12 + 10 cold damage, and the
    target is pushed 6 squares and immobilized (save ends); *Miss:*
    Half damage, and the target is pushed 3 squares.
↩ **Disintegration Breath** (minor; recharge ⚄ ⚅; all breath
    weapons share one recharge roll)
    Close blast 10; +40 vs. Fortitude; 4d12 + 10 damage, and 15
    ongoing damage (save ends).; *Aftereffect:* Ongoing 10 damage
    (save ends).
↩ **Misty Breath** (minor; recharge ⚄ ⚅; all breath weapons share
    one recharge roll) ✦ **Polymorph**
    Close blast 10; +40 vs. Will; the target is stunned, weakened,
    and transformed into fine mist (save ends all). While the target
    is in this mist form, enemies can move through the target's
    space freely.
↩ **Bloodied Breath** (free; when first bloodied; encounter) ✦ **Cold**
    Bahamut's breath weapon recharges, and he uses *polar breath*,
    disintegration breath, or *misty breath*.
↩ **Frightful Majesty** (minor; encounter) ✦ **Fear**
    Close burst 20; targets enemies; +38 vs. Will; the target is
    stunned until the end of Bahamut's next turn. *Aftereffect:* The
    target takes a -2 penalty to attack rolls (save ends).
Discorporation (when bloodied)
    When Bahamut becomes bloodied, he discorporates and is
    unable to take physical form for a time.
Alignment Lawful good   **Languages** Supernal
Skills Arcana +31, Athletics +33, Diplomacy +32, Endurance +34,
    Heal +32, History +31, Insight +32, Intimidate +32, Religion +31
Str 31 (+28)   **Dex** 23 (+24)   **Wis** 28 (+27)
Con 33 (+29)   **Int** 27 (+26)   **Cha** 29 (+27)

ASPECT OF BAHAMUT

BAHAMUT CAN CREATE AN ASPECT OF HIMSELF from
the willing sacrifice of a powerful metallic dragon
worshiper. The dragon dies, but rises anew as an
aspect of the Platinum Dragon itself, remembering all
of its previous life and now utterly bound to Bahamut.

Bahamut prefers for his dragon worshipers to
remain dragons rather than sacrificing themselves in
this manner, but he sometimes uses aspects as long-
term guardians, ambassadors for crucial diplomatic
efforts, or extraplanar authorities who bring to justice
villains too powerful for anything less than an aspect
of the god of justice.

Aspect of Bahamut	Level 18 Solo Soldier (Leader)
Huge immortal magical beast (dragon)	XP 10,000

Initiative +11   **Senses** Perception +18; darkvision
HP 704; **Bloodied** 352; see also *bloodied breath*
AC 35; **Fortitude** 32, **Reflex** 29, **Will** 30
Resist 20 cold, 20 fire
Saving Throws +5; whenever an attack causes an effect on an
    aspect of Bahamut that a save can end, it immediately makes a
    saving throw. The aspect of Bahamut also makes saving throws
    at the end of its turn as normal.
Speed 10, fly 10 (hover), teleport 5
Action Points 2
⊕ **Bite** (standard; at-will)
    Reach 3; +25 vs. AC; 2d10 + 8 damage, and ongoing 10 damage.
⊕ **Claw** (standard; at-will)
    Reach 3; +25 vs. AC; 2d10 + 8 damage.
† **Draconic Fury** (standard; at-will)
    The aspect of Bahamut makes two claw attacks and one bite
    attack.
† **Snatch** (immediate interrupt, when an enemy moves into a
    square adjacent to the aspect of Bahamut; at-will)
    +20 vs. Reflex; 2d10 + 8 damage, and the target is grabbed.
    First Failed Escape Attempt: The aspect of Bahamut automatically
    hits the target with its bite attack.
↩ **Polar Breath** (standard; recharge ⚄ ⚅; all breath weapons
    share one recharge roll) ✦ **Cold**
    Close blast 5; +20 vs. Reflex; 3d12 + 10 cold damage, and the
    target is immobilized (save ends). *Miss:* Half damage.
↩ **Disintegration Breath** (standard; recharge ⚄ ⚅; all breath
    weapons share one recharge roll)
    Close blast 5; +20 vs. Fortitude; 3d12 + 10 damage, and 10
    ongoing damage (save ends).
↩ **Misty Breath** (standard; recharge ⚄ ⚅; all breath weapons
    share one recharge roll)
    Close blast 5; +20 vs. Will; the target is stunned, weakened,
    and transformed into fine mist (save ends all). While the target
    is in this mist form, enemies can move through the target's
    space freely.
↩ **Bloodied Breath** (free; when first bloodied; encounter)
    The aspect of Bahamut's breath weapon recharges, and it uses
    polar breath, *disintegration breath*, or *misty breath*.

BAHAMUT'S PALACE

The shining castle Bahamut calls home rests atop Mertion,
one of the seven mountains of Celestia, the astral domain
of the good and just. This grand structure is more than
just a palace—it's also Bahamut's hoard. The walls, inlaid
with copper and ivory on the inside and platinum on the
outside, reflect the eternal light of Celestia and make the
castle appear like a beacon on the horizon. The walls are
made of mithral tiles, and the windows of gemstones set
in silver and gold. Bahamut viciously pursues (usually by
proxy) anyone who attempts to steal from his great castle.
He might be a good god, but he's also dedicated to justice
and is a dragon. It's best not to mess with his hoard.

↶ **Frightful Majesty** (minor; encounter) ✦ **Fear**
  Close burst 10; targets enemies; +20 vs. Will; the target is stunned until the end of the aspect of Bahamut's next turn. *Aftereffect:* The target takes a -2 penalty to attack rolls (save ends).

Alignment Lawful good   **Languages** all
Skills Arcana +18, Diplomacy +19, History +18, Insight +18, Intimidate +19, Religion +18
Str 22 (+15)	**Dex** 14 (+11)	**Wis** 19 (+13)
Con 24 (+16)	**Int** 18 (+13)	**Cha** 20 (+14)

Aspect of Bahamut's Tactics

Like Bahamut, an aspect uses one of its breath weapons whenever able. The rest of the time it flies over its enemies and harries them with melee attacks. It uses one of its action points early in the battle to use both a breath weapon and *draconic fury*. It saves *frightful majesty* for the round after it uses *bloodied breath*, and saves its last action point for a getaway or a last-ditch attack.

Kuyutha, Exarch of Bahamut

THE LAST AND GREATEST PALADIN from the ancient dragonborn empire of Arkhosia, Kuyutha did his best to gather and protect the scattered dragonborn clans after the empire's fall. In recognition of Kuyutha's ceaseless efforts to safeguard his people, Bahamut granted him a spark of divinity and bade him train a new order of knights on Mount Mertion itself.

Since that day centuries ago, Kuyutha has acted as Bahamut's ambassador to the dragonborn race. He crisscrosses the world, shepherding dragonborn clans that find themselves in dire straits and brokering honorable accords when two clans have a dispute they cannot resolve. Kuyutha also seeks out the bravest among the dragonborn to train with him on Mount Mertion—and takes the vilest dragonborn villains to face their judgment before Bahamut.

Kuyutha, Exarch of Bahamut	Level 23 Elite Controller (Leader)
Large immortal humanoid, dragonborn	XP 10,200

Initiative +15   **Senses** Perception +22; darkvision
HP 430; **Bloodied** 215
Dragon Affinity aura 10; each ally within the aura has resist 10 radiant.
AC 37; **Fortitude** 35, **Reflex** 34, **Will** 36
Resist 10 cold, 10 fire, 15 radiant
Saving Throws +2
Speed 6, fly 6 (clumsy)
Action Points 1
⊕ **Dragontalon Blade** (standard; at-will) ✦ **Weapon**
  Reach 2; +28 vs. AC; 3d6 + 9 damage.
† **Legion Attack** (standard; at-will)
  Kuyutha makes a *dragontalon blade* attack, and one ally within 10 squares of Kuyutha and of 25th level or lower slides 1 square and makes a basic attack.
† **Bahamut's Blade** (standard; recharges when first bloodied) ✦ **Radiant, Weapon**
  Reach 2; +30 vs. AC; 4d6 + 9 damage, and the target takes ongoing 10 radiant damage and is blinded (save ends both).

↗ **Draconic Healing** (minor; recharge ⚁ ⚂ ⚃) ✦ **Healing**
  Ranged 20; targets one ally; the target regains 20 hit points.
↶ **Coldfire Breath** (standard; recharge ⚁ ⚂ ⚃) ✦ **Cold, Fire**
  Close blast 6; +27 vs. Reflex; 4d12 cold and fire damage.
↶ **Will of Bahamut** (standard; encounter)
  Close burst 5; +25 vs. Will; the target is stunned until the end of Kuyutha's next turn.
Dragonborn Fury (only while bloodied)
  Kuyutha gains a +1 racial bonus to attack rolls.

Alignment Lawful good   **Languages** Common, Draconic
Skills Athletics +24, Diplomacy +25, Heal +22, History +23, Insight +22, Intimidate +25, Religion +23
Str 27 (+19)	**Dex** 18 (+15)	**Wis** 22 (+17)
Con 23 (+17)	**Int** 25 (+18)	**Cha** 28 (+20)

Kuyutha's Tactics

Kuyutha's *coldfire breath* recharges quickly, so the "melee or breathe" decision comes up more frequently. In general, use *coldfire breath* if it has recharged and Kuyutha can hit at least two enemies with it; otherwise, attack with *legion attack* or *Bahamut's blade* (if you haven't used it yet). Occasionally, Kuyutha uses *legion attack* to move an ally out of danger, sliding the ally away from a foe and having that ally either skip the basic attack or make a ranged basic attack.

Otherwise, Kuyutha fights like a dragon, using *will of Bahamut* (his version of *frightful presence*) when beset by multiple flanking enemies, and then moving away to a place where he can catch as many stunned enemies as possible in his next blast of *coldfire breath*.

Kuyutha rarely fights alone, preferring to form a larger band so he can use his leader abilities. He uses *draconic healing* for his allies, and grants them attacks using *legion attack*. His *dragon affinity* aura protects his allies against enemies using radiant damage (usually users of the divine power source). This can come as a surprise to enemies who are accustomed to encountering foes that have other resistances.

Encounter Groups

Treat Bahamut as a solo in the truest sense of the word. He's a god, and he should be just fine on his own. Kuyutha, on the other hand, fights alongside dragons (sometimes including Bahamut) and dragonborn.

Level 21 Encounter (XP 20,200)
✦ Kuyutha, exarch of Bahamut (level 23 elite controller)
✦ Aspect of Bahamut (level 18 solo soldier)

Level 25 Encounter (XP 42,300)
✦ Kuyutha, exarch of Bahamut (level 23 elite controller)
✦ 3 dragonborn champions (level 26 soldier, *MM* 87)
✦ 4 angels of light (level 23 minion skirmisher, *MM2* 9)

Because steel dragons respect humans' achievements, adaptability, and ambition, they protect humans and impel them to rise against tyranny. The interests of the steel dragon Jalanvaloss, however, reflect less lofty ideals. A schemer, trickster, and manipulator, she lives for upheaval and unpredictability, endeavoring to keep her city dynamic.

In human form, Jalanvaloss usually appears as a slim female human with long, straight, black hair and steel-gray eyes. With the trademark catlike grace of steel dragons, she wears the latest fashions, entertains guests at her homes, and attends parties of the city's elite.

Jalanvaloss alters her appearance to assume any of a dozen identities. She takes her dragon shape the least often of all her forms.

In her dragon form, Jalanvaloss is long and sleek, with glossy scales, spines that fall straight like hair, and delicate whiskers. Her large, intelligent silver eyes accent her expressive face.

Jalanvaloss	Level 18 Solo Controller
Adult steel dragon	
Large natural magical beast (dragon, shapechanger)	XP 10,000

Initiative +13   **Senses** Perception +19; darkvision
HP 692; **Bloodied** 346; see also *bloodied breath*
AC 31; **Fortitude** 29, **Reflex** 27, **Will** 31; see also *illusory double*
Resist 20 force
Saving Throws +5
Speed 8, fly 10 (hover), overland flight 12; see also *dimension step*
Action Points 2

ⓐ **Arcane Claw** (standard; at-will)
  Reach 2; +23 vs. AC; 2d8 + 7 damage, and Jalanvaloss slides the target 2 squares.

ⓐ **Bite** (standard; at-will) ✦ Force
  Reach 2; +23 vs. AC; 2d8 + 7 damage plus 1d8 force damage.

⊣ **Double Attack** (standard; at-will)
  Jalanvaloss makes two *arcane claw* attacks.

⊣ **Burst of Force** (immediate reaction, when an enemy moves into an adjacent square; at-will) ✦ Force, Teleportation
  Close burst 1; +22 vs. Fortitude; 2d8 + 7 damage, and the target is knocked prone. *Effect:* Jalanvaloss teleports 4 squares.

JALANVALOSS AND THE FORGOTTEN REALMS

Jalanvaloss originates from the city of Waterdeep in the FORGOTTEN REALMS setting. Fickle but not malicious, she manipulates merchants and adventurers in her efforts to expand her power and holdings.

In the years leading up to the Spellplague, Jalanvaloss's wealth and control over Waterdeep expanded, but the disaster dashed her economic fortunes along with the fortunes of other nobles and merchants. To make matters worse, she lost considerable arcane power to the blue fire. In the past century, she has spent her dwindling fortune in rebuilding what she lost.

↢ **Breath Weapon** (standard; recharge ⚄ ⚅) ✦ Force
  Close blast 5; +21 vs. Fortitude; 4d6 + 8 force damage, and the target is dazed (save ends). *Miss:* Half damage.

↢ **Bloodied Breath** (free, when first bloodied; encounter)
  Breath weapon recharges, and Jalanvaloss uses it.

↢ **Frightful Presence** (standard; encounter) ✦ Fear
  Close burst 10; targets enemies; +22 vs. Will; the target is stunned until the end of Jalanvaloss's next turn. *Aftereffect:* The target takes a -2 penalty to attack rolls (save ends).

✳ **Steel Sting** (standard; at-will) ✦ Force
  Area burst 1 within 20; +22 vs. Reflex; 2d6 + 5 force damage.

✳ **Scattergloom** (standard; encounter) ✦ Necrotic, Zone
  Jalanvaloss makes three area burst attacks, and the bursts can't overlap: area burst 1 within 20; +22 vs. Fortitude; 2d6 + 5 necrotic damage. The burst becomes a zone of draining darkness until the end of Jalanvaloss's next turn. Any creature except Jalanvaloss that starts its turn within the zone takes 5 necrotic damage. The zone blocks line of sight for all creatures, and any creature entirely within the zone is blinded until it leaves the zone. Jalanvaloss is immune to the effects of the zone. *Sustain Minor:* The effect persists.

Change Shape (minor; at-will) ✦ Polymorph
  Jalanvaloss alters her form to appear as a unique human (see "Change Shape," MM2 216).

Dimension Step (move; encounter) ✦ Teleportation
  Jalanvaloss teleports 10 squares.

Illusory Double (minor; encounter) ✦ Illusion, Teleportation
  Jalanvaloss becomes invisible and teleports 4 squares. In the space she left, an illusory double appears and moves 8 squares. The double vanishes and Jalanvaloss becomes visible at the end of Jalanvaloss's next turn.

Alignment Unaligned   **Languages** Common, Draconic
Skills Arcana +19, Bluff +22, Diplomacy +22, History +19, Insight +19, Streetwise +22

Str 24 (+16)	Dex 18 (+13)	Wis 20 (+14)
Con 21 (+14)	Int 20 (+14)	Cha 26 (+17)

Equipment fine clothing, wand, ritual book

JALANVALOSS LORE

History or Streetwise DC 13: One of the best-known nobles in the city (Waterdeep, Sharn, or another city of your choosing), Lady Jalanvaloss is a powerful merchant. She commands a mercantile empire that has holdings throughout the city. Having come to prominence years ago, she retains her youthful beauty, which leads to speculation about her longevity. Rumors say that dark powers have touched her or that she is something other than she seems. Her vast fortune has saved the city, sponsored adventurers, recovered relics, and raised the city's prominence.

History or Streetwise DC 20: According to legend, a steel dragon protects the city from enemies inside and without; however, no one has seen the dragon since a great calamity (the Spellplague, the Mourning, or some other catastrophe) beset the land. At that time, the dragon, called the Wyrm of Many Spells, defended her community from unchecked magic and destruction; however, tales paint the dragon as an avaricious busybody, noted more for manipulation and trickery than for noble deeds.

History or Streetwise DC 25: The legends are correct: the fabled Wyrm of Many Spells is Lady Jalanvaloss. She has lived here for two centuries, using guile and magic to amass a fortune from real estate, business ventures, and sponsored expeditions. Other citizens suspect a hidden identity, but only those close to her know the truth. She defends the city from attack, but protecting her investments is as important to her as safeguarding its citizens.

Jalanvaloss gained the moniker "Wyrm of Many Spells" because of her training with the mortal archmage Rythtalies. The wizard raised her from a hatchling and taught her the rudiments of magic so she could serve as his guardian and steed.

After Rythtalies's exceptionally long life, the young steel dragon traveled to a place abundant with humans, the creatures she knew best. She assumed the identity of a human traveler and forged connections in every echelon of society, favoring adventuring types because they reminded her of her deceased master. She gathered her hoard in the form of real estate and investment enterprises.

History or Streetwise DC 30: Jalanvaloss does not have a traditional lair. Comfortable as a human, she owns houses throughout the city and beyond, including residences for her other personas. If she is discovered, she can remain in the city in such a residence and cut her losses.

As greedy as a red dragon, Jalanvaloss justifies her behavior on the grounds that she grants everyone the opportunity for success. She dreams of founding a kingdom where she will rule as queen, so her people might live without fear; however, she likes her current arrangements and does little to disrupt her lifestyle.

JALANVALOSS'S TACTICS

Jalanvaloss is a schemer, not a warrior. When she must fight, she chooses the time and place.

She opens combat by using *change shape* and smashing enemies with her *breath weapon*. If most foes avoid becoming dazed, she spends an action point to use *frightful presence*. Otherwise, she spends an action point to use *scattergloom*. While waiting for her *breath weapon* to recharge, she uses *dimension*

step to gain an advantageous position and hits her enemies with *steel sting*. When near defeat, she uses *illusory double* to create a distraction and slip away undetected.

ENCOUNTER GROUPS

Jalanvaloss has connections throughout her city and calls on assistance from a variety of adventuring groups that owe her favors. To protect her lairs, she keeps battle guardians in top fighting form.

Level 20 Encounter (XP 14,800)
✦ 3 battle guardians (level 17 controller, *MM* 149)
✦ Jalanvaloss (level 18 solo skirmisher)

WILLIAM O'CONNOR

JALANVALOSS'S ENEMIES

Only when enemies threaten to ruin Jalanvaloss's way of life—when she reaches the brink of collapse—does she take dragon form and attack directly. Characters might incur such ire by acting on behalf of a third party that has a grudge against Jalanvaloss, by provoking Jalanvaloss as a side effect of a quest, or by trying to topple the dragon from her position.

In the distant, frigid north, the scattered communities have long lived in fear of a vicious, barbaric tribe the natives have named the Talons of Winter. For long generations, the Talons emerged but rarely, guided by their frost giant masters to raid and slaughter. But now, the tribe grants its fealty, its devotion, even its worship to a new lord, a draconic horror named Niflung dwelling deep in the nearby glacier, a creature whose only purpose is to see his "children" grow strong—at the expense of everyone else.

Niflung, who has accepted the title of god given him by the Talons of Winter, looks much like other cobalt dragons. Observation of the dragon in motion, however, or a close study of his fearsome form, reveals peculiar anomalies. His limbs, his neck, his tail, and his wings seem unduly long in proportion to his body—not dramatically so, just enough to give him an unnatural gait and a subtly disturbing silhouette. His scales hang loosely on his body, occasionally jutting out at odd angles, as though he had spent ravenous years starving inside his own shell. And perhaps he once did, for his obsession with proving his own strength, and that of his "worshipers," leads him to extremes that even other cobalt dragons would consider excessive.

Niflung never holds entirely still; when he is conversing with others, at rest, or even asleep, his tail twitches, his claws flex, his jaw clenches. When he speaks with other creatures, his attention seems frequently to wander, yet he appears fully capable of following the flow and details of the conversation.

NIFLUNG LORE

History DC 15: In the frozen north, a cobalt dragon named Niflung has recently emerged from the glacier called the Road of Sleet. He has taken over the Talons of Winter, a fearsome tribe of shifters and giants, and he has increased their raids against civilized communities fivefold.

History DC 20: What occurred in Niflung's life before he emerged from a long slumber within the caves of the glacier is unclear. Something, however, has made him different from other cobalt dragons. His abilities, although similar, differ in several profound respects, and his obsession with strength and dominance crosses the line into megalomania.

Niflung is not unwilling to speak to visitors, but they must show the proper deference. Any insult—any perceived insult—to his strength or abilities results in an immediate, enraged attack.

History DC 25: Niflung basks in the adulation of the Talons of Winter, using them to expand his own domain, but he also seems genuinely determined to make them as strong as they can be. He truly believes (or at least seems to believe) that he's doing

what's best for his "children," and that he can guide them to a position of strength and dominance in the region. He allows outsiders to attack the tribe, hoping to strengthen them through combat, but he grows enraged if an enemy takes what he considers "unfair advantage" when battling them. (What that "unfair advantage" might be varies with Niflung's mood, but he does object strongly to the use of powerful fire magic against his tribe.)

Niflung	Level 20 Solo Controller
Elder cobalt dragon	
Huge natural magical beast (dragon)	XP 14,000

Initiative +14   **Senses** Perception +19; darkvision

Aura of Chill Mist (Cold) aura 2; each creature that enters the aura or starts its turn there takes 10 cold damage. The ground in the aura is difficult terrain, and the squares of the aura are lightly obscured.

HP 772; **Bloodied** 386; see also *bloodied breath*

AC 34; **Fortitude** 34, **Reflex** 30, **Will** 31

Resist 25 cold

Saving Throws +5

Speed 8 (ice walk), fly 10 (hover), overland flight 15

Action Points 2

⊕ **Bite** (standard; at-will) ✦ **Cold**
Reach 3; +25 vs. AC; 2d6 + 8 damage, and ongoing 10 cold damage (save ends).

⊕ **Claw** (standard at-will)
Reach 3; +25 vs. AC; 1d10 + 8 damage.

↯ **Niflung's Pounce** (standard; at-will)
Niflung makes a bite attack, shifts 2 squares, and then makes two claw attacks against a different target. If both claw attacks hit, Niflung pushes the target 5 squares, and the target is knocked prone. Niflung can push a creature restrained by his own breath weapon.

↯ **Wing Crush** (immediate reaction, when an adjacent enemy hits Niflung with a melee attack; at-will)
+24 vs. Reflex; 2d6 + 8 damage, and the target is pushed 3 squares and falls prone. Niflung can push and knock prone a creature restrained by its own breath weapon.

⬳ **Breath Weapon** (standard; recharge ⚄ ⚅) ✦ **Cold**
Close blast 5; +24 vs. Fortitude; 4d8 + 8 cold damage, and the target is restrained and takes ongoing 10 cold damage (save ends both). *Aftereffect:* The target is slowed (save ends). *Miss:* Half damage.

⬳ **Bloodied Breath** (free, when first bloodied; encounter)
Breath weapon recharges, and Niflung uses it.

⬳ **Chilling Presence** (standard; encounter) ✦ **Cold, Fear**
Close burst 10; targets enemies; +24 vs. Will; the target is stunned until the end of Niflung's next turn and gains vulnerable 10 cold (save ends).

Savage Opportunist
Niflung gains a +2 bonus to attack rolls, and deals 1d8 extra damage, when making a bite, claw, or *wing crush* attack against an enemy that is immobilized, slowed, or granting combat advantage to Niflung.

Alignment Unaligned		**Languages** Common, Draconic
Skills Athletics +23, Endurance +22, Intimidate +20		
Str 27 (+18)	**Dex** 19 (+14)	**Wis** 19 (+14)
Con 25 (+17)	**Int** 14 (+12)	**Cha** 20 (+15)

NIFLUNG'S TACTICS

Niflung's array of abilities differs from those of other cobalt dragons—perhaps due to the same experiences that altered his physical form. Despite his many controlling abilities, he prefers to fight from the midst of his enemies, moving in close, engaging them in melee, and allowing his aura to wreak havoc. He is not shy about using his *breath weapon*, but unlike other dragons, he prefers to save his *chilling presence* (his equivalent of *frightful presence*) until he's surrounded by strikers and defenders. He despises showing weakness, but if he's severely wounded and most allies are dead, self-preservation inspires him to flee.

ENCOUNTER GROUPS

Encounters with the Talons of Winter don't normally involve Niflung. Only when invaders come near his lair on the glacier, or when he's accompanying his worshipers in battle against a truly devastating foe, does he participate.

Level 22 Encounter (XP 21,200)
✦ 3 frost giants (level 17 brute, *Monster Manual 2* page 122)
✦ 1 ice archon rimehammer (level 19 soldier, *MM 20*)
✦ Niflung (level 20 solo controller)

HISTORY AND DOMAIN

Deep in the frozen regions sometimes called the Frostfell, one particular glacier stretches in a near straight line from a towering row of mountain peaks. Called the Road of Sleet, this glacier has long been known as the home of various fearsome creatures, including the barbarian tribe called the Talons of Winter. This tribe consists primarily of heavily furred shifters, far more vicious than their civilized cousins. The tribe is—or rather, was—ruled by a frost giant jarl (chieftain) named Eilchost. Eilchost was a shaman of some sort, though tales differ as to whether he devoted his worship to one of the primordials or to the demon prince Kostchtchie.

In recent years, the tribe has devoted itself to the dragon Niflung, whom they call the god in the glacier; Eilchost has become his lieutenant and high priest. Precisely why the frost giants chose to dub Niflung a god—a title that they bestowed upon him, not one he claimed on his own—is unclear. Perhaps Eilchost believed him to have been sent by whatever power the tribe previously worshiped. Whatever the case, Niflung's presence has had a profound effect on the tribe. Once, the Talons of Winter were known for their brutal but sporadic raids against the other communities that existed at the base of the glacier; now, those attacks have grown far more frequent, and spread far wider, than ever before.

Today, the tribe consists of a wide array of shifters (ranging from those detailed in the *Monster Manual* to far tougher, more advanced specimens), a number of frost giants and frost giant ice shapers related to Eilchost by blood or marriage, and a pack of trained winterclaw owlbears.

The Road of Sleet is as much of a mystery as the dragon who came from it. Legends say it has a great many tunnels throughout its frigid center and that an entire ancient city lies within, most of it crushed but portions perfectly preserved by the ice.

Note: This information is available with a DC 20 History check.

CHIPPY

SOME DRAGONS—PARTICULARLY SILVERS and benefi-cent golds—are great and noble protectors of lesser races. They might even grow too enamored, bringing about tragedies such as that of the dragon D'Argent, called Silvara.

In draconic form, Silvara looks like other silver dragons of her age. Her scales gleam, and her broad, muscled wings tense into great shields. Only her sor-rowful eyes suggest something unusual about her.

In her elf form, which she prefers, Silvara is a silver-haired woman. She wears tribal garb or leather armor.

dragons. She is particularly fond of elves and eladrin, because, like her, they live long lives relative to other humanoids.

History or Nature DC 24: In her elf form, Sil-vara fell in love with an elf warrior-prince who fought alongside a band of heroes against Tiamat's armies. The prince returned her affections until circum-stances forced Silvara to reveal her true nature.

For a while, the pair remained together, despite the prince's inner turmoil as he sought to reconcile his conflicting emotions and to keep Silvara as an ally against Tiamat. In the end, he asked Silvara to depart.

Silvara still mourns the loss. In her battles against evil, her motivations conflict. Does she seek to protect

Silvara	Level 24 Solo Soldier
Elder silver dragon	
Huge natural magical beast (dragon, shapechanger)	XP 30,250

Initiative +19   **Senses** Perception +23; darkvision
HP 908; **Bloodied** 454; see also *bloodied breath*
AC 40; **Fortitude** 37, **Reflex** 36, **Will** 36
Resist 30 cold
Saving Throws +2
Speed 8, fly 8 (hover), overland flight 15
Action Points 2

⊕ **Bite** (standard; at-will)
    Reach 3; +31 vs. AC; 4d6 + 9 damage.
⊕ **Silver Claw** (standard; at-will)
    Reach 3; +31 vs. AC; 3d6 + 9 damage.
✦ **Dragon's Onslaught** (standard; at-will)
    Silvara makes a claw attack against each enemy in reach.
✦ **Wing Slice** (immediate reaction, when an enemy attacks Silvara while flanking her or attacks one of Silvara's allies; at-will)
    Reach 3; +31 vs. AC; 3d6 + 9 damage.
⟵ **Breath Weapon** (standard; recharge ⚄ ⚅) ✦ **Cold**
    Close blast 5; +29 vs. Reflex; 3d8 + 9 cold damage, and the target is slowed and gains vulnerable 5 to all damage (save ends both). *Miss:* Half damage.
⟵ **Bloodied Breath** (free, when first bloodied; encounter)
    Breath weapon recharges, and Silvara uses it.
⟵ **Frightful Presence** (standard; encounter) ✦ **Fear**
    Close burst 10; targets enemies; +29 vs. Will; the target is stunned until the end of Silvara's next turn. *Aftereffect:* The target takes a –2 penalty to attack rolls (save ends).
Enfolding Wings (immediate interrupt, when an enemy within 3 squares of Silvara attacks an ally that is also within 3 squares; at-will)
    The target of the attack slides to a space adjacent to Silvara, and the attack targets Silvara instead.
Change Shape (minor; at-will) ✦ **Polymorph**
    Silvara alters her form to appear as a unique female elf (see "Change Shape," MM2 216).

Alignment Good   **Languages** Common, Draconic, Elven
Skills Arcana +22, Bluff +24, Diplomacy +24, Insight +23

Str 28 (+21)	Dex 25 (+19)	Wis 22 (+18)
Con 27 (+20)	Int 20 (+17)	Cha 25 (+19)

Equipment leather armor, hunting club, obsidian dagger

SILVARA LORE

History or Nature DC 16: A silver dragon named Silvara has dwelt among mortals for generations. She prefers the company of humanoids to that of other

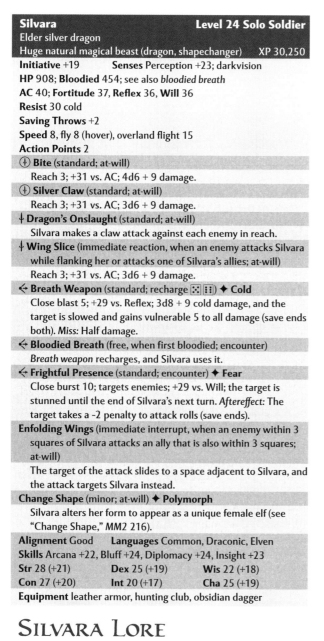

TOMÁS GIORELLO

the innocent, to impress and win back her lover, or to end her pain in death?

History or Nature DC 29: Silvara sporadically battles against Tiamat's forces (including Cyan Bloodbane; see *Draconomicon: Chromatic Dragons*, page 234). She has protected several elven communities and the tomb of an ancient hero, replete with relics. She helped to convince metallic dragons to join Bahamut's side rather than sit out the war. Evil chromatic dragons hate her for her role in the conflict.

History or Nature DC 34: Since the dissolution of her relationship with her lover, Silvara rarely joins in the conflict between good and evil—and then only in her elf form or in the form of a human knight. She reveals her true nature only in desperate circumstances.

"Silvara" is a name she frequently uses. Her birth name transliterates to Common as "D'Argent." Her first elven name, taken when she joined a primitive elven community, was "Silvart." Called "Silvara" by more civilized elves when the tribes began to interact, she adopted the name to avoid association with savagery. Finally, in her guise as a human knight, she answers to the name "Arlena Plata."

SILVARA'S TACTICS

Silvara in dragon form is less brutal and slower to attack than other silver dragons. Her time among mortals has rendered her more interested in protecting her allies than in slaying her enemies. She remains near her allies, guarding them with *wing slice* attacks and *enfolding wings*. She unleashes her *breath weapon* against foes that attack en masse.

As long as her allies are in danger, Silvara does not retreat from battle. If her allies escape, she flees with them. If she has no one to protect, Silvara sees little need for combat.

ENCOUNTER GROUPS

Silvara favors solitude, where she can suffer alone and mourn what might have been, but she fights only alongside others. Any champion of good or of Bahamut is a potential ally.

Level 25 Encounter (XP 39,850)
+ 3 ghaeles of winter (level 21 artillery, *MM* 103)
+ Silvara (level 24 solo soldier)

SILVARA'S ORIGINS

Silvara appears throughout the DRAGONLANCE series of novels. In her first appearance, in *Dragons of Winter Night*, she poses as one of the Kagonesti, the primitive "wild elves," and falls in love with the elf Gilthanas, ruler of the Qualinesti elves. During the war with Takhisis (Tiamat) and through the ages and trilogies to follow, she reappears as a tragic champion of good. In a later novel, Silvara and Gilthanas reunite, but the information given here predates that event.

The following text is an excerpt from *Dragons of Winter Night*, in which Silvara reveals her true nature.

"Hold the torch there . . ." she instructed, guiding his hand so that the light blazed right before her. "Now—look at my shadow on the wall behind me," she said in trembling tones.

The tomb was silent; only the sputtering of the flaming torch made any sound. Silvara's shadow sprang into life on the cold stone wall behind her. The companions stared at it and—for an instant—none of them could say a word.

The shadow Silvara cast upon the wall was not the shadow of a young elfmaid.

It was the shadow of a dragon.

"You're the dragon!" Laurana said in shocked disbelief. She laid her hand on her sword, but Theros stopped her.

"No!" he said suddenly. "I remember. That old man—" He looked at his arm. "Now I remember. He used to come into the Inn of the Last Home! He was dressed differently. He wasn't a mage, but it was him! I'll swear it! He told stories to the children. Stories about good dragons. Gold dragons and—"

"Silver dragons," Silvara said, looking at Theros. "I am a silver dragon. My sister was the Silver Dragon who loved Huma and fought the final great battle with him—"

"No!" Gilthanas flung the torch to the ground. It lay flickering for a moment at his feet, then he stamped on it angrily, putting out its light. Silvara, watching him with sad eyes, reached out her hand to comfort him.

Gilthanas shrank from her touch, staring at her in horror.

Silvara lowered her hand slowly. Sighing gently, she nodded. "I understand," she murmured. "I'm sorry."

Gilthanas began to shake, then doubled over in agony. Putting his strong arms around him, Theros led Gilthanas to a bench and covered him with his cloak.

"I'll be all right," Gilthanas mumbled. "Just leave me alone, let me think. This is madness! It's all a nightmare. A dragon!" He closed his eyes tightly as if he could blot out their sight forever. "A dragon . . ." he whispered brokenly. Theros patted him gently, then returned to the others.

"Where are the rest of the good dragons?" Theros asked. "The old man said there were many. Silver dragons, gold dragons—"

"There are many of us," Silvara answered reluctantly.

"Like the silver dragon we saw in Ice Wall!" Laurana said. "It was a good dragon. If there are many of you, band together! Help us fight the evil dragons!"

"No!" Silvara cried fiercely. Her blue eyes flared, and Laurana fell back a pace before her anger.

"Why not?"

"I cannot tell you." Silvara's hands clenched nervously.

IN THE SKIES ABOVE CIVILIZATION and wilderness alike, an astounding sight floats amid the clouds: an enormous oval island of stone covered in jagged peaks. The Floating Mountain, as it is called, is the home of Valamaradace, a gold dragon who has become far more interested in vengeance against the forces of evil than in the safety and well-being of the lesser creatures she used to zealously protect.

The Queen of the Floating Mountain is longer than most gold dragons of her age (not that there are many to compare her to), but she has substantially less mass. Valamaradace is more serpentine in build than most other golds, and she seems to wind her way through the air like a snake when she flies. Her claws are long and narrow, looking almost like humanoid fingers, and grant her impressive manual dexterity and grace when casting rituals.

As with other ancient golds, her scales seem to gleam with an inner radiance. Her eyes do as well, with glowing slitted pupils that almost blend into the golden orbs that house them.

VALAMARADACE LORE

History or Nature DC 28: For long centuries, the Floating Mountain hovered over, or near, the community of Silverymoon (or any other city appropriate to your campaign). Valamaradace and her consort—a silver dragon whom the people below called "Silverwing"—served as guardians and protectors of the region, and they frequently collaborated with the city's ruler, a potent spellcaster in her own right.

Initially, Valamaradace saw herself as the queen of the region, as a guardian responsible for ensuring the healthy growth of all creatures in her domain. She sought to harm none, to understand all living beings, and to use her shapeshifting to better appreciate their lives. Eventually, however, her interest in her domain waned. She was more interested in countering possible evils than in safeguarding the good of any particular creatures, and she had come to think that she had learned all that the humanoids could teach her. Silverwing remained more involved with the people. Over the years, he grew more protective of them while Valamaradace grew more detached. Her focus shifted to her magic and to the spread of evil elsewhere in the world.

Valamaradace is an extremely skilled caster. It is said that her spellbooks hold every ritual known to mortals and several that no human, eladrin, or gnome has ever heard of. Legend claims that her skills at divination and scrying are so great that no enemy can possibly take her unawares.

History or Nature DC 33: Over the years, the two dragons grew apart as their interests and feelings for the people below diverged. The ruler of the city below, and all the other mortals Valamaradace knew, grew old and died. Their heirs proved ever less impressive in the gold dragon's eyes. Slowly but steadily, the Dragon Queen's interest in those below her waned further. Finally, when the region was rocked by a catastrophe that shook the foundations of the earth and of magic itself, Valamaradace dedicated herself to what she called "a greater purpose" than the protection of a few insignificant lives. She and Silverwing went their separate ways (though they still cooperate on occasion), and Valamaradace allowed the Floating Mountain to drift free so she could scour the land in search of great, world-shaking threats.

Valamaradace	Level 30 Solo Artillery
Ancient gold dragon	
Gargantuan natural magical beast (dragon)	XP 95,000

Initiative +22   **Senses** Perception +27; darkvision

Searing Flame (fire, radiant) aura 2; each enemy that starts its turn within the aura takes 20 fire and radiant damage and takes a -2 penalty to attack rolls until the start of its next turn.

HP 1,088; **Bloodied** 544; see also *bloodied breath*

AC 42; **Fortitude** 40, **Reflex** 44, **Will** 42

Resist fire 30, radiant 20

Saving Throws +5

Speed 8, fly 12 (hover), overland flight 15

Action Points 2

⊕ **Bite** (standard; at-will) ✦ **Fire, Radiant**
Reach 4; +35 vs. AC; 1d8 + 13 damage plus 2d8 fire and radiant damage.

⊕ **Claw** (standard; at-will)
Reach 4; +35 vs. AC; 2d8 + 13 damage.

⊗ **Golden Light** (standard; at will) ✦ **Fire, Radiant, Teleportation**
Ranged 20; +35 vs. Reflex; 2d8 + 13 fire and radiant damage, and Valamaradace teleports the target 4 squares.

↗ **Curtain of Light** (free, when an enemy starts its turn within 5 squares of Valamaradace; at-will)
Valamaradace uses *golden light* against the triggering enemy.

↗ **Twin Gleaming** (standard; at will)
Valamaradace makes two *golden light* attacks.

↞ **Breath Weapon** (standard; recharge ⚅ ⚅) ✦ **Fire, Radiant**
Close blast 7; +35 vs. Reflex; 4d10 + 13 fire and radiant damage, and the target is blinded (save ends). *Miss:* Half damage.

↞ **Bloodied Breath** (free, when first bloodied; encounter)
Breath weapon recharges, and Valamaradace uses it.

Beguiling Light (minor; encounter)
Until the end of Valamaradace's next turn, any creature that takes radiant damage from her attacks is dazed (save ends).

↗ **Searing Mark** (minor; recharge ⚅ ⚅) ✦ **Fire, Radiant**
Ranged 20; +35 vs. Fortitude; the target gains vulnerable 20 fire and vulnerable 20 radiant (save ends).

Change Shape (minor; at-will) ✦ **Polymorph**
Valamaradace can alter her physical form to take on the appearance of any Large or smaller humanoid or beast (see "Change Shape," MM2 216).

Alignment Unaligned	**Languages** Common, Draconic, Elven, Supernal

Skills Arcana +33, Diplomacy +29, History +33, Intimidate +29

Str 25 (+22)	**Dex** 24 (+22)	**Wis** 24 (+22)
Con 24 (+22)	**Int** 36 (+28)	**Cha** 28 (+24)

History or Nature DC 38: Valamaradace's efforts to destroy what she considers to be great threats—and none are quite certain what her criteria might be—do not take into account the good of other, lesser creatures. She is willing to obliterate innocent bystanders if doing so is the most effective way to defeat an enemy, and her zeal to defeat powerful tyrants has left more than one community in the throes of anarchy afterward. She expects all creatures to obey her without question, and those that do not risk being lumped in with her enemies in her mind.

Valamaradace rarely assumes humanoid form anymore, but when she must, she most often travels as an elf by the name of Targarda.

VALAMARADACE'S TACTICS

Valamaradace prefers to devastate her enemies from a distance. Indeed, over many years—and many mystical endeavors—her abilities have diverged from those of other gold dragons, allowing her to do just that. She never engages her foes in melee if she can avoid it, partly because of her combat abilities, and partly because she wants to avoid "sullying herself" by close contact with lesser creatures.

She uses *beguiling light* and *searing mark* early in the fight to make her *golden light* and *twin gleaming*

attacks more effective. She holds her *breath weapon* in reserve for foes that manage to move near her despite her *curtain of light*.

Valamaradace, despite her sense of innate superiority, is willing to flee combat if a foe proves too difficult or impossible to keep at a distance. She then uses her mastery of rituals to study that foe and better prepare her for their next encounter.

When you run Valamaradace in combat, portray her as though she already has a full understanding of the characters' abilities. The Dragon Queen is a master of almost every ritual known—including divinations and scrying—and unless her enemies have been incredibly secretive, odds are that she has learned of them and studied them from afar.

ENCOUNTER GROUPS

Valamaradace fights alongside any creatures willing to follow her orders and swear fealty to her cause. She prefers allies that can move in close, allowing her to keep her distance from the fray.

Level 32 Encounter (XP 143,000)
✦ Valamaradace (level 30 solo artillery)
✦ 2 dragonborn champions (level 26 soldier, MM 87)
✦ 1 godforged colossus (level 29 elite brute, MM 44)

THE ORIGINS OF VALAMARADACE

Valamaradace first appeared in the FORGOTTEN REALMS campaign setting as the "Dragon Queen of Silverymoon." Allied with Alustriel, Valamaradace and Silverwing battled against many evil forces of that setting, including (among others) the Cult of the Dragon and the Zhentarim. However, Valamaradace rarely featured in these efforts, remaining in the background while her consort and Alustriel performed

most of the great deeds. With the changes discussed here, however, Valamaradace becomes a far more active figure and can be the driving force behind many an adventure.

Valamaradace's story was written to fit into any campaign setting. If you choose to use her in Faerûn, however, the magical and natural catastrophe mentioned in the Lore section likely refers to the Spellplague.

KEREM BEYIT

ELITE DRAGONS

When a party fights a dragon, it's usually the entirety of the combat. But what should you do when you want to have the dragon accompanied by other creatures? You could use a dragon of a much lower level than the party, but that might result in a combat in which the dragon is mostly ineffectual–the dragon's attack bonuses and defenses will be too low to threaten the party. In these cases, you need an elite dragon.

Creating an elite dragon is similar to applying a template, with a few extra steps. Powers need to be simplified to tone down the dragon's strength. First, the dragon's ability to recharge a *breath weapon* in combat requires more tracking than an elite creature should require, so *breath weapon* becomes an encounter power. The second aspect that needs to be removed is the attack that occurs as an interrupt, minor, or move action; this ability is what allows a solo creature to have an extra attack aside from its standard action.

Prerequisite: Solo dragon

Elite Dragon	Elite Any
(Dragon)	XP by level

Saving Throws +2 (instead of +5)
Action Points 1 (instead of 2)
Hit Points 16 + (Constitution score × 2) + (level × 16)
← Breath Weapon (standard; encounter) ✦ **(keywords unchanged)**
  Use the original *breath weapon*, but change it to an encounter power rather than a recharge power.
Nonstandard Attack Power
  Remove an interrupt attack power, minor attack power, or move attack power from the dragon (see the tables).
Healing and Self-Damaging Powers
  Adjust powers that heal the dragon or cause it to damage itself to half the original value. (For example, a young bronze dragon would regain 41 hit points instead of 82 hit points using *restorative dive*.)

Consider reducing the size of the dragon to indicate that it is a weaker member of the kind, especially if you intend to include the full-strength dragon as a solo encounter at another point during the adventure. Also, this system isn't perfect, so make a reality check to ensure that the monster's abilities are reasonable for its level and the party's capabilities.

CHANGING DEFENSES

Monsters from before *Monster Manual 2* were created using a slightly different method, which gave elites and solos higher defenses than other monsters. If you're making an elite dragon based on one from the *Monster Manual, Draconomicon: Chromatic Dragons,* or a different older source, consider reducing its defenses so they're close to the values given in *Dungeon Master's Guide 2*. In a pinch, just reduce all the dragon's defenses by 2.

CHROMATIC ADJUSTMENTS

Variety	Power Removed	Variety	Power Removed
Black	*Tail slash*	Green	*Tail sweep*
Blue	*Wingclap* (ancient only)	Purple	*Dominating gaze*
		Red	*Tail strike*
Brown	*Sand spray*	White	–
Gray	*Warding tail*		

METALLIC ADJUSTMENTS

Variety	Power Removed
Adamantine	*Wing buffet*
Brass	*Wing buffet*
Bronze	*Wing smash*
Cobalt	*Wing flurry*
Copper	*Cutwing step*
Gold	*Fiery wing riposte*
Iron	*Wing block*
Mercury	*Quick snap*
Mithral	*Wing buffet*
Orium	*Tail coil* (elder or ancient only)
Silver	*Wing slice*
Steel	*Wing scatter*

SAMPLE ELITE DRAGON

Turning a young iron dragon into an elite requires lowering its saving throw bonus and action points, reducing its hit points to 134, and cutting out the *wing block* immediate reaction attack power.

Elite Young Iron Dragon	Level 5 Elite Lurker
Large natural magical beast (dragon)	XP 400

Initiative +8   **Senses** Perception +8; darkvision
HP 134; **Bloodied** 67; see also *bloodied breath*
AC 19; **Fortitude** 19, **Reflex** 17, **Will** 16
Resist 15 lightning
Saving Throws +2
Speed 8, fly 8 (hover), overland flight 10
Action Points 1
① Bite (standard; at-will) ✦ **Lightning**
  Reach 2; +10 vs. AC; 2d8 + 4 damage plus 1d8 lightning damage.
① Claw (standard; at-will)
  Melee 2; +10 vs. AC; 1d10 + 4 damage.
✦ Double Attack (standard; at-will)
  The dragon makes two *claw* attacks.
← Breath Weapon (standard; encounter) ✦ **Lightning**
  Close blast 5; +6 vs. Reflex; 2d6 + 4 lightning damage, and the dragon pulls the target 3 squares. *Miss:* Half damage.
← Bloodied Breath (free, when first bloodied; encounter)
  Breath weapon recharges, and the dragon uses it.
← Frightful Presence (standard; encounter) ✦ **Fear**
  Close burst 5; targets enemies; +6 vs. Will; the target is stunned until the end of the dragon's next turn. *Aftereffect:* The target takes a -2 penalty to attack rolls (save ends).
Alignment Unaligned   **Languages** Common, Draconic
Skills Acrobatics +9, Athletics +8, Stealth +9

Str 13 (+3)	**Dex** 14 (+4)	**Wis** 12 (+3)
Con 19 (+6)	**Int** 12 (+3)	**Cha** 11 (+2)

ALTERNATIVE POWERS

The statistics blocks in this book and in *Monster Manual 2* show common, iconic powers of metallic dragons. Dragons might develop other powers through training, environment, or magic, allowing you to create surprising adversaries.

SHAPECHANGING DRAGONS

Mercury and steel dragons are natural shapechangers, but other metallic dragons, particularly golds and silvers, can also learn to change shape. Even a few chromatics have this ability.

Adding *change shape* (see *Monster Manual 2*, page 216) to a dragon does not dramatically increase the dragon's power, but shapechanging can serve your story. If you want to have a shapechanging dragon, you need not replace another power with it. If you want the characters to have a chance of being able to discern the dragon's true nature, you can limit the ability or have the dragon retain a hint of its draconic appearance. (Also see the "Unmasking the Dragon" skill challenge on page 50.)

ADAMANTINE DRAGON POWERS

Masters of surface caves and the caverns of the Underdark, adamantine dragons are tyrants that bring lightning to the depths. The following powers bring out their brash and destructive nature.

ADAMANTINE CHARGE

By forgoing its ranged attack prowess, an elder or ancient adamantine dragon can boost its melee attack. This power replaces *painful resonance*.

⊹ Adamantine Charge (standard; at-will)
> The dragon makes a charge attack: level + 5 vs. Fortitude; 1d10 + one-half level damage, and the target is knocked prone. The target cannot stand while the dragon remains adjacent to it.

PUNISHING THUNDER

An adamantine dragon can magically bind thunder from its breath to its scales and unleash the thunder when struck. This power replaces the "Effect" section of an adamantine dragon's *breath weapon*.

⬅ Punishing Thunder (free, after using *breath weapon*) ✦ **Thunder**
> Close burst 5; each enemy in the burst is marked by the dragon until the end of the dragon's next turn. Until the end of the dragon's next turn, any creature that hits the dragon with a melee attack takes 10 thunder damage.

BRASS DRAGON POWERS

Despite their curiosity, brass dragons avoid great pain and do not tolerate insolence. The following powers allow brass dragons to punish anyone that crosses those bounds.

BURNING BLOOD

A brass dragon can increase the temperature of an attacker's blood. This power replaces *wing slam*.

Burning Blood (free, when the dragon takes damage from a melee attack; at-will) ✦ **Fire**
> The attacker takes ongoing fire damage equal to 5 + one-half the dragon's level (save ends).

FIRE CLOAK

An elder or ancient brass dragon can gain a protective fire aura after using a flame attack. This power replaces *ignite*.

Fire Cloak (free, after hitting with *breath weapon* or *fire stream*; at-will) ✦ **Fire**
> Until the end of its next turn, the dragon is hidden, and any creature that attacks it takes 10 fire damage.

BRONZE DRAGON POWERS

Bronze dragons do not suffer fools. A bronze's great sense of self-worth grants its words the power to twist thoughts or control elements.

IMPERIOUS COMMAND

Bronze dragons that want to subjugate others develop the following power instead of *frightful presence*. Any bronze can manifest this power, but young bronzes rarely do so.

⊹ Imperious Command (immediate interrupt, when an enemy damages the dragon; recharges if *imperious command* misses) ✦ **Charm**
> Level + 3 vs. Will; the dragon takes half damage from the attack, and the triggering enemy is dominated until the end of the dragon's next turn.

WATER NIMBUS

Elder and ancient dragons can surround themselves with magical water that hangs in the air. This power replaces *pinning claw*.

⬅ Water Nimbus (minor; recharge ⚄ ⚅) ✦ **Zone**
> Close burst 3; the dragon creates a zone of water in its space and in the burst. Any creature within the zone except the dragon gains vulnerable 5 lightning and uses its swim speed or Athletics (DC 15) to move. If the dragon is ancient, increase the vulnerability to 10, and the Athletics DC to 20.

COBALT DRAGON POWERS

Cold and sullen, a cobalt dragon believes that good fences make the best neighbors. It can form its breath into a frigid wall or draw upon dark powers of the Shadowfell.

ICE WALL

An ancient cobalt can shape a wall of ice from its breath. This power replaces *rimedeath fog*.

> ✳ **Ice Wall** (minor; encounter) ✦ **Cold, Conjuration**
> Area wall 10 within 10; the dragon conjures a solid wall of ice 10 squares long and 10 squares high. The wall blocks line of sight and prevents movement through it. Any creature that starts its turn adjacent to the wall takes 15 cold damage and is slowed until the end of its turn.

SHADOW HAIL

Cobalt dragons that live in the Shadowfell can mix their innate cold powers with necrotic energy from the realm of the dead. This power replaces *savage mauling*.

> ✳ **Shadow Hail** (standard; recharges when first bloodied) ✦ **Cold, Necrotic**
> Area burst 2 within 20; level + 5 vs. Fortitude and Reflex; if the attack hits Fortitude, one-half level necrotic damage, and the target takes a -2 penalty to attack rolls (save ends); if the attack hits Reflex, one-half level cold damage, and the target is knocked prone.

COPPER DRAGON POWERS

Copper dragons have tricks up their proverbial sleeves. The following powers allow coppers to stop foes in their tracks . . . or to outsmart them.

BREATH WEAPON: ACIDIC MORASS

A copper dragon's *breath weapon* can melt the earth into acidic mud. This power replaces the dragon's normal *breath weapon*.

> ⇠ **Breath Weapon** (standard; recharge ⚃ ⚁) ✦ **Acid, Zone**
> Close blast 5; level + 1 vs. Reflex; acid damage equal to that of the dragon's normal breath weapon. The blast creates a zone of acidic morass until the end of the encounter. The squares within the zone are difficult terrain. Any creature that starts its turn within the zone takes acid damage equal to one-half the dragon's level and must make an Acrobatics or Athletics check (DC 10 + one-half the dragon's level) or become immobilized until the start of its next turn. The creature can attempt another Athletics check as a move action.

CAUSTIC ESCAPE

When a copper dragon moves, it can leave behind an acidic shadow of itself. This power replaces *cutwing step*.

> **Caustic Escape** (immediate reaction, when an enemy moves adjacent to the dragon; recharge ⚄ ⚁) ✦ **Acid, Zone**
> The dragon flies its speed. The space it left becomes a zone of acidic mist until the end of the encounter. The zone is difficult terrain and lightly obscured. Any creature that enters the zone or starts its turn there takes 5 acid damage. For a dragon of 11th level or higher, the damage increases to 10, and for a dragon of level 21 or higher, the damage increases to 15.

GOLD DRAGON POWERS

Monarchs and other regents revere the gold dragon for its majesty, strength, fortitude, and luck. The following powers enhance a gold dragon's defenses or luck.

GOLD BARRIER

A gold dragon can learn to manifest a golden sphere of protection instead of learning to counterattack. This power replaces *fiery wing riposte*.

> **Gold Barrier** (immediate reaction, when hit by an adjacent creature; at-will)
> The dragon gains resistance equal to one-half its level to all damage until the start of its next turn. If the triggering attack scored a critical hit, increase the resistance by 5.

TREASURED LUCK

An adult or older gold dragon can hamper its foes' luck. This power replaces *burning tomb*.

> ✳ **Treasured Luck** (minor; recharge ⚁)
> Area burst 2 within 20; targets enemies; level + 3 vs. Will; the first time the target attacks the dragon each round, the target rolls d20 twice and takes the lower result (save ends). If that attack misses, the target grants combat advantage to the dragon on the dragon's next attack.

IRON DRAGON POWERS

The ill-tempered iron dragons value their privacy. The pricklier ones release arsenals of iron spikes or blinding breath upon creatures that dare to attack.

IRON-SPARK LIGHTNING

An iron dragon can diffuse its lightning breath to create a blinding flash of light. This power replaces *frightful presence*.

> ⬧ **Iron-Spark Lightning** (standard, or minor if *breath weapon* is available; at-will) ✦ **Lightning, Radiant**
> Ranged 20; level + 2 vs. Reflex; 1d6 + one-half level lightning and radiant damage, and the target is blinded until the end of the dragon's next turn.

➹ **Mercury Tendril** (minor 1/round; at-will) ✦ **Poison**
Ranged 10/20; level + 3 vs. Reflex; 1d6 + one-half level poison damage, and the dragon slides the target 1 square.

MITHRAL DRAGON POWERS

Mortal concerns of space and distance do not confine mithral dragons. These astral creatures can temporarily phase out of existence, gaining strength from mysteries that lie beyond.

INTERPLANAR STASIS

A mithral dragon can become trapped between the world and the Astral Sea and turn into a ghostlike figure frozen in time. This power replaces *wing buffet*.

Interplanar Stasis (minor; recharges when first bloodied) ✦ **Healing**
The dragon goes into stasis and is insubstantial, restrained, and weakened. If the dragon is in stasis at the start of its turn, it regains 2 hit points per level and is then no longer in stasis.

MITHRAL MISTS

An elder or ancient mithral dragon can teleport other creatures and rearrange a battle. This power replaces *mithral prescience*.

⬅ **Mithral Mists** (minor; encounter) ✦ **Teleportation**
Close burst 3; level + 5 vs. Will; the target is teleported to a square within 10 squares of the dragon. *Effect:* The dragon teleports 10 squares.

ORIUM DRAGON POWERS

Reclusive masters, orium dragons sit among the ruins of lost empires. From ancient stories, they reproduce powers once used by dragons of old.

TAIL SWIPE

An elder or ancient orium dragon can learn to attack with its tail more effectively than with its bite. This power replaces the dragon's bite attack. *Draconic fury* also uses this power instead of the bite attack.

⬅ **Tail Swipe** (standard; at-will)
Close blast 3; level + 6 vs. AC; 1d6 + one-half level damage, and the target is knocked prone.

VAPOROUS TENTACLE

An orium dragon can create a vaporous serpent that has acidic tentacles. This power replaces the bite attack of the dragon's vaporous serpent.

✦ **Vaporous Tentacle** (standard; at-will) ✦ **Acid**
Level + 4 vs. Fortitude; acid damage equal to that of the vaporous serpent's bite attack – 5, and the target is grabbed by the vaporous serpent.

IRON SPIKE DEFENSE

Elder and ancient iron dragons can transform their scales into jagged iron spikes. This power replaces *iron wing defense*.

Iron Spike Defense (minor; recharge ⚄ ⚅)
Until the end of the dragon's next turn, any creature adjacent to the dragon that attacks it takes ongoing damage equal to one-half the dragon's level.

MERCURY DRAGON POWERS

Fluid in body and disposition, mercury dragons can learn to exude versatile tendrils. Tendrils can grab, pierce, or drag enemies.

FLOWING GRAPPLE

A mercury dragon can adapt its shapeshifting ability to ensnare and drag a creature. This power replaces *quicksilver form*.

✦ **Flowing Grapple** (standard; encounter)
Level + 3 vs. Reflex; 4d6 + one-half level damage, and the target is grabbed. *Effect:* The dragon shifts its speed. If it is grabbing a creature, it pulls the creature with it and places the creature in any space adjacent to it at the end of the movement (and the creature is still grabbed).

MERCURY TENDRIL

A mercury dragon can create tendrils that pierce and stagger its enemies. This power replaces *frightful presence*.

KEREM BEYIT

4

Silver Dragon Powers

Compassionate and honorable to friends, silver dragons show no mercy to enemies. This ruthlessness can manifest in varying powers.

Bloodied Onslaught

A silver dragon can gain a power similar to *bloodied breath* for its *dragon's onslaught* or *furious dragon's onslaught*. This works best for Huge and larger dragons because of their long reach. This power replaces *bloodied breath*.

> ✦ **Bloodied Onslaught** (free, when first bloodied; encounter)
> *Dragon's onslaught* or *furious dragon's onslaught* recharges, and the dragon uses it, gaining a +2 bonus to the attack rolls.

Breath Weapon: Immobilizing Breath

Silver dragons can adapt their freezing breath to immobilize foes. This power replaces the dragon's normal *breath weapon*.

> ⟵ **Breath Weapon** (standard; recharge ⚄ ⚅) ✦ **Cold**
> Close blast 5; level + 1 vs. Reflex; 1d10 + one-half level cold damage, and the target is immobilized (save ends). Each time the target makes a saving throw against this effect, it takes cold damage equal to one-half the dragon's level.

Chill Recovery

When an elder or ancient silver dragon recovers from a harmful effect, it unleashes a triumphant burst of cold. This power replaces *unstoppable*.

> ⟵ **Chill Recovery** (when the silver dragon succeeds on a saving throw; at-will 1/round) ✦ **Cold**
> Close burst 3; level + 3 vs. Reflex; the target is immobilized (save ends).

Steel Dragon Powers

Living in disguise means being evasive. Steel dragons can grow paranoid and seek possible escapes in all situations.

Entrapping Retreat

A skilled elder or ancient steel dragon can trap a foe in a sphere of force and then retreat. This power replaces *force prison*.

> ✦ **Entrapping Retreat** (move; recharges when the dragon uses breath weapon) ✦ **Force, Zone**
> 5 + one-half level vs. Reflex; the target's space becomes a zone of force until the end of the dragon's next turn. The target doesn't have line of effect to squares outside the zone and can't leave the zone. No creature has line of effect to the target.
> *Effect:* The dragon shifts its speed.

Steel Swath

A steel dragon can develop its fighting ability in human form. This power replaces *dragon's suggestion*.

> ✦ **Steel Swath** (standard, when the dragon is in human form; recharge ⚄ ⚅) ✦ **Weapon**
> The dragon makes two attacks: level + 5 vs. AC; 2d8 + one-half level damage. The dragon shifts its speed between the two attacks.

ABOUT THE DESIGNERS

RICHARD BAKER is an award-winning game designer who has written scores of D&D® adventures and supplements, including *Manual of the Planes*™ and *Divine Power*™. Rich is also a best-selling author of FORGOTTEN REALMS® novels, including *Swordmage* and *Corsair* in the Blades of the Moonsea series.

PETER LEE works as a game designer for Wizards of the Coast, where he splits his time between RPG design and leading the design for D&D® Miniatures.

DAVID NOONAN has an extensive list of RPG credits, including *Martial Power*™, *Scepter Tower of Spellgard*™, and contributions to the 4th Edition core rules. He lives in Washington state with his wife and two children.

ROBERT J. SCHWALB works as a freelance designer for Wizards of the Coast. His recent credits include *Martial Power*, *Draconomicon*™: *Chromatic Dragons*, and the FORGOTTEN REALMS *Player's Guide*. Robert lives in Tennessee with his wife, Stacee.

ARI MARMELL is a novelist and freelance writer, who has been working on both fiction and role-playing games for almost ten years and has published material through companies such as Paizo, White Wolf, Green Ronin, and Wizards of the Coast. His 4th Edition D&D credits include *Draconomicon: Chromatic Dragons*, the EBERRON® *Player's Guide*, the EBERRON® *Campaign Guide*, and numerous articles for *D&D Insider*™. His fiction credits include *Agents of Artifice* for the Magic: The Gathering® line, and *The Conqueror's Shadow* (forthcoming from Bantam Spectra).

NEW MONSTERS

Every new monster in this book appears on the following list, which is sorted alphabetically by level and monster role. Monster leaders are indicated with an (L).

Monster	Level and Role	Page
Brass Dragon Wyrmling	2 Elite Artillery	175
Goblin Cursespewer	2 Artillery (L)	88
Baaz Draconian	2 Soldier	190
Goblin Sentry	2 Soldier	89
Ferak Draconian	3 Brute	191
Cobalt Dragon Wyrmling	3 Elite Controller	177
Iron Dragon Wyrmling	3 Elite Skirmisher	179
Brass Dragon, Young	4 Solo Artillery	156
Chevkos's Crossbowman	4 Artillery	94
Kobaaz Draconian	4 Controller	192
Kapak Draconian	4 Lurker	192
Mercury Dragon Wyrmling	4 Elite Lurker	180
Thraeshk	4 Solo Lurker	90
Chevkos's Lackey	4 Minion Skirmisher	94
Copper Dragon Wyrmling	4 Elite Skirmisher	177
Chevkos's Guard	4 Soldier	94
Bozak Draconian	5 Artillery	191
Bronze Dragon Wyrmling	5 Elite Brute	176
Silver Dragon Wyrmling	5 Elite Brute	183
Cobalt Dragon, Young	5 Solo Controller	161
Dragonkin Channeler (Kobold)	5 Controller	198
Steel Dragon Wyrmling	5 Elite Controller	183
Dragonkin Zealot (Kobold)	5 Lurker	198
Iron Dragon, Elite Young	5 Elite Lurker	218
Adamantine Dragon Wyrmling	5 Elite Soldier	174
Chevkos	6 Artillery	96
Cave Stirge Swarm	6 Brute	104
Wyrmling Vaporous Serpent	6 Minion Brute	182
Mercury Dragon, Young	6 Solo Lurker	163
Korzinalikur	6 Elite Skirmisher	96
Adamaaz Draconian	6 Soldier	189
Orium Dragon Wyrmling	6 Elite Soldier	182
Bronze Dragon, Young	7 Solo Brute	159
Dragonkin Champion (Kobold)	7 Brute	198
Gold Dragon Wyrmling	7 Elite Controller	179
Steel Dragon, Young	7 Solo Controller	172
Wyrmguard Sentinel (Kobold)	7 Soldier	199
Vaporous Serpent, Young	8 Minion Brute	170
Aurak Draconian	8 Controller (L)	189
Sivak Draconian	8 Skirmisher	192
Baaz Draconian Foot Soldier	8 Minion Soldier	190
Orium Dragon, Young	8 Solo Soldier	170
Wyrmguard Scout (Kobold)	9 Artillery	200
Vulture Drake	9 Brute	194
Zanathakla Vaporous Serpent	9 Minion Brute	106
Mithral Dragon Wyrmling	9 Elite Skirmisher	181
Zanathakla	9 Solo Soldier	106
Three-Tooth (Kobold)	10 Elite Artillery	201
Brass Dragon, Adult	11 Solo Artillery	156
Gargoyle Harrier	11 Lurker	112
Mithral Dragon, Young	11 Solo Skirmisher	166
Cobalt Dragon, Adult	12 Solo Controller	162
Aelathric Sahuagin Guard	12 Minion	123
Liondrake	12 Skirmisher	194
Aelathric Sahuagin Priest	13 Artillery	120
Vaporous Serpent, Adult	13 Minion Brute	170
Mercury Dragon, Adult	13 Solo Lurker	164
Orium Dragon, Adult	13 Solo Soldier	170
Sand Knives Bandit	13 Minion Soldier	203

Monster	Level and Role	Page
Bronze Dragon, Adult	14 Solo Brute	159
Uvokula	14 Elite Brute (L)	120
Xyphreneus	14 Solo Brute (L)	122
Steel Dragon, Adult	14 Solo Controller	172
Couatl Rogue Serpent	14 Skirmisher	186
War Shark	14 Skirmisher	121
Vanathia	14 Solo Soldier	116
Andraemos	15 Solo Artillery	202
Gold Hollow Dragon	16 Solo Brute	184
Drakkensteed	16 Skirmisher	196
Brass Dragon, Elder	18 Solo Artillery	157
Jalanvaloss	18 Solo Controller	210
Mithral Dragon, Adult	18 Solo Skirmisher	167
Aspect of Bahamut	18 Solo Soldier (L)	208
Cobalt Dragon, Elder	19 Solo Controller	162
Vaporous Serpent, Elder	20 Minion Brute	171
Niflung	20 Solo Controller	212
Hoard Guardian Sentinel	20 Soldier	137
Orium Dragon, Elder	20 Solo Soldier	170
Grave-Born Drakkensteed	21 Artillery	196
Bronze Dragon, Elder	21 Solo Brute	159
Galzaik	21 Elite Controller	134
Steel Dragon, Elder	21 Solo Controller	173
Mercury Dragon, Elder	21 Solo Lurker	165
Death Thrall Attendant	22 Minion Brute	147
Methenaera	22 Solo Brute	128
Kuyutha, Exarch of Bahamut	23 Elite Controller (L)	209
Angel of the Sigil and Word	23 Soldier	134
Couatl Redeemer	24 Artillery	186
Askaran-Rus	24 Elite Brute (L)	144
Gold Hollow Wyrm	24 Solo Soldier	184
Silvara	24 Solo Soldier	214
Astridaria	25 Solo Skirmisher	136
Mithral Dragon, Elder	25 Solo Skirmisher	167
Brass Dragon, Ancient	26 Solo Artillery	158
Venomous Remnant	26 Minion Artillery	153
Cobalt Dragon-Bred Drakkensteed	26 Skirmisher	196
Death Giant Soulfire Hurler	27 Artillery	142
Cobalt Dragon, Ancient	27 Solo Controller	162
Vaporous Serpent, Ancient	28 Minion Brute	171
Golgorax	28 Elite Controller (L)	146
Mercury Dragon, Ancient	28 Solo Lurker	165
Orium Dragon, Ancient	28 Solo Soldier	171
Bronze Dragon, Ancient	29 Solo Brute	160
Steel Dragon, Ancient	29 Solo Controller	174
Tananzinaen	29 Solo Lurker	152
Valamaradace	30 Solo Artillery	216
Mithral Dragon, Ancient	31 Solo Skirmisher	168
Bahamut	36 Solo Soldier (L)	208
The Old Man with the Canaries	36 Solo Soldier (L)	206

IMPROVE YOUR GAME WITH A BOOKMARK.

Add D&D Insider™ to your Favorites and bring more to your characters and campaigns with a constantly growing source of new content, tools, articles, applications, and more.

Whether you're a player, a DM—or both—D&DI™ will help you spend less time prepping for your game and more time playing it.

SUBSCRIBE NOW AT DNDINSIDER.COM

D&D
INSIDER™
NEVER SPLIT THE PA[

All trademarks are property of Wizards of the Coast LLC. ©2009 Wizards. Restrictions apply. See site for details.